D1000349

# *Furthering Talk*

## Advances in the Discursive Therapies

# *Furthering Talk*

## Advances in the Discursive Therapies

Edited by

TOM STRONG
*University of Calgary*
*Alberta, Canada*

and

DAVID PARÉ
*University of Ottawa*
*Ontario, Canada*



KLUWER ACADEMIC/PLENUM PUBLISHERS
NEW YORK, BOSTON, DORDRECHT, LONDON, MOSCOW

Library of Congress Cataloging-in-Publication Data

Furthering talk: advances in the discursive therapies / edited by Thomas Strong, David Pare.
p. cm.
Includes bibliographical references and index.
ISBN 0-306-47907-9
1. Psychotherapy. 2. Narrative therapy. I. Strong, Thomas. II. Pare, David.
RC479.S74F875 2004
616.89'14—dc22 2003060441

ISBN: 0-306-47907-9


233 Spring Street, New York, New York 10013

http://www.wkap.nl/

10 9 8 7 6 5 4 3 2 1



Printed in the United States of America

To Arista—for all the conversations ahead of us
*from Tom*

To Sijbrigje
*from David*

# Contributors

*Harlene Anderson* • A founding member of the Houston Galveston Institute and Taos Institute, is internationally recognized for her contributions on the applications of a postmodern collaborative approach to therapy, organizational consultation, and education. She is the author of *Conversation, Language and Possibilities: A Postmodern Approach to Therapy* (Basic Books) and a founding director of the Taos Institute.

*Johnella Bird* • Is a therapist in private practice at The Family Centre in Auckland, New Zealand. After training in Psychological Medicine, she was registered as a Child Psychotherapist, and for the past twenty years has focused on the concerns that effect young people and their families; women and men who have suffered the effects of physical, emotional and sexual abuse; and the numerous issues that impact on adult relationships. She is presently particularly interested in the ideas and strategies for engaging with Power Relations in management. Johnella has taught hundreds of clinicians over the past 15 years in New Zealand, Australia, and North America, and is author of the recent book, *The Heart's Narrative*.

*J. Paul Burney, Ph.D.* • Is a Clinical Psychologist in private practice in Conroe, Texas. He is a marriage and family therapist, a professional mediator, consultant, and is adjunct faculty for Our Lady of the Lake University and Sam Houston State University.

*Thomas Conran, Ph.D.* • Serves the community as a family therapist who has founded *Epiphany Partners*, a public foundation for compassion education. He also serves as an Adjunct Professor for the Department of Counseling and Family Therapy for Saint Louis University and a consultant for violence prevention and family development programs. He is attempting to bridge connections between the wisdom of historical figures such as Moses, Jesus, Buddha, and Mohammed and the postmodern insights of social constructionism and non-essentialist neurobiology. This co-evolution may assist us to remember and develop anew practical possibilities for compassionate intervention into arduous problems of trauma, violence, disease, and the loss of hope in chaotic times.

*Peter Finck* • Has a broad base in the field of organizations and corporations. Aside from his degree in Criminology from Simon Fraser University, Peter has twenty years of practical experience in the Human service field. Peter is perhaps best known for his re-visioning of the modern corporation and organization put into practice in his Community Vision. Peter is co-founder, with Christopher Kinman, of Rock the Boat, an organization that concentrates its efforts toward the building of community life, whether in neighborhoods, corporations, or other types of organizations. Peter is a busy family man with three small children. His friends all know him as a man with an abundant sense of community and life.

*Jerry Gale, Ph.D.* • Is Director of the MFT Doctoral Program at The University of Georgia. He has written over 40 papers and chapters and authored the book, *Conversation Analysis of Therapeutic Discourse* and co-edited the book, *Constructivism in Education*. He has presented at national and international conferences on topics ranging from qualitative research, postmodern approaches to research, Ericksonian hypnosis, family mediation and improvisation. Jerry has been married over twenty years to Barbara, and together, they are over-indulging parents to their 3 year old daughter, Hannah Elizabeth Chu Rui. Jerry enjoys parenting, yoga, racketball, and improvisational theater.

*Bill Hanec, M.S.W., R.S.W.* • Has worked for the past 20 years as a psychiatric social worker in Alberta, Canada. He is currently a family and group therapist in the Young Adult Program at the Foothills Hospital in Calgary. Bill has developed a range of programs in forensic psychiatry incorporating constructivist theory into clinical work with men who have perpetrated both physical and sexual abuse on women and children.

*Lois Holzman, Ph.D.* • Is a founder of the East Side Institute for Short Term Psychotherapy in New York City and serves as its director. Along with Fred Newman she is the major theorist of social therapy and its methodology. With Newman, she has authored *Lev Vygotsky: Revolutionary Scientist*; *The End of Knowing*; and *Unscientific Psychology*. Other books on social therapy and other postmodern approaches to psychology and education, include *Schools for Growth: Radical Alternatives to Current Educational Models*; *Performing Psychology: A Postmodern Culture of the Mind*; and (with John Morss) *Postmodern Psychologies, Societal Practice and Political Life*. Her most recent work (with Rafael Mendez) is *Psychological Investigations: A Clinician's Guide to Social Therapy*.

*Arlene M. Katz, Ed.D.* • Is an Instructor in the Department of Social Medicine at Harvard Medical School. As Director of the Community Councils Project at the Cambridge Health Alliance, she collaborated with community elders and professionals to develop a unique program to address ageism by creating a Council of Elders to help teach residents and nurse practitioners about their lived experience of aging (Katz, et.al., 2000). This is a continuation of a series of participatory ethnographic research projects involving the development of 'resourceful communities' of those involved in clinical practice, training and in mentorship programs, in part to address issues of inequality, access to care and to increase a sense of answerability to our communities. Her work has emphasized hearing the 'voice' of the patient and the community in care, training and research. Reports of these studies include papers with John Shotter on a "social poetics" approach to the understanding and elaboration of diagnostic practices in primary care as well as in the process of mentorship. She emphasizes the importance of socially informed dialogic practices in health care, psychotherapy, and organizations. Dr. Katz has authored many articles on mentoring and relationship-centered, collaborative methods of care, research and training and has lectured on these subjects nationally and internationally.

*Christopher J. Kinman, M.Sc., M.Div.* • Was born in Ibadon, Nigeria. He has lived in numerous places throughout his life, including England, Michigan, Chicago, and—in Canada—Saskatchewan, Alberta and British Columbia. He is married with three children and loves to spend time by the sea. He has been heavily involved as a consultant to human service organisations in the fields of proposal preparation, program design, qualitative research, as well as program delivery and evaluation. Christopher is also well known for his work with young people and families. He has been involved in the development of a number of youth-services programs, and he has an international reputation as a consultant in youth services.

*Glenn Larner, B.A., Dip., Psych.* • Is a senior clinical psychologist from Sydney, Australia, with 30 years experience in child and adolescent therapy. He is an associate editor for the Australian and New Zealand Journal of Family Therapy, has published widely on the topic of deconstruction and therapy and is co-editor with David Pare of *Collaborative Practice in Psychology and Therapy* (Haworth, 2003).

*John Lawless, Ph.D.* • Is Assistant Professor at Drexel University's Programs in Couple and Family Therapy. He utilizes postmodern/poststructural epistemologies in his practice as a therapist, teacher, and supervisor. He is currently exploring methodological convergence between critical race theory and discursive methodologies to help examine the institution of couple and family therapy. Outside of academia, John is married, Kathryn, with three children, Quinn, Aidan, and Connor. He enjoys studying Northern Wu Taijiquan, running, backpacking, and kayaking.

*Sheila McNamee, Ph.D.* • Is Professor of Communication at the University of New Hampshire and holds the University's Class of 1944 Professorship. She is a founding member of the Taos Institute (www.taosinstitute.org.) Her work is focused on dialogic transformation within a variety of social and institutional contexts including organizations, education, health care, psychotherapy, and communities. She is author of *Relational Responsibility: Resources for Sustainable Dialogue*, with Kenneth Gergen (Sage, 1998). Other books include, *Therapy as Social Construction*, with Kenneth Gergen (Sage, 1992), *Philosophy in Therapy: The Social Poetics of Therapeutic Conversation*, with Klaus Deissler (Carl Auer Systeme Verlag, 2000), and *The Appreciative Organization*, with her co-founders of the Taos Institute (Taos Institute, 2001). Professor McNamee has also authored numerous articles and chapters on social constructionist theory and practice. She actively engages constructionist practices in a variety of contexts to bring communities of participants with diametrically opposing viewpoints together to create liveable futures. Professor McNamee lectures and consults regularly, both nationally and internationally, for universities, private institutes, organizations, and communities.

*Gerald Monk, Ph.D.* • Is a mediator in San Diego, California. He is also a Professor at San Diego State University in the College of Education. Prior to this, he worked as an academic at the University of Waikato in New Zealand and conducted a successful practice in counseling psychology and mediation for 20 years. Gerald publishes in the area of discursive psychology and its applications to daily life. Gerald is internationally known for his work with the development and application of narrative approaches to counseling and mediation. He has co-authored three books on this subject: *Narrative Therapy in Practice: The Archaeology of Hope* (1997); *Narrative Counseling in Schools: Powerful and Brief* (1999) and *Narrative Mediation: A New Approach to Conflict Resolution* (2000). Gerald has led numerous workshops in New Zealand, Australia, Canada, Iceland, Austria, Mexico, and the United States.

*Fred Newman, Ph.D.* • Is a practicing psychotherapist, founder of the East Side Institute for Short Term Psychotherapy and artistic director of the Castillo Theatre, New York City. Trained in philosophy of science and language, he left academia in 1968 for community and political organizing. Since then, hundreds have joined him in creating an activist community of developmental psychological, cultural and political projects. Academic works (with Lois Holzman) are *Unscientific Psychology: A Cultural-Performatory Approach to Understanding Human Life*; *Lev Vygotsky: Revolutionary Scientist;* and *The End of Knowing: A New Developmental Way of Learning*. Newman has also written popular books (*Let's Develop: A Guide to Continuous Personal Growth* and *Performance of a Lifetime: A Practical-Philosophical Guide to the Joyous Life*) and 30 plays.

*David Paré, Ph.D.* • Is a psychologist and counsellor educator at the University of Ottawa as well as co-director (with Mishka Lysack) of The Glebe Institute,

A Centre for Constructive and Collaborative Practice, in Ottawa, Ontario, Canada. For the past decade his work has focused on the 'postmodern turn' in family therapy and psychotherapy. David has a particular interest in narrative ideas and practices; in addition to writing and presenting widely on that topic, he offers training and supervision to practitioners interested in developing collaborative therapeutic practices. He is currently conducting participatory action research with students into the processes of teaching and learning collaborative therapy. David's work is made possible through the support of his partner Susan, and children, Casey and Liam. David enjoys canoeing, hockey and tennis, and playing music—occasionally with his colleague Tom Strong.

*Peter Rober, Lic.* • Is clinical psychologist, family therapist and family therapy trainer. He is co-director of the training institute Feelings & Context (Antwerp, Belgium). He also works at the Relationship and Family Studies department of the Faculty of Psychology at Ghent University (Ghent, Belgium). Peter is member of staff of the C.G.G.Z. MenSana (Antwerp, Belgium) and member of the family therapy training team of Kern (Sint Niklaas, Belgium). He has published several articles on family therapy in professional journals in the USA and Europe. He is also member of the editorial board of the *Journal of Marital and Family Therapy*. Peter lives in Antwerp (Belgium) with his wife Greta, who is a professional painter, and their 6 year old son Nemo.

*John Shotter* • Is a professor of interpersonal relations in the Department of Communication, University of New Hampshire. His long term interest is in the social conditions conducive to people having a voice in the development of participatory democracies and civil societies. John's extensive writings make him one of the premier articulators of social constructionist philosophy. His recent books include *Cultural Politics of Everyday Life: Social Constructionism, Rhetoric, and Knowing of the Third Kind* and *Conversational Realities: The Construction of Life Through Language*.

*Stacey L. Sinclair, Ph.D.* • Is a counselor educator at San Diego State University. Her research interests include social constructionist and postmodern feminist epistemology, narrative approaches to counseling and therapy, research on and for women, deconstruction and discourse analysis, and cultural constructions of gender, ethnicity, sexuality, and the body. Stacey has led workshops and published on these subjects, and she is a nationally certified counselor whose training specializes in postmodern approaches to family therapy.

*Hans Skott-Myhre, Ph.D.* • Has over 25 years experience as a therapist, administrator, consultant and academic in the field of psychotherapy. He holds a Ph.D. in Work Community and Family Education from the University of Minnesota with a dissertation on Youth Subcultures as Performances of Post-Colonial Hybridity (focusing on Punks and Skinheads) and is completing a second doctorate in Cultural Studies with a focus on recuperating psychotherapy as a political project. He is an assistant professor of Child and Youth Studies at Brock University in Ontario where he is working on developing models of radical youth work. He and his colleague Reginald Harris provide workshops and trainings in culturally based approaches to creating Radical Psychotherapies.

*Tom Strong, Ph.D.* • Is a psychologist and counsellor educator at the University of Calgary. Formerly a practitioner throughout northwestern British Columbia, he recently re-entered academic life to explore the possibilities of discursive and postmodern thought for collaborative practice. Inspired by dialogic thinkers like Bakhtin, Garfinkel and Wittgenstein, his writing explores pragmatic and ethical issues such thought holds for psychotherapy, health conversations, and counsellor education/supervision. Tom is also involved in the Discursive Therapies ("The Virtual Faculty") graduate program offered online from Massey University in New Zealand. He is a part-time father to 13 year old Arista and, away from work, he can be found outdoors or engaged in some musical activity in his new hometown: Calgary.

*Nick Todd, M.Ed.* • Is a psychologist who has worked mainly in the areas of addictions, family therapy and domestic violence. For the past eight years he has worked in the Men's Crisis Service, an outreach service of the Calgary Women's Emergency Shelter. He has a particular interest in how language can be used to mitigate or highlight responsibility for violent behavior.

*Allan Wade, Ph.D.* • Works as a therapist and researcher in private practice. As a therapist, Allan specializes in consultation with individuals, organizations, and communities who are faced with difficulties stemming from interpersonal violence. As a researcher, Allan is particularly interested in therapeutic and legal discourse, and particularly the connection between language and violence.

*Jaakko Seikkula* • Is Senior Assistant at the University of Jyvaskyla and Professor at the Institute of Community Medicine in the University of Tromsso. He has been involved in the team in the Finnish Western Lapland for developing the Open Dialogue approach for severe psychiatric problems. He is mostly interested in Bakhtinian understanding of dialogue and its application to psychotherapy.

*Catherine Cook* • Is a counselling practitioner at Auckland University, New Zealand. She brings to her work a keen interest in the ways in which feminism and social construction inform practice and their intersections with gender and the body.

*Kathryn Roulston, Ph.D.* • Is an assistant professor in the Qualitative Inquiry Program, Department of Educational Psychology, at The University of Georgia where she teaches courses in qualitative methodology. Her research interests are conversational and ethnomethodological approaches to data analysis, qualitative research methodology, and qualitative approaches to music education research. She has published in *Qualitative Inquiry*, *Qualitative Research*, *Text*, and *Music Education Research*. Her current research interests include investigations of young children's music preferences and beginning music teachers' perceptions of their work.

*Martine Renoux, Ph.D., M.S.W.* • Is French and moved to England in her early twenties. She finds learning a different language and living in a different culture a fascinating experience. Martine has been registered with the United Kingdom Council for Psychotherapy and worked in private practice and in the National Health Service as a psychotherapist. She conducts training sessions in stress management and team building for medical centres and works as consultant to the Complementary Health Trust in London. She wrote the *Trust's Code of Ethics*, *Guidelines to Support Patients Who May be Suicidal*, and *Internal Disciplinary Procedure*. Martine became interested in Brief Therapy in 1994. She joined the Ericksonian Society in London and later became a workshop organizer. As an Integrative Psychotherapist, Martine enjoys mixing different approaches. Currently she is writing a book. She likes to read popular science books on neurology, mathematics, physics and astronomy.

*Craig Smith* • Is a Marriage and Family Therapist in private practice at the Solana Beach Counseling Center in San Diego County. He also teaches counselors at San Diego State University, supervises at various local agencies, and does trainings in collaborative therapy. Craig is co-editor of Narrative Therapies with Children and Adolescents with Dave Nylund.

*Bradford Keeney, Ph.D.* • Is Vice President of Cultural Affairs, Ringing Rocks Foundation, Philadelphia. He is also Cultural Anthropologist at the Mental Research Institute in Palo Alto and an Adjunct Professor with California State University, Fullerton. Author of *Aesthetics of Change*, *Mind in Therapy*, and a number of books on shamanistic healing practices.

*Donald Baker, B.A. Soc.* • Has worked with youth for seventeen years in a variety of settings including youth detention, group homes and doing groups with male abusers. He is currently working for the Youth Services Bureau of Ottawa as a youth and family counsellor.

*Jess Skott-Myhre* • A student, is a bi-racial transgender dyke boi who is an activist in queer, transgender and human rights work. She is currently a student at the University of Minnesota, the administrator of the activist non-profit MIR and the author of the Strange and Amazing Grrly Dyke Boi comic.

*Kathleen Skott-Myhre, M.A.* • Is a feminist therapist with an interest in Ericksonian hypnotherapy who has worked with young people in emergency shelters, street-based drop-in programs and college counseling centers. She is a doctoral candidate at the University of St Thomas where she is writing her dissertation on The Multigenerational Transmission of Feminine Power in Young Women of Irish Ancestry. She teaches psychology and youth studies.

*Reginald Harris* • Is the co-founder of Rhizomatic Transitions, a non-profit that works towards liberatory change. He works at Youthlink, a non-profit youth service agency in Minneapolis as the arts coordinator for Culture Club and as a case coordinator with homeless youth in the Archdale Apartments, a transitional living program for homeless youth. He is a poet and spoken word artist.

*Lynn Hoffman, ACSW* • Is an internationally known lecturer on family therapy and author of *Techniques of Family Therapy* (with Jay Haley); *Foundations of Family Therapy*; *Milan Systemic Family Therapy* (with Luigi Boscolo, Gianfranco Cecchin, and Peggy Penn); and *Exchanging Voices*. Her most recent book is *Family Therapy: An Intimate History*. She has taught at the Ackerman Institute for the Family and Hunter College in New York, the Smith School of Social Work in Northampton, MA, and the Family Therapy Program at St. Joseph's College in West Hartford, CT. During her nearly forty years in the field, Hoffman has led or taken part in hundreds of workshops and conferences in the U.S., Canada, South and Central America, the United Kingdom, Europe, Australia and Japan. In 1988, she was awarded the Life Achievement Award for Distinguished Contribution to the Field of Family Therapy by the American Association of Marital and Family Therapy, and in 1994 the Massachusetts MAMFT gave her an award for Distinguished Contribution. In 1995, she was a 'State of the Art' speaker at the Milton Erickson Foundation's Evolution of Psychotherapy Conference in Las Vegas.

*Lois Shawver, Ph.D.* • Is a clinical psychologist who publishes on postmodernism as it relates to therapy. She is a contributing editor for the American Journal of Psychoanalysis and for the New Therapist, an external faculty member for the Virtual Faculty in New Zealand and with VIISA Institute in Marburg Germany. She is also the host of a popular online community for therapists who are interested in postmodernism and for associated online publications such as: http://www.california.com/~rathbone/pmth.htm.

# Foreword

Recently, a client coming in for her second appointment, told me the story of how she had been volunteering her time for the past several years to free several innocent prisoners from Illinois prisons. She told me how tenaciously and persistently she had to work against politicians who did not want these releases to take place. I was so struck by her dedication and personal sacrifice of time, money, and energy.

At the end of her story, I thanked her. I said there were many times when I heard some story of injustice on the news and I thought to myself how I should get involved or at least write a letter. But somehow other matters would take precedence, my anger would dissipate and soon the issue would slip my mind. Listening to her I felt grateful that there were people like her to take up the cause and put energy and voice to my concerns. I looked at her and thanked her again.

Reading this manuscript I was reminded of this story. Editing a book on postmodern thinking and ways of being with clients is certainly not the same as confronting politicians or taking on power structures in a justice system. But nonetheless, after reading this manuscript I found myself grateful to Tom Strong and David Pare for their taking the time and committing the energy to the collection. This is a book that should have been written. It is timely and moves ideas forward. This is a very worthwhile endeavor and the product reflects their dedication to contemporary ideas.

Readers sometimes scoff at edited books, as if being an editor is just a matter of convincing a group of people to write your book for you. However, I think the skill of editing this book has been in selecting the present authors, suggesting and structuring a postmodern conversational format, and then somehow creating a finished product that is exciting, useful, and coherent. Editing means pushing for deadlines and here and there making suggestions to better the contributions and make them relate or fit together. In this book individually and collectively the chapters take the conversation forward about different ways of being with clients.

Knowing some of the authors and being familiar with the work of others, I appreciate not just what they have written but also the struggle and excitement of transition from modernist beginnings to the freedom of contemporary ideas.

For me this transition was both difficult and inspiring. In the eighties, I was in love with, if not married to, what I thought were the truths of cybernetics and the Brief Strategic and early Solution-focused models. I could not imagine ever thinking any differently or of another way of thinking ever being any better.

What was unsettling and inspiring for me was listening to the late Harry Goolishian as he described the many "truth" stages of his career. I was struck how many transitions he had made and how he was fascinated no longer by cybernetics and family therapy but by client stories. He was fascinated not by how the stories represented family or intrapsychic structures, but rather just as stories. I was inspired by his fascination with how these stories changed and possibilities emerged in the telling and retelling of the stories in the context of dialogue he hoped always to create.

I began to listen to stories with a different ear. I was often amazed how client responses to problems, tragedies, or crises were stories of courage. These courage stories I had not heard when the stories of tragedy or problems crowded them out. As I listened to just the stories and not how they fit into my previous categories, I was much more touched by the client's experience and my own responses were more heartfelt and encouraging. I began to listen more carefully as I heard client stories of courage and hope and I became more curious of clients' heartfelt desires and hopes for the future of themselves and their families.

I began to read more postmodern philosophy and postructural writers. Finally, I coauthored with Jane Peller our own ideas in "Recreating Brief Therapy: Preferences and Possibilities" (2002). In this book we moved our own pragmatic approach out of its formerly strategic language and fully into social constructionist and new pragmatist philosophies. We became committed to a dialogical approach. At the same time we found that just as others might facilitate a deconstruction of client problem or complaint narratives, we found possibilities as we deconstructed client stories of their desired futures.

We also became committed to redefining our field by suggesting an alternative to the word "therapy" with all it medical model and disease baggage. We suggested that regardless of discipline that helping professional call themselves personal consultants. By adopting a different title, professionals would be making a dramatic statement about adopting a new vocabulary for the field, one that highlighted collaboration, the possibility of multiple stories of courage, strength, resiliency, and client directed conversations. This would also mark the abandonment of protocols of mental status examines, drug and alcohol assessments, and risk assessments that put pathology and information gathering before the creation of a collaborative relationship.

As we were writing this book we were haunted and guided by the questions of two friends of mine. What is this postmodern stuff and how does it make a difference to you and your clients?

This is what this book is all about. What is this postmodern stuff? How is it different? How does it make difference to personal consultants and how they are with clients? How does it make a difference to the client and the conversations they have? How do these ideas push the conversations of the field forward or in different directions? Each chapter of this book speaks to these questions. Let me give you a few of the highlights.

First off, I was fascinated with the play of the title, "Furthering Talk". I thought if I put the emphasis on the action of this title, it means this book is about pushing the conversation within the field further or forward. On the other hand, the meaning could be on the talk, that is, the products of each chapter. Perhaps the meaning is that each chapter is talk that has been advanced, the cutting edge ideas of these authors within this movement. This book does both.

I was also struck by the format of the book. Tom and David put discursive ideas into the medium of the book. Each chapter is a summary of not just the author or coauthors' ideas but the summary of a conversation. Each chapter includes a conversational partner who contributes to the chapter by listening carefully and offering reflections and questions to further a presentation of ideas. The author or coauthors then respond. The chapter is thus expanded by the conversational partner's supplement or query. Practically, I found this to be engaging. Conversational partners often made similar comments or raised similar questions that I would have. In that case I felt affirmed and more engaged. In cases where the conversational partner made different comments I was delighted by the contrast and curious of what was to come.

Different chapters conversed about different topic areas, some theoretical, some ethical, some defined by population or problem. The advantage of this edited book is that you the reader can read what interests you first without worrying about the reading being out of sequence.

I cannot review or forward each chapter. I do not have the space and Tom and David do that in their chapter. So let me talk about one in particular as an example of what to expect from others. Being in a new position where I am working with clients involved with violence or abuse, I went to those chapters first. I was intrigued with Todd, Wade and Martine Renoux's chapter. Their work produces what I would call victimnesses and offendernesses, expansions of traditional essentialist notions of victim and offender. Their deconstruction of victim redefines the victim not just by symptoms or effects but by the responses of the individual to the offense. These responses include various forms of resistance, resilience and active protest to what happened. By exploring these notions within a session, both counselor and client can regain or create stories that are alternatives to the very limited traditional constructs of a passive, weak, and perhaps partially willing victim. Clients may walk away with a sense of themselves consistent with their self respect by having done everything they could to resist the violence. This is in contrast to the self doubt, confusion and helplessness that can accompany the traditional and exclusive construct of victim by virtue of what has been done to them.

The chapter also analyzes the language of the judicial system and mental health discourses for the subtle ways that language subtlely blames the client and diminishes the responsibility of the offender.

Other chapters in like manner talk of different ways to be with a client because of expanded or deconstructed counselor dispositions or languages.

After finishing this book and reflecting on the experience, I again came back to the title. The language and conversations within the book were definitely "furthering." They carried me into new ways of thinking, stimulated me to think of my present client sessions in different ways, and led me to already different conversations and anticipated conversations. Again, thanks to the many authors.

JOHN WALTER
Consultations, Evanston, IL
Coauthor with Jane Peller of "Recreating Brief Therapy: Preferences and Possibilities" Norton, 2000

# *Preface: Welcome to the Multilogue*

Within these pages you will encounter a *multilogue*—exploratory and deliberately unfinished dialogic exchanges, conversations about the conversational potentials of therapy. We hope that you will not merely witness them, but enter into them, carrying them forward and transforming our multilogue with your questions and critical reactions in your further dialogues.

This book explores conversation as the central resource and medium of therapeutic helping. And to avoid merely talking *about* talk, and to demonstrate its workings throughout these covers, we've made lots of room for conversational exchanges within the bounds of a medium that fixes ink on paper. It's our attempt to nudge textual conventions in a multivocal direction, while approximating robust dialogue.

You will notice this conversational motif within our introductory chapter, which unfolds as a dialogue between us, Tom Strong and David Paré. Resisting the temptation to adopt a definitive stance and "tell" you what Furthering Talk and discursive therapy are all about, we conversed about these things in a series of exchanges that spanned many months and many miles. Our conversation occasionally baffled and frequently frustrated us, but ultimately rewarded us by surfacing differences in understanding, and by contributing to new perspectives and distinctions neither of us anticipated prior to this multilogue. We invite you to join us as an active listener and to note your own points of convergence and divergence.

Beyond our introductory exchanges, all chapters in Furthering Talk are constructed as dialogues (or multilogues) between main contributing authors and "conversational partners". In our experience such understandings meld and diverge in the great conversation that is life. We hope that this is a generative book for you, one to turn to as much for others' ideas, as those provoked for you by the multilogues, and one you carry forward in your own conversations. Welcome to the multilogue.

TOM STRONG AND DAVID PARÉ

# *Acknowledgments*

This book marks an important crossroad in a conversational journey I began almost five years ago. I was traversing the wild roads of northwestern British Columbia as a psychologist. While the internet afforded conversations on listserves with people who continue to figure hugely in my life. And, I became quite inspired by people like Ken Gergen, John Shotter, Lynn Hoffman, Michael White and Jonathan Potter who were clarifying possibilities for postmodern conversation that seemed more hopeful and respectful than those I found in mainstream of psychotherapy practice. An opportunity to teach at my region's university came up (University of Northern British Columbia) and three years there gave me the academic freedom and support I needed to discuss, probe and adapt the collaborative and therapeutic potentials of discursive ideas, while my conversational circle widened. By the time I arrived at University of Calgary, in the fall of 2001, to now, these conversations had become central to my professional life.

For contrast, envision this journey's 'starting place' (Smithers) where picking up the mail was a social event that could unfold into myriad actual conversations. Then, fast forward to my university office computer showing a morning swack of e-mails—my cyber-conversations. David's and my conversations date back to my first year at UNBC and in him I found a colleague with whom I could hatch grand schemes like this book. And, from that point onward, my conversations were greatly furthered by the vital connection Lois Shawver continues to provide at her Postmodern Therapy listserve. But, UNBC also offered me a chance to pilot these ideas, and to work with students (especially you: Margaret Fuller, Kristi Smith, Elaine Colgate, Bev Read, and Andrew Burton) and colleagues (Peter Macmillan and Bryan Hartman) who helped me find legs for this new journey. Coming to Calgary meant another huge shift I'm still adjusting to. And, here I'm well on my way in making a new home, in finding great students (Shari Couture, Don Zeman) new colleagues, friends and a supportive university to work with.

But, this journey began from Smithers. In my last year there I was betwixt and between. I had a beautiful home and great friends in an idyllic setting, but I was so often on the road with my practice, while getting what one UNBC colleague called 'itchy brain' as I participated in online discussions about Bakhtin and Wittgenstein. I've been seeking that feeling of community since departing, for the new community that is still developing before me. My cyber-buddies became more than that as we found ways to present together or meet at conferences (Lois Holzman, Fred Newman, Tom Conran, Jerry Gale and John Lawless, Sheila McNamee, Harlene Anderson, Gerald Monk, Allan Wade, Chris Kinman), and I'm still conniving ways to see the others involved in this book. Big thanks to Sallyann Roth, for your early encouragement, to Stephen Madigan for those Vancouver Narrative therapy conferences, to Karl Tomm for helping make Calgary a postmodern therapy Mecca, to my journalistic exploits with John Soderlund (at New Therapist), to research conversations with Janet Bavelas, and to you, Andy Lock, for beaming me aboard your wonderful project at the Virtual Faculty (a Graduate program in Discursive Therapies). Finally, the last five years have been made a lot less lonely by longtime friends (Christo Holmes, Angus Macdonald, Carey Petkau, Don Davidson, you Smithers lot), my daughter (Arista), sister (Heather) parents (Irv and Irene), and for my growing group of new friends I prefer not to e-mail here in Calgary. To, you, David: we didn't nearly play enough guitar on this project, did we? We'll have to remedy that.

TOM STRONG

Working with so many talented contributors on this book has reminded me again that the words we write and speak are never our "own"—we borrow them, and shape them to our own intentions guided and inspired by the way they've been used by others. Those "others", for me, include the fresh thinkers and daring practitioners represented between these covers. Each has illuminated new territories for me.

I'd like to mention my co-editor, Tom Strong, in particular. Tom and I started out as e-mail correspondents, separated by several hundred miles in Western Canada. After scheduling a day in Vancouver just to walk and talk, we became collaborators and (guitar) pickin' partners. Tom's relentless curiousity and voracious appetite for ideas has inspired and challenged me over the years. This book owes much to his energy and passion.

I've been sustained, too, by my work with Mishka Lysack, my co-director at The Glebe Institute, whose sojourns into Bakhtin and Vygotzky will no doubt fuel many projects to come. The conversations Mishka and I have had with a growing community of Ottawa practitioners devoted to respectful and collaborative practice encourage me to go forward.

This book was made possible by the support I've received from The Faculty of Education at the University of Ottawa, and from the Social Sciences and Humanities Research Council of Canada. I'm grateful for Canada's continuing commitment to public funding for research devoted more to service than any particular bottom line.

Thanks as well for the patience and thoroughness of Charu Malhotra, James Galipeau, and Marina Nedashkivska, who took turns proofing and formatting the manuscript for *Furthering Talk*.

And finally, to Susan, Casey and Liam, who have graciously accommodated and even made light of my sometime distractibility: guys, it all matters because of you.

DAVID PARÉ

# *Contents*

## Chapter 1

# *Striving for Perspicuity*

## Talking Our Way Forward

Tom Strong and David Paré

***DAVID:*** Tom, it makes sense to me that a conversation with you is an apt starting point to this book, but conversations aren't the typical point of departure for edited collections. Maybe it would be helpful if you could start by saying something about what the word "discursive" means for you?
***TOM:*** David, this word keeps evolving for me. In this book it takes on different forms, as our authors regard the 'discursiveness' of their practices in some distinctive ways. Nowadays, I see it referring to how particular conversations give form to particular meanings and practices. It partly relates to a question of Tullio Maranhao's (1986): "is the representation of reality in language reconcilable with the intervention over reality by means of language?" (p. xii). Said another way, can we use talk (our primary way of understanding experience) to change our experience? But discursive also relates to how we use language to re-present experience to each other and ourselves. We aren't all tethered to the same meaning system, so we need to hear how the specific meanings people live by work/don't work for them, to talk beyond those not working.
***DAVID:*** That fits for me, and it goes both ways, too: in addition to conversations giving form to meanings and practices, cultural meanings and practices give form to the kinds of conversations we have. I think that distinction illuminates one area of diversity as it pertains to talking about discourse in this book. Some contributors hold a magnifying glass up to conversational exchanges, while others are more oriented to the broad social contexts within which those exchanges occur. These are variations on "discursive" and Jerry Gale and John Lawless (Chapter 8) are a rich source of vocabulary for describing them.
***TOM:*** Yeah, in our lifetimes we could point to the cultural meanings of gender or even (DSM) psychiatric labels (homosexuality in, then out), to see discursive

influences at work. We could see these in monolithic terms ('culture' prescribes this), or we could see particular conversations that produce such cultural monoliths (see Paula Caplan's 1991 report on articulating personality disorders for the DSM-IV). This isn't just about words, of course. People think and act differently as such discursive changes take place, or are pursued. We can't simply coast on pre-established meanings, however. We seek perspicuous meanings, those optimally fitting our shared circumstances and purposes, but usually settle for adequate ones that take us forward.

***DAVID:*** I'm increasingly astonished by the way the meanings we attribute to words can diverge significantly. This goes for the various sites of conversations, too, from public debates to intimate two-way talk. You and I and the contributors to this book explore conversation in a variety of ways, from the macro (cultural discourse) level down to the micro (two way talk) level. The emphasis varies, but what is shared is that attention to the ways that meaning is constructed in dialogue. It's one of the distinguishing features of any discursive orientation to therapeutic practice.

***TOM:*** Yeah, subtitling this book, "Advances in the discursive therapies" gave all of us a challenge to rise to. One unifying theme of the book—played out in our discussions—is that talk is inescapably consequential. That is, we talk some understandings into being, while contesting or passing over others—and we do this in consequential ways for how our discussion and relationship proceed. So we hope to promote a richer sensitivity to these constructive and deconstructive aspects of talk in and out of therapy.

***DAVID:*** That too: this textual conversation of ours is much more than a mere "reporting" of alternate points of view—it's been a construction site for new understandings. We've reserved space to review the twists and turns of that process at the end of this exchange. Despite our shared interest in discourse, we've also encountered points of divergence made palpable by our efforts to hear and be heard. For me, a central point of tension has hinged around the distinction between the ways we are all constrained *by* discourse, and the ways we are shapers *of* discourse. While we agree both views are important, my talk drifts to the constraints of broader cultural discourses, and yours to the possibilities for new construction that emerge from a specific conversation.

***TOM:*** Yes, and it is in how we talk through these differences that interests me. Perhaps, you meant something like this when you mentioned conversation giving "rise to" meaning. For me, such language insufficiently reflects the people's efforts when constructing meanings. For example, we both like Bakhtin's (1984) notion about words in any dialogue being "half mine". One could see the 'other half' as taken up by prior speakers (in our cultural discourses), but here is another way of seeing this: what I am about to say will influence what you say next. While I see historical inertias and constraints of culture in our discourses (the macro-view), I also see a performative (micro) dimension in talk—like improvisational theatre—where my talk plays some role in how you perform yours. Both 'halves' seem important, to me. When clients present understandings and actions at least half-determined by their cultural experiences, therapists need to think about the unspoken other 'half'.

***DAVID:*** While we're being busy teasing out some of these intriguing distinctions among approaches which also share a significant number of features, here's another one: discourse as noun and discourse as verb. That macro view you referred to often depicts discourse as socially and historically entrenched structures of thought and practice: hence "noun". A leaning towards the micro brings out another dimension of the word so that "engaging in discourse" is something we *do* when we talk to each other: hence "verb".

***TOM:*** David, this noun/verb distinction of discourse is important. Seeing discourse as a noun can lead to essentializing and generalizing about "it", as if we could say what a discourse really is or does in some objective sense. But, it can also present static ways to understand and relate to our experience. In hearing, "*this* is how things *are*", we are hearing about a particular way to understand, talk about and relate to some experience that has held up under repeated use—with other possible versions of 'how things *are*' passed over. A noun view of discourse and words highlights how conversations give form to and privilege some ways of understanding over others. Discourse, as a verb, looks at the activity of communicating and making sense; where understanding and relating is seldom static or fixed. It refers to how seemingly finalized meanings are often in conversational play or negotiation, for their adequacy or alternatives. I like Ian Hacking's (1999) view on this noun/verb distinction, that in postmodern times we need a tension between our best representations of experience, and how we continually modify them.

***DAVID:*** I like all of what you're saying about extending apparently finalized meanings and I'm *also* comfortable speaking about people as "inhabiting" established cultural discourses. Discourses are pervasive in our lives—we're the fish, discourses the water. I see discourses (as noun) contributing to how we make meaning, and sometimes in ways we only notice with the help of someone else. Sometimes one discourse blinds us to another—Salman Rushdie said that every story is form of censorship. To me, generative dialogue is not only about refashioning existing discourses. It may involve sharing and exploiting previously unconsidered ones, opening up new universes of understanding. Or it might involve "unmasking" an unhelpful discourse, challenging assumptions previously taken to be "truths".

***TOM:*** David, your word "inhabit" implies a determinism I only partly accept (e.g., "the discourse *made* me think/act this way"). I still see value in probing discourses for limiting cultural prescriptions clients may adhere to unaware, especially in the narrative mediation work of Monk and Sinclair (Chapter 10). And, conversation analysts and ethnomethodologists (e.g, Heritage, 1984; Sacks, 1995) give what we are discussing a slightly different, less determined, emphasis: we are *shaped by and shapers of* the conversations in which we participate.

***DAVID:*** I think we're tracing our way here across the map of the territories traveled by contributors to this book. Moving away from a preoccupation with a purportedly objective world, discursive therapists place talk itself at the centre of the process. As Berger and Luckmann have said, "language marks the co-ordinates of my life in society and fills that life with meaningful objects" (1967, p. 22.). Those are the "nouns" that surround us. But it doesn't end there: talk also furnishes us with tools for the coordinated action of "worldmaking" (Goodman, 1978).

***TOM:*** Staying with Berger and Luckmann (1967), I like their phrase: "the most important vehicle of reality-maintenance is conversation." (p. 152). I think our authors highlight how we construct and *sustain* our understandings and ways of relating via our ways of talking. A simple view of discursive therapy involves changing how talk occurs (discourse as verb part) so that other understandings and actions are made possible (discourse as noun). To me, it is important to see what we 'talk into being' and how we keep talking our familiarities 'into being'.

***DAVID:*** Yes. . . changing the talk can alter a dominant cultural meaning. Meanings are "pre-made" to an extent, and we *also* make them in conversation, through the performance that is speech. I prefer to keep visible both the fine-grain view of conversational utterances *and* the cultural context in which those exchanges take place.

***TOM:*** I'm with you here. We join a world in conversation, and take up particular ways of talking and relating within it. Our common sense, in this way, arises from our common use of particular ways of talk. And, until such ways of talk are seen as inadequate we generally continue using them, common-sensically. I still wrestle, however, with how laden my talk, and that of clients is with psychological discourse (see Danziger, 1997) that essentializes such phenomena as emotions as properties of (or inside) the individual, as if "my sadness" was 'mine' alone. By seeing psychotherapy's back-and-forth as a performance clients and therapists are afforded opportunities to reflect and try on other compelling forms of talk and common sense.

***DAVID:*** That notion of talk as performance is something I hope readers will hold as they engage with the writings here. You and I aren't just talking *about* conversation, we're *performing* it right now in the exchange between us, working out meanings as we go. Talk is action, and conversation is coordinated action.

***TOM:*** Coordinated action captures that sense of telling and doing for me, David: *what* people talk about, and *how* they do that talking. I'm doing that now as I respond to you, and I could throw off our 'coordinated action' if I threw in a non sequitur. This coordination between us (a choreography we work out in what we say, and how) is what John Shotter (1984) has referred to as "joint action" (see his chapter with Arlene Katz).

***DAVID:*** For me, it makes sense to view our contributions as invitations to further dialogue, including contradictory or complementary views. You and I don't share identical views, and yet our conversations have given birth to distinctions never before uttered by us—novel ways of talking, new possibilities for going forward. That's what good therapy does.

***TOM:*** Yes, it seems odd that therapy is generally not seen as conversation. From Fred Newman and Lois Holzman (1997, & Chapter 5) I've come to see words as 'tools' possibly customized by the people using them—and indexed to how they make sense of each other. Indexicality is an ethnomethodology term referring to how understandings are contextualized in this manner. So, when I say, David, "remember what finishing grad school was like?"—we index somewhat different experiences, though social convention treats them as if they are the same.

***DAVID:*** "9/11" comes to mind.

***TOM:*** There's another. And we can *use* words in novel ways. Think of all the ways "9/11" was construed. Those who see language as an unambiguous "tool" for accurately and correctly transmitting understandings—their understandings—will be at odds with those who see things "correctly". It is a recipe for conflict over "how things are". Still, people tend to use language in resourceful and poetic ways particular to their cultural histories and relational circumstances.

***D12:*** Your description of words as tools helps illustrate how we may actively construct meaning together in the moment *despite* the surrounding context of cultural understandings that give certain resonances to the words we use. Poetic talk involves "languaging" in novel ways. Within a psychiatric language, "fidgeting" may be understood as a "symptom" of "attention deficit disorder". But choosing a competence-oriented language makes room for speaking of the habit as an indication of "abundant energy". Some discourses constrain meaning making, others expand it; which shall we choose? In Chapter 7, Peter Rober talks of paying attention to our inner conversations in selecting which words to bring to the therapeutic dialogue. The poet's creation is an ethical act.

***TOM:*** I like that, and its flipside occurs when someone names our experience 'for us', and that naming (or discourse from which it was derived) doesn't fit. Critical discourse analysts and narrative therapists (example, Johnella Bird in chapter 4) suggest we cultivate this kind of ethical sensitivity to meaning, especially since discourses offer incomplete and value-based ways to understand and relate our experiences to each other. Therapy, seen this way, focuses on the "conceptual resources" (e.g., words, metaphors) afforded or constrained by different discourses. For example, if I conceptualize bereavement in a technical or psychological discourse, neither may afford the conceptual resources available in poetic or spiritual discourse.

***DAVID:*** I think Nick Todd and Alan Wade richly portray this (Chapter 9) by showing how persons who've been abused may conceptualize their actions as "evidence of victimhood", while by drawing on an alternate discourse they may ponder their active and courageous resistance to the abuse. I think sometimes the therapist's role is to offer up a discourse as a resource in the service of constructing more helpful meanings.

***TOM:*** I'm fine with that, David and hope therapists invite clients into a practical-critical stance where meaning-making is a rigorous activity of scrutinizing any language for its fit or adequacy. No question, some discourses can be more helpful than others in this regard, and I like the notion that therapy can help clients become more discerning about the words and languages they use in and beyond therapy.
***DAVID:*** That process of settling on which languages to use in the therapeutic conversation-at-hand intrigues me. There is much to be said about making room for the client's language and this may get more attention in what you called the "micro" realm of discursive work (as in the chapter by Katz & Shotter). On the other hand, practitioners like Monk and Sinclair (Chapter 10) have their eyes trained on the macro level, the broader social setting for those micro-exchanges. They're more inclined to invite clients to reflect on the negative fallout of dominant language they use for representing their experiences, and introduce them to new ways of speaking about their lives. The measure of truly collaborative practice is in how we settle in on these various ways of talking together.
***TOM:*** Yes, and about your ("settle") comment: there is usually some negotiability in what we say and how we say it. This fits my view of collaborative practice, whether in language we propose for understanding client problems or solutions, or in the kinds of conversations we invite clients to join. Most people (helping professionals included) use language unaware of its constraining and value-based influences on helping conversation. So, settling how we talk with clients—in our shared descriptions or ways of talking—can be key to a collaborative partnership.
***DAVID:*** In a sense, when we "plug in" to particular discourses, they light up different territories. But who gets to hold the plug; who chooses the socket? This is an ethical question: an orientation to discourse unveils the moral dimensions of the conversational craft. Glenn Larner (Chapter 2) elaborates on this in developing Levinas' (1969) notion that we are fundamentally ethical beings. The word "collaborative" takes on much significance in this context, when talk is seen as action that inescapably enacts values and impacts on others.
***TOM:*** Collaboration asks us to revisit what it means to coordinate our interactions with clients, to fit their preferences and circumstances while not abandoning our morals and ethics. Many hit a conceptual and ethical wall here. Once we acknowledge that our talking plays a role in constructing understandings (example: how different is the church official's "I christen you. . . " from the therapist's "you have disorder X"?—both are examples of J. L. Austin's, 1962, 'performatives') and actions we face ethical questions like how 'monological' we will be with clients. How much do our pre-understandings and accustomed professional ways of talking shunt our conversations with clients into *our* familiarities?
***DAVID:*** I wonder if you could say more about how this pertains to monologue versus dialogue, Tom, and how these relate to ethical concerns.
***TOM:*** Here things can get complicated, depending on how one defines dialogue. Most definitions of dialogue identify a conversation of reciprocal influence. So

much of mental health practice can feel pre-scripted, because aside from an initial discussion of clients' concerns or goals in seeing the practitioner, things can get quite monological from that point onward. For theorists like Foucault (1973), or Deleuze and Guattari (1987), this is where therapeutic conversation becomes *institutionalized*—as we fit client meanings into our (not their) interpretive frameworks. Improvised dialogues based on collaborations particular to the emergent preferences and resourcefulness of clients and therapists sound dangerous by contrast (Strong, 2002). Like any dialogue, they might take clients and therapists to unexpected places.

***DAVID:*** The word "improvisation" itself suggests the end point's up in the air, and implies a faith in the client's resourcefulness and good intention because it involves letting go of the institutional roadmap. Bill Hanec (Chapter 12) co-creates improvised scenarios in his mens' groups. By his account, it's difficult to predict how the ideas he brings will get played out, although they typically open up on what for some men are unfamiliar territories of respect and mutuality in relationships. The improvisation loosens the grip of certain discourses the men typically play out in violence and abuse, opening the door to very different conversations about their experience.

***TOM:*** I appreciate this and remember Harlene Anderson (1997, see her chapter with Paul Burney) writing about conversations in therapy needing to be different from those that clients have been having with themselves and others. Paraphrasing Bateson (1980), needed are conversational differences that make a difference. The impatience some have with talk therapies is that people can stay conceptual, and not practically engage with change. Often needed are extra-ordinary conversations that are intentionally creative that break from stale, resource-impoverished, or fetishized discourses in which stuck actions and understandings can be embedded.

***DAVID:*** I think this is particularly important with discourses that pathologize or marginalize in some manner. Many entrenched ways of describing and acting that may ill-serve the persons they're intended to help formed around institutional considerations (budget restraints, scheduling logistics, waiting lists, drives for standardized service delivery, and so on). Sometimes that breaking free you speak of is the rejection of stereotyping, categorizing, and other practices that dishonor people and render their uniqueness invisible. In some cases, discursive practice takes on libratory dimensions.

***TOM:*** Yeah, discourse analysts and narrative therapists are great for taking us to taken for granted "sites of contestable meaning". For example, an expert's language like that in the DSM-IVTR can offer a symptom-based way of conceptualizing and responding to clients' concerns. In contesting this discourse as the *only* way of understanding, we negotiate space for other discourses offering different solution pathways. I'm not suggesting that all understandings require such reflection or deconstruction, to see or question what supports them. And, I see our conversation (like others) as one we sometimes sustain or extend, and sometimes *negotiate* as we propose and work out new content or directions.

***DAVID:*** Your comments highlight, for me, differences in the way discursive practitioners engage with that negotiation. Macro-oriented practitioners are more inclined to import some unusual ideas and practices into conversations. This may include deliberately inviting clients to critique apparently unhelpful ideas, or speaking about problems as external to persons, even though this way of speaking defies linguistic convention. I think discourses (as noun) are not only constraining, as we've mainly emphasized here—they're also potentially useful resources that emerge from cultural traditions. We can learn and benefit from bodies of thought and practice that precede us. But they must be held lightly, to avoid adopting a dogmatic stance that may sideline the client in the negotiation of meaning.

***TOM:*** David, this relates to the meaning units central to how we practice. There is a tradition in therapy to go after what Lynn Hoffman (2001) has referred to as "the thing in the bushes", what we see as the 'culprit' causing problems or constraining solutions. A "thing in the bushes" attitude can concern me here should therapists indict particular words or discourses as those "things". You've spoken about this in how therapists can 'colonize clients with their passions', hi-jacking therapeutic conversation for particular ideological purposes (Paré, 2003). And, therapists can become disrespectful should they see clients as dupes needing their knowing deconstructive and reconstructive guidance.

***DAVID:*** Point taken: the notion of some thing or other "in the bushes" might be useful to a client to makes sense of events, and it might not. We need to check, and in doing so we adopt . a not-knowing stance, while simultaneously bringing ideas to the dialogic table, as it were. Despite the risks of what our contributors Todd and Wade have called "psycolonization" (Todd and Wade, 1994), I do believe it's precisely because our ideas *are* different from our clients that creative and constructive dialogue ensues. I think we discursive practitioners sometimes get overly preccoupied with the purported ills of ideas and practices associated with modernist traditions when we could be learning more about how to join with clients in evaluating the pragmatic worth of *any* ideas and practices (modern *or* postmodern) we bring into therapeutic dialogues. Again, this brings us to ethics and an issue that Glenn Larner (Chapter 2) has articulated for some time now.

***TOM:*** This common presumption that we speak the same language can create "differends" (Lyotard, 1988), impasses where my discourse and yours can be conceptually and evaluationally different, the stuff of parallel discursive worlds. In whose discourse will therapy be conducted in? Whose evaluations should count? Therapeutic conversation is not unlike many conversations between strangers in everyday life. They work out a shared discourse, to bridge differences and similarities in their ways of understanding and talking. They can't commandeer the conversation to the familiarities of their own conversational turf; they make room for and work out their differences, using whatever words and ways of talking are helpful to moving forward.

***DAVID:*** "Helpful" is a word that resonates strongly for me; I appreciate its pragmatic ring. We arrive at what is helpful through our dialogue and may discover to our surprise that there's a piece of an institutional narrative that a person finds very useful to them. This calls on us to loosen our grips on pre-set givens, whether "dominant" discourses or well-intentioned libratory ones (Paré, 2003). A discursive orientation frees me from the futile quest to get "to the bottom of things". It's what is helpful in moving us forward that counts—and evaluating that is all part of the dialogue.

***TOM:*** "Moving forward" was a phrase Wittgenstein (1958) repeatedly used to describe how we might overcome our problems with language, David. We've been word-smithing our way forward here, and therapy strikes me similarly. Crafting shared intentions, shared understandings, shared ways of going forward are linguistic activities where we work out a language that can take us forward. These conversations reflect the moral, aesthetic and other considerations that conversations, cultural and face-to-face, work out (Taylor, 1989). People can be pretty generous in how they understand and develop shared intentions and actions together. They might disagree over perspicuous understandings, but in shifting from "correct meanings" to adequate or effective meanings, going forward becomes more attainable.

***DAVID:*** And that looks different every time; therapeutic conversations have an exquisitely idiographic quality. By idiographic, I mean specific and particular: instead of viewing clients as one of a 'class' of persons identified by a particular population marker or presenting problem (e.g., "anorectics"), we cherish their uniqueness. We orient to the suprises they bring, rather than turning to our bookshelves, to learn what their "type" thinks, feels, and needs in order to change. When we experience a person as a "type" we are blinded to their resourcefulness, dulled to the aliveness of our encounters with them. Of course now I'm clearly falling out of line with one contemporary thrust towards one-size-fits-all, manualized treatment targeted at specific population subgroups.

***TOM:*** Yeah, that one-size-fits-all approach seems *monocultural*, a particular descriptive/prescriptive worldview. This is my nightmare for therapy, (a dream for some?): mental health maps out all problems using professional language like the DSM, to which we hitch authorized prescriptions for intervening, addressing each possible diagnosis thusly. In short, therapy would be pre-scripted, with client responses slotted into pre-established categories. This, ostensibly, is what some see as required, to put therapy on the same footing as medicine (Rose, 1990). From there questions of competent and ethical practice can be answered by turning to what is pre-set, by how closely practitioners adhere to these conversational protocols. In this book we have authors critiquing variations on this way of institutionalizing practice (see Chris Kinman & Peter Finck Chapter 14, and Hans Skott-Myhre's

Chapter 13). But, let me reverse this, and ask you if some might read anarchy into discursively practiced therapy that doesn't operate from a unified body of knowledge and practices.

***DAVID:*** My concern is that in the quest for uniformity, that flight from so-called anarchy, we banish that specificity which may be our most precious resource. It's the texture and tone of the particular that opens unforeseen possibilities. There is no manual for such things. In the precisely non-universal dimensions of these encounters, we find new ways forward. If this is anarchy, there's gold in them there hills.

***TOM:*** David, Ken Gergen (2002) recently described this as the "suppression of cultural hybridity", ways our professions limit dialogue by sanctioning a narrow range of professional conversation. Therapy has many 'aporectic' moments where the possibilities for new ('golden') meanings abound. "Aporia" refers to indeterminate meaning, and that opens up the concept of how meanings are 'determined'. "Nailing things down", determining them with authoritative meaning seems imperialistic, especially when it crowds out other fitting idioms we might work out for relating to shared experiences, and each other.

***DAVID:*** Which brings us back to your nightmare, and mine. In many respects, the trend that you darkly refer to is about wringing the ambiguity out of the world, and out of the word. There is so much richness and opportunity for creativity in that vertiginous place between pre-set meanings. Does this nudge us towards the slippery slope to anarchy? I don't think so. But it does lead us away from the kind of large scale empirical studies which factor the idiographic out of the picture in order to render a conclusion somehow untainted by local variation. But do we really want to strive for a homogeneous world? I'd rather see us assume that what lies out there is more like an ecological reserve full of mystery and complexity, and develop habits of relationship that minimize the chances of us eradicating species, as it were, in our earnestness to be helpful.

***TOM:*** This stance of respectful curiosity seems central to the discursive therapies; if we are not surprising ourselves in how clients respond to us we're probably just extending our own narratives, with what they tell us. Levinas (1969) sees ascribing meaning as *violent* when we "totalize" with our meanings—by closing down other possibilities for talking or understanding.

***DAVID:*** I think you're getting at what I view as an (appropriately) massive disjuncture between natural science and discursive therapeutic practice. I think it's fair to say that your nightmare's projection of one trend in the therapeutic domain looks a lot like the final colonization of conversation by natural scientists. The challenge, which Sheila McNamee (Chapter 15) articulates, is to demonstrate that a preferable way forward may not be to apply empirically-validated, packaged interventions, but to co-invent therapeutic directions *in conjunction with* clients. And our therapist training programs should make more room for these collaborative conversational practices, alongside the perhaps more common therapist-driven models and descriptive snapshots of the makeup of certain "client populations". This pertains to Multicultural Counselling, too. As much as I'm encouraged by the rapid growth of attention to multicultural concerns, we need to be careful not to reify taxonomies of culture that look like periodic tables in a different guise.

***TOM:*** 'Periodic tables' seem a penultimate reification, and they privilege the general over the particular, and product over process. When we have empirically validated treatments (EVTs) that are supposed to work regardless of context, or client preference, what should one make of the particularizing or customizing thrust of how discursive therapies could be practiced?

***DAVID:*** That pointing to what *could* be is how I prefer to see what we're doing with this book, Tom: it's a temporary stopping point in the ever-flowing conversation about how talk figures in generating possibilities. . This doesn't feel like an end-point by any means in *our* conversation, but perhaps is a place to turn the mirror on ourselves and see what we notice about the exchange we've had over these many months. I think we've confirmed that a textual medium is very handy indeed for portraying discourse as noun: our chapter overflows with the "product" of a generative conversation. But in the tidy parade of edited exchanges we see no evidence of the *verb*: the dialogic process—sometimes arduous, sometimes exhilarating—that produced this chapter. How about if we take a moment to render that process more visible (in retrospect) by debriefing on it here?

***TOM:*** David, today (April 1, 2003) I got your April Fool's message ("let's scrap the dialogue chapter") and for an angst filled moment I believed you. Dialogue can sound so wholesome until you're in there (like us) trying to be understood, avoiding misrepresentations, haggling over words, provoking and countering ideas, while still trying to move forward in mutually satisfying ways. We weren't talking down tubes where the accuracy of our transmission and reception was the issue (Maturana and Varela, 1987); that overlooks the rhetorical and moral dimensions of our talk as our way of resolving matters of "right and good" (Billig, 1996; Gergen, 1999). If I'd turned to you at any point and said in reference to 'my' words and ideas, "David, you don't get it, this is how things are"—what could I have turned to, to make such a claim? In the absence of universal standards to adjudicate conversations like ours a discursive approach asks us: how do we come up with shared and meaningful ways of going forward together?

***DAVID:*** Tom, I think that among other things, what kept us in the conversation are the choices we continuously made in responding to each other. Of the various voices I could identify in my inner conversations accompanying our exchanges, some drifted towards dismissal—much like the "you don't get it" you mentioned. This to me is a milder version of what happens when a therapist, frustrated in the attempt to "engage" a client, resorts to a diagnostic label such as borderline personality disorder. The therapist is thereby exonerated, because the failure to coordinate is placed in the lap of the pathologized client. I think we also do this more globally when we suspend talks because one party is "evil". I experienced the two of us as avoiding this entrenchment by choosing to speak of "missing each other"—an invitation to the other to speak more, the announcement of a commitment to listening more. Not to say it's been a cakewalk. For me, our prolonged exchange has surfaced numerous differences between us—in terms of both what we prefer to talk about and how we prefer to talk about it.

***TOM:*** I'd go back to Wittgenstein's 'perspicuity' here—language to optimally represent how we mutually want to be understood and go forward together. Of course, we bring different criteria for what 'optimal' means but it took hard conversational work to arrive at ways of going forward that were inclusive and meaningful for both of us. There were times when I thought things important to me were glossed in these exchanges and, in a frustrated moment, I even wrote that you had a "conceptual allergy" to ideas I was trying to include in our discussion. Of course, that sort of talk doesn't serve either of us well. How are you feeling about our personal efforts toward perspicuity here?

***DAVID:*** I've experienced those efforts happening on various fronts. It has probably been most evident for me in our striving for agreement on word meanings: I can think of a prolonged discussion we had that hinged on the word "instrumental". This relates to what Garfinkel (1967) says about the indexicality of language—until we saw that we were indexing the word to different contexts, using it differently for different purposes, we missed each other. For me, this discovery changed everything, and what felt like an impasse dissolved. But there were other ways we needed to coordinate our talk that we may never have named, but which we "danced" together. I'm thinking particularly of phone conversations that often shifted the tenor of our interactions—both written and spoken. The tone and volume of our voices, our phrasing and pacing and silences, communicated our concerns and vulnerabilities in ways that our e-mails could not, and I always went away from those spoken exchanges feeling more synchronized with you and more ready to go forward again together.

***TOM:*** For me, David, we are talking about dialogue's adequacy, what makes conversation good enough for us both so we can move forward. Of course, there's always more room for meaning, and no final word on what we say. I've been seeing our stuckpoints as challenges in finding perspicuity. At times, I felt that your attempts to highlight our seeming points of convergence insufficiently acknowledged nuances that mattered to me. I would respond hoping that these nuances could be better reflected in our shared efforts, and we worked this out, into something adequate for moving on. I think this parallels what goes on in therapy or any other conversation that's meaningful to those having it. We strove for perspicuity and usually settled for adequacy.

***DAVID:*** "Adequate" has a forgiving ring to it—something like "good enough". I've been struck—astonished at times—by the seemingly endless layers of meaning in our conversations with each other and in the conversations *about* those conversations. We've 'pinged and ponged" (as you once put it) back and forth, and I've witnessed a gradual movement towards what has felt like adequately mutual understanding. But I mean something more than "you (mostly) get me and I (mostly) get you". There's more: our exchanges over these months have increasingly contained echoes of the *other's* utterances. The contours of what may have started as "my view" and "your view" altered in response to one another so that we've come to a place of "we (mostly) get *us* better". Is "better" good enough? It's "adequate", for going on, but as you said, there's always room for more meanings. Our exchanges have also surfaced many new mysteries yet to be explored.

***TOM:*** And still we grapple for adequate words. Let's not forget the many places where we said something later, and retraced (behind the scenes, so to speak) our steps, inserting concepts that weren't there before. Now, why should this matter? Personally, I like the idea that we can go back to some meanings, revise them as we see fit, and move on, all the better for those revisions.

***DAVID:*** That helps to remind me how different an edited textual exchange is from spoken conversation; for me, this experiment has highlighted many of those distinctions. It's also rendered more apparent a variety of processes that I think equally apply to spoken talk. I've been aware of a different conversational "pace" between us, with you typically responding much quicker. Our vocabularies, going into the exchange, also showed some interesting contrasts and have been subject to much discussion as we've attempted to articulate our (opening) views without obliterating the others'. At this point, my vocabulary from speaking about dialogue has expanded, courtesy of yours. There's also a *shared* vocabulary that's emerged, so that the two of us can "go more places together" as it were. And as we have, we've encountered *new* nuances, new distinctions: I certainly don't feel any nearer to closure.

***TOM:*** I think that is part of our postmodern predicament: we live with tensions and possibilities that keep us talking, without getting in any final word.

***DAVID:*** Well, here's to future conversations, furthering talk.

## REFERENCES

Anderson, H. (1997). *Conversation, language and possibilities*. New York: Basic Books.

Austin, J.L. (1962). *How to do things with words*. (J.O. Urmson, Ed.). Cambridge, MA: Harvard University Press.

Bakhtin, M. (1984). *Problems of Dostoevsky's poetics*. (C. Emerson, Ed. & Trans.). Minneapolis, University of Minnesota Press.

Bateson, G. (1980). *Mind and nature: A necessary unity*. New York: Bantam Books.

Berger, P., & Luckmann, T. (1967). *The social construction of reality: a treatise in the sociology of knowledge*. New York: Doubleday.

Billig, M. (1996). *Arguing and thinking*. (Second edition). New York: Cambridge University Press.

Caplan, P. (1991). How do they decide who is normal? The bizarre but true tale of the DSM-IV process. *Canadian Psychology*, 32, 162–170.

Danziger, K. (1997). *Naming the mind: How psychology found its language*. Thousand Oaks, CA: Sage.

Garfinkel, H. (1967). *Studies in ethnomethdology*. Cambridge, UK: Polity Press.

Deleuze, G. & Guattari, F. (1987). *A thousand plateaus: Capitalism and schizophrenia*. (B. Massumi, Trans.). Minneapolis: University of Minnesota Press.

Foucault, M. (1973). *Birth of the clinic: An archaeology of medical perception*. New York: Pantheon.

Gergen, K. (1999). *An invitation to social construction*. Thousand Oaks, CA: Sage.

Gergen, K. (2002). Psychological science as culture. Presentation at the American Psychological Association 110th Annual Convention. August 23. Chicago.

Goodman, N. (1978). *Ways of worldmaking*. Hassocks, England: Harvester Press.

Hacking, I. (1999). *The social construction of what?* Cambridge, MA: Harvard University Press.

Heritage, J. (1984). *Garfinkel and ethnomethodology*. Cambridge, MA: Polity.

Hoffman, L. (2001). *An intimate history of family therapy*. New York: WW. Norton.

Larner, G. (2003, in-press). Towards a critical therapy. *International Journal of Critical Psychology*, 6, 9–29.

Levinas, E. (1969). *Totality and infinity: An essay on exteriority*. (A. Lingis, Trans.). Pittsburgh, PA: Duquesne University Press.

Lyotard, J-F. (1988). *The differend: Phrases in dispute*. (G. Van Den Abeele, Trans.) Minneapolis, MN: University of Minnesota Press.

Maranhão, T. (1986). *Therapeutic discourse and Socratic dialogue: A cultural critique*. Madison, WN: University of Wisconsin Press.

Newman, F. & Holzman, L. (1997). *The end of knowing*. New York: Routledge.

Maturana, H. & Varela, F. (1988). *The tree of knowledge: Biologic roots of human understanding*. Boston, MA: Shambhala.

Paré, D.A. (2003, in press). Discursive wisdom: Reflections on ethics and therapeutic knowledge. *International Journal of Critical Psychology*.

Rober, P. (2002). Constructive hypothesizing, dialogic understanding and the therapist's inner conversation: Some ideas about knowing and not-knowing in the family therapy session. *Journal of Marital and Family Therapy, 28*(4), 467–478.

Rose, N. (1990). *Governing the soul: The shaping of the private self*. New York: Routledge.

Sacks, H. (1995). *Lectures on conversation*. (G. Jefferson & E. Schegloff, Eds). Oxford: Blackwell.

Shotter, J. (1984). *Social accountability and selfhood*. Oxford: Blackwell.

Strong, T. (2002). Dialogue in therapy's 'borderzone'. *The Journal of Constructivist Psychology, 15*, 245–262.

Taylor, C. (1989). *Sources of the self: The making of the modern identity*. Cambridge, MA: Harvard University Press.

Todd, N. & Wade, A. (1994) Domination, deficiency, and psychotherapy. Part I *The Calgary Participator*, Fall, 37–46.

Wittgenstein, L. (1958). *Philosophical investigations*. 3rd Edition. (G.E.M. Anscombe: Trans). New York: MacMillan.

*Chapter* 2

# *Levinas Therapy as Discourse Ethics*

GLENN LARNER WITH CONVERSATIONAL PARTNERS
PETER ROBER AND TOM STRONG

## INTRODUCING LEVINAS

In this chapter I introduce the ethical philosophy of Levinas and consider its implications for therapy as a discourse ethics, providing practice examples along the way. Emmanuel Levinas who died in 1995 is one of the most significant Continental philosophers of our time (Critchley and Bernasconi, 2002). Like French contemporary Jacques Derrida (1999) his thinking has influenced diverse fields of poststructuralist study including more recently psychology and therapy (Kunz, 1998; Gantt and Williams, 2002). Levinas's unique contribution is the notion that first and foremost we are ethical beings. This *ethics first* philosophy was to some extent a personal response to the horrors of the Second World War and the holocaust. As Levinas (1995) says: "To overcome the ethical is the beginning of all violence. To acknowledge this is very important after the events of 1933 to 1945" (p. 58).

Though for Levinas the ethical is overridden not just by physical violence but by a Western philosophy of being, which effaces persons by reducing them to concepts like reason or intentionality. War and philosophy can have similar effects, indeed the former is "fixed in the concept of totality, which dominates Western philosophy" (Levinas, 1969, p. 21). To reduce the lived experience of another person to finite categories of our understanding is a totalizing act that does them violence through language. We no longer see the *person* but an idea or representation of their being as defined by cultural, gender, physical, racial, psychological attributes, and so on. Whether you are a Nazi or a philosopher (in the case of Heidegger disturbingly both), to reduce the other to an idea or concept is dehumanizing and compromises their difference and freedom.

## The Saying and the Said

A person is not an abstract concept, a biological entity or cognitive being but someone we speak *to* as part of a relational act; by placing them under a category or label we step outside the relationship and cease to participate in a conversation. Acting as outside observers we impose a totalizing meaning or rule of the same, an objective way of talking and thinking *about* a person, that Levinas calls the *Said*. In simplistic terms the Said is the objective content of what we say, the ideas, meanings and observations we want to communicate. This form of discourse is totalizing and violent when it forces meaning on a person ignoring what is uniquely different about them. It deploys what Martin Buber famously called 'I-It knowledge' rather than 'I-Thou dialogue'. This treats "the other person as a thing under my power" seizing the relationship in a total act of comprehension (Levinas, 1993, p. 40).

By contrast Saying is the relational context for speaking and communicating *with* another person, the here and now dialogic encounter with another human being. The focus is less what is said and more the *how* or process of saying it. The intent is vocative: to engage others in dialogue rather than use language in a way that treats them as objects. Here discourse is an ethical process of making space for the voice of the other in dialogue and conversation[1]. The self is defined not as I or It but as *thou* where language breaks through as "the very bursting forth of thought dialogically coming out of itself" (Levinas, 1993, p. 40).

Yet for Levinas both the Saying and Said are needed: "Without the Said there is no philosophy and, more importantly, no society, justice, judgement or ethics either" (Davis, 1996, p. 79). In ethical relation, knowledge, technology and power that define the Said are still there, but there *for* the other. I will comment on this later in relation to how discursive therapists use language and knowledge in therapy.

## Facing the Other

The ethical relation celebrates a person's difference or otherness or as Critchley and Bernasconi (2002) say: "Ethics is the location of a point of otherness . . . that cannot be reduced to the same" (p. 15). What contributes most to another person being different is the fact they have a body and especially a face, which establishes

[1] This meaning of discourse derives from the Latin *curro curs*-run 'to let things run' as in 'rambling, digression, expatiating or copious speaking and talking' (The Australian Pocket Oxford Dictionary, p. 202). However the term also refers to a professional or technical language based on prescribed beliefs and covert practices of power.

they are completely *Other* from me. This is something we experience or *feel*: "The other's otherness is what makes me feel and makes me think what I feel "(Diprose, 2002, p. 137). Ethical relation begins with my experience of another person as physically separate from and yet proximate to me; this is a spiritual-like awareness of the singularity and separateness of human beings[2].

For Levinas what is most Other about a person is their face as a powerful expression of personhood and a focal point for interpersonal communication. Here Critchley and Bernasconi (2002) note: "The central task of Levinas's work, in his words, is the attempt to describe a relation with the other person that cannot be reduced to comprehension. He finds this in what he famously calls the 'face to face' relation (p. 8)". Infant attachment research shows mutual gazing at the face is an essential component of bonding between parent and baby. Though for Levinas the face is my whole experience or encounter with another person in so far as they transcend the knowledge or concept I have of them: "The way in which the other presents himself, exceeding *the idea of the other in me*, we here name face" (Levinas in Critchley and Bernasconi, p. 15). What the face speaks to is our *failure* to comprehend the other, it is "an epiphany that resists conceptual grasp" (Wyschogrod, 2002, p. 195). A person has a body and face beyond my concept or understanding and cannot be captured within a prescribed system of meaning and language.

## DISCOURSE ETHICS

In other words when we engage in discourse persons have a singular and individual presence that defines them as other and not me, a body and face that allows relationship and conversation to be possible. Because persons already have a meaning we have to be mindful about using language to totalize their experience: "The neighbour is precisely what has a meaning *immediately*, before one ascribes one to him" (Levinas, 1987, p. 119). This is why for Levinas (1995) the first move of discourse is always ethical: "Language is fraternity, and thus a responsibility for the other (p. 123)". In the physical presence of another there is a welcoming and reaching out, a gesture that acknowledges the person as other.

This is what Levinas calls the 'place offered to the stranger', which provides refuge or hospitality to a fellow human being: "the welcome of the other or of the face as neighbor and as stranger, as neighbor *insofar as* he is a stranger, man, and brother" (Derrida, 1999, p. 68). Discourse begins with the welcoming of the other as separate or different from me. The other is my neighbor with a body that requires

[2] For Levinas the ethical is also the spiritual. As Derrida (1999) notes in his eulogy, *Adieu To Emmanuel Levinas*, "ethics" is a Greek equivalent "for the Hebraic discourse on the holiness of the separated (*kadosh*)" (p. 61).

nourishment and a face that speaks and calls for a welcome. Ethics is a welcoming of the stranger as physically separated or other, and from such fraternity dialogue or discourse begins.

## The Self is Ethical

Personhood begins *with* the neighbor; persons are not disconnected thinking beings but in dialogue with and responsible *for* each other. The self is not structured as *I*, but as *you, I* or persons' in dialogue and relationship; self is defined in the process of reaching out to and welcoming the other in language, conversation and discourse. Persons are constituted by responsibility and ethics: "The word *I* means *here I am*, answering for everything and for everyone "(Levinas quoted in Derrida, 1999, p. 55). What comes first is not self but the other, an emptying out or giving up of oneself that Levinas (1987) calls an "ethical event of "expiation for another"" (p. 124).

## Ethics before Discourse

Ethics is presupposed by discourse or as Levinas says: "This responsibility is prior to dialogue, to the exchange of questions and answers . . . (quoted in Derrida, 1999, pp. 56–7)". What makes discourse possible is first of all an ethical reaching out to the other, who is put before oneself. This simple humility or interpersonal generosity as an interest in a person's otherness, as in a cultural, ethnic or gender sense, provides the conditions for discourse as a mutual exchange between persons. For Levinas ethics as a responsibility towards the other is a condition of discourse. From ethics, discourse follows. Or as Diprose (2002) comments on Levinas: "And this giving of one's self-possession amounts to the opening of myself beyond myself through discourse, conversation, language" (p. 140).

The talking or discursive person is first of all ethical and to be ethical is to acknowledge the physical presence of the other particularly their face. Before I speak, I welcome the other. Before language and subjectivity is ethics: "To approach the Other in discourse is to welcome . . . " (Levinas, quoted by Derrida, 1999, p. 18). Before I, before the word, comes the other as a Saying between us. *I other*. The other constitutes my self as a communication in gestures or words. While persons are discursive beings, discourse depends first of all on ethics[3]. Because the self is first of all ethical, welcoming the other is always the starting point for discourse. This is what Derrida (1999) following Levinas calls an ethic of hospitality, where "discourse, justice, ethical uprightness have to do first of all with *welcoming* (p. 35)".

[3]This has important implications for social constructionist theory I am unable to develop here.

## THERAPY AS DISCOURSE ETHICS

What does this mean for a discursive therapy? An ethical encounter is not merely discursive but presupposes a physical and non-verbal experience of the other person. Before anything can be said or done the therapist is first of all *there* for the other, like a mother's face is there for her infant before words are spoken. This form of relating *takes in* freely, it is unconditional; it is the non-discursive condition of the discursive, the bridging of a chasm between two persons through what is unsaid and cannot necessarily be put into words, what Frosh (2001) refers to as the *unsayable* in therapy. Cohen (2002) describes this pre-discursive sensibility using Levinas's concept of 'maternal psyche': "The other morally encountered is "in-me" as if the other were literally in my body, the other's pain my pain, the other's suffering my suffering "(p. 46). Here the self is defined ethically as an obligation to the other as if they were present *in* me.

Discourse in therapy begins with this pre-discursive welcoming or taking in of the other. The therapist knows and thinks *with* the person in a way that is ethically and dialogically responsive, more than empathy this being-in- the other defines what it is to be human. First there is an orientation to the person as different followed by a desire to learn their language or culture and participate in discourse. Here the therapist's use of a professional language is tentative and depends on first learning and becoming fluent in the language of the other, such as the descriptive terms and metaphors they use. What clients say is put *before* what therapists say and do; their words and meaning are taken in by the therapist. This allows the possibility of a reciprocal gesture, where the client is open to taking in what therapists have to say and offer. This dialogic process is a face-to- face exchange and sharing of meaning, a flow of conversation between persons that allows a common language of understanding to evolve. Whatever professional or client languages are spoken this mutual welcoming is what defines therapy as a discourse ethics.

## PRACTICE EXAMPLE 1

(The following practice illustrations are composites of dialogue with real clients using fictional names).

*Jay is a highly intellectually gifted 14-year-old boy referred because of his chronic negativity, self-denigration, oppositional behavior, social isolation, academic under-achievement and almost total non-compliance with class or home-work, all issues of several years standing. In the initial family interview I asked why they had come to see me.*

*Jay:* *I'm insane; my parents brought me here to stop me from being insane.*
I asked Jay what might lead them to think that.

*Jay:* *They're stupid.*

Mother: *It's complex. He's not coping at school, reluctant to engage in lessons, unwilling to learn and not inviting people over.*
Jay: *I have no friends mum.*
Mother: *He's not pursuing sport.*
Jay: *All this means I'm lazy.*
Mother: *And worse of all, he has hurt himself scratching his arm on a few occasions.*
Father: *With a craft knife.*
Jay: *I'm high on the insanity list.*
Mother: *He is extremely bright but very unhappy in the school environment. He's happy being at home if we're not talking about school.*
Jay: *If it involves thought or energy.*
At this point I asked what the father thought.
Father: *I am a depressive personality. The systems of the world don't suit us.*
Mother: *Jay is also a depressive.*
Jay: *The world is a hole.*

## A Welcoming Stance

Jay spoke with an extreme sense of sarcasm and irony and was particularly scornful about counseling. Later I found out the father had a long history of severe depression involving medication and like Jay didn't take kindly to school or therapists. In this first interview I strongly *felt* both were extremely sensitive about labels like sane/insane, as evident from the way they continually introduced them in the conversation. Thus an essential part of welcoming this family was not to apply them; the challenge for me was *not* to be a therapist, to intervene by not intervening, to do therapy without doing therapy. In Levinasian terms this path *between* knowing and not knowing leaves meaning open and puts the person first before the language of therapy.

At the end of the session I told the family in the face of such complexity (as the mother termed it), I could not presume to offer a solution where none had been found, but we could talk more if they were willing. After one year we still meet together weekly for family therapy, a multisystemic approach that has included regular meetings with the school and Jay's closest friend. Jay is now significantly less depressed and oppositional, making friends, showing more interest in his work and participating at school. In discussing these changes the parents confirmed my ethical stance of not applying labels was crucial.

Here a relational stance of welcoming Jay and his family as other *is* the therapy. A therapist can be reflective or interpretive in the session and even suggest strategies for change but the crux is *how* this is done? In ethical relationship the therapist's voice is one among others. There is a collaborative sharing of ideas, insights, thinking and understanding, where meaning is not final or total but there is respect for its complexity. In the midst of a never ending riposte of words between Jay and his parents, I was given space to talk and contribute my own thoughts and reflections. For example, in one session I interpreted intense hostility between Jay and his mother in terms of attachment issues and they were prepared to listen because I had first listened to them. From my welcome I was welcomed, which meant whatever therapy I provided was more likely to be accommodated. Later the mother was astounded when Jay actually requested to speak to me alone about his school situation.

## The Relation to the Other

In these terms, therapy is first of all the enactment of a person-to-person relationship. Whatever a therapist says or does, what matters most is how he or she *is* towards the other. The therapist is hostage or host to the other welcoming him or her in a spirit of hospitality. This ethic is the substratum of therapy. Therapy is not a mere technology imposing a language of expertise and knowledge but first enacts a relational ethics. This is a gesture of hospitality, a welcoming of the other to a place where dialogue as a speaking between persons can occur. Whatever happens after that, in the form of therapeutic techniques, strategies or approaches is secondary to face to face Saying and dialogue.

This accords with outcome research showing what contributes most to change is not therapeutic technique or model but "common factors" across all approaches, like the therapeutic relationship and whether the therapist is perceived as empathic, caring and compassionate (Miller and Duncan, 1998; Larner, 2001). Change is not the result of a detached instrumental knowledge but emerges from the Saying between persons in the room. The language of therapy is not forced on others but a welcoming vehicle for discursive sharing. By taking care not to impose a preferred discourse from a position of power, the therapist helps persons to speak and construct their own language of change. Here therapy enacts a process of relational discourse; a shared language of understanding that allows agreement about the purpose of therapy, where there is less risk of a client resisting a therapist's language and interventions.

## A Thinking Space

Through ethics therapy becomes a talking or discursive space in which thinking is possible, where client and therapist learn to think and reflect together. The first step for the therapist is to be welcoming to what others say. Here thinking is not private but occurs in the presence of others, but it is also to be *disturbed* by the other. It is because the other is other and not me that I am obliged to respond and enter discourse. The other disturbs my self-sufficiency, forcing a relationship beyond myself through discourse. This disruption of my autonomy, which brings me into relation with others, *is* ethics. By welcoming what is strange and other my usual schemas are disrupted and new thinking and learning is possible. Thus with

Jay and his family I was forced to confront my own values and beliefs about what therapy can be or achieve. If I merely applied labels (like oppositional–defiant disorder) and corresponding treatment, they would have refused to participate[4]. If I was to help I had to encounter them face-to-face and in turn they were invited by my presence and words to reflect upon possibilities for change.

This ethical relation is distinct from a code of ethics all therapists are obliged to follow, like confidentiality and respecting personal boundaries (Sullivan, 2002). Over and above a professional ethics it is present at every interactive moment as a welcoming and speaking *to* the other. Whatever else is said or done in therapy the ethical relation prefigures *how* persons are to speak to one another. Here therapists model an ethical process, where persons are defined by their responsibility in discourse with each other.

## PRACTICE EXAMPLE 2

*Kino is a 13 year old boy with mild cerebral palsy, chronic encopresis, enuresis and lack of self-care skills in dressing and toileting. His physical disability is not severe enough to account for these difficulties; rather he refuses to care for himself. At school he is unable to learn or complete schoolwork. Kino presented as an affable, talkative lad adopting an 'I'm okay' posture saying he enjoyed school with no problems in his academic, social, personal or family life. The message from the parents was the exact opposite; they were exhausted by a daily regime that included putting him on the toilet to prevent soiling and wiping his bottom, which he refused to do. This latter issue became the focus of family therapy and after several interviews I shared my thinking about Kino's predicament.*

In reflecting with the family I suspected he was reluctant to grow up (which he freely admitted) and connected this life choice to parental anxiety about his disability from an early age. A wider systemic issue was the mother's role as a caregiver for her aged parents in the family home. I suggested Kino's refrain was opposite to the steam train *Puffing Billy* in the children's book, who struggling up the mountain repeats: "I think I can", I think I can". For Kino it was: "I can't therefore I won't". Yet like all adolescents Kino wished to be seen as normal and cool, particularly by peers and in this sense he was Janus-faced, with one face looking back to the safety and security of childhood and the other ahead. Nonetheless I said I could understood why Kino may not want to grow up and recounted a personal memory of my own soiling incident in early childhood, where like Kino I experienced the pleasure of sitting in one's pooh oblivious to the world. Here the therapist encountered Kino face to face; in struggling with his personal

[4] Outcome research shows multisystemic family therapy is an effective intervention (Cunningham and Henggeler, 1999) and this professional knowing can be integrated into the primary ethical stance I am advocating here.

dilemma about growing up, metaphorically speaking, I was in him and he was in me.

Next I asked the family: "What might entice a boy of Kino's age to grow up?" Kino replied he would 'love' (the first expression of enthusiasm I heard) to be five years older so he could access advanced technology like computer games. An animated relational exchange between Kino and his father followed that was different and surprising, particularly as I had not sensed a strong attachment between them. I asked what else being grown up might mean and to the astonishment of all Kino said in the future he fully expected to wipe his own bottom. The mother said this was the first time she had *ever* heard Kino talk in such a mature, self-aware and responsible manner. I asked whether technology might be accessible for Kino sooner rather than later and suggested a behavioral reward system using star charts for soiling, as the family had used them under previous therapists. For six months Kino has not soiled his pants and has wiped his bottom every day.

How do we explain such change? At one level it can be seen in terms of family therapy combined with behavioral techniques (Carr, 2000) part of a systemic process that explored the meaning of the problem; at another it enacted an ethical relationship pivotal to the change process. The *welcome* I accorded to Kino and his family allowed my reflections and a shared Saying about growing up in his personal and family story. Here the sharing of my own personal experience and a book about steam trains and other possibilities gently involved Kino in a discourse of change where he became more responsible to others and for himself.

## MODERN/POSTMODERN DISCOURSE IN THERAPY

> "Of course we inhabit an ontological world of technological mastery and political self-preservation. Indeed without these political and technological structures of organization we would not be able to feed mankind. This is the great paradox of human existence: we must use the ontological for the sake of the other, to ensure the survival of the other we must resort to the technical-political systems of means and ends . . . We have no option but to employ the language and concepts of Greek philosophy even in our attempts to go beyond them" (Levinas, 1984, p. 64).

In this section I discuss some implications of Levinas and discourse ethics for the modernist/postmodernist debate in therapy. I assume what Levinas here calls the *ontological* is manifest in a totalizing use of language in modern psychology and therapy today, which assumes an objective knowledge of psychological being. Otherwise known as the scientist-practitioner model or evidence-based practice in therapy, personal experience is diagnosed as individual pathology and treated in standard cost-effective ways, like biological psychiatry or cognitive therapy. Postmodern or discursive therapists deconstruct this paradigm in favor of narrative, social constructionist and relational understanding of persons in the world (Gergen, 1999). They critique the neglect of personal and relational context in modern therapy and emphasize the role of culture, gender, politics and spirituality in psychological well-being (Larner, 2001). Modern therapists in turn debunk non-evidence-based psychotherapy as wooly, unsubstantiated and ineffective.

## The Postmodern Fallacy

Now to use Levinas to support postmodern *as opposed to* modern therapy would be misleading as the above quote suggests. This commits what I call the postmodern fallacy, which paradoxically sets up a violent opposition or forced duality between narrative *and* science, the modern *or* postmodern. However this institutional or foundational move repeats the very totalizing that defines modernity; it is the same old politics of exclusivity where therapists belonging to one school of thought totalize and dismiss another (Larner, 2003). A science of therapy needs ethics to give it a human face, but it is not simply a matter of one replacing the other, one *or* the other, but a more complex situation of *both/and*.

As Levinas (1984) says ontology is "necessary but not enough (p. 64)", we may not be able to escape its language but we can introduce the ethical relation into it. Here the language of ethics and being co-exist (albeit uneasily) as the *ontological for the sake of the other,* a paradox that Levinas (1984) sees as providing a "golden opportunity for Western philosophy to open itself to the dimensions of otherness and transcendence beyond Being "(p. 64).

## Both Science and Ethics

Levinas notes if people are starving ethical relations are no use to anyone; without a technology of being there would be no persons or ethics at all. Likewise in therapy an ethical relation to the other behooves us to address psychological pain and suffering using the best modern technological means possible. For example, if a client is seriously depressed or psychotic, best practice such as hospitalization or medication may be life-saving. Ethical therapists have pragmatic concerns to apply what works best in therapy while acknowledging outcome research that establishes the therapist's relational stance as central; as my practice examples illustrate, what we do in therapy may be less relevant than *how* we do it.

## Therapy for the Other

Just as for Levinas the Saying and Said go together, in therapy there is a two way relationship between ethics and science or discourse and model, so that one enriches the other. Technology in therapy can be integrated as part of "the *thou* to describe a human encounter" (Levinas, 1963, p. 359). The challenge is *how* to apply knowledge and technology in an ethically sensitive way, that is, where what therapists say and do is in the service of the other. In ethical relation the person comes first before theory, knowledge and technique; these take second place to the person, the therapeutic narrative and the therapy relationship.

The various theories and techniques of modern psychology and therapy are still there, but there *for the other* (Williams and Gantt, 2002). Following Derrida I call this both/and stance an ethic of hospitality (Larner, in press), another name for it is discursive wisdom (Paré, 2003, in press) or collaborative influence (Strong, 2000), which respects all languages and discourses in psychology and therapy (Paré and Larner, in press).

> *Tom Strong: Lately I've been thinking of discourse as a conversational or conceptual immune system—a conditional way of being in the world or in the language you've shared here, it is a privileging of particular versions of the Said over the Saying. Extending this concept, it seems that some forms of 'the Said' serve us in both protective and growth-oriented ways, like particular traditions do. Many constructionists use the language of "resources" when they speak about these forms of the 'Said' (stories, concepts, discourses). How might Levinas have advocated for a therapy that combines the resourcefulness of some forms of the 'Said' AND therapist/client involvement in the 'Saying' of therapeutic conversation?"*
>
> *Glenn Larner: "I like your metaphor of discourse as a kind of conceptual immune system, which introduces the language of biology and the body into discursive thinking, which as you know has been neglected at least within family therapy and social constructionist circles. (Flaskas, 2002a). Discourse is not everything and Levinas puts great emphasis on body and face, the physical presence of the person before me as other who is experienced in the Saying between us. Now whatever is Said becomes a Saying or is translated into relational discourse and in this sense Levinas opens up the whole field of therapeutic knowledge to be available for the discursive therapist; we can utilize whatever therapy training and knowledge we have, which is there for the other. And in this day and age it would be irresponsible for therapists not to utilize particular resources of the Said, for example, best practice interventions for victims of trauma, violence, depression, self-harm, anxiety and so on. For example, a suicidal young person first requires protection and safety for their person; discourse can follow later (Larner, in press).*
>
> *What makes the difference for discourse ethics is how therapeutic knowledge is used, whether I put thou as ethical relation to the other first? It is not that Levinas denies knowledge; rather It proceeds from ethics. Because we fail in our attempt to completely know the other, a more humble way of knowing is required. As an ethical therapist I draw upon the training and knowledge of my discipline in a way that opens up what I know to not knowing or the otherness of the other. This means the resources of the Said, the technology and knowledge of therapy, become integrated as Saying in therapy conversation.*

## PRACTICE EXAMPLE 3

*A 14 year-old boy was referred to me because of chronic stealing and lying in the home. He had been adopted by an Australian family at the age of 5 years after spending his infancy and preschool years in an orphanage in Vietnam. Now while his behavior falls under psychological categories like conduct and reactive attachment disorder, to stop there tells us little, particularly as outcome research on treatment of these disorders is primitive(Carr, 2000). As I hear this boy's personal narrative I realize his symptoms relate not only to a serious disruption of early attachment but also to an extreme trauma and deprivation, where stealing and lying in the orphanage was essential to survival. In conversation with the adoptive family further systemic and cultural meanings emerge. The parent's have high Christian moral standards and judge stealing and lying as the most shameful behavior possible and this has led them to question their own parenting capacity and to doubt the whole adoptive venture. This has significant implications for ongoing attachment issues as well.*

### Knowing not to Know

Such reflection opens up the possibility of a rich *integrative* approach to therapy that includes psycho-education concerning attachment and trauma, behavioral management of stealing, family therapy, individual therapy and discussion of cultural and ethnic differences (Larner, in press). The ethical relation provides a link between these various languages. Here modern and postmodern therapy sit together *for* the sake of the other, which allows relevant psychological knowledge from neuropsychology, trauma and infant attachment research, cross-cultural adoption studies etc. to be treated with the fascination and respect they deserve. Like all therapists, discursive therapists have a professional responsibility to offer the wisdom of what is known and works, the difference is it is applied in a non-totalizing way. Ethical therapists do not relinquish knowledge and power but use it for justice, to empower others (Larner, 1995), which is part of the paradox of power (Kunz, 1998).

The person is more than the description but this does not mean I cannot have descriptions; rather there is room for us to *fail* in comprehending another person. In a stance of not knowing therapists still know but what is important is *how* they know, in a way that is responsive to the person. Ethical relations involve a position of not knowing *and* knowing, a therapy stance I call 'knowing not to know' (Larner, 2000). Here my therapeutic skills and professional knowing as the Said are utilized *for* the other as a Saying. I know *when* to know and when to let the client do the knowing. There is interplay between different ways of knowing that allows a mutual relationship of influence to evolve in the conversation. At one point the client knows, then the therapist knows or both can know at the same time, but what is important is for each to be willing to hold their knowing humbly or in abeyance long enough to speak with each other. In sharing therapeutic knowing in a non-totalizing way the therapist demonstrates ethics or how to be there *for* the other.

This process of curious, open, transparent, flexible and creative enquiry is an interchange between knowing and not knowing that Rober (2002) calls 'constructive hypothesizing'. Here knowing is the thinking of therapists in the presence of others, bursting forth as dialogue and language. Thus Kino's story above inspired me to share my own experience and in response Kino could share his knowing and become more responsible in the process. The inner thoughts therapists have in response to others becomes outer talk as a Saying in the session; expertise and knowing is shared and the client is encouraged to do likewise. With Kino I introduced my hypothesis into the family conversation as a tentative attempt to think in the presence of others. This immediate face-to-face response to another person in discourse is ethics. My encounter with Kino helped him to be more responsible for self and others. Though as Levinas might say in ethical relation I do not think or know so much as tremble. It is the saying of the other in me.

## The Paramodern

This integration between knowing and not-knowing bridges the usual dichotomy between the modern and postmodern, a both/and positioning I call *paramodern* (Larner, 1994a). This addresses the fact that discursive therapists often work within modern mental health organizations that demand accountable practice as a condition of funding or employment (Larner, 2003). Thus as a postmodern social constructionist or narrative therapist I am professionally required to work with colleagues *within* the orbit of modern therapy discourses such as biological psychiatry and cognitive therapy. Here the deconstructive challenge is how to be ethical *and* apply evidence-based therapy as technology, which enhances best practice for all. Ethical therapists can speak a particular therapeutic language and apply techniques while emphasizing the therapeutic relationship and what is unique and different about a personal narrative (Larner, in press).

> *Peter Rober: In your chapter you reflect as a therapist on philosophical sources and inspirations. This is what family therapists have been doing the last 30 years. What strikes me most, however, is the importance of ethics in your chapter, and the (almost) absence of epistemological questions. This is rather uncommon in family therapy literature. You write: "In these terms therapy is first of all the enactment of a person-to-person relationship. Whatever a therapist says or does, what matters most is how she is towards the other." Indeed, sometimes we forget that therapy is, in the first place, a meeting of two (or more) mortal human beings trying to make sense out of their lives. While reading your chapter I started to wonder why family therapist have put so much energy into discussing epistemological questions and so little with ethical questions. Maybe you have thoughts on that?*

*GL: Thanks for your reflections which I briefly speak to below in order. As you say family therapy has put epistemology before ethics, which I suspect reflected the modern philosophical impulse in which the discipline was founded by Bateson and his colleagues in postwar systems thinking. Family therapists then began to appreciate the aesthetic basis of knowledge, instead of acting upon family systems it was enough to be with persons in a stance of curiosity and systemic wisdom. With the narrative metaphor we began to appreciate stories and locate therapy in a wider contextual, cultural and political ethos. The ground was set for ethics and social justice to become paramount: we know because we are in relation to and responsible for the other. So I see family therapy as having gradually moved towards an ethical epistemology, which is why Levinas may be so relevant now. Of course my argument is we need both knowledge and ethics.*

*PR: Another thing that fascinated me is your idea that thinking occurs in the presence of others, but that it also is being disturbed by the other's difference. In my words, I would talk about surprise: what surprises me in the contact I have with my clients makes me think and try to understand. I often use this surprise as the starting point of a conversation and a collaborative search for understanding. It's nice to read that you call this surprise, this disruption of my autonomy, ethics.*

*GL: Being surprised or disturbed by the other goes along with an ethical relation as a face-to-face encounter with another person. This exposes therapists to a point of vulnerability and fragility both within themselves and others. The protective shell of the therapist's knowing is intimately and experientially informed by the other; in other words you feel their suffering, which is disturbing, but this being with the other expands possibilities for change. In your chapter Elly putting a needle into her mother was surprising to you and this 'play' invited you to participate more fully in the family experience. From your disturbance or surprise new thinking and reflection followed. A similar process happened with Kino where I was disturbed enough to think my own soiling story and this self-disclosure opened up a wider conversation with the family.*

*PR: Thirdly, what I found less surprising (since I read other publications of yours), but very important is your struggle with the modernist/postmodernist dualism. Especially your warning that postmodernism sometimes totalizes (when it presents itself as the better approach, and tries to replace modernism), and that we need a both/and position in this debate. Also in other discussions you search for a both/and position. For instance: your view on power as inevitable, but also as an ethical responsibility: 'how can I use my power and expertise humbly, respectfully, and in the service of the client's wellbeing,' What I like about this is that you have a very ethical view of the therapist, but not a restrictive view. In your view of therapy there is room for family therapy, psycho-education, attachment theory, play therapy, and so, as long as they are used in a non-violent, non-totalizing way.*

*GL: Nicely put and here I consider myself a pragmatist much like my family therapist colleague in Australia, Carmel Flaskas (2002a, b). As a practitioner for nearly thirty years I find many therapeutic approaches fascinating and valuable or as I have said previously, change whether at the level of persons or the universe is a multi-faceted, complex and mysterious affair (Larner, 1994b). Here modern and scientific approaches to therapy like cognitive therapy, neuropsychology research or biological psychiatry have a role to play. I want to see the therapy field as a whole becoming more discursive and ethical, I believe this will happen and is what this book offers. Following Levinas the overriding question for me is how knowledge can be ethically situated or used for the other.*

## Therapy as Other

In other words, there is a technology of being *and* a language of the ethical that opens it up to transcendence and the Other; both sit together despite the tension. Science is not discarded; rather transcendence enters of its own accord. Often in real life therapy the finely tuned package of therapists is disturbed by otherness, the person doesn't quite fit the formula and the cookbook solution doesn't apply. Therapy becomes an extra-ordinary experience; there is a break in the ordinary and everyday application of therapeutic knowledge or expertise: "The otherness or strangeness of the other manifests itself as the extra-ordinary par excellence: not as something given or intended, but as a certain disquietude, as a *derangement* which puts us out of our common tracks (Waldenfels, 2002, p. 63)".

As Levinas would describe it, the ethical relation is what transcends or breaks into any therapy as completely *Other*. The application of an approach like cognitive or family therapy is interrupted and we come up against the person beyond the therapist's grasp or understanding. The therapist is brought into a strange relationship with the Other where another way forward is possible. Sometimes change can appear out of the blue in the form of random yet mysteriously fated events I call 'miracles' or 'narratives of destiny' (Larner, 1994b, 1998).

# CONCLUSION

One has to be careful not to set out a kind of ethical ontology of therapy based on prescribed rules and procedures which would go against the grain of Levinas's work. Nonetheless there are practice implications of an ethical approach to therapy. For Levinas the beginning point for ethical discourse is how another person *affects* me at a face to face level. Here the physical presence of others and the importance of welcoming is emphasized as well as what transpires at a nonverbal level of the body. The ethical therapist is attuned to inner experience, which can inform thinking and reflection in the presence of others. Likewise the Levinasian therapist is open to being disturbed or surprised by the Other and the unique meaning and story of persons in the world. This includes what happens both inside and outside of therapy.

To represent another purely in terms of a psychological category or concept does them violence; it is to take over another human being with a language or approach. A therapist simply applying a technique or model stands outside the other and is not in an ethical relationship where the person is put first. Therapists who disregard this ethical relation risk violence in their therapy whatever approach they use[5]. At the same time a Levinasian therapist would not deny objectivity or science in therapy but ask how technology or professional knowledge can be applied ethically? Here the ethical relation can be seen not as *one* way of doing therapy but a stance adopted *within* any therapy approach or model of choice. Ethical therapists are sensitive about *how* they use a therapeutic language; the relation to the other always takes precedence over theory, technique or method. What is deconstructed is the totalizing approach of a modern therapy that overrides the personal, rather than the techniques themselves which means a therapist's prior training and expertise can remain an integral part of an ethical approach.

While Levinas would have more affinity with relational, contextual and meaning based therapies like narrative and family therapy or psychoanalysis (Cohen, 2002), an ethical stance can be adopted within modern scientific approaches such as cognitive therapy and biological psychiatry. Insofar as therapists working within these models demonstrate a collaborative relational awareness and a non- totalizing use of language they are ethical in a Levinasian sense. This means all therapeutic approaches are available to the discursive therapist who by adopting a stance of hospitality towards different therapies can engage in respectful conversation with more scientifically-minded colleagues about the centrality of ethical narratives (Larner, in press).

In other words from a Levinasian perspective an advance in discursive therapy might manifest as a return to modern therapy and psychology in consolidating what is useful in the service of others. As Paré (2003) notes discursive therapy is not the "New Brand X", rather the ethic more than the model is key; what makes the difference is *how* interventions are applied. My professional training happens to be in psychodynamic and family therapy, but this does not prevent me using aspects of behavioral and cognitive therapy as part of an ethical relation. In this sense discourse ethics straddles the Saying and the Said or the modern and postmodern as *paramodern*.

When the therapist allows the voice of the other to be heard above the clamor of one's own, whether it is the inner dialogue of reflection or the spoken knowledge and wisdom of the profession, therapy enacts ethics. Whatever language of therapy is spoken, it belongs first to the other; the therapist is there *for* the other. Derrida says that Levinas thinks and rethinks the same idea in copious forms comparing his work to a sea lapping at the same shore (Davis, 1996). If so, the land is called Other, an infinite world beyond our comprehension where the ethical relation is sacrosanct.

[5] It is interesting that recent research shows an ethical attitude of egalitarianism, altruism and hospitality rather than divisive self-interest benefits others in terms of prosperity and well-being (Fehr and Gachter, 2002).

## REFERENCES

Carr, A. (2000). Evidence-based practice in family therapy and systemic consultation. I Child-focused problems. *Journal of Family Therapy*, 22, 29–60.

Cohen, R.A. (2002). Maternal Psyche. In E. Gantt & R.N. Williams (eds.). *Psychology for the other: Levinas, ethics and the practice of psychology* (pp. 32–64). Pittsburgh, PA: Duquesne University Press.

Critchley, S. & Schroeder, W.R. (eds.) (1999). *A companion to continental philosophy*. Oxford: Blackwell.

Critchley, S. & Bernasconi, R. (eds.) (2002). *The Cambridge companion to Levinas*. Cambridge: Cambridge University Press.

Cunningham, P.B. & Henggeler, S.W. (1999). Engaging multiproblem families in treatment: Lessons learned throughout the development of multisystemic therapy. *Family Process, 38*, 3: 265–281.

Davis, C. (1996). *Levinas: An introduction*. Cambridge: Polity Press.

Derrida, J. (1999). *Adieu: To Emmanuel Levinas*. Stanford, CA: Stanford University Press.

Derrida, J. (2001). *Cosmopolitanism and forgiveness*. London: Routledge.

Diprose, R. (2002). *Corporeal generosity*. Albany: State University of New York Press.

Fehr, E. & Gachter, S. (2002). Altruistic punishment in humans. *Nature, 415*: 137–140.

Flaskas, C. (2002a). *Family therapy beyond postmodernism: Practice challenges theory*. New York: Brunner-Routledge.

Flaskas, C. (2002b). Practice experience and theory boundaries: An argument for theory diversity in family therapy. *The Australian and New Zealand Journal of Family Therapy*, *23(4)*, 184–190.

Frosh, S. (2001). Things that can't be said: Psychoanalysis and the limits of language. *International Journal of Critical Psychology*, *1*, 28–46.

Gantt, E. & Williams, R.N. (Eds.) (2002). *Psychology for the other: Levinas, ethics and the practice of psychology*. Pittsburgh, PA: Duquesne University Press.

Gergen, K.J. (1999). *An invitation to social construction*. London: Sage.

Kunz, G. (1998). *The paradox of power and weakness: Levinas and an alternative paradigm for psychology*. Albany NY: State University of New York Press.

Larner, G. (1994a). Para-modern family therapy: Deconstructing post-modernism. *Australian and New Zealand Journal of Family Therapy*, *15*, 11–16.

Larner, G. (1994b). A miracle narrative for family therapy. *Australian and New Zealand Journal of Family Therapy*, *15*, 208–214.

Larner, G. (1995). The real as illusion: Deconstructing power in family therapy. *Journal of family therapy*, 17, 191–217.

Larner, G. (1998). Through a glass darkly: Narrative as destiny. *Theory and Psychology*, *8*, 549–572.

Larner, G. (2000). Towards a common ground in psychoanalysis and family therapy: On knowing not to know. *The Journal of Family Therapy*, *22*, 61–82.

Larner, G. (2001). The critical-practitioner model in therapy. *Australian Psychologist*, *36*, pp. 36–43.

Larner, G. (2003). Towards a critical therapy. *International Journal of Critical Psychology*, *6*, 9–29.

Larner, G. (2003, in press). Integrating family therapy in child and adolescent mental health practice: an ethic of hospitality. *Australian and New Zealand Journal of Family Therapy.*

Levinas, E. (1969). *Totality and infinity*. (A. Lingis, Trans.) Pittsburgh, PA: Duquesne University Press.

Levinas, E. (1984). Emmanuel Levinas. *Dialogues with contemporary continental thinkers*. Manchester: Manchester University Press.

Levinas, E. (1987). *Language and proximity, collected philosophical papers*. Dordrecht: Martinus Nijhoff.

Levinas, E. (1993). Outside the subject. Stanford, CA: Stanford University Press.

Levinas, E. (1995). Emmanuel Levinas Atlantic Highlands, NJ, In F. Rotzer (Ed.), (G. E. Aylesworth,) *Conversations With French Philosophers*. Humanities Press.

Miller, S.D & Duncan, B.L. (1998). Paradise lost: From model-driven to client- directed, outcome-informed clinical work. *Journal of Systemic Therapies*. *19*, 20–35.

Paré, D.A. (in press, 2003). Discursive wisdom: Reflections on ethics and therapeutic knowledge. *International Journal of Critical Psychology*.

Paré, D.A. & Larner, G. (in press). *Collaborative practice in Psychology and Therapy*. New York: Haworth.

Rober, P. (2002). Constructive hypothesizing, dialogic understanding and the therapist's inner conversation some ideas about knowing and not-knowing in the family therapy session. *Journal of Marital and Family Therapy*, *28*, 467–468.

Strong, T. (2000). Collaborative influence. *Australian and New Zealand Journal of Family Therapy*, *21*, 144–148.

Sullivan, K. (2002). Ethical beliefs and behaviors among Australian Psychologists. *Australian Psychologist*, *37*, 135–141.

Waldenfels, B. (2002). Levinas and the face of the other. In S. Critchley & R. Bernasconi (eds.). *The Cambridge companion to Levinas*. Cambridge: Cambridge University Press.

Wyschogrod, E. (2002). Language and alerity in the thought of Levinas. In S. Critchley & R. Bernasconi (Eds.). *The Cambridge companion to Levinas*. Cambridge: Cambridge University Press.

# *Chapter* 3

# *Acknowledging the Otherness of the Other*

## Poetic Knowing in Practice and the Fallacy of Misplaced Systematicity

ARLENE M. KATZ AND JOHN SHOTTER WITH CONVERSATIONAL PARTNER JAAKKO SEIKKULA

"The 'otherness' which enters into us makes us other" (Steiner, 1989, p. 188).

"This is connected, I believe, with our wrongly expecting an explanation, whereas the solution to the difficulty is a description, if we give it the right place in our considerations. If we dwell upon it, and do not try to get beyond it" (Wittgenstein, 1981, no. 314).

"You really could call [a work of art], not exactly the expression of a feeling, but at least the expression of feeling, or felt expression. And you could say too that in so far as people understand it, they resonate in harmony with it, respond to it. You might say: the work of art does not aim to convey *something else*, just itself" (Wittgenstein, 1980a, p. 58).

There are certain special kinds of involved, reciprocally responsive, meetings with others which, when they occur, can give rise to special and distinctive feelings in us, feelings which can 'tell' us something about the unique nature of an other's 'inner world', and which can thus shape our responses to them in ways that matter to them. In a moment, below, we would like to try to describe the special nature of such meetings or engagements, and also, to spend some time outlining some of the prior attitudes and expectations that can prevent such engaged meetings from ever taking place. For it seems to us that certain orientations—often to do with demands made on us by our training as professionals—can lead us to impose already existing demands and requirements on all our meetings, externally, and it is just these external impositions that can prevent these special kinds of involvement from ever emerging.

In the next section below, we would like to present in a degree of concrete detail, a number of such meetings. We will then turn to try to identify and describe some of the crucial features of engaged, respectful meetings, with the aim of outlining some of the prior attitudes and expectations that can prevent such engaged meetings from ever taking place. For it seems to us that it is here—in the prior attitudes forced on us by the *after the fact* need to legitimate our practices to our professional colleagues—that we can begin to slip back into the external imposition of already existing demands and requirements on our meetings with clients, and it is just these external impositions that prevent fully engaged involvement from ever emerging. We turn next to some exemplars in which such a kind of involvement is at work.

## EXEMPLARS OF ENGAGED MEETINGS

### The Spangler in Feasance

Meetings early in training may be striking; they may be carried over as resourceful reminders of what matters most in relationally responsive care. The first involved one of us as an intern in psychology(AMK).[1] The setting was an acute psychiatric clinic in a general hospital, where anyone could (and did) walk in off the street. The client, a man in his 50s, had written on his 'face sheet' in the space for employment, "I am the Spangler in feasance, of taoist economics, with a titter to the population.". I looked around the waiting room, wondering which person he was, among those reading magazines, pacing, looking at watches, gazing at a fixed point in space. The senior psychiatrist, with whom I was sitting-in, came in, the face sheet in one hand, guiding the patient in with other, and gestured for him to sit down. He began the interview in the 'usual' way: what brings you in today? (aka "chief complaint"); how long have you been feeling this way? has it varied in intensity? [aka "History of Present Illness (HPI)].

Precise questions, random answers. More precise questions, more (seemingly) random answers. What was unusual, however, was the client's response. He had something to say, and he said it, then said it again, sometimes more slowly and sometimes more intensely: "I am the Spangler in feasance . . . " He repeated his words at seemingly random intervals. The more he did so, the more focused and pointed came the clinician's questions. An uncanny yet predictable rhythm emerged.

[1] At such points in the text as these, we will switch to first-person accounts.

As he asked questions, I wondered, what was a Spangler? what were feasance reports? and, perhaps, did he want us to know more about them?

After a certain point in the proceedings the psychiatrist asked him to go back into the waiting room, then turned to me and said, 'What do you think?" and, "I don't think we'll be able to get him back in again . . . " "I think," I dared to say, "that he wanted to show us his feasance reports . . . and perhaps if we talked with him about those . . . "

There's an expression that passes over someone's face when they're just not quite sure of what you're saying, an expression of intrigued but not yet well oriented curiosity. The psychiatrist looked at me as if he wasn't at all sure whether I was now talking in the same way as 'the Spangler'. I tried to get more specific. He looked at me again, drew a breath and said, "I'm not sure exactly what you are talking about, but, bring him back in, and have a try!" I began to talk with the Spangler: "Help me understand . . . could you tell me, what is in the word 'Spangler' . . . what is in the words 'feasance reports' . . . oh, the opposite of malfeasance . . . do you want to bring them in? Pause . . . "You want to see them?" he asked. "Yes, I would like you to; can I bring them in next week?"—and he did.

But what was uncanny in our exchange was that once he felt met, once he felt attended to by us responding seriously to his utterances, he shifted in his expressions to a clear, understandable 'language' . . . in contrast to the previous rote repetitive discourse of (normal expert) Professional Psychiatrist and (schizophrenic patient) Spangler. "If someone only listened," he said, "I wouldn't have to write the feasance reports." If someone had only asked to see his feasance reports, I thought, he would have known that what mattered to him mattered to us also. By dwelling with him, rather than glancing off, the seemingly too different otherness of this other, a whole landscape of meaning began to be created as I let his otherness touch me, and we entered into the space between us.

## Hearing English Spoken in a Foreign Country

In a reflecting team consultation (Andersen, 1991) with Tom Andersen, after hearing the comments of a reflecting team, the wife, in a halting but increasingly clear voice, offered the following reverie: "It's the tenderness . . . that's something that is real easy to lose sight of . . . it gives me the ability to take a deeper breath and go back into the world . . . It's like hearing English again in a foreign country . . . " (Katz & Shotter, 1998).

We find, in the dwelling that followed the reflections, in the moment of her response, the woman expressing a felt sense that those around them were 'there' for her, were 'with her', in a way that made her feel connected with her surroundings in a way that mattered to her. But rather than gaining any new 'information' though, the woman now felt in contact with a new resource, something she could draw on that enabled her 'to go back into the world'.

## Being Rendered 'Invisible'

In a moving meeting, an 8 year old girl, Sophia, sat next to her mother, and began to tell her story of recent events . . . Then mom began telling of the changes that had affected both of their lives . . . a husband who had moved to another state, the sale of the only home that Sophia had known as her own . . . and mom's move with the kids to another state. Shortly thereafter came father's announcement that he no longer wanted the marriage. And when asked what she needed, Sophia replied, "to feel settled, to know where I am living, going to school and whether my parents would get back together again." But later, another story emerged. . . as Sophia began to re-live the moment when ". . . one time when Mom was away, another woman came over to see my Dad. And Dad was different then, he and she were all light and sparkly—he is usually dark. They made me feel invisible," and she added thoughtfully, "if they *saw* me, how could they do that in front of me?"

What is it to be seen, to be noticed? . . . and what is it to be rendered invisible, unseen, unheard? Sophia was struck that the person she knew, and how she knew him to be, was suddenly different. How could it be that Dad was now light and sparkly, but almost seeing past her? Not only did 'they make me feel invisible', but further, she asked them to be answerable—'how could they do that in front of me?' if they saw me? Long, long before children can tell triangles from squares and circles, children know when those around them are attentive and responsive to them or not. What was remarkable about Sophia was her ability to articulate her sensitivities in this respect in such a distinct manner.

The cases we outline above are all similar in style to Bill, the now well-known case of the revolving door schizophrenic recounted by Anderson and Goolishian (1993). Immediately upon meeting him, Bill sensed that Harry Goolishian was simply talking *with* him, rather than asking him what Bill called "conditional questions" (p. 25)—clearly, Bill *felt* that Harry Goolishian was *there*, *present*, in a personal relationship with him, rather than, so to speak, *standing over against him*, observing him from a distance, like his previous therapists.

Indeed, all these clients (we surmise) had, in the moments we outline, a felt sense of their therapists being there 'with them' in a way that was special for them, that made them feel connected in a way that mattered to them, that made a difference to them. The Spangler thus felt it important to turn up for his next appointment. The woman too gained more than mere information, more than facts; she gained access to a certain kind of resource, something to draw on that enabled her 'to go back into the world'. Bill felt a mattering connection with Harry Goolishian that was so strong, that he felt that here was someone he could, so to speak, be 'real' with, someone he could trust. While the little girl reminds us of the importance of being "seen", and what is at stake when you are suddenly rendered invisible. As Seikkula, J. et al. (1995) note, "as long as the physician searches for answers only in order to accept or reject his/her own hypotheses, the interactional context stays monological . . . [Often], in a consultation with a physician, only the physician has the possibility to determine the actual meaning of the symptoms the patients describes" (p. 66). It is only in the shift to "open dialogue," as they describe it, that language can become "true between oneself and the other speaker" (p. 66). In an *open* dialogue, "utterances are constructed to answer previous utterances and also to wait for an answer from utterances that follow" (Seikkula, 2002, p. 268). Indeed, adds Seikkula (2002), "hearing is witnessed in our answering words" (p. 283).

*Jaakko Seikkula: I have been working to develop an entire public psychiatric system to make the kind of engaged meetings discussed above possible. This project has been located in the Finnish Western Lapland, where since early 1980s the staff from Keropudas hospital reorganized their way of admitting a patient into the hospital.*

*In first trying to create a family centered system based on ideas of systemic family therapy, we realized that our efforts were not successful. This was due to our thinking that we first had to devise a treatment plan in a staff meeting, and after that, to organize family therapy session on the basis of the plan—if we thought it necessary. Only a minimal number of families could participate in this procedure, and many either refused to enter into the family therapy meetings, or discontinued them too early.*

*After dissatisfaction and frustration with our attempts we heard that at the psychiatric clinic in the University of Turku, Professor Yrjö Alanen with his team had started to organize open treatment meetings both to analyze the problem and to create the treatment plan, with both the patient and the family being present from the very first words in the conversation. This was the answer to our questions: to integrate all the available resources, to bring the resources of everyone related to the case into the treatment arena.*

*Although the idea is a simple one, it took several years to see the specific issues central to this approach. We early realized that it was no longer possible to have control over the treatment processes by treatment plans or by family therapy interventions. We could "only" adapt our behavior to the way family was used to behave. Several years after, the ideas of dialogism by Mikhail Bakhtin, Lev Vygotsky and Valentin Voloshinov made it possible to create a description of the processes initiated in these open meetings.*

*To be successful in these open meetings and to generate the patient's own resources and those of the family, means that we as therapists must also become involved in engaged meetings. As in Bill's case above the new way of interviewing made it possible for him to see himself as an agent in the treatment story, so in our meetings, patients become to see themselves as agents able to influence their own lives. Traditional psychiatric treatment by check list, defining the symptoms, and diagnoses, is aimed at having an explanation for the problem and thus control over it. Coming into engaged meetings, or dialogical meetings (as we started to call them), means giving up the idea of primarily having control over things and, instead, jumping into the same river or rapids with our clients, trying to survive by taking each other's hands. Working as a team makes available to us all the opinions and ideas of all, and meeting the patient and family without any pre-planning makes the network a co-agent in the story. We really need each other.*

## ALIENATION FROM INTERACTION

The special kind of engaged or involved, reciprocally responsive, *meetings* with others that both we—and Jaakko Seikkula—discuss above, have also been discussed by Goffman (1967) as entailing what he calls "joint spontaneous involvement" (p. 113). We mention Goffman's work here for, under the heading of *alienation from interaction*, he discusses those moments in which participants become disoriented, awkward, and feel that they have committed an offense, or have been offended against, in terms of a conversation's "involvement obligations." Only if 'you' respond to 'me' in a way sensitive to the *relations* between your actions and mine can 'we' act together and sustain the sense of a collective-we between us, with its own distinctive and firm sense of reality. "And this kind of feeling," Goffman (1967) notes, "is not a trivial thing... When an incident occurs and spontaneous involvement is threatened, then reality is threatened... [If] the illusion of reality will be shattered, the minute social system that is brought into being with each encounter will be disorganized, and the participants will feel unruled, unreal, and anomic" (p. 135).

Thus, if we sense you as not being sensitive to our utterances in an expressively responsive way, then we can feel immediately offended in an ethical way—we feel that you lack respect for 'our' affairs. But again to quote Goffman (1967), the satisfaction of our involvement obligations in an exchange is not a simple matter, it cannot be done according to a plan or check-list:

> "The individual's actions must happen to satisfy his involvement obligations, but in a certain sense he cannot act *in order* to satisfy these obligations, for such an effort would require him to shift his [sic] attention from the topic of the conversation to the problem of being spontaneously involved in it. Here, in a component of non-rational impulsiveness—not only tolerated but actually demanded—we find an important way in which the interactional order differs from other kinds of social order" (p. 115).

In other words, we cannot just decide on our own to be involved; it is a matter of all involved 'working themselves into' each other's rhythms, into each other's tempos, each other's styles. But to orient oneself toward doing this *spontaneously* requires a quite different approach.

Just as we immediately know, have a felt sense, that someone across a room is looking at us, or, that someone we are talking to at a party has 'left us', and is looking over our shoulder for their next port of call, so (sometimes at least) we can also have a felt sense that someone now, at this moment, is 'with us' in a way that is special for us, that makes us feel connected to (or disconnected from) them in a way that matters, that makes a difference to us. Similarly all these clients and therapists (we surmise) had a felt sense that the other was at that moment 'with' them in a way that was special for them. As we see it, in all these episodes, as George Steiner (1989) puts it, the Other before us, is an "'otherness' which enters into us and makes us other" (p. 188).

As professional experts, adopting the stance of uninvolved external observers, relating ourselves only in a monological fashion to our surroundings, we can find it very easy not to take our involvement obligations into account. But, as we will argue further below, we cannot justify our failure to honor them on the grounds of our need for scientific objectivity—such so-called 'objectivity' is a socially constructed achievement that rests for its authority, as we have seen above, on our shared ways of acting in anticipation of what might next follow a present action. Appeals to objectivity cannot be used to *trump* one's involvement duties without causing justifiable resentments by one's "involvement offenses" (Goffman, 1967, p. 125)—as exemplified in Bill's reaction to always being asked "conditional questions" (Anderson and Goolishian, 1993, p. 25). For such "conditional-question talk" was, of course, offensive to Bill as it was to the Spangler, as it was *external to* the ongoing talk between each and their therapist. They had no constructive role to play in it, and could not contribute to any of the new possibilities for being that might become available within it. It was a professional or scientific knowledge that was being sought; the means-ends, problem solving talk of professionals intent upon applying their 'theories', and, on the basis of their 'observations', of coming to an accurate 'picture' of a 'patient's' supposed 'inner mental state'. Where, it was hoped, of course, that the possession of such a 'picture' will provide the knowledge of what 'caused' his mental state, thus to re-cause it in a new and better configuration.

*JS: In open dialogue, two elements become central: 1) working as a team is emphasized, as well as 2) meeting first with the social network of the client before going into individual meetings or any other way of meeting the problem. What happens in the Finnish Western Lapland, in an optimal context, is that for every new crisis a unique team is created. The team consists most often of staff members from different units, e.g., one psychologist from an outpatient clinic, one nurse from the wards, and one doctor from the crisis emergency service. The team is polyphonic in that there is not a single authority having to tackle the case, but all the necessary authorities from a multi-problem situation are involved in the same process. The therapists are speaking in many voices, but in response to all the others in their surroundings, and thus dialogically integrate the fragmented reality that the patient has met after having to be in contact with many separate helpers. But having the social network now included in the crisis, means that it is possible for all those who have been involved in the life and perhaps even in the incidents of which the patient is speaking in his/her psychosis, to start together to create words for those experiences which have not yet had any other words than psychotic hallucinations.*

All this forms an exciting tension at the very beginning, and this "nuclear loading[2]" is verified in the meeting, in that most often the one behaving in a psychotic way discontinues this way of behaving in the meeting. He/she becomes heard and psychotic-speak is no longer needed in the context of the meeting. When therapists are working as a team, they have to become responsive to and thus connected with each other's language in the presence of the context of the patient's social network. The patient too is speaking in the presence of those who most probably are the core persons in the difficult experiences in their lives. Together with the therapists, they form a new, mutually responsive community for, not only living through the crisis, but able also to construct a new, joint language for the not-yet spoken experiences.

This is a complicated issue from the philosophical perspective, too. It can be said that our task is to be present for those who need help in their crisis. We have to be present for the others but we cannot be present for them without them. This task is the same one for our clients, too. They have to be present for us in order to guarantee that their stories are heard as they wish them to be heard. If clients meet a doctor with a pre-established diagnostic language, they have to adapt themselves to that language to become heard, whereas in engaged meetings our clients have to find (or create) another type of connectedness to their experiences.

Theoretically, being involved in engaged meetings seems to me be the only possibility, if we are to draw on the patient's own resources—and the resources of all those with relevant understandings—in discovering ways to recover from a crisis.

Yet many other psycho-educational programs have reported improvement in treatment of psychotic problems. How is this possible?

Perhaps the way that help is structured in some psycho-educational programs forms one step in the right direction. For, in structuring the program, psychiatrists have to take the patient seriously, in following their behavior, to see if the program is working. But a second part of this could be to do with re-thinking what is recovery. I think that recovery is being able to make use of one's own psychological and social resources. Whereas, we know that the traditional treatment in mental hospitals, with high doses of medication, can both prevent recovery and risk the setting in of a process of chronicity. Yet, some structured programs may still aid recovery,

[2] A Finnish phrase meaning, metaphorically, a concentrated source of powerful energy as in nuclear energy.

because the therapist becomes more predictable for the patient. Being predictable means security for one's own reasoning and acting. More space for herself is left in the process.

Thus the question can be put: Are dialogical meetings the only ones that can help patients in their own work in testing reality and in coming back to the demanding world with a high responsibility of each act you take?

## THE CENTRALITY OF OUR ENGAGED MEETINGS: DWELLING AND GRAMMAR

Wittgenstein (1981) warns us that the challenge we face in our inquiries into human difficulties and disquiets, is a matter of what stance to adopt: does a disquiet present us with a problem needing solution, or with a problem of orientation—we suffer confusion as to how to 'go on' in our current circumstances? If it is a problem of the latter kind, then the way to enter into the different worlds of others is not through seeking explanations, but by '*dwelling*' with them for a while in our meetings with them. He presents the character of such problems to us as follows:

> . . . the difficulty—I might say—is not that of finding [a] solution but rather that of recognizing as the solution something that looks as if it were only a preliminary to it. 'We have already said everything.—Not anything that follows from this, no, *this* itself is the solution!' This is connected, I believe, with our wrongly expecting an explanation, whereas the solution to the difficulty is a description, if we give it the right place in our considerations. If we dwell upon it, and do not try to get beyond it. The difficulty here is: to stop (no. 314).

It is only in our 'dwelling' on or with the other person's expressions of their disquiets, in our interactive explorations of their expressions in relation to our's, that they reveal their inner lives to us—and this is where Wittgenstein's (1953) emphasis upon the relevant explorations being of a *grammatical* kind becomes crucial.

For the shared anticipations and expectations we exhibit in our meetings with each other have a *style* or a *grammar* to them in the ways in which we spontaneously respond to the events occurring around us. For we respond, not in terms of their objective actuality (as observed by third-person external observers), but in terms of immediately shared anticipations of next possibly happening events. And it is from the direct and spontaneous nature of such momentarily shared understandings as these that our acts gain their unique and particular meanings. Yet, there is an *after the fact* tendency to attribute the orderliness in that style or grammar to an external organizing agency, or to an already existing systematic set of abstract rules or principles beyond history and institutions.

To show how an activity's style or grammar can spontaneously emerge in the course of its conduct, and need not exist prior to it, we must explore further the nature of the expressive responsive, bodily reactions spontaneously occurring between people in their meetings with the others and othernesses in their surroundings.

As a first step in coming to a grasp of their nature, let us just note that when we and a neighbor both look over a visual scene, a landscape, or another's face, our eyes flick and jump from one point of fixation to the next. Yet, irrespective of the actual pattern of our individual looks and looking, we both still see, more or less, the same seamless whole, a 'something', a 'landscape', to which we can both relate ourselves. Similarly, when we both read a written text made up of quite separate printed elements, we both develop a sense of all the elements as contributing toward or as playing a participant part in a similar meaningful whole; and so on. In other words, in many such temporally unfolding circumstances (although not in all), there is something special in the sequencing of our activities, in their temporal succession.

If the separate elements we encounter seem to unfold in a special way, not just haphazardly but according to a certain *style*, they give rise in all who encounter them, prior to any thought or deliberation on their part, i.e., spontaneously, a *shared* or at least *shareable* background sense in terms of which all our individual actions in such circumstances, can have meanings intelligible to others.

This claim, that our human activities are not just formless, that not just anything can follow or be connected with anything, is clearly connected with Wittgenstein's (1953, 1978) claim, that most of our activities on investigation seem to have a "grammar" to them. And as he sees it, it is their *shared* grammar that we *must* observe if our expressions and utterances are to be intelligible to those around us. It is this—not the constraints imposed on us externally by an already existing physical reality—that makes it impossible for us just to talk as we please. "Grammar is not accountable to any reality," he claims, "it is grammatical rules that determine meaning (constitute it) and so they are not answerable to any meaning and to that extent are arbitrary" (Wittgenstein, 1978, no. 133, p. 184).

Now to many, this might seem an outrageous claim. After the claim that there is no prior, already fixed and categorized physical reality to which to appeal in adjudicating the worth of our claims to truth, it might seem to add insult to injury. But it has two very important implications:

(1) Any claims that we might as individuals address to those around us regarding the character of things and events in our surroundings, must all be couched in a certain shared style. If they are not, then they will not be properly understood by those to whom they are addressed; they will be confusing or misleading. This alone is a very important point. For it is only too easy for us to think that when we talk about such things as 'the individual', 'the person', 'identity', 'thought', 'speech', 'language', 'perception', 'motivation', 'social constructionism', 'narrative', etc., that we all know perfectly well what the 'it' is that we are talking about, or that we are researching into. We find it difficult to accept that 'objects' such as these are not

already 'out there' in the world in some primordial naturalistic sense. To ignore the need for a shared grammar is to ignore the crucial 'glue' holding everyone's separate, individual activities together within a meaningful whole. The task is not to speculate or theorize but to bring to light, as Wittgenstein suggests, what is really possible *before* all new discoveries and inventions.

(2) This orients us toward an even more important implication. To the extent that all such claims are in some sense expressive of people's responsive relations to events in their surroundings—and not merely claims occasioned by a speculative theory—others should also be able to dwell on, or with, such circumstances to find within them the same possibilities also. So although one might not yet be able to formulate such possibilities within a theoretical framework, to state them as facts, one draw an other's attention to them with a practice that is shaped by being responsive to them. And just as this is Wittgenstein's intent in his philosophy, so it can be our intent in psychotherapy. Wittgenstein's "grammatical remarks" can direct our attention outwards in the same way to 'teach' us previously unnoticed relations between our actions and their surroundings—and similar such events can occur at any time between those involved in 'open dialogues'. This is their power.

In other words, although there may be no prior criteria to which one can appeal in judging the truth of a person's stated claims—for their truth is not a matter of their representational accuracy—there are criteria immediately available as to their intelligibility in the context of their utterance, criteria expressed in terms of what they allude to or gesture toward. And these criteria will arise out of the fact that all the elements involved are mutually determining, interwoven, or inter-related with each other in a certain way, according to a certain style or grammar.

It is this, we feel, that has been missed in many of the new therapies. Our capacities to understand each other as we communicate, are not dependent on already agreed social conventions or rules, but are much more to do with our being influenced by people's expressive responsive bodily activities in a *gestural* fashion. And it is that which that makes it possible for us to be moved by unique others, in uniquely new circumstances, in uniquely new ways in a manner intelligible to both them and us. But missed also, we feel, is the very strange way in which the living activities of two related individuals are intertwined—it is to the 'creative' nature of these intertwinings that we next turn.

*JS: An interesting example of the need to accept entirely the reality of the other is the way of behaving we call psychotic. In a psychotic experience the one having hallucinations does not share reality in the same way as most of those around them do. For them, physical reality may include extremely individual and specific meanings, and the only possible way for others to share in that experience is to accept it as it is. Having psychotic "symptoms" is one form of chiasmically or dialogically-structured activity. But, to treat such activity in this way is a long step from the traditional way of trying to search for reasons and explanations for the psychosis, psychotic behavior is one voice among others in the present dialogue. Here, instead of thinking that psychosis is caused by something for which there is a logical or general systematic reason, psychotic behaviors become seen as responses to the actual situation within which the patient, with his/her network, is present. Most often it is an ongoing, dialogical response to immediate circumstances and past experiences, along with the emotions connected with them.*

Psychotic behavior is a good example of an embodied action. Hallucinations are possible to every one of us in a stressful enough situation, and there is no precondition to psychosis (Karon, 1999; Karon & Vandenbos, 1981; Seikkula et al., 2001). In hallucinations people often speak of incidents that actually have happened in the past. Actually this means that a psychotic behavior may be the first time that these experiences, which could only be expressed in psychotic speech, become possible to handle. This means that we as therapists should be extremely sensitive to the task of listening to those parts of the narrative which are presented in a psychotic form. For at that point, the patient reaches something that has been living in the memory of his/her body, and which now, in becoming formulated into both spoken narrative and thought, affords or allows the patient to become more of an agent in his/her own difficult experiences. But such experiences are always unique experiences. Thus, we have to orient ourselves in the landscape of the patient to have an alliance with them and the possibility of sharing in their reality—this is a presupposition for their becoming "cured" from psychosis.

In dialogue this means not at all challenging the reality of the patient, or becoming "reality oriented," as was said in the past. It is the opposite: in speaking of psychotic experiences or behavior in a way in which one wonders even if it is a psychotic act, allowing 'it' to become one voice among all the other voices in the present dialogue, is to treat psychotic-talk as one treats the talk of any other voice. We even started to call this a "normalizing discourse," in the sense that all those incidents and forms of behaving that seemed in the beginning impossible to understand, start to have meaning as a way of responding to real life incidents. Initially confusing behavior can start to be seen as a "normal" response to stress situation, and not as symptoms of schizophrenia. Although we perhaps are speaking of phenomena not possible to understand, we have begun now to speak of it in a way similar to any other phenomena.

## THE 'CHIASMIC' STRUCTURE OF OUR ENGAGED MEETINGS

Besides their possession of an immanent grammar, the living activities occurring in our engaged meetings are dialogically-structured or, as we shall suggest in a moment, *chiasmically*-structured. The most remarkable characteristic of the special kind of interweaving or intertwining occurring in such activities is that, in mutually influencing each other's activities, people create between (and around) themselves, a unified flow of temporally unfolding activity to which they can all be responsive in their own way—but still in ways intelligible to the other participants within it. This unified flow of activity, within which they all momentarily have their being, involves a complex and intricate intertwining of not wholly reconcilable, mutually influencing movements. It contains within itself, as Bakhtin (1981) notes, both 'centripetal' tendencies inward toward order and unity at the center, as well as 'centrifugal' ones outward toward diversity and difference on the borders or margins. It is the importance of the uniquely organized dynamic complexity of this unfolding, emerging stream of living activity, occurring afresh in each of our meetings, that we feel has not yet been recognized as such in constructionist therapies and discourse. And it is this failure—as Wittgenstein (1981) noted above—which prevents us from recognizing "as the solution [to our problem] something that looks as if it were only a preliminary to it" (no. 314). For, to repeat, our problem is often of an orientational kind—to do with how to 'go on'—and not a matter of explanation. We need to 'know our way around' inside such realities.

To characterize their unique chronotopic (time-space) nature, we shall say that they involve a *chiasmatically* organized flow of living activity. In using the word *chiasm* here, we are following Merleau-Ponty (1968) who in his posthumously published last book remarks at the beginning of Chapter 4, entitled: "The Intertwining—The Chiasm:" "If it is true that as soon as philosophy declares itself to be reflection or coincidence it prejudges what it will find, then once again it must recommence everything, reject the instrument's reflection and intuition had provided themselves, and install itself in a locus where they have not yet been distinguished, in experiences that have not yet been "worked over," that offer us all at once, pell-mell, both "subject" and "object," both existence and essence, and hence give philosophy resources to redefine them" (p. 130).

In other words, such joint- or dialogically-structured activities cannot easily be characterized in classical philosophical terms: they have neither a fully orderly nor a fully disorderly structure, neither a completely stable nor an easily changed organization, neither a fully subjective nor fully objective character. Indeed, to the extent that the temporal unfolding of intertwined activity in this realm is shared in by all, it is non-locatable; it is neither 'inside' people, but nor is it simply 'outside' of them; it is 'spread out' or distributed amongst all those participating in it. Indeed, to the extent that it is undifferentiated as to whose it is, we could say that they all have their being 'within' it—such, for instance, is the character of all our truly engaging conversations. And, to the extent that they all have their own unique, temporally unfolding character, we can say, to repeat, that they all can give rise (for those involved within them) to a 'grammar', to a "structure of feeling" (Williams, 1977) to do with the anticipation of 'ways of going on' within them. Consider, for instance, singing the unfolding sequence of sounds to yourself out loud:

di-di-di-der/ di-di-di-daa/ di-di-di-der/ di-di-di-d..?.. None of us have any trouble in making at least a first attempt at continuing the sequence by offering 'daa'.

In other words, most importantly, the *invisible* but nonetheless *felt* forms, created in the interplay of living activity between us, are neither wholly alive (as self-maintaining organisms) nor wholly dead (as self-contained, inert objects). Taking our lead from George Steiner (1989), we will call these invisible forms "Real Presences." And what is of crucial importance about a "real presence" is not that you 'get the picture', so to speak, but that it 'calls' you to respond in a certain way: a greeting with a greeting; a question with an answer; a request with a compliance, etc. In short, a real presence, although it is invisible and impalpable, *has agency*, and can exert the force of an agent upon us.

But there is more to such real presences than their agency, and this is why we want to call this kind of influence upon us "chiasmic." In choosing this term, we are following Merleau-Ponty (1962, 1968) and Gregory Bateson (1979), who both take binocular vision as paradigmatic of the special nature of our living relations to our surroundings. To quote Bateson (1979): "The binocular image, which appears to be undivided, is in fact a complex synthesis of information from the left front in the right brain and a corresponding synthesis of material from the right front in the left brain . . . From this elaborate arrangement, two sorts of advantage accrue. The seer is able to improve resolution at edges and contrasts; and better able to read when the print is small or the illumination poor. More important, information about depth is created . . . In principle, extra "depth" in some metaphoric sense is to be expected whenever the information for the two descriptions is differently collected or differently coded" (pp. 68–70).

In other words, much much more is happening here than the mere blending or interweaving of separate constituents which remain identifiably separate even when complexly interwoven. Something utterly new and novel is being continuously created. Every ordinary everyday event that matters to us, is not just simply the repetition of an event that is already in some way known to us. Sometimes, it is true, events do matter to us because they fall into one or another well known category. But those events that in-form us of the unique 'inner lives' of the others around us are just the opposite: they matter to us because they are continually happening, as Garfinkel (1967) puts it, for "another first time" (p. 9). Indeed, this is what we think is most difficult to accept against the background of our classical scientific thinking. If an event has never before occurred, how can we understand it? Well, if we think of understanding as a special inner mental event—to do, perhaps, with information processing, computation, or a process of inner picturing, or whatever—we cannot. But if we think of it as a matter of responding bodily, as if to an other's gesture (to look in the direction they are pointing, say), then perhaps it is not too difficult. For although to gesture may be familiar, what is pointed to in our surroundings is unique to what our present surroundings are.

Hence Wittgenstein's (1980) claim that "the origin and primitive form of the language game is a reaction" (p. 31). Where, what he means by the word "primitive" here is that, as he notes elsewhere, "this sort of behavior is *pre-linguistic*: that a language-game is based *on it*, that it is the prototype of a way of thinking and not the result of thought" (Wittgenstein, 1981, no. 541).

Elsewhere, we have drawn on this fact—that the beginnings of new language games can be found in "striking moments"—to set out the methods of what we have called a "social poetics" for use in drawing attention to crucial events occurring in our meetings together that might be useful in refining and elaborating their nature.[3]

## CONCLUSION: THE FALLACY OF MISPLACED SYSTEMATICITY

What we have been trying to do in this article, is to bring to prominence, not only the importance of the interpersonal, relational gains made in the early days of the turn to constructionist therapies, but also how the urge to legitimate practices by attempting to base them on a set of systematic principles is utterly misplaced. For, as is becoming more and more clear, our capacities to understand each other as we communicate are not dependent on rules or upon already agreed social conventions, but are much more to do with our understandings being an extension of our expressive responsive bodily abilities to influence the actions of those around us in a *gestural* fashion (Merleau-Ponty, 1962, 1964; Vygotsky, 1978, 1986; Wittgenstein, 1953, 1980a). It is this, we feel, that has been missed in many of the new therapies. But it is this that allows us when in uniquely new circumstances, with unique others, to invent afresh socially shared forms of activity in terms of which we can influence each other in a manner intelligible to both them and us. If we are responsive to what matters most to them and to the voicing of our words to those others, then in talking 'with' those others in this way, they will be able to find something that matters to *them* in *our* words. But to communicate with others in this way, in terms which allows them to express their own unique nature, means that the task of understanding here is not a matter of "recognizing the form used, but rather [of] understanding it in a particular, concrete context, [of] understanding its meaning in a particular utterance, i.e., it amounts to understanding its novelty and not to recognizing its identity" (Voloshinov, 1986, p. 68). Without this possibility, we would have no chance of expressing to each other

[3]We have outlined these methods and their application in a number of articles elsewhere (Katz, A.M. and Shotter, J., 1996a; Katz, A.M. and Shotter, J., 1996b; Katz, A.M., Conant, L., Inui, T., Baron, D. and Bor, D., 2000; Shotter, J. and Katz, A.M., 1996; Shotter, J. and Katz, A.M., 1998; Katz & Shotter, in press).

the meaning of aspects of our own unique personal lives—the crucial meaning in a woman's life of saying it's the tenderness . . . it's like hearing English again in a foreign country, would be lost to us.

But there are utterances that connect and utterances that disconnect, and wordings that touch and wordings that wound. Words can be more than mere discourse, more than mere disquisitions on bodies of knowledge, more than the mere telling of facts. They can very directly acknowledge or violate the other, and in so doing, can enrich us or degrade us. This is what we have been exploring above: that if we are to respect the otherness of the other in our exchanges with them, then we must allow the flowing interplay of living, expressive, bodily responsivity to occur freely between us. But here, in our concluding comments, we want to explore what can shut that possibility down.

Strong and Paré in recruiting us for this book, suggested that although many of us began the new constructionist approach some twenty years or so ago with great hopes, "some of this excitement has now waned." For us, the opposite is the case. Our excitement has increased.

We value even more the importance of creativity especially in these days when the systematicity of 'evidence based' practices, with their algorithms and externally driven accountability, is being imposed on us all. It is important to put this move in context: Voloshinov (1986) captured our age of formalism and systematicity brilliantly well. No doubt commenting on the age of Stalinism in Russia, he describes it as follows:

> "The typical distinguishing marks of [this] kind of thinking [is that it is] focused on a ready-made and, so to speak, arrested object . . . Characteristically, what undergoes systematization is usually (if not exclusively) someone else's thought. True creators—the initiators of new ideological trends—are never formalistic systematizers. Systematization comes upon the scene during an age which feels itself in command of a ready-made and handed-down body of authoritative thought. A creative age must first have passed, then and only then does the business of formalistic systematizing begin—an undertaking typical of heirs and epigones who feel themselves in possession of someone else's, now voiceless word. Orientation in the dynamic flow of generative process can never be of the formal, systematizing kind . . . Formal, systematic thought about language is incompatible with living, historical understanding of language. From the system's point of view, history always seems merely a series of accidental transgressions" (p. 78).

And as we commented above, we see the very nature of academic debate over theory and metatheory as leading us all in exactly this direction.

Above, then, we have tried to show by reference to the work of such thinkers as Wittgenstein, Merleau-Ponty, Bakhtin, and Voloshinov, that there is an important pre-intellectual, bodily aspect to the living of our practical, everyday lives together. They show that as a sphere of activity, joint spontaneous involvement, when it occurs, is a very special sphere of human activity that has, so to speak, a 'life of its own', an active agentic nature quite different from the other two great spheres of human activity so far studied in Western philosophy—the deliberate actions of individuals done for *reasons*, and *caused* behavior. It can be called joint- or dialogically-structured activity, but we to make its very special nature have called it *chiasmically* structured activity. This is what we are excited about.

Turning to its study, a whole new world of human being and activity comes into view, requiring a quite new and unfamiliar set of concepts and set of methods in its investigation. And our chapter has been oriented precisely toward the task of bringing this new world into view. Talk in relation to such a world—an indivisibly unified world of felt "real presences" rather than seeing representations, of internally responsive versus externally driven activities, of 'knowing from within' rather than objective knowledge—will require a new sensibility and a new body oriented vocabulary, one quite distinct from our current, intellectualistic forms of 'mind'-talk. While the unidentified Cartesianism present in current investigations into discursive practices has led us into the continual, monological rediscovery of *sameness*, a move to the dialogical and chiasmic can lead us into creative relations with the *otherness* of the *other* not previously explored. Rather than waning, the true excitement to be got from the exploration of living relational processes has hardly yet begun.

## CODA

> "You might say: the work of art does not aim to convey *something else*, just itself" (Wittgenstein, 1980a, p. 58).

We end with the words of 8 year old Sophia . . . It had become a part of how we talked with each other, a kind of talk that allowed for and indeed invited spaces for reflection—for the not yet known. Sometimes a pause was incredibly important, as when she reflected on the kind of conversation she might have with her father, to again be *seen* by him. On our last meeting, she mused on the nature of such 'hard questions' and proceeded to pose some of her own: Do you see other kids who have the same problem I do with my family? What do they say? And the next, after showing some of her artwork, 'What is art?" After a pause, she began, what became another kind of multi-voiced dialogue as she said "'*It*' is . . . ". then, together, '*it* creates magic'.

*AMK:* "*It* happens in a fleeting moment."
*Sophia:* "You write something down and there it is—how did I do *that*? There is the spirit of *it* and that's it"

## REFERENCES

Andersen, T. (1991). *The reflecting team: Dialogues and dialogues about the dialogues*. New York: W.W. Norton.

Anderson, H. & Goolishian, H. (1992). The client is the expert: A not-knowing approach to therapy. In S. McNamee & K.J. Gergen (Eds.). *Constructing therapy: Social construction and the therapenutic process* (pp. 25–39). London: Sage.

Bakhtin, M.M. (1981). *The dialogical imagination*. M. Holquist (Ed.), (C. Emerson, trans.). Austin, TX: University of Texas Press.

Bateson, G. (1979). *Mind in Nature: a necessary unity*. London: E.P. Dutton.

Descartes, R. (1968). *Discourse on method and other writings*. (Trans. by F.E. Sutcliffe). Harmondsworth: Penguin Books.

Garfinkel, H. (1967). *Studies in ethnomethodology*. Englewood Cliffs, NJ: Prentice-Hall.

Goffman, E. (1967). *Interaction ritual*. Harmondsworth: Penguin.

Katz, A.M. & Shotter, J. (1996a). Hearing the patient's 'voice': Toward a social poetics in diagnostic interviews. *Social Science and Medicine, 46*, 919–931.

Katz, A.M. & Shotter, J. (1996b). Resonances from with the practice: social poetics in a mentorship program. *Concepts and transformations*, 2, 97–105.

Katz, A.M & Shotter, J. (1998). 'Living moments' in dialogical exchanges. *Human Systems, 9*, 81–93.

Katz, A.M. & Shotter, J. (2003, in press). Methods of a 'social poetics' in people becoming 'present' to each other and to themselves. In Larner G. & Paré D. (Eds.). *Critical knowledge in psychology and psychotherapy*. New York: Haworth Press.

Katz, A.M., Conant, L., Inui, T., Baron, D., & Bor, D. (2000). A council of elders: Creating a community of care. *Social Science and Medicine, 50*, 851–860.

Karon, B. (1999). The tragedy of schizophrenia. *The General Psychologist, 32*, 3–14.

Karon, B. & Vandebos G. (1981). *Psychotherapy of schizophrenia: The treatment of choice*. New York: Jason Aronson.

Merleau-Ponty, M. (1962). *Phenomenology of perception* (C. Smith, Trans.). London: Routledge & Kegan Paul.

Merleau-Ponty, M. (1964). *Signs*. (R.M. McCleary, Trans.). Evanston, IL: Northwestern University Press.

Merleau-Ponty, M. (1968). *The visible and the invisible*. Evanston, IL: Northwestern University Press.

Seikkula, J., Aaltonen, J., Alakare, B., Haarakangas, K., Keranen, J. & Sutela, M. (1995). Treating psychosis by means of open dialogue. In S. Freidman (Ed.). *The reflecting team in action: Collaporative practice in family therapy* (pp. 62–80). New York: Guilford Press.

Siekkula, J., Alakare, B. & Aaltonen, J. (2001). Open dialogue in first-episode psychosis II: A comparison of good and poor outcome cases. *Journal of Constructivist Psychology, 14*, 267–284.

Seikkula, J. (2002). Open dialogues with good and poor outcomes for psychotic crises: examples from families with violence. *Journal of Marital and Family Therapy, 28*, 263–274.

Shotter, J. & Katz, A.M. (1996). Articulating a practice from within the practice itself: establishing formative dialogues by the use of a 'social poetics'. *Concepts and Transformations*, 2, 71–95.

Shotter, J. & Katz, A.M. (1996). "'Living Moments' in Dialogical Exchanges," *Human Systems, 9(2)*, 81–93, 1998.

Steiner, G. (1989). *Real Presences*. Chicago, IL: University of Chicago Press.

Voloshinov, V.N. (1986). *Marxism and the philosophy of language*. (L. Matejka & I.R. Titunik, Trans.) Cambridge, MA: Harvard University Press, first pub. 1929.

Vygotsky, L.S. (1978). *Mind in society: The development of higher psychological processes*. M. Cole, V. John–Steiner, S. Scribner, & E. Souberman (Eds.). Cambridge, MA: Harvard University Press.

Vygotsky, L.S. (1986). *Thought and Language*. (A. Kozulin, Trans.). Cambridge, MA: MIT Press.

Williams, R. (1977). *Marxism and literature*. Oxford: Oxford University Press.

Wittgenstein, L. (1953). *Philosophical investigations*. Oxford: Blackwell.
Wittgenstein, L. (1969). *On certainty*. Oxford: Blackwell.
Wittgenstein, L. (1978). *Philosophical grammar*. Oxford: Blackwell.
Wittgenstein, L. (1980). *Remarks on the philosophy of psychology*, Vols. 1 & 2. Oxford: Blackwell.
Wittgenstein, L. (1980). *Culture and value*. (P. Winch, Trans.). Oxford: Blackwell.
Wittgenstein, L. (1981). *Zettel* (2nd. Ed.), G.E.M. Anscombe & G.H.V. Wright (Eds.). Oxford: Blackwell.

# Chapter 4

# Narrating the Difference

JOHNELLA BIRD WITH CONVERSATIONAL PARTNER
CATHERINE COOK

The long-standing interest I have in the politics of therapy acted as the impetus for the development of therapeutic practices which circumvent the potential for an imposition of meaning within therapeutic conversations. This imposition is particularly relevant where individuals believe in a version of life events even though this version undermines their sense of well-being and sometimes their very existence. In these circumstances we can feel stuck between two positions. These positions are reflected by these two questions (Avis, 1985, p. 36):

- Do I expose these ideas by presenting an alternative version/explanation for life events? If I don't do this will I be supporting the ongoing oppression of these people (clients)?
- If I do expose these ideas, will people (clients) experience me as another agent of control?

Consequently I have developed a linguistic practice where the advantages and disadvantages of a particular version of life events is discovered through dialogue. I believe our engagement with an attitude of discovery is a critical determinant in supporting our (therapists') willingness to listen for and generate the metaphoric descriptions of life events that are fractional and contradictory. This is in contrast to a clinical practice where the listening and making sense process confirms stereotypes or the dominant viewpoint.

The attitude of discovery I use is complimented by the recognition of the power relationship inherent within the therapeutic relationship (Bird, 2000, pp. 128–136). A lack of acknowledgement of this power relation creates the conditions where an imposition of meaning can subject people to experiences of powerlessness, blame, shame, categorisation and silence. We (therapists) are particularly vulnerable to subjecting people to this imposition of meaning whenever people's (clients') lived experiences are very different from our lived experience knowledges (which includes the professional theories we hold).

In this article I will introduce the concept of relational consciousness, which is a central tenet of my therapeutic work. Relational consciousness is generated through a conversational process I call the relational linguistic practice. When we create a relational consciousness through relational languaging we are able to move beyond the binary constructs of right and wrong, respectful and not, collaborative and not. We are able to reconstruct an experiential metaphor into relational language which in turn generates the relational space for us (client and therapist) to consider the following position, "this linguistic metaphor is in relation to me, it is not intrinsically me." Once relational space is created, it is possible for us (therapist and client) to contextually explore this metaphoric representation of lived experience. The contextual exploration exposes the social and political implications of this metaphoric representation of lived experience to us (therapist and clients). We are able to engage in the present moment with a central linguistic theme as a relational construct which is situated contextually and thus specifically within each person's life.

I bring to this work a belief that "the power to define reality is more in the hands of some social groups than others" (Unger, 1989, p. 30). Consequently I have developed this practice over the last 12 years in order to reduce the risk of imposition by creating the conditions where we can explore the following:

- the exposure of the institutional power relations which constitutes some individuals as bad, mad, inadequate, failures, incapable and others as good, sane, adequate, successful, capable;
- the exposure of the effects of and ongoing negotiation of the power relation inherent within the therapeutic relationship. This power relationship is subject to the multiple and fractional complexities of class, (including the professional classes), gender, culture, age, sexuality.
- the engagement with the process of making sense of the contradictory, fractional, intimate experiences of our lives;
- the engagement with the intricacies of narrating through dialogue;
- the creation of metaphoric positions that support us to name and then research experiences beyond the binary positions available to us within the conventional usage of the English language. I have described this as creating the language of the in-between, (Bird, 2000, pp. 20–25). For example, through the conventional structure of the English language, we are often positioned within a binary, i.e.: I am confident/I lack confidence; I am trusting/I can't trust; I am committed/I am unable to commit.

The therapeutic practice which I have developed privileges *the making of meaning* in the present moment within a therapeutic relationship. This process of making meaning occurs through the negotiation and renegotiation of the everyday language metaphors which emotionally resonate for people. The meaning making negotiation requires an engagement with these languaging practices:

- The creation of relational consciousness through a relational linguistic practice.
- The constructing of the continuous present.
- The constituting through language of the I that is active.
- The generating of the metaphors of movement.
- Processes for escaping the binary.

I use these languaging practices in order to constitute a therapeutic approach which is more than these languaging practices. The space constraints of this chapter limit the discussion I can have in regard to these languaging practices.[1] This chapter will primarily consider the constructing of self through language. I will draw the distinction between the effects on the construction of the self using the conventional English language structure with the construction of the self through the creation of a relational linguistic structure.

Through this focus I hope to illuminate a process which supports therapists/counsellors to negotiate with people the possible meanings available for lived experience while exposing "the differential nature of social power" (Unger, 1989).

*Catherine Cook: Johnella, I'm interested to know more about your thoughts on how therapists might actively cultivate a climate of discovery in their work. I notice that while I hold a dedication to this idea, in practice it is easily overshadowed by my own reactions/responses to the experiences clients bring. These responses (such as a fear of asking a question which might be too provocative) brings a caution that easily stalls the work.*

*Johnella Bird: Catherine, one of the most common issues for people practising this counselling style is asking questions which are too big. What I mean by "a too big question" is a question where the therapist has leapt ahead of the conversational flow by coming to a conclusion, i.e. "this means this". The person (client) often experiences this question as jarring. It informs the person of the therapist's theory conclusion or preoccupation. Given the power relation in the therapeutic relationship, the person may concede to the therapist's professional knowledge or disagree through silence, a "yes but" or a direct challenge, e.g. "do you think I'm to blame?"*

*I'm imagining the awareness you hold of the above possibility seems to contribute to the experience you have of this fear. The form of questioning I'll be exploring in this chapter helps to address this fear because it invites persons into a collaborative exploration, and avoids the imposition of meaning upon them. For instance, Simon says he'd never marry his girlfriend if she wasn't a virgin, yet he has had numerous*

[1] A detailed discussion of these languaging practices together with an explanation of the therapeutic practice that I use can be found in *The Heart's Narrative* (2000) and 'Relational Consciousness, A Living Practice', to be published 2003.

*partners. The fear of alienating Simon informs me that the questions need to step towards exposing this cultural value, e.g. "Simon, how do you explain the different valuing of virginity for women and men? How did you come to this conclusion? If Sarah (his girlfriend) held the same virginity value for you—i.e. you must be a virgin—what would you think, feel, do? What role does love play in the prioritising of this value in relationships? When does this value come to the forefront for you as you get to know someone?"*

*As I step towards exposing this culturally determined gender-value, I attend to the emotional content of the conversation, i.e. I may identify doubt, fear, confusion, anger, which we can then engage with in relational terms.*

## AN INTRODUCTION TO THE RELATIONAL LINGUISTIC PRACTICE

The relational linguistic practice evolved as a consequence of the clinical work I focussed on from 1988 to 1999. Through this time I found myself exploring with people the effects of sexual, physical and emotional abuse. I began this particular work supported by the many clinical knowledges and skills I had collected over the years, (i.e. Bateson,1972; Watzlawick, Weakland, and Fisch, 1974; Fisch, J.H. Weakland, and L. Segal, 1982; Avis, 1985; Goldner,1985; Hare-Mustin,1978; Hare-Mustin, Rachel, and Mareck,1988; Hoffman, 1981; Selvini Palazzoli, Boscolo, Cecchin, and Prata, 1980; Gilligan, 1982; White, 1988;1988/89). I was particularly intrigued by Feminist writers (Spender, 1980) who critiqued the production of meaning through language. These writers included Feminist Family therapists who reviewed the invisible power relation inherent in Family Therapy models, particularly in relation to language (Bograd, 1988).

I discovered relational languaging and thus relational consciousness through the work with individuals who had suffered traumatic life injuries. This work was initially supported by the technique of "externalising the problem" and exploring "the unique outcome", (White, 1988; 1988/89). I had found externalising the problem concept and technique very useful in the work with children and families as it challenged the totalisation of the child as "the problem". In the work with children I was particularly inspired by David Epston's (1989) practice.

However, early on in the work I was doing with individual adults and couples I discovered that the concept of identifying the problem became problematic. This was particularly noticeable when the identity or self was regarded or known as the problem, i.e. "I'm bad, mad, dirty, wrong, responsible for the abuse, crazy, ungrateful, weak, sick, deserving of punishment, seductive, etc." Nor did it fit for me to therapeutically take up a *generalised externalisation*.[2] A generalised externalisation

[2] I have detailed the distinction between externalising practices and the relational linguistic practice in a chapter, titled "The Historical Development Of A Relational Linguistic Practice" in the book *Relational consciousness: A living practice* (in press 2003).

is generated whenever a significant metaphor, e.g. ambition, is considered "the problem" and is thus externalised. This generalised externalisation process can occur without the development of a consensus of meaning between therapist and client regarding this metaphor. In the work with children, the externalisation is more often connected to behaviour, i.e. the temper, the worry, the stealing. In the work with adults who have suffered traumatic life injuries, fixing a metaphor as "problematic" without developing a consensus of meaning, has the potential to be either ineffectual and/or dangerous.

## LANGUAGE MATTERS

Most counselling and/or therapeutic practices are mediated by and through language. It was apparent to me that the traditional structure of the English language acted to totalise and internalise lived experience, thus creating a failed, sick, injured and deficit self. This consequently obscures the contextual and social conditions which impact on individuals' sense of well being. For example:

> *Internalisation*—Do you feel self critical or are you critical of yourself?
> *Externalisation*—How have you stood up to self-criticism? or, What does self-criticism try to tell you about yourself?
> *Relational Linguistic Practice*—How would you describe the words which make up this experience you have of criticism? When you notice the words of criticism, what do you do, think, feel?

In the above internalising example, the self is constituted as *self-critical*. In the externalisation example, criticism is separated from the self and is positioned as acting against the self. There is also an assumed consensus of meaning re. the construct self criticism. In my view, this languaging structure thus acts to generalise experience thereby limiting an appreciation of the intricacies of each person's experience.

The externalising process as described and defined by Narrative therapists, (Dickerson & Zimmerman, 1996; Epston & White, 1992; Freedman & Combs, 1996; Monk, Winslade, Crocket & Epston, 1997; Morgan, 2002; White, 1989; 1995), positions the problem, (e.g. self criticism) as the central construct which is separated from the self, i.e. the problem is the problem, not the person (White, 1989, p. 55). For example, Morgan (2002) moves a statement "I'm a worrier" into this externalised statement or question, "What does the Worry say?" "How does it (the problem) affect your motivations?" Consequently Narrative therapists construct agency through the person's ability to act on this problem construct. In contrast, the relational linguistic practice has an emphasis on relationally constructing a central meaning making metaphor for the person to consider, ie., this is in relation to you, however, it is not the total of you.

For example, "I'm a worrier" is reconstructed as, "How would you describe or put words to these worries that you experience?" This relationally constructed metaphor "these worries that you experience" may be centralised temporarily by the therapist. In other words, I choose this metaphor from the many possibilities revealed in the therapeutic conversation to establish a consensus of meaning with people while also re-searching the metaphor's significance. The choice I make is shaped by the listening process (Bird, 2000, p. 14) and the person's answer may act to shift or change the metaphor which is centralised. The movement generated through this enquiry process allows me to engage with the complexities of people's lives while finding language which more accurately reflects and shapes people's lived experience.

Agency is generated in the relationship people (clients) have to an idea and/or practice. The relational linguistic practice thus generates an "I, which is constituted through and by the relationship I have to the ideas and practices of criticism or worry." In other words, the metaphoric description, e.g. criticism, is relationally constructed as "in relation to the I but not the total of the I." It becomes, for example, "this experience I have of criticism" or "this critical idea ("You'll never make it in life") that I hold". For example[3]:

*JB:* *What are the words which make up the sense of criticism that you experience?*

*Maureen:* *They are things like "you'll never get it right, you're stupid, give up now before you make a complete fool of yourself".*

*JB:* *When you hear these words, what are the feelings that come forward?*

*Maureen:* *Despair I suppose. I begin to think I should just give up.*

*JB:* *Do these critical words bring forward an experience of despair which in turn introduces the idea "I should just give up"?*

*Maureen:* *That's right.*

*JB:* *This idea "you'll never get it right", has this idea come forward into your life recently?*

*Maureen:* *Yes, actually I was thinking about it in the waiting room before our session.*

*JB:* *Do you mind if we get to know a little more about what supports the appearance of this idea in your life?*

*Maureen:* *That would be good. Look, Johnella, I suppose I worry that you'll give up on me.*

*JB:* *That's interesting Maureen. Did the idea "you'll never get it right" come before or after this worry you hold that I'll give up on you?*

*Maureen:* *I think the worry came first.*

*JB:* *If we find a way to address this worry you hold, "I'll give up on you", what do you think will happen to the idea "you'll never get it right"?*

*Maureen:* *I think it wouldn't be there.*

*JB:* *Do you think its possible that these critical ideas like "you'll never get it right" are a sign that you are suffering under the weight of worry?*

[3]The examples of dialogue in this chapter have primarily been collected through consultation processes with consultees. They are partial representations of conversations produced to demonstrate a theoretical construct or highlight technical skills.

In this example, I am attempting to demonstrate the creation of a relational linguistic practice through the reconfiguration of the grammatical structure of the everyday language we use to construct and reflect the reality of our lives. This method of languaging supports me to engage with an enquiry process where people's lived experience descriptions are both privileged and reconfigured into a relational construct. For many people (including children), words are and have been meagre representations of their experience. When we privilege the language of the everyday, while reconstructing it through a relational linguistic strategy, we (therapists and clients) are provided with an opportunity to experientially negotiate and renegotiate the language that more closely represents people's (clients') unique lived experience.

In many instances we (therapists and clients) are *making language* or remaking language within the present moment. Consequently, I think of this way of working as a "living practice". When we orient to the descriptions that are shaping of our lives relationally, we are positioned as observers to a metaphoric description. From this position we can experience the effects of this way of languaging lived experience, and these effects tell us of the accuracy of the metaphoric descriptions we hold. We thus have an opportunity to renegotiate the meanings inherent in these descriptions while exposing the benefits of one description over another for the self, others, or institutions. Together (therapist and client) we can participate in creating multiple linguistic possibilities which have differing consequences and effects on the meaning made of individual's lived experiences. For example, consider the metaphoric descriptor, "trust":

## Conventional English Language Construction

*JB:* *(therapist) Do you trust me?*
*Suzy:* *(client) Yes, I think so.*
*JB:* *If you didn't trust me, could you tell me?*
*Suzy:* *Look, there's no reason why I shouldn't trust you. Its just crazy. I don't know how it happens.*

The above example represents an exploratory conversation/dialogue using the conventions of the English language. These conventions create an internalising process. Trust is thus positioned as an attribute of self which is primarily constructed through a binary, i.e. do you trust me *or not*.

The traditional grammatical use of the English language which produces internalisation and binary positions severely limits the negotiation of the power relation within therapeutic relationships. In the above example, Suzy may be unwilling to subject the therapist to the effect of totalisation:

*JB:* *(therapist) Do you trust me?*
*Suzy:* *No I don't trust you.*

The desire to protect the therapist from a totalising description can shape Suzy's response for numerous reasons:

- The definitive "I don't trust you" may represent a position which has limited accuracy in relation to Suzy's lived experience of the relationship.
- Suzy may want to protect a valued relationship from the effect of a totalising position and thus may side with the other side of the binary, "Yes I do trust you."
- Suzy may want to protect herself within a power relationship, i.e. "What will happen to me if I tell her (the therapist) I don't trust her?".
- Suzy may have limited life experience in considering the contribution others make to the creation of relational environments, i.e. throughout childhood she was held responsible for the abuse perpetrated by valued adults in her life.

## RELATIONAL LINGUISTIC PRACTICE

When the development of relational consciousness is the overarching tenet which shapes the therapeutic conversation, we are positioned to construct a relational linguistic grammar. Through the use of this relational linguistic grammar I can temporarily centralise "the trust" metaphor. The following example reflects an exploration of trust using a relational linguistic practice. Notice the emphasis on both the exploration of consensual meaning and the contextualising of the trust experience:

*JB:* *You have described other therapeutic relationships where you have experienced a sense of disappointment in the relationship. If there was an experience of disappointment in this relationship, what would be the first sign?*
*Suzy:* *I'd start to not trust you.*
*JB:* *As you experienced this movement away from trust in this relationship, what would I notice?*
*Suzy:* *I'd get really quiet and fidgety.*
*JB:* *Could you tell me that there was a movement away from trust in the relationship?*
*Suzy:* *I don't know, I don't think so.*
*JB:* *If I notice these signs you've described, quietness and fidgeting, and asked if there is a movement away from trust, what would that be like, could you answer?*
*Suzy:* *I think I could.*
*JB:* *If we then explored what had contributed to the movement away from trust, would that be useful?*
*Suzy:* *Yes, I think just doing that would build trust again.*

*CC: Johnella, I noticed the detailed care given to the engagement with and unfolding of the therapeutic relationship. The use of this relationship as a resource in the therapy has been given very little attention in therapies that draw on social constructionist ideas. Could you say more about the way you conceptualise the therapeutic relationship that enables you to attend to this relationship with such dedicated rigour?*

*JB: Catherine, many of the people I work with are alienated from family and sometimes, community resources. The therapeutic relationship thus becomes a principal site for discovery, as people negotiate a relationship to and with trust, hope and safety. I cannot provide trust, give hope or construct safety for people. Instead we (therapist and client) negotiate the conditions which generate this. We can capture experiential moments which occur in the therapy and we can create ways to build on these discoveries outside the therapeutic environment. These fragments of hope, trust and safety are sometimes tenuous and fleeting. I remain alert to their appearance through tone of voice, eye contact, body posture, energy, animation and feelings. Once noticed, I can negotiate what I've noticed with people in order to construct joint meaning.*

## THE CREATING OF RELATIONAL CONSCIOUSNESS THROUGH LANGUAGING

The processes through which we engage with the making or creating of relational consciousness was first described in *The Heart's Narrative*, (Bird, 2000, pp. 7–14). I wrote of moving that which is subjectified, i.e "I am sad", into a relational construct by using a noun which is positioned in relation to the self, i.e. "the sadness that you are experiencing". This noun can then be moved to a demonstrative adjective and/or pronoun with the introduction of this, these, that, those, e.g. "*this sense of sadness* that you are carrying" or "these ideas that bring forward the experience of sadness." Constructing language in this manner acts to create a relational I. This relational I is produced when the interviewee is positioned in relation to the relational construct. For example, "I am sad" is reconfigured to become "the sense of sadness that I am carrying about the loss of the relationship". Thus I am able to reflect on the self who is carrying this sense of sadness. I am positioned to re-search in relation to my life the following:

The I ↔ carrying ↔ this sense of sadness ↔ about the loss of the relationship.

In this instance, the I is constructed as active or an agent in that the I is carrying something—*this sense of sadness*. These linguistic constructions allow me to re-search the particular contextual environment which I inhabit at this point in time. This relational languaging confirms the self as active or as an agent in life. This focus on the self as active or as an agent is particularly important when people are subjected to psychological conditions that renders them as power-less.

## CONSTITUTING THE "I" THAT IS ACTIVE

The relational linguistic enquiry which constitutes an active "I" occurs when we introduce language that positions people in relationship to the self, the other, the relationship and the language constructs we are exploring. In this manner we are creating the conditions to challenge that which has been subjectified through language and thus experienced as the *totality* of a person, i.e. I am sad, mad, unhappy, etc. In the generation of relational language the person experiences this relationship, rather than being totalised by the description or separated from the description (e.g. externalisation).

In relational consciousness, a person is positioned to reflect/experience/feel/know the I that is active in relation to a metaphoric category. In turn, this metaphoric category is created, explored and recreated in an attempt to closely represent actual lived experience.

## A COMMON TRAP

In the teaching I do, I have noticed that practitioners often embrace the notion that relationships are important. Consequently students often begin by asking questions which introduce the word "relationship" as the principle generator of the relational linkage. This introduction of the word "relationship" isn't generative of either a relational consciousness or a relational linguistic enquiry. For example: "What is the relationship you have to anger/sadness/fear?". When the inclusion of the word "relationship" is the principle language strategy used, it maintains the linguistic separation between the person and the concern or the person and the issue.

In contrast, when creating relational consciousness through relational languaging, we are constructing a linguistic relationship which emphasises the person as both contextually constructed *and* as active in relating to this context. For example: "How does this watching for signs of rejection which you do, how does this impact on the relationship you have with Jack?", or "In the taking of the first step towards this speaking of your mind, what feelings or thoughts came forward?".

The language I use to create an active self while also generating relational linkage between the self and the linguistic metaphor includes the following concepts:

*Supporting:* What did you do to support the relationship decision for . . . ?
*Acting:* If you act on the decision to . . . who or what would support that?
*Engaging:* When you are engaging with this life-long protection strategy of pretending to be happy, who notices?
*Using:* When you use this determination to succeed. . .
*Sensing:* This sense of freedom from despair that you describe. . .
*Moving toward:* What are the feelings that come forward as you take up this commitment to challenge these persecutory ideas?
*Holding:* If you were to hold the idea "He loves me", what feelings or thoughts come forward?
*Moving Away:* In moving away from the possibility that life is controllable, toward the possibility that I can control, what have you discovered?

*Making:* When you found yourself making the decision to take a stand to . . .
*Experiencing:* When you experienced this glimmer of hope five minutes ago . . .
*Coming to:* These feelings that come forward when you consider the possibility of living rather than waiting to die . . .
*Collecting:* When you collect the evidence for this position you have taken . . .

This relational linguistic practice supports the discovery of the ideas, practices and traditions influencing people's knowing of, sense of, and experience of the self while considering the advantages and disadvantages to this. For most people, the therapeutic environment provides an opportunity to reconsider and or re-experience that which they considered fixed. Once people embark on this experiential process there is an inevitable shift, bringing forth other possibilities for both considering life events and engaging with the self. These may include possibilities the therapist hasn't thought of or considered.

## GENERATING THE METAPHORS OF MOVEMENT

Binaries promote either/or positions that generate definitives which in turn obscure the fractional nature of experiences. Instead, I attempt to identify the fractional by creating movement through a variety of approaches to language: languaging to create the continuous present; constituting the I as active or as an agent in life; positioning the relational "I" contextually.

In a supervision consultation, process Gail is describing a young boy, (Stephen, 10 years old), who has a long history of stealing. In the conversation Gail has with the parents, she finds herself stuck when they conclude "he doesn't have a conscience; maybe he's a sociopath". The stuck place she found herself in reflected the position she inhabited within a binary, i.e. "Given his behaviour he doesn't seem to have a conscience, maybe he doesn't have one. I don't think its ok to go along with that, but I don't have an alternative."

On reviewing the above situation I suggested researching other metaphoric possibilities with all the family members. For example:

*The Types of Conscience:* The convenient conscience; one-sided conscience; conscience that reflected care of others; conscience found then lost; selective conscience; the ten years old type of conscience.

*The Development of Conscience:* The partial development of conscience; first steps towards a conscience position; the conscience building strategies; the conscience coach; the supports to and for a movement toward a new conscience position.

This partial list indicates the rich therapeutic enquiry that is available to us if we can constitute metaphoric positions beyond binaries. In this example with Gail, the relational linguistic enquiry generates metaphoric possibilities beyond binaries. In re-searching these metaphoric possibilities we (therapists and clients) can produce a place which Stephen can occupy, know, be proud of, re-search. From this place we can then consider the possibility of building on this knowledge and experience. The generation of these metaphoric possibilities supports an enquiry process where I can contribute to the *making of difference* through relational languaging. This making of difference is constituted in the present moment as we reflect on the past relationships to the present, the present relationship to the future or even the five minutes before the relationship to the now.

## ESCAPING BINARIES: FOCUSING ON "WHAT IS"

People (clients) who experience difficulties in their lives tend to describe/ experience those difficulties as "other than normal". The other than normal descriptions and/or experiences create a comparative process which has as its focus *what is not*. This is described and/or experienced by people as "I am not coping", "I am not an achiever", "I'm not normal", and so on.

Geoff (therapist) was exploring with Debbie (client) the effect of Gender difference, i.e. as a male therapist working with a woman client, on the counselling process. Debbie responded to his questions by saying "I don't feel uncomfortable with you", "I don't feel silenced by you". Geoff felt he could have engaged with this further, he just didn't know how. In a consultation process I demonstrated other inquiry possibilities through centralising what is, i.e. "comfort": "How do you think we have both contributed to the sense of comfort you feel in this relationship? If you were to put words to this experience of comfort what would the words be? Has this comfort place been experienced by you from the beginning of this relationship? If you were to notice a reduction in the experience of comfort you have in this relationship, what would be the first sign?", and so on.

These are imagined and possible enquiry resources for Geoff. The questions are only potent if they build on Debbie responses. However, I'm attempting to illustrate the rich resources available to Geoff and Debbie if the enquiry process focusses on "what is" using a relational linguistic grammar.

The "I am not this" position can refer to small life considerations, e.g. "I am not confident" or it can refer to totalising life considerations, e.g. "I am nothing," "I am a waste of space". The effects on people of the "I am not" position can range from discomfit to hopelessness and frequent suicide attempts. When people attend counselling/therapy this absence is to the forefront of their experience. If we focus on this we can find ourselves collecting copious evidence for this despair position or lack position.

Relational languaging provides the linguistic structure to centralise "*what is*" and explore it contextually in order to expose the environment which is both generative and undermining of "*what is*". This environment includes an exposure of the power relation inherent in what and whom, is culturally supported or undermined.

When we centralise "*what is*" we are assuming that when people carry a knowledge of what is absent in their lives, they also carry a knowledge of what it is or may be to have this in their lives.[4]

This knowing may be fragmented, fleeting, located in the dreams which come from observing others' lives. It may be strongly rooted in past relationships and family knowledges and experiences. It may come and go with the advent of unpredictable or traumatic life experiences. Nevertheless this knowing exists once it is *languaged into existence*. The focus of the conversation is to fully get to know this knowing, including what supports the person and or the relationship to move toward this, and what contributes to movement away from this knowing.

## THE RELATIONAL LINGUISTIC PRACTICE IN A CLINICAL CONTEXT

Conventional grammatical structure of English creates the logocentric self which acts to obscure both the fractional and contradictory nature of lived experience together with the implications and effects of social power. Thus psychological theories and practices that use a conventional grammatical structure inevitably capture the individual as solely responsible and culpable for the psychological development of concerns. The individual is thus available for scrutiny, evaluation, diagnosis and intervention by the detached psychological expert. The conventions of the English language thus generate the traditional professional position which captures these people as "other". The "other" is outside of normal, often medicated in an attempt to find normal, and counselled back to normal.

In this transcript of a consultation process, I am reviewing the therapeutic direction that Elizabeth (therapist) and Jessica (client) are taking, as both Elizabeth and Jessica have indicated that the counselling is in a stuck place. I have attempted to draw a distinction between the relational grammatical structure and conventional English grammar which constitutes an internalising process.

*JB:* *What I heard Elizabeth saying was that there's a strategy you've been using for a long time in your life which is to 'get on with things"?*

*Jessica:* *Yeah.*

*JB:* *Right and this getting on with things, when this strategy is being used by*

[4]I have extended the thinking and practice I engaged with since I wrote about the linguistic movement from what isn't to what is (Bird, 2000, p. 240). These ideas/practices owe a primary allegiance to the direct experience I have had of otherness on my life and on the lives of the people I work with, together with the work of Rachel T. Hare-Mustin and Jeanne Mareck (1988), Jane Flax (1990), Rhoda K. Unger (1989). I consider Sampson's (1989) description of Derrida's ideas, i.e. A is both A and not A (p. 8) as also a pertinent way to provide a theoretical meaning to this clinical practice.

*you, what happens to the feelings or the thoughts or the experience you've had?*

Jessica: *Well, they get squashed down, and I feel I'm isolated, like I just don't, I get on with things, I get into surviving you know, so I end up being alone and I feel ashamed and blame and self-blame myself. That's very powerful in terms of whenever I look back on some of those things.*

JB: *Right. O.K.*

Jessica: *And I think what's happened is when I get on with things, it's come out in other ways. It comes out in nightmares, it comes out in panic.*

JB: *Is this strategy that you use of getting on with things, has this entered into the therapeutic relationship between you and Elizabeth, is this what happens as part of this relationship or do you find yourself able to do something different in this relationship?*

Jessica: *Umm. . . . When I look back on the time with Elizabeth, I actually had or when I first talked about the rape I couldn't take anymore and I left the counselling and umm thought that I've just got to get on with it and it was just too much to be talking about and it was just too painful, and then I came back to it about six months later when I broke up with my partner. I knew I didn't have enough support at home to be looking at those things but then things got really bad so I came back to counselling. So I suppose I do think I should get on with things in the counselling as well.*

JB: *How would you know that in this relationship things were moving towards being a bit too much again?*

Jessica: *Oh, I'd just be overwhelmed by strong feelings. When I get in touch with what happened I become very upset and down and bad tempered and it was really difficult.*

JB: *Is there a way that you can tell in this relationship now as you begin to challenge the strategy of getting on with things and start talking about things, is there a way that you know that you're coming up to the edge of this too strong a feeling?*

Jessica: *Umm that's a good question. I think I'm probably more ready to look at things now. I'm not sure if I know when its going too far.*

JB: *Okay, so if something was moving towards going too far, what do you imagine might be a feeling response? Like a feeling response that might tell you.*

Jessica: *Overwhelmed, I think.*

JB: *Getting overwhelmed.*

Jessica: *Yeah, and life is pretty overwhelming at times anyway in terms of what I've been dealing with and the way I've been dealing with it is by not caring and putting things to the back burner, i.e. "I can't deal with that right now, I'll just deal with this."*

JB: *So if you feel this sense of being overwhelmed and this was happening in the room, would that show itself in a body feeling?*

Jessica: *I'd start to panic.*

JB: *An experience of panic would start to come forward?*

Jessica: *Yeah, panic would come forward. Umm, its interesting that panic hasn't come forward as much in the last few sessions so I'm not sure if I, and I've been talking about some pretty scary things. I'm not sure what's happened. I've been a bit more relaxed with it.*

JB: *What was different in those last two sessions that's brought forward less panic. Do you think its the way you've been talking about the memory or something that's happening in this relationship that makes it easier?*

Jessica: *It might be something, I might be trusting Elizabeth a little bit more. I'm not sure, ummm, yes, I'm not sure.*

JB: *So if we were going to put words to that possible trust that you're experiencing, how would we describe it, what sort of trust is happening in this relationship do you think?*

Jessica: *Well, in my conversation I think I trust her in some ways and not in others. In fact no one, no one person knows everything about me, so umm yeah, there's some trust.*

JB: *Okay. You consider this relationship as a place where there's some trust, would you consider there's limited trust in this relationship?*

Jessica: *I think so, I think so.*

JB: *How would you describe the limits of this trust you have in this relationship?*

In this two minutes of transcript using a relational linguistic dialogue, I am interested in exploring the experiences Jessica has of the therapeutic relationship. The therapeutic relationship can potentially provide Jessica with an environment for discovery within which she experiments with herself as having agency or being active in relation to the negotiation of safety and trust. The "limited trust position" once known, can be negotiated re its effects on Jessica, the therapeutic relationship, Elizabeth (therapist) and the "getting on with things" strategy. The following diagram (Fig. 1) represents the possible avenues for enquiry when I centralise through the enquiry process "the strategy of getting on with things" which Jessica uses. At any point in the enquiry another metaphoric may possibly may be centralised.

In the interview with Jessica the metaphor which is centralised shifts and changes with the ebb and flow of a conversational process. The initial metaphor which I used, i.e., "the strategy of getting on with things" is held and put to one side as we centralise "the limits of the trust Jessica has and/or holds in this relationship". Fig. 2

After an exploration of the thoughts, feelings, actions and effects on Jessica and the relationship she's in of this limited trust position, I might also enquire about the relationship between this limited trust and "the strategy she uses of getting on with things". In exploring the gendered implications of the development of and use of this strategy of getting on with things, Jessica says "Sometimes its easier to just go along." I could therefore at some point centralise *the going along decision that she makes*. I have described this conversational process as the weaving

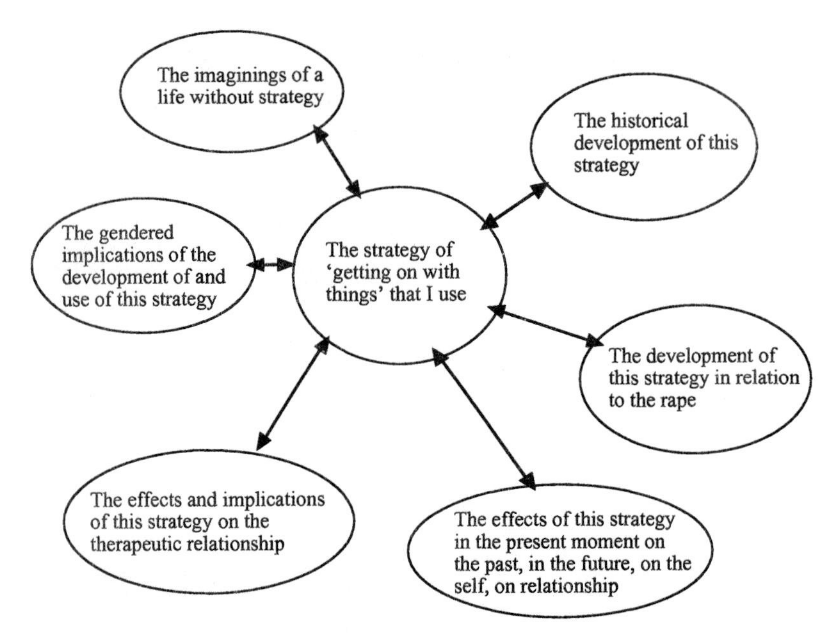


**Figure 4.1.** Possible Avenues for Enquiry: Getting on with Things.

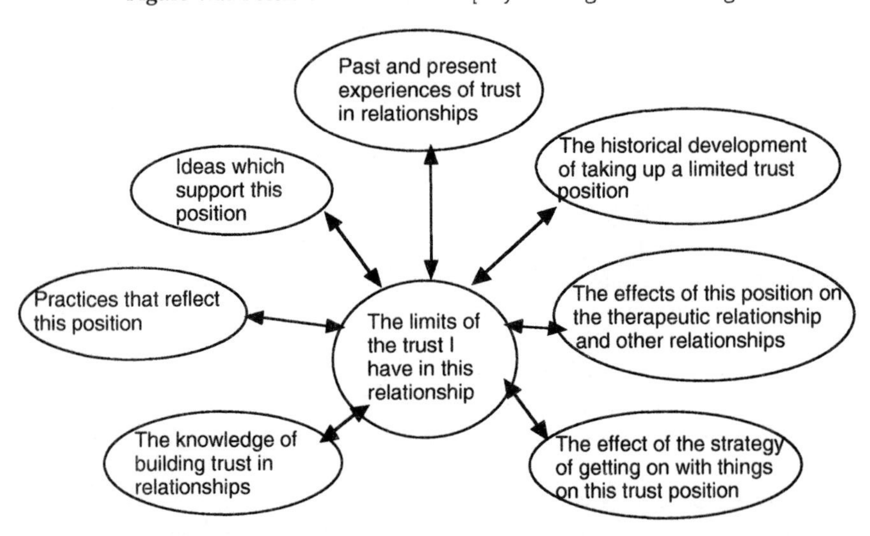


**Figure 4.2.** Possible Avenues for Enquiry: Limits of Trust Jessica had/holds in this Relationship.

of meaning, others have considered it tapestry like. The two dimensional page limits the demonstration of the ebb and flow construction and reconstruction, dismantling and making meaning at the same time, quite unlike the living practice of therapeutic conversation.

*CC: Johnella, as I read I am aware of the extent to which you draw upon the feeling experiences clients have in the embodiment of whatever they are living with. It often appears to me that in the relationship with the feeling, body is left out of therapeutic conversations informed by social constructionist ideas. Could you elaborate more on engaging with body talk as a resource for the therapy?*

*JB: Catherine, in the work with people who have suffered traumatic life injuries, I found it was essential to engage in experiential conversations. Words were such "a meagre representation of actual lived experience" (Bird, 2000, p. 29) and as such often contributed to people's sense of hopelessness, confusion and worthlessness. The words people use to describe lived experience are a beginning point for an exploration which holds the spoken words while wondering. For example*[5]*:*

*Q: As you listen to these words "it wasn't such a big deal", what feelings, thoughts or images came forward?*
*A: Anger actually, I think no-one deserves that.*
*Q: When you said "the words won't come", where do they stop? Are the words in the mind or do they getting stopped somewhere in the body?*
*A: They get stopped in my throat. I've got a something in my throat.*

When we listen to and for the body, the mind, feeling states, sensations, visions, smells, we are better prepared to step cautiously with people into terrain that can hold both the promise of liberation and the terror of annihilation.

In contrast, internalising language can construct the following enquiry process:

*Person:* *I've just got to get on with things*
*Therapist:* *How have you come to that conclusion?*

Or perhaps the following:

*Person:* *I can't think like that, it would be too much, I'd be overwhelmed. Well I've tried everything but I'll give it a go.*
*Therapist:* *I think we could help you face the past and the rape differently.*

Whenever the conventions of the English language or internalising language are used, problems are experienced as a deficit of self. In this deficit place we look to others for guidance. In my view, therapists who use internalising language will counter the deficit in the other with advice drawn from the expert position which is predominately shaped by the dominant discourses of human psychology.

The relational linguistic process positions Jessica as an observer to herself in relation to significant meaning making tenets. I believe this position supports us (therapist and client) to expose and establish the conditions which generate certain experiences, thoughts, feelings which she has. In exposing these conditions we are

[5]The tone of voice, body posture and tension will all influence how these questions are received. For this question to be effective the emotional environment needs to be one of intense curiosity. Anger or fear will shift the meaning made of this question.

positioned to challenge the essentialist notions of autonomous, self-determined self. In contrast the internalising languaging process acts to centralise Jessica as the central determiner of experiences, thoughts and feelings. This constructs the individual as solely culpable for success/failure, wellness/illness, despair/happiness.

## CONCLUSION

The concept of relational consciousness which is generated through a relational linguistic practice allows me to engage in a living practice, where we (therapist and client) are *making difference within the present moment* through dialogue. This process is particularly important in the therapeutic work with people who have traumatic and/or marginalising experiences while believing themselves to be responsible for the life circumstances they are in.

I believe it is not enough to just listen to the story they carry and speak of, as this story is often one of blame, shame, inadequacy, failure—descriptions that are in fact totalising of the self. Instead I engage with those words and descriptions which people use to describe lived experience as relational constructs. Once we have generated a relational construct I am in a position to ask questions which contextualise and reconstruct these descriptions of lived experience, making language as we go. The effect of this relational enquiry is to generate a relational consciousness which reveals the shaping of the individual by the social context. We thus unmask the advantages and disadvantages which are generated through an adherence to the conventional structure of the English language which act to internalise experiences, while generating a logiocentric self. The taken-for-granted or the common sense nature of the language used to describe lived experience is reconfigured through a relational enquiry. This in turn generates the possibility for the exposure and negotiation of the power relation inherent in the taking up of meaning.

Through the relational languaging process we are making and re-making the relationship people have with the lived experiences that are shaping of their lives. This making and re-making occurs in the present moment within a therapeutic relationship, through the process of dialoguing. I am privileging the process of journeying, composing or narrating with people. In this process I often have a destination in mind, however this is held as one possibility amongst many as we (therapist and client) discover the intricacies of lived and experiential knowledges.

## REFERENCES

Avis, J.M. (1985). The politics of functional family therapy: A feminist critique. *Journal of Marital and Family Therapy, 11*, 127–138.

Bateson, G. (1972). *Steps to an ecology of mind*, New York: Ballantine Books.

Bird, J. (2000). *The heart's narrative*. Edge Press, New Zealand

Bograd, M. (1988). Emeshment, Fusion or Relatedness? A conceptual analysis in *A guide to feminist family therapy*, edited by Lois Braverman, Harrington Park Press, pp. 65–80.

Dickerson, Victoria, C. & Zimmerman, Jeffrey. L. (1996). *If problems talked: Narrative therapy in action*, the Guilford Press.

Epston, D. (1989). *Temper tantrum parties: Saving face, losing face or going off your face*. Dulwich Centre Newsletter, Autumn, pp. 12–26.

Epston, D. & White, M. (1992). *Experience, contradiction, narrative and imagination: Selected Papers of David Epston and Michael White* 1989–1991, Dulwich Centre Publications.

Fisch, R., Weakland, J.H. & Segal, L. (1982). *The tactics of change: Doing therapy briefly*. San Francisco, Jossey-Bass.

Flax, Jane. (1990). 'Postmodernism and Gender Relations in Feminist Theory' in *Feminism/ Postmodernism* edited by Nicholson L.J. Routledge.

Freedman, J. & Combs, G. (1996). *Narrative therapy—The social construction of preferred realities*, WW Norton.

Gilligan, C. (1982). *In a different voice: Psychological theory and women's development*. Cambridge: Harvard Press.

Goldner, V. (1985). Feminism and family therapy. *Family Process*, *24*, 31–47.

Hare-Mustin, R. (1978). A feminist approach to family therapy. *Family Process*, *17*, 181–94.

Hare-Mustin, Rachel, T., Mareck, Jeanne. (June 1988). The meaning of difference, gender theory, postmodernism and psychology, *American Psychologist*.

Hoffman, L. (1981). *Foundations of family therapy*. New York: Basic Books.

Monk, G., Winslade, J., Crocket, K., & Epston, D. (1997). *Narrative therapy in practice: The archaeology of hope*, Jossey Bass Inc.

Morgan, A. (2002). Discerning between structuralist and non-structuralist categories of identity: A training exercise. *The International Journal of Narrative Therapy and Community Work*, (4).

Sampson, E.E. (1989). "The deconstruction of the self" in *Texts of Identity*, edited by John Shotter and Kenneth J. Gergen. London: Sage Publications Ltd.

Selvini Palazzoli, M., Boscolo, L., Cecchin, G., & Prata, G. (1980). Hypothesising-circularity-neutrality: *Family Process, 19*, 3–12.

Spender, D. (1980). Man *made language*. Boston: Routledge and Kegan Paul.

Unger, Rhoda K. (1989). *Sex, gender and epistemology in gender and thought: Psychological perspectives* edited by Crawford, M. and Gentry, M. Stringer-Verlog, New York.

Watzlawick, P., Weakland, J. & Fisch, R. (1974). *Change: Principles of problem formation and problem resolution*. New York: Norton.

White, Michael. (1988). *The process of questioning: A therapy of literary merit?* Dulwich Centre Newsletter, Winter.

White, Michael. (1988/89). *Externalising the problem*, Dulwich Centre Newsletter, Summer.

White, M. (1989). *Selected papers*, Dulwich Centre Publications.

White, M. (1995). *Re-authoring lives: Interviews and essays*, Dulwich Centre Publications.

# *Chapter 5*

# *Power, Authority, and Pointless Activity*

## The Developmental Discourse of Social Therapy

LOIS HOLZMAN AND FRED NEWMAN WITH CONVERSATIONAL PARTNER TOM STRONG

If excitement about postmodern and discursive therapies has recently waned, as editors Tom Strong and David Paré suggest, perhaps this is because, for the most part, these therapies are all talk! This is, paradoxically, their strength relative to mainstream modernist therapies and their limitation relative to what is needed if we human beings are to transform our emotionality so as to prevent our killing ourselves off (whether quickly or painfully slowly).

We have been asked to speak concretely and practically to readers, to show our therapeutic approach—social therapy—in action, to stay grounded in our practice—and we will. However, we must, as well, situate ourselves as "on the left" of the postmodern spectrum, both methodologically and politically—which, we hope to show, is neither a characteristic nor the "location" of social therapy, but its activity. To do so, we need to speak to the issue of power.[1]

[1] In presenting our understanding of power and subsequently of social therapy, we recognize that our position is but one of many on the broad landscape. Our "assertions" are, in the best postmodern sense, not Truth, nor even local truths, but our opinions given expression to in a particular discourse.

## POWER AND AUTHORITY REVISITED

Among the more thoughtful Marxist critiques of postmodernism is Ian Parker's "Against Postmodernism: Psychology in Cultural Context," which appeared in *Theory & Psychology* (Parker, 1998). Parker's critique of postmodernism is, as we understand it, valid. What is his criticism? Essentially, that most versions of postmodernism avoid or deny the issue or question of *power*. Parker has leveled this attack against postmodernism in general and, we must add in the name of intellectual honesty, at virtually all of our positive writings on postmodernism. Some postmodernists avoid the issue (question, topic, etc.) of power, we imagine, because they take power to be the fundamental flaw of modernism and, therefore, it is precisely what postmodernism must get rid of (as if avoiding something gets rid of it!). Others, with varying degrees of sophistication, deconstruct and discard power as a necessary component of social life. We have always been somewhat bewildered by Parker's critique of our efforts since we regard all that we have written—and far more importantly, what we have organized or created—as a postmodern explication/expression of power. For we believe that the matter of power (not to mention the power of matter) must be postmodernized if we are to go beyond postmodernism as a mere stage of modernism (Jameson, 1984).

Power (or the word "power" if you prefer), no doubt, has multiple meanings. But, as we have long argued, the socio-political sense of power is best understood in its dialectical relationship to *authority*. First, some simpleminded remarks. Authority goes from the top, down. It is imposed. Most importantly, it must be known. Power comes from the bottom, up. It is expressed. It is created. Obviously, in ordinary language, power and authority are often treated as synonymous. Yet nothing could be further from the truth (in our view, everything is actually equidistant from the truth, viz. an infinite distance!). But the commonplace confusion of the two, power and authority, says a great deal about the *authoritarian* structure of our ontic, now worldwide, culture. For not only are commodities fetishized—turned into god-like authorities, à la Marx—but *everything* is commodified. Hence knowledge, scientific and otherwise, is God-like here in late-modernism/early postmodernism.

The fetishization of knowledge has led some philosophers (for example, Rorty, 1982, 2000; Newman, 1999; Newman and Holzman, 1996) to abandon it, and others (for example, Davidson, 2000) to attempt to rehabilitate it. But even "getting rid" of knowledge is not enough. The more serious issue (activity) is eliminating the *authority of knowledge* in favor of the *creativity of power*—not to mention the power of creativity. Even Davidson, the supreme rehabilitator, recognizes the defect of knowing as an authoritarian conception. He believes we can overcome that defect analytically, i.e. philosophically, and he is no doubt right (he almost always is!).[2]

[2]Donald Davidson, one of the foremost contemporary American philosophers, engages in a dialogue with Richard Rorty in which Davidson argues that in order to make sense of our interpretations of

But it would make no difference, since philosophy (analytical or otherwise) has for many years now had little or nothing to do with the activities and the struggles of ordinary people. Philosophy has no one to blame for that except contemporary philosophers. Newman and Rorty have not abandoned philosophy. Rather, they are unwilling to abandon people in the name of the ever-shrinking academic niche into which philosophy has retreated. Unless postmodernism wishes to become as irrelevant as institutionalized philosophy, it must (we believe) move beyond a *deconstruction* of knowing (which, in its extreme form, is an *elimination* of knowing, Newman and Holzman, 1997) to an active reconstruction of power—*the activity of power*.

In its historic roots (religious, legal, scientific, civic, etc.) authority is dominantly individualistic. The "author" is, for the most part, an individual, an actor, an agent. There is, strictly speaking, no activity of authority. It is fundamentally *regulatory*. Authority is an inactive negative for essentially inhibiting growth and development in the name of those in control—or, as we sometimes confusedly say, in the name of those "in power." But being "in power" (somewhat ironically) does not at all involve the activity of power. It is, rather, the commodification of power (labor power) into authority. And while commodities can be sold, they do not develop; they are consumed. Authority stifles growth. It is not a necessary evil. It is an unnecessary evil. What is necessary for development is the activity of power, the exercise of power, the development of power by the many—collectively, democratically and creatively. It is the work of the laborer, Marx teaches us, that creates value (Marx, 1967). It is the authoritarian commodification of this process that yields a *realization* of this value which, in turn, maintains the authority of the owners of the means of production.

But authority (vs. power) goes well beyond the economic sphere. It is constantly present, under capitalism, in the psychological sphere. The human capacity to authoritarianly commodify oneself is in constant psychological struggle with the human desire and capacity to exercise power *without commodification*, i.e., freely. This understanding, first articulated by one of us in a vulgarly ultra-left political form in *Power and Authority* (Newman, 1974), has been refined in practice, over decades, into what is now identified as *social therapy*.

Our efforts to give meaning to the concept of power led us to practicing and speaking of the *activity* of power rather than either a *definition* of power (a classical modernist mistake) or the *use* of power (a revisionist understanding of Wittgenstein). In our view, a careful and sympathetic reading of Wittgenstein (such as that of Baker, 1992) suggests that it is not meaning and use which are equatable, but meaning and the *activity of using*. Meaning is a *doing*, not an interpretation.

others in meaningful discourse, we must have a notion of turth. Davidson's essays, along with others by Jürgen Habermas, Hillary Putnam, Daniel Dennett and others, appears in *Rorty and His Critics* (Brandom, 2000).

("the *speaking* of language is part of an activity, or of a form of life," Wittgenstein, 1953, p. 11). The use of something, on the other hand, is a functional interpretation (an Aristotelian essence)—What is a chair used for? To sit on? The activity of using is, in point of fact, what the chair *is* used for (standing on it to swat a mosquito). The meaning of a term is not its interpretive use but what it is (*in activity*) used for. Wittgenstein's "slab" examples (Wittgenstein, 1953) make this point precisely because the function of the "slab" is unknown (indeed, unknowable). The endless "ordinary language" analyses, based presumably on Wittgenstein's later writings, bear little or no resemblance to the pointlessness of Wittgenstein's "slab" examples—indeed, to the pointlessness of all of Wittgenstein's later thinking. Thus, it is the activity of power, not the pointedness of power, that interests us in social therapy and, indeed, throughout our organized postmodernist community.

Postmodernism must be an organized activity—it must be performed—if it is to be truly powerful. The temptation to keep postmodernism unorganized, or even disorganized, is a misunderstood libertarianism, an anti-power perspective—ultimately, a liberal authoritarian perspective. Postmodernism must reorganize the world in anti-authoritarian ways, i.e. in *power*ful ways. But powerful ways must be activities. As with Aristotle's practical syllogism, "the conclusion" of postmodernist understanding must be an action (more precisely, an activity). For postmodernist understanding is a moral discourse. It goes from descriptive premises to a normative activist conclusion (in Aristotle's language, an action). It is not a mode of thought going from description (interpretation) to description (interpretation). It is a journey from "what is" to "what ought to be." As such, it is creative and powerful.

While Aristotle's practical syllogism (which was, for him, the form of the ethical statement)[3] is an interesting prefiguration of our activist manifesto, Aristotle was, of course, the grandfather of dualism (in postulating the particular-universal dualistic distinction). And modernism is, arguably, little more than dualism writ large. From Lovejoy to Dewey to Quine to Davidson to Rorty, and on and on and on, dualism has been under attack for a century. Still, it flourishes, largely because, as we noted earlier, philosophy (including critical philosophy) is so alienated from the popular culture. Postmodernism's efforts to present a critique of deadly dualism in a more popular voice has brought nasty self-serving criticism from the establishment intellectual community—including, of course, the philosophers. In their efforts to defend themselves from these vicious pseudo-intellectual attacks, postmodernists have for the most part noticeably avoided the theoretical psychological writings of Lev Vygotsky, no doubt because he was a Marxist—and a Soviet Marxist at

[3]The search for method becomes one of the most important problems of the entire enterprise of understanding the uniquely human forms of psychological activity. In this case, the method is simultaneously prerequisite and product, the tool and the result of the study. (Vygotsky, 1978, p. 65).

that. But, in our view, Vygotsky's critique of psychological dualism is potentially of great value in understanding the activity of power and the creation of a new psychology.

First, Vygotsky gave us a new conception of method, one that is not dualistically instrumental—tool for result—but monistically dialectical—*method as simultaneously tool-and-result* (Vygotsky, 1978, p. 65).[3] With this, the scientific community could have finally ended the theory-practice debate, yet still it persists, even among postmodernists. Second, his *zone of proximal development* offered psychology a way out of the conundrums generated by its dualistic framework: person-environment, self-other, internal-external, to name the most longstanding (Vygotsky, 1978). As we understand Vygotsky, learning and development in early childhood is a tool-and-result activity in which learning leads—dialectically, not linearly—development, a phenomenon made possible by the social, collective construction of the environment that makes learning-and-development possible (Newman and Holzman, 1993). Creating such zones of proximal development is the activity of power.

Third, Vygotsky deconstructed the centuries-old dualism between thought and word and, in so doing, he provided a means for the rejection of not only the pictorial but also the pragmatic view of language. His position can be seen in the following remarks:

> The relationship of thought to word is not a thing but a process, a movement from thought to word and from word to thought . . . Thought is not expressed but completed in the word. We can, therefore, speak of the establishment (i.e., the unity of being and nonbeing) of thought in the word. Any thought strives to unify, to establish a relationship between one thing and another. Any thought has movement. It unfolds. (1987, p. 250)

The structure of speech is not simply the mirror image of the structure of thought. It cannot, therefore, be placed on thought like clothes off a rack. Speech does not merely serve as the expression of developed thought. Thought is restructured as it is transformed into speech. It is not expressed but completed in the word. Therefore, precisely because of the contrasting directions of movement, the development of the internal and external aspects of speech forms a true unity. (1987, p. 251) There are not two separate worlds, the private one of thinking and the social one of speaking. There is, instead, the dialectical unity, speaking/thinking. Children would not be able to perform as speakers, and thereby learn to speak, if thinking/speaking were not a *completive social activity*. Like Wittgenstein, Vygotsky provided the basis for a non-dualistic (non-expressionist, non-descriptive) conception of language and a method for moving beyond epistemology (even a social one) to a new ontology of activity. Social therapeutic practice is in many ways a synthesis of Wittgenstein's and Vygotsky's approach to language and human subjectivity (Newman and Holzman, 1996, 1997). "Completion" is far more than a critique of dualism. It is a positive (postmodern) move (an activist move) beyond dualism. It is not, like dualism, secretly value laden. It is not pointed. It is (like Wittgenstein) properly pointless. As such, it is a useful frame of reference for a value-free psychology—indeed, for an infinitude of value-free psychologies. Creating these psychologies—actively creating new psychologies—is, in our view, the critical work (the revolutionary activity) of postmodernism.

Socal Therapy is pointless, powerful and paradoxical. If you have been following our argument, you may have spotted some seeming paradoxes. Two are of particular relevance to the doing of social therapy. One, if individuals have become commodified selves, how can they exercise their power freely, i.e., uncommodified? Two, we seem to be saying that morality and moral discourse can and ought to be pointless and value free, but aren't these the very things that comprise morality and moral discourse? We will take each of these in turn.

Typically, people come into therapy groups, as they come into any group setting, individuated. They want help and think that the way to get it is individualistically—a perfectly understandable notion, given that in our culture people are socialized to an individuated learning and development model. They say things like, "I had this awful fight with my mother last night. I was furious . . . and I'm really upset right now." They look to the therapist for some advice, solution, interpretation, explanation or, in more postmodern approaches, leadership in a collaborative process that might generate some new understanding of themselves. They are, again understandably, appealing to *authority*—that of the therapist, of knowledge and of language. To the extent that *power* is a relevant concern to them, they want only to "feel more powerful," by which they typically mean that they want, *as individuals*, to have "more control" over their lives.

People come to social therapy with similar understandings and expectations, even if they might have heard that it isn't like "ordinary" therapy. Social therapy is not designed to help individuals with their individual problems, nor to help individuals feel or become more powerful, since we believe that only authority—and not power—is ascribable to individuals. It is, rather, designed to help people *exercise* their collective power to create new emotional growth, a process that requires deconstructing the sense of self (an authoritarian commodification) and reconstructing the concept of social relationship.

Our experience is that this comes, not from some abstract ideological commitment, but from a participatory process in which people actually construct something together—namely, the group. The key focus in social therapy is building the group. Groups are typically composed of 10–25 people, a mix of women and men of varying ages, ethnicities, sexual orientations, professions and "problems." Most groups are ongoing (although we do some time-limited groups) and meet weekly for 90 minutes. Members' length of time in group varies; some people remain for years, others for shorter periods of time, and new members join periodically.

Power is the creative capacity of the group—by the exercise of its emotional labor—to generate new environments; authority is the societally overdetermined[4] predisposition of the individuated members of the group to passively accept class-dominated, patriarchal emotive environments. Conflict between the two gets played out in social therapy groups, where the unit of transformation/change/growth/learning is the group, and the therapist is simultaneously the organizer of the group's emotive labor power and the potential (or even actual) repository of the group members' "authoritarian instincts." The ongoing process of social therapy is the working out of this relationship; as the group engages in the activity of building the group, it is changing its relationship to power and to authority and becoming more powerful. As one social therapy group member, a man in his early 40s, put it: "The social therapy term 'building the group' is probably the one that drives people crazy more than any other. It's so hard to get your head around! There's a vagueness and a clarity about it at the same time. It's what's going on in group. Early on, you can't see it even though you know something's happening."[5]

In this process people come to appreciate what—and that—they can create. Simultaneously, they come to realize the limitations of trying to learn, grow and create individually and that growth comes from participating in the process of building the groups in which one functions. This new learning rekindles development—development by virtue of the group growing. In social therapeutic terms, human development is the activity of creating the conditions for development (Vygotsky's zone of proximal development) and the unit that engages in this activity is the group (the collective).

A recent social therapy group began with a woman, very upset, asking for help. She described what was going on at her job as a teacher in an inner city school, things she and the group members found oppressive and oppressing. Some members of the group responded that they would like to help but that how she was asking was all about herself and her problem and wasn't connected to them or to the work the group had been doing for weeks. The woman acknowledged various group members' comments, but persisted in being upset and saying she needed help with this problem. At one point, she turned to the therapist and asked him for help. He suggested that she respond to the group. She kept pursuing her agenda and group members were becoming exasperated. One long-time member of the group burst into an impassioned and very moving "speech" about how she too comes to group wanting to be taken care of, given advice, etc. for what's going on with her, but she never gets it. Instead, she said, the therapist insists that help

[4]For us, "overdetermined" refers to the use of a conception in ordinary discourse without seriously considering the assumptions of that conception.

[5]This and subsequent quotations from social therapy clients are taken from an ongoing interview project.

comes from building the group, the struggle over that ensues, people do some building, and she leaves group every week feeling very loved and helped from the work.

Then a woman new to the group said that she knew she couldn't get help with her personal problems in social therapy, but that this was OK with her. One or two group members—including the upset woman who had begun the group and had been its focus for much of the time—supported her, others disagreed, and the group went around on this topic for awhile. The therapist then said that as he understood it, those who believed that social therapy doesn't deal with people's personal problems had a misunderstanding. Indeed, it does—*building the group* is how social therapy helps people with their personal problems. He contrasted how people go to therapy with how they go to a medical doctor. You might go to a medical doctor for a pain in your eye, he said, but if after some conversation and examination, he tells you he has to treat your kidney, you might be surprised but you probably won't fight with him and insist that he must help you in "your way." The social conventions of medicine and illness and health are such that we accept the doctor's way of helping us. But therapy, evidently, is a different story. People come to therapy not only with their personal problems, but also committed to a particular way of getting help with them. The group then worked with another group member who wanted help with problems he was having dealing with his young son; they experimented and played with ways of talking (asking for help) so as to contribute to the growth of the group.

This particular social therapy group session highlights—in both form and substance—the group's active struggle with its power (of collective creativity) and authority (of individual knowing). It also suggests the activistic and collective way that the social therapist responds to therapy talk. She or he conveys, in varying ways, that what is being said ("I had a fight; I'm upset; I need help") is of no interest (qua social therapy) except in so far as the group can make use of it in the activity of creating itself into a new socialized helping environment, i.e., in its exercise of power. The task of the group is to *do* something with what people say in therapy, something that contributes to the social process of development. The social therapist works with the group (not the individuated selves that, reductionistically speaking, comprise the group) to organize itself to engage in this process of building the group. In this process the group becomes an *emotional zone of proximal development (emotional zpd)*. The various members, each at different levels of emotional development, are encouraged to create a new unit with a new level of emotional development, i.e., the group's level of emotional development.

This process involves a qualitative change of therapeutic focus—from the individuated self who discovers deeper insights into his or her consciousness to the collective engaged in the continuous activity of creating a new social unit, the emotional zpd. The overriding question transforms from "How is each individual doing?" to "How well is the group performing its activity?" A longtime social therapy group member speaks to how this impacts: "The focus in social therapy on the group and not the individual is really helpful. It helps you get out of yourself. It changes your orientation to the world, how things are organized in the world."

Social therapy's ultra-focus on activity, specifically on the activity of speaking, i.e., on the conversation, transforms meaning itself. Reconsidering Wittgenstein from a Marxian and Vygotskian activity-theoretic vantage point, social therapy rejects the equation of meaning and use that is common among many followers and students of Wittgenstein in favor of the dialectical relationship between meaning and activity. Meaning is created, Vygotsky has shown, through the activity of speaking completing thinking. Social therapy extends ("completes") Vygotsky's picture in the following manner. If thinking-speaking is a continuous process of completing, then the "completer" need not be the same person who is doing the thinking. *Others can complete for us*. When people speak, participate in a dialogue, discussion or conversation (or write), we are not simply *saying* what's going on but are *creating* what's going on. And we understand each other by virtue of engaging in this shared creative activity. As one newcomer to social therapy commented, "Social therapy is like a new practice of relationship. In our group the creating of our conversation is the activity of our interconnectedness."

Inevitably, and nearly continuously, the group confronts the conflict between our socio-culturally constructed adherence to authority and our world-historic capacity to exercise power, as we saw in the group session discussed above. *"How can we talk so that our talking helps build the group?"* This question encapsulates the group's process of discovering a method of relating to talk relationally rather than individualistically—in Wittgenstein's terms, as "activity, or a form of life;" in Vygotsky's terms, "completively" not expressively. It is the activity of talk—not the substance of talk (its aboutness) nor the use of talk (its societal pragmatic function)—that is the focus of the group's activity. The authority of language (as expressive of truth, reality and self) is challenged explicitly as people falteringly attempt to converse in this new way, to create meaning together. Commenting on her group, one woman said, "The group creates a different language in the course of a group [session]. I never realized that the meaning of words is so contextualized. We create a vocabulary and a language that's particular to each group." In this process, group members come to see that what they are saying to each other has no meaning other than what they create. Like poets, they become meaning makers, creators of language and of a new conception of language, one that is non-essentialist and non-descriptive. It is in the creating of their poem, the therapeutic conversation, that the group exercises its power.

A woman began a recent group saying that she still hated her father. She couldn't be absolutely sure, but she thought he was always out to abuse her, he looked at her in a certain way, etc. The initial response of several group members—a line of questioning that is typical in this kind of situation—was to ask for details (what happened, when, for how long, etc.) in order to find out what "really" happened, was she "really" abused, etc.—that is, in order to get to the "truth." After about twenty minutes, the group began to question what this woman meant by some of the words she was saying and how it was that she was saying them ("What do you mean when you say 'you hate him'; what do you mean by 'abuse'; why are you saying this to us now," etc.), and these words and their contextualization (the group's *doing* of meaning) became the focus of the conversation.

At this point, the group had abandoned the pursuit of truth in favor of exploring the activity of their speaking together. This changed activity—from trying to find the truth to creating meanings—created a group sense of new meaning rather than a collective sense of truth. Engaging in this activity, the group gains a heightened understanding that finding truth is not possible, that meanings are created collectively and that they have the power to create meanings. In the words of one group member, "The challenge in our group is always to not take what's said as truth. We don't always succeed! It's very freeing, though, when I can hear and see what so-and-so is saying and doing and not experience it as 'This is really what they're doing and so this is what I have to do in response.' People say words and we don't know what they mean until we create their meaning. The group grows a lot by taking ownership of what it creates."

All we have said thus far relates to the question of the place of morality in postmodernism in general and postmodern therapies in particular. Morality as we know it is authoritarian—it comes from the top, it is imposed and it must be known. Certain behaviors, acts, values and beliefs are wrenched out of the ongoing life process and reified into a code or system of conduct. People (or peoples) are then judged by how well they conform to the code or system. Moral discourse is always in reference to authority (the knower or the known, a god, truth, dogma, belief, system or rule, etc.). In trying to escape authoritarianism, much of postmodernism accepts or embraces alternative moralities (i.e., codes or systems of conduct). For this, it is accused by some of being "rampantly relativist" and/or amoral (Parker, 1998; Rosenau, 1992). And we agree that it is, so long as it fails to reject the ontological premise of modernist morality. Why it hasn't is unclear to us, for there surely is no evidence that human beings require a moral system in order to know what to do. Throughout history, countless terrible things have been done in the name of moral systems (and people seem no better able to know what to do for having such a system). Human beings no more need a code of ethics in order to live morally than children need rules of grammar in order to speak. Neither activity requires an *appeal* to any authority. It is human activity that produces both.

With activity as the ontological unit of human life, social therapy rejects morality (an authoritarian code or system) in favor of *moral activity*. Ordinary people create morality in ordinary ways every day. When it is not commodified into a finished product or code (and then imposed on its creators by others, usually those "in power"), but is allowed to be continuously created and developed by its creators, then moral activity is another tool-and-result of the social process of making meaning. It is then not authoritarian but powerful.

Sharing his experience in social therapy, a man in his early 30s brought up the topic of morality: "There's a certain morality to social therapy. It's not so judgmental, not into 'people should be a certain way.' It opens up space for people to be *all* the ways they are. The question is what people do together, not how they are. I'm much closer to people now. It used to be that my relationships were based on what people said five minutes ago or five months ago. But that keeps you distant. In group, we're freed up to have certain kinds of dialogues not based on your interpretation of what people say or on how you're feeling or how they're feeling. It challenges us to be open to bringing something into the mix so we can constantly create something."

In so far as it is realizable, human freedom lies in our collective ability to create meaning, not in our individualistic capacity to discern truth. In social therapy we "make the problems vanish" (following Wittgenstein, 1980) by changing their meaning through an appeal to the collective capacity, responsibility and creative power of the group.

And why isn't all of this just a vulgar idealism? Because, in practice, the philosophically religious dualism, Realist-Idealist, is rejected in favor of an activity-theoretic *world* (more accurately, *life*) view. Social therapy is a humanistic radical rejection of all forms of reductionism. This leaves us with only one tool to build with: human activity. And that tool is a tool-and-result. The anthropological discovery of humans as tool users was the theoretical basis of humanistic Marxism. The psychological discovery of moral humans as tool-and-result users is the theoretical basis of humanistic postmodern Marxism. All creative power to the activity of the people!

> *Tom Strong: I could read social therapy as a badly needed response to the excesses of individualism that have been with us since the Enlightenment, especially from Locke and Descartes whose views Western society has enshrined. In that sense you invite participants in social therapy to join a very different language game from normal ones where individual views, especially those referenced to objective truths, are 'played'. You locate development in group activity, not in intellectual and other accomplishments engineered by individuals. But, in so doing it seems to me you create another dualism, that of individual/social. Where that gets challenging for me in reading your work, is in seeing how groups do their group building. Things get ouija board-like for me if you say that individuals aren't contributing to this building process. Where I think I can understand you is that it takes two people giving up a significant piece of their individuality to dance in-sync with each other, a good marriage requires thinking as one in some places and not in others would be another example. Do you want to say more about this individual/social dualism?*

> *Lois Holzman & Fred Newman: Back to dualism again. We are not denying that there are multiple things in the world, including individuals and groups. What we*

*are rejecting is reducing one to the other. And what we're interested in is the dialectic relationship between them. Speaking of the "excesses of individualism," one of the most pernicious elements of individualism in our culture is that individual implies ownership, which makes it impossible to engage/experience/create sociality. The subject of our work is activity and in activity theoretic terms the interesting question is the nature of the relationship between individuals and groups and how to shape that relationship in such a way to maximize people's learning and development.*

*TS: I pulled out my Ian Parker writings after reading your comments, including those you had with him on the points you raise early in your chapter. In reading you here, you tackle power after describing it as having multiple meanings. Here you have offered one version of power: authority: power as the focus of your chapter. I like that in one sense but see other forms of power others would say you are not speaking to, such as the power that arises in violent circumstances, or the power differentials that economically divide people. Parker, as I read him, would claim that constructionists, by focusing on interpretive and constructive activities involved in being human, subvert the claims of those experiencing such power-based experiences—they relativise them away. How does social therapy deal with such things as people living in violent or impoverished circumstances? Are there other meanings for power beyond the authority-power meaning you described here that you see as relevant to people's lives and social therapy?*

*LH & FN: Although understandable, your question seems to us to be a non sequitar unless you believe that the violent and impoverished circumstances that people live with can be done away with therapeutically. Maybe you do. We don't. Such things will be done away with by social-economic-political transformation that does away with the need on the part of some for the continuance of such condition. What you're raising is a political issue. Social therapy doesn't deal with these kinds of issues. It is people that can transform the world. What we think therapy can do is help people—the changers—change.*

*TS: I grapple with what you have advocated elsewhere as an 'end to knowing'. When I read that I can think of claims to objectivity, which Humberto Maturana once described as "absolute demands for obedience". I think this is what you refer to as truth-referential discourse, something you discourage in the practice of social therapy. But, beyond a way of looking at knowing as "objective" it strikes me there are some humbler forms of knowing that we make use of all the time, traditions or forms of knowing that we can selectively use or disregard, and they have some potential value to how people go forward in their lives. Can you say more about your stance on knowing in this regard.*

*LH & FN: Again, when it comes to knowing, we're extremists. Others (you, here, we think) ask for a slight variation on our claims and method so as to include a bit of or a form of knowing or truth. We won't do it, but we can live with this difference of approach and opinion. We think doing that is revisionist, while others think it's accurate and that we go too far. So, we don't think there are any humbler forms of knowing. All knowing is authoritarian. It's just that some forms of knowing are articulated by humble people! We fully support Rorty on this matter. In responding to his critics, he successfully articulated ways of understanding various claims without ever relying on a concept of knowing (Brandom, 200). For example, in his debate with Davidson when Davidson rehabilitates truth for logical purposes in relation to understanding language, Rorty responds by showing that one need not rehabilitate truth, that no appeal to truth is needed. We think that abstract conceptions like truth are talked "about" more than they are actually employed in everyday life. They're used in descriptions, but not much in doings. Children don't employ them until they get to a certain age when description becomes very important. And then what happens, unfortunately, is we learn to reduce our doings to our descriptions of what we do (another dualism). Social therapy tries to help people break out of this dualism.*

*TS: So, "knowing" won't work for you, and I'm sympathetic to that should this word conjure up synonyms like certainty or capital "T" TRUTH. But, people rely on community forms of understanding (stopping when traffic signals are red) or the forms of wisdom (e.g. that there might be things one can learn about parenting from others) from which they can resourcefully draw and coordinate their shared existence together. When one abandons notions of apodictic TRUTH, can there still be room for the kinds of 'truths' some refer to as useful fictions, fictions that may need to be revisited and revised as time and circumstance change? Or, do you mean that people should literally approach life unaware in every respect?*

*LH & FN: No, we do not mean that people should approach life unaware. But what you are calling community forms of understanding and wisdom are among the social cognitive processes that don't require knowing. Human beings understand without knowing and without truth, and surely the human learning process must be possible without awareness. Of necessity, children learn before they come to know. Then, at a certain point in the life process, "knowing" gets added on—for authoritarian reasons. In our work, we resist turning such understanding into authoritarian forms like "kinds of truths," "knowing," "wisdom," etc.*

*TS: A final and related question comes out of what could be problematized as the focus for therapeutic work and how that problematizing might occur in the group's activities. I raise this point because I'm trying to better understand the kinds of collaboration involved, how the therapy keeps from being coercive for any member as other group members interact with him/her. Is there a role social therapists play in keeping things from achieving a kind of "tyranny of the group"?*

*LH & FN: This question makes us aware that we have left out an important element of our work that may help to clarify some of what we've been saying—and so we're thankful to you for raising it. Unlike many (most?) therapy groups, social therapy groups are located within a community—a community of groups—(of all kinds—work groups, learning groups, performing groups, to name a few)— and it is this community that works against "the tyranny of the group" you refer to. It's the broader environment in which social therapy is located that structurally mitigates against the parochialism that can be generated by group therapy. Concretely, within some organizations or private practices, therapy groups are quite isolated from the rest of the world, sometimes intentionally, sometimes not. Some groups have rules disallowing speaking about what goes on in the group with non-group members or socializing with group members. Social therapy has no such rules. Even without rules, often it's the case that group members don't have adequate or supportive contexts in which they can talk about their group experience. People in social therapy groups do have these supportive contexts. In our community, talking about what goes on in therapy is standard practice—a regular and lively topic of conversation for many. So, it's the community that plays the role of keeping things from achieving a kind of tyranny of the group. That's where the power resides—not in the therapist. The therapist can't play this role because s/he is bound by confidentiality. But the clients are not.*

## REFERENCES

Brandom, R.B. (Ed.) (2000). *Rorty and his critics*. Oxford: Blackwell.

Davidson, D. (2000). Truth rehabilitated. In R.B. Brandom (Ed.). *Rorty and his critics*. Oxford: Blackwell.

Jameson, F. (1984). Postmodernism, or the cultural logic of late capitalism. *New Left Review, 146*, 53–93.

Marx, K. (1967). *Capital* Vol 1. New York: International Publishers.

Newman, F. (1999). One dogma of dialectical materialism. *Annual Review of Critical Psychology, 1*, 83–99.

Newman, F. (1974). *Power and authority: The inside view of class struggle*. New York: Centers for Change.

Newman, F. & Holzman, L. (1993). *Lev Vygotsky: Revolutionary scientist*. London: Routledge.

Newman, F. & Holzman, L. (1996). *Unscientific psychology: A cultural-performatory approach to understanding human life*. Westport, CT: Praeger.

Newman, F. & Holzman, L. (1997). *The end of knowing: A new developmental way of learning*. London: Routledge.

Parker, I. (1998). Against postmodernism: Psychology in cultural context. *Theory & Psychology, 8(5)*, 621–647.

Rorty, R. (2000). Universality and truth. In R.B. Brandom (Ed.), *Rorty and his critics*. Oxford: Blackwell.

Rosenau, P.M. (1992). *Post-modernism and the social sciences: Insights, inroads and intrusions*. Princeton, NJ: Princeton University Press.

Vygotsky, L.S. (1978). *Mind in society*. Cambridge, MA: Harvard University Press.

Vygotsky, L.S. (1987). *The collected works of L.S. Vygotsky. Vol. 1*. New York: Plenum.

Wittgenstein, L. (1953). *Philosophical investigations*. Oxford: Basil Blackwell.

Wittgenstein, L (1980). *Remarks on the philosophy of psychology*. Oxford: Blackwell.

*Chapter* 6

# *A Postmodern Collaborative Approach*

## A Family's Reflections on "In-the-Room" and "On-the-ChallengeCourse" Therapy. It's all Language

HARLENE ANDERSON AND J. PAUL BURNEY WITH CONVERSATIONAL PARTNER SUE LEVIN

In our experience a postmodern collaborative perspective allows for a multitude of possibilities for therapists and clients. Because therapy is "locally" informed by its participants, each therapy is an unique endeavor that takes its shape along the way and maintains relevance for each person. Here we illustrate this uniqueness and relevance with a family's story of their therapy with Paul—in-the-therapy-room and on-the-challenge-course as they told it in a reflective "interview conversation" with Harlene after the completion of therapy. We first highlight our therapy premises and describe a challenge course. We then illustrate with extensive excerpts from the conversation which provide a glimpse of the family's explanation of how therapy was helpful and the flow of the conversation. The reflections, comments, and questions of Sue Levin, a conversational partner at the Houston Galveston Institute, are interspersed throughout the chapter.[1]

[1] We thank Kristina Fernandez for transcribing the video interview and Becky Weaver for operating the video camera and her valued suggestions for the chapter.

## OUR POSTMODERN PREMISES

For us, postmodern philosophy is relevant to the rapid social transformation in which our world is involved, including its more noticeable diversity and increasing complexity. Evolving from the social sciences and humanities, postmodernism offers a challenge and alternative to traditional therapist understandings and practices in these changing times. Postmodern is an umbrella term that refers to a philosophical direction based in a perspective of knowledge and language: knowledge, what we know, or think we might know, is a communal activity and is socially constructed[2] in language. Language, any kind of spoken and unspoken communication, is formative, creative, and generative. Language is the primary vehicle through which we construct and make sense of our world. It creates social reality and knowledge, rather than reflects them. Meaning, as in how we understand or make sense of our world, relationships, others, and ourselves is not in the word itself. Rather, meaning develops through our use of words in spoken, written, and other forms of communicative interaction, and it develops within the broader social cultural context. In this communal perspective, knowledge and the knower are interdependent and knowledge is dynamic and ever changing. Local knowledge and language—the meanings constructed within a particular context and its relevance specific to the participants—are priviledged. Universal knowledge is acknowledged but it is not prized and is always open to questioning. Likewise, inherent in postmodernism is a continual self-critique that acts as a safeguard against it assuming a meta-narrative status. Combined, these premises spotlight the relational and dialogic nature of knowledge and language and their inherent transforming or generating nature.

## TRANSLATING OUR PREMISES TO THERAPY: A PHILOSOPHICAL STANCE

The premise that knowledge and language are relational and generative and therefore inherently tranforming and generating informs the way that we think about therapy, the people we meet in therapy, and our relationship with them. It informs what we refer to as our *philosophical stance*: a way of thinking about, experiencing, acting, repsonding, and talking with others (Anderson, 1995, 1997, 2000, 2001). The stance represents a belief that is demonstrated in attitude, posture, and tone that communicates to the other that they are a unique human being, not a category of people, and that they are recognized and have something to say worthy of hearing. If a therapist authentically holds this belief, it becomes a

[2] In this chapter we use the term postmodern and place social construction theory under this umbrella.

spontaneous, natural way of being in relationship and conversation—of connecting, collaborating, and creating with others—rather than a technique (Anderson, 1992, 1997). And, though the stance has distinctive characteristics, it is unique to each therapist and human system, their circumstances, and what is required. Interrelated characteristics associated with the phlosophical stance include:

## Conversational Partners

The client and therapist become conversational partners who engage in collaborative relationships and dialogical conversations. That is, they engage in a two-way process: a back-and-forth, give-and-take, in-there-together connection and activity where people talk and respond *with* rather than to each other. Inviting this kind of partnership requires that the client's story take center stage and that the therapist constantly listens, learns, and tries to understand the client from their perspective and in their language. This therapist learning position acts to spontaneously engage the client as a co-learner or in what we refer to as a mutual or shared inquiry in which each voice adds to the conversation, cogenerating newness in understanding and meaning. In this kind of participation members have a sense of belonging and ownership that in turn invites shared responsibility. Said differently, conversations and relationships go hand in hand: the kinds of relationships we have form and inform—enhance and limit—the kinds of conversations we have and vice versa (Anderson, 1997; Boyd, 1996).

The focus is on the conversation, not its content. That is, the process of generating knowledge supersedes the importance of the knowledge itself. In such a conversation the content cannot be determined or predicted ahead of time since it emerges in the current, moment-to-moment exchanges between people.

## Client as Expert

The client is the expert on his or her life and is the therapist's teacher. The therapist invites, appreciates, and takes the client's story seriously, including its content and the manner in which it is told. For instance, the therapist does not expect a story to unfold in chronological order, be told at a certain pace, or be bounded by time. The therapist asks questions, comments, or other utterances to facilitate the storytelling and participate in a conversation with a client. The therapist does not expect answers to questions and does not judge answers as direct or indirect, right or wrong.

## Not-Knowing

Not knowing refers to how the therapist thinks about his/her knowledge and expertise and the intent with which they use it (Anderson & Goolishian, 1988;

Anderson, 1997). The therapists do not possess superior knowledge or a truth monopoly. They offer their knowledge and voice, including their professional and personal experiences, values, and biases; and their questions, comments, opinions, and suggestions in a tentative manner as simply food for thought and dialogue. And importantly, the therapists remain willing to have their knowledge questioned and changed.

## Being Public

A therapist's words and actions are often informed by private thoughts—professionally or personally and theoretically or experientially informed—such as diagnoses, judgments or hypotheses that are not shared with the client but influence how a therapist listens, hears, questions, and so forth. From a collaborative stance, the therapist makes his/her invisible thoughts visible. For instance, ideas and opinions are shared, but as indicated earlier, they are offered as food for thought and dialogue. It is not a matter of whether a therapist can or cannot say or ask about something, but rather the manner, attitude, and timing in which he/she does. Keeping therapists' thoughts public minimizes the risk of therapist and therapist-client monologue—being occupied by one idea about a person or situation (Anderson, 1986; Anderson & Goolishian, 1988). Monologue may subsequently and inadvertently lead to therapist participation in the creation or maintenance in what is often attributed as internal characteristics of clients such as 'resistance' and 'denial.'

## Mutual Transformation

Change or transformation is not unilateral. Therapists are not expert agents of change and they do not change others. Rather the therapist's expertise is in creating a space and facilitating a process for collaborative relationships and dialogical conversations. In this space and process, both client and therapist are shaped and reshaped—transformed.

## Uncertainty

Being a collaborative therapist invites and entails uncertainty. When a therapist accompanies a client on a journey and walks along side him/her, neither can know the direction in which the story will unfold or the outcome. The newness develops from within the local conversation and is mutually created, and therefore is uniquely tailored to the person(s) involved. How transformation occurs and the shape it takes varies from client to client, therapist to therapist, and situation to situation. Put simply, collaborative therapy is improvisational in the sense that the therapist must be flexible and do what the occasion demands.

## Everyday Ordinary Life

Combined these characteristics influence a therapy that is more participatory and collaborative and less hierarchical and dualistic, which in turn helps dilute inherited power differentials. Therapy resembles more the everyday ordinary concerns that any of us may have and the relationships and conversations that most of us prefer. Inherent in this approach is an appreciative belief that most people value, want, and strive toward healthy successful relationships and qualities of life.

Clients and problems are not categorized as challenging or difficult, or in need of solving or curing. Each client is simply thought to present with a dilemma of everyday ordinary life rather than a problem in the usual sense of dysfunction, pathology, or deficit. This does not mean that therapy is chitchat, without agenda, or simply a friendship. Therapy relationships and conversations occur within a particular context and purpose.

Theory is not put into practice and there are no therapist techniques and skills as is common in most therapies. Instead, the philosophical stance becomes the "*guiding ethic.*"

# A POSTMODERN COLLABORATIVE APPROACH AND CHALLENGE COURSES: ITS ALL LANGUAGE

Our therapy philosophy has some similarities to performative psychology or social therapy (Holzman, 1999; Holzman & Morss, 2000; Wadlington, 2001). Peformance is used in the sense of the "language of performance," rather than in the sense of performing an activity. Social therapist Fred Newman suggests that human beings are performatory species and that activity is performance (Holzman and Mendez, 2003). Newman takes the word performance from the theater and substitues it for behavior to indicate that life, including human growth and development, is a performance and that performance is a social activity with the capacity to transform. We learn to live our lives differently by doing it. Doing can involve out loud talking or not; there is no distinction.

Therapy conversations are, for the most part, spoken language-oriented and occur in office settings. Although both spoken and unspoken language are always present in therapy conversations, the role of silent language [e.g., movements and gestures] is most evident in experiential activities. Experiential activities, like challenge courses, are simply one kind of generative environment or space for talking and being.

Challenge courses emerged during World War II to teach British seamen survival training and emphasized team work, problem solving, and communication.

Public school educators later integrated the concept to supplement traditional classroom education (Schoel, Prouty & Radcliffe, 1988). Challenge course programs are used worldwide in schools, businesses, and in therapy with groups of individuals (i.e., students, business teams, and families).

A challenge course is typically a series of out-door low and high obstacles that create physical and mental challenges. Physical ability and strength, however, are generally not factors since the activities are conducted in as noncompetitive manner as possible and with the aim to not discriminate by characteristics such as age and gender (Burney, 1998). In traditional challenge courses, facilitators guide the participants' activities and discussions. A facilitator may be a therapist but often is not; Paul is both a therapist and a trained challenge course facilitator.

Philosophically, Paul approaches in-the-room and on-the-challenge course therapy from a postmodern collaborative philosophical stance (Anderson & Burney, 1997). The idea for the direction of therapy, including its focus, membership, and form evolves from the local conversations between the client and Paul and remain relevant to what the client desires to accomplish and how they think a therapist can best help. Paul has no prescribed design for a challenge course experience. Although there are pre-existing structures and formats, every effort is made so that by Paul and the family codevelop a specific structure and format that fit the members' defined agendas and expectations, thereby valuing, respecting, and accommodating their uniqueness. Paul offers beginning ideas about activities, but all activities remain to be mutually fine-tuned and tailored to the family. Likewise, subsequent course facilitation requires Paul to remain flexible and able to continually adjust the activities based on the family members' changing needs and expectations as the experience unfolds (Burney, 1998).

Family members' experiences are more important than the mechanics or techniques of the activities. There are no right or wrong "solutions." Emphasis is on the family, their focus (i.e., roles, relationships, communication, decisions, feelings), and the meaning they develop through conversation and interaction with each other during and after the course experience.

> **SL:** *Over the last several years there has been increasing conversation in the postmodern discourse about performance as a modality and alternative way of thinking about behavior (Holzman, 1999). Currently, therapists at the Houston Galveston Institute are using performance and improvisational games with groups of divorcing families to explore the implications of this format for theory and practice, and for growth, community, and change. So Harlene and Paul's chapter is of special interest to me and it raises many thoughts, questions, and distinctions. The distinctions I highlight include,* ***suggestions*** *(or possibilities) and* ***imperatives****, the* ***expertise of the client*** *and the* ***expertise of the therapist****, being* ***"in the room"*** *and* ***"out of the room"****, and* ***pursuing ideas*** *rather than* ***adopting them or dismissing them cursorily****.*

## A FAMILY'S REFLECTION ON THEIR IN-THE-ROOM AND ON-THE-CHALLENGE COURSE THERAPY

To illustrate our therapy-in-action we will share a family's reflections on their in-the-room and on-the-challenge course therapy and the relevance it had for them. Paul provides a first-person introduction to the family; then we provide selected excerpts from Harlene's after-therapy reflective conversation with the family and Paul and intersperse our joint comments.

### Paul's Narrative: "How we Worked or did not Work Together"

The Smith's are a blended family with five children: Sally, the mother, has three daughters Megan, age 16; Alice, age 22; Pam, age 24; and one son, Tom age 10, from previous marriages. Bob, the father, has one son Mark, age 14, from a previous marriage. Megan, Mark, and Tom live with Bob and Sally. Bob's son Mark, who previously lived with his mother, recently moved in with Bob and Sally after they, Mark's mother, and Mark discussed what might be best for him. Pam is employed, Alice is a university senior, and Megan is a high school sophomore. Before their marriage of six years, Sally, a school administrator, was a single parent for four years and Bob, a sales executive, was a single parent for eight years.

Bob and Sally initially came to therapy to address conflicts in their marriage. During the third visit they discussed Bob's son, Mark. They believed their differences about how to raise Mark were the main cause of their marital discord. At one point, I asked Bob what Mark might say if he were present. They speculated but did not know. I wondered if they thought Mark might come to a session with them so that we could hear his ideas about their concerns. Both thought it would be helpful. Subsequent sessions included various combinations of family members with the exception of Pam who travels extensively. Bob, Sally, Alice, Megan, Tom, and Mark attended the challenge course session and the interview with Harlene.

> ***SL:*** *Shifts in membership of the therapy sessions and problem descriptions are not unusual in our work (Anderson & Goolishian, 1986, 1988; Anderson, 1997). We do not differentiate therapy based on the social system (e.g. couple, individual, or family) or on a problem designation. In our experience, the membership shifts along with the focus of the conversation. Who is included in a session and what is discussed are mutually determined by the conversations participants, not solely by the therapist (Anderson & Goolishian, 1986, 1988).*

As it turned out, Mark and his father came to the next session. During the session as I was learning about Mark's interests, he mentioned that his class had spent a day on a challenge course. Mark said that he had a great time and enjoyed being out-of-doors and working with the other students. He thought the experience had helped him and his classmates learn more about each other and ways to get along better with one another. I mentioned that I trained facilitators for challenge courses and had worked with different types of groups and families on courses. As we talked I wondered if Mark thought he and his family might be interested in spending a couple of hours on a course and if he thought it would be helpful to them. Mark and Bob both liked the idea. They went home to discuss the possibility with Sally who agreed.

> **SL:** *Paul's experience as a challenge course trainer naturally fed his curiousity about Mark's experience. The idea for the invitation emerged from "inside" the local conversation rather than "outside" it. Paul did not have an agenda to steer the direction of therapy, nor did he believe that the course experience was a technique to "fix" the family. Like the invitation to Mark, Paul offered the challenge course as a possibility. He had no investment or hidden agenda and had Mark not been interested in talking about his challenge course experience, Paul would have set his curiosity free. All offerings are presented in the spirit of food for thought and dialogue without agenda except to facilitate collaborative relationships and dialogical conversations.*

I had another appointment with Bob and Mark and then Sally joined us for the next one. The idea of the challenge course remained part of the conversation and arrangements were finalized with Bob, Sally, and Mark. They thought it important to include Sally's three children. With the family members' permission, I asked a colleague, who is also a challenge course facilitator and therapist, to video tape the course experience. I facilitated and my colleague videotaped and then joined us at the end to offer his reflections. Several weeks later, I invited the family and my colleague to watch the video tape. The family members were fascinated watching themselves on the course and reflecting on their experiences or as one member described it, "How we worked or did not work together."

> **SL:** *Reflecting on therapy conversatons with our clients and our colleagues is a normal part of our practices and another example of shifting membership. We often invite colleagues and students to participate during and after the conclusion of therapy as visiting or reflecting therapists (Anderson, 1997) and find that there are endless varieties of ways to include reflectors. For instance, we invite clients and therapists to reflect with each other at the end of sessions; we invite clients and therapists to return after therapy is completed to together reflect on their therapy experience or with a visiting therapist such as in this instance with Paul's challenge course colleague and Harlene. Clients and therapists consistently report that reflecting conversations are helpful.*

Important for us is the conceptual objective of reflecting practices: to invite a multiplicity of voices and to make those voices public so that the client can hear the different views and choose what strikes them, what invites further outer and inner conversation, or what they deem irrelevant. Also important is that the various reflecting processes invite therapists to be thoughtful about their practices and encourage research as part of everyday practice (Andersen, 1997; Anderson, 1997; Schon, 1983).

> ***SL:*** *When, how and why to accept alternatives to "in the room" therapy? Here, the idea of going on the challenge course came from a conversation between Mark, who had found a course experience helpful, and Paul who had experience as a challenge course facilitator. Paul followed-up on Mark's comment, asking if he thought the family would be interested. If Paul had not had the challenge course experience and Mark had not been interested, would this option have been pursued? The emphasis Paul and Harlene place on conversation helps with this question. Paul had continuing conversations about going on the course with other family members and with one of his colleagues, who agreed to videotape and offer reflections on the experience. These "follow-up steps" are inherent in a collaborative language systems approach, as all members of the invested group pursue any idea toward further clarification and definition. For instance, if a ten-year old child wanted the therapy system to convene at a swimming pool, this wish would be explored with equal sincerity. Of importance and interest to the therapist is not only the wish but also the meaning and intent associated with it. In collaborative language systems therapy* ***ideas are pursued rather than cursorily dismissed****. No matter how absurd, irrelevant, or "out of the ordinary" a client's idea might seem, giving merit and attention to newness and creativity can generate sacred moments that offer the possibility for people to move in new directions.*
>
> *A related issue is our notion of "what is therapy?" We challenge ourselves to be open and stretch, and to imagine that therapeutic experiences can take place in settings other than the therapy room. Our professional values and belief systems come into question as we imagine therapy in-homes, in-schools, on playgrounds, on challenge courses, at conferences, in theaters, at restaurants, and in swimming pools. It is important that we examine these beliefs and consider what the costs and benefits might be to shifting the grounds where we are most familiar.*

## THE AFTER THERAPY REFLECTIVE INTERVIEW: "*ARE WE GOING TO BE MISERABLE TOGETHER? OR, ARE WE GOING TO BE HAPPY TOGETHER?*

Two months after the family's therapy concluded, Paul invited them to a reflective interview with Harlene to learn about their therapy expectations and experiences. The family members readily agreed to come and to videotaping. We present segments from the transcript of Harlene's conversation with Paul and the family and intertwine our summaries and comments. We invite you to think about the characterisitics of our philosophical stance as you read along.

We met in Paul's office. We arranged the chairs in a semicircle for the videotaping, though we usually prefer a circular arrangement. As we do in therapy sessions, we allowed the family members to select their seats, then we took the two remaining ones. We do not have an investment in who sits where and we do not interpret seating arrangements. The family seated themselves in the inner portion of the semicircle; we then took the end chairs.

Harlene asked the family members to introduce themselves to our imagined audience. Each made his or her unique introduction, commenting on their role and birth order, and volunteering other information. The introductions faded into the purpose of the interview. We reiterated ours intentions and learned the family members' agenda, never assuming participants share the same agenda or that agendas remain the same over time. Harlene then asked Paul what he told the family when he invited then to come for the interview. Paul iterated that he had told them that we were writing a chapter for a book and that we were interested in their experiences of therapy with him.

Harlene: *So, to add on to what you were saying earlier—what we like to do is reflect on our work with families. We invite them to come back in and talk about what the experience was like for them as a way for us to learn—I know very little about you. What I know is that you live in the area and that you have met with Paul seven or eight times and in different family member combinations. If I remember correctly, Sally, Paul said you initially called.*

Sally: *Yes.*

Harlene: *And when you called what did you have in mind?*

Sally: *Hum, let me remember now. It's been awhile... I had some concerns that I thought he may be able to help me work through. It involved Bob, at that time, and it involved Mark, at that time. At different times, we were all pulled in.*

Harlene: *So you had some concerns that involved you as a wife and as a mother?*

Sally: *Yes.*

Harlene: *So, who came in first to meet with Paul?*

Sally: *We came together. Bob and I came together.*

Harlene: *And then there were different combinations after that depending on what you were talking about. Let's see, some of you were only on the challenge course [all hands go up] OK, so all of you.*

*Bob summarizes the membership and says that Paul was highly recommended by a friend.*

Harlene: *What were your expectations before you came [to therapy]?*

Bob: *We knew we had some things to work through. If you talked to me, you would hear one thing. If you talked to Sally you would hear something else. If you talked to the kids, you would probably hear a different story. So we decided to get a third party. As we named him on our ropes class, he was our "little board." I think on the ropes course you were our "little board" [Addressing Paul]. He came to be "the little plank" [The family and Paul laugh]... I think it gave us each a chance to hear you, what we all thought. It was very difficult. For me, it was difficult to voice my frustrations and then hear myself say it. For me, it was the ability of Paul to say, "Well, what do you mean by that?" So many times when you are in the midst of something, you don't really hear what the person means, just what he is saying. That is the biggest problem in our relationships, especially ours [Indicating Sally] is hearing what the mouth is saying but not really what the person is saying. I think it gave us the ability to weave through that.*

*Harlene:* *So, two expectations. One, helping you put those thoughts into words and express yourself so you could convey what you wanted the other person to hear. And two, providing a forum in which people could hear each other. Is that right?*

**SL:** *Harlene asks questions to learn about the family's experience and to check-out her understanding. She often poses comments punctuated with question marks. The family members join with each other and with Paul and Harlene in a mutual inquiry.*

The family talks about at home and in public manners. Sally relates that Alice suggested after the ropes course that they should try harder to have better manners.

*Sally:* *For me, as you said earlier, the reflecting, reflection. Just having a mediator, having someone that really didn't know us . . . He's a good listener . . . Bob and I are not good listeners. That's one of the things that we are having to learn is to be better listeners for each other. We both verbalize a lot and we are both strong willed and we want to be heard and we don't listen well. So just having someone put it into perspective and repeat back to you what you are saying. It sometimes makes you feel very silly, when you hear what you have said, especially, when it is said back to you and you go," hum, I guess that I did say that."*

*Bob:* *He [Paul] was very careful not to choose sides.*

*Sally:* *Right, right. He was very fair.*

*Harlene:* *You really felt in a way that he was on both sides?*

*Sally:* *Yes.*

*Harlene:* *You never felt he was on one side and you were on another?*

*Sally:* *No, no, and Bob didn't feel that way either.*

*Harlene:* *So, the first time you came together and then out of that conversation, Mark came?*

*Sally:* *We saw Paul several times before Mark came.*

*Bob:* *One of the main issues between us [Pointing to Sally] and especially on Sally's side was the raising of Mark. Mark is my son by a previous marriage and her only step-child. Megan is my adopted daughter, and Tom is Sally's son by a previous marriage and Alice from another marriage. So, these are my step-children here [Indicating Tom and Alice].*

*Sally:* *It's confusing, isn't it? [Laughing] We are very much a blended family.*

*Bob:* *So we decided that it would be very beneficial, I think for Dr. Burney. He just started asking questions, "Well, what does Mark think?" We didn't really know what Mark thinks. We didn't know what Tom thinks. We don't listen to them! We're on our own wave length. So, Paul brought it up and said, Well, let's just bring Mark in here if you all don't mind and ask him some questions. See if Mark wants to come.*

Mark: *I thought he was going to read my mind [Everyone laughs].*

Harlene: *Were you disappointed when you came in and he didn't read your mind, or did he?*

Mark: *I'm glad he didn't. I was kind of shocked.*

Harlene: *You didn't know what you were getting into. So did you feel like you were dragged in or coerced in?*

Mark: *No, it really didn't bother me.*

Harlene: *It didn't bother you. When you came in what was it like? What was Paul like?*

Mark said that the things they had talked about "seemed useful at the time," but at home he was soon "doing the same old stuff." Bob added that he and Sally did likewise. Sally, however, thought in the "long haul" that their therapy work had been productive and that they had "made gains." They agreed with each other that the three of them had worked through some parenting concerns and that things were much better. They also agreed that if problems arose in the future they would want see Paul again.

Paul: *You felt it was a big issue.*

Sally: *A big issue.*

Mark: *Because I was moving around so much.*

Sally: *Yes, I do remember telling Paul at the ropes course, when we were out there the first time or when we went back to view the video, that the decision had been made that Mark was going to be living with us on a permanent basis, and that he would have regular visitations with his mother. I felt like it would benefit our relationship [Sally's and Mark's] and I felt good about it. [To everyone] Do you remember us talking about that? That this was home and that is where he would be. And, it's what I wanted. [All of the children nodded in agreement.] Making that decision was it.*

Alice: *Yes.*

Sally: *That was not going to be another way.*

Bob: *See Sally is a very much, "I want to know what it is, I want to know where it is" person.*

Alice: *Yes.*

Paul: *I was just curious about something, I wanted to ask Alice. I heard you make a comment. You thought it was beneficial for Mark to be in the home with Bob and your Mom?*

Alice: *I don't live there much any more but I think I was there a lot then and I know there was a lot to conflict. Where is Mark, or who is going to pick him up? But now it is like he lives here and it [Mark being a permanent member of the family] is the responsibility of everyone in the family. Now he goes to see his mother.*

*Tom:* *Now he goes to see his Mom every other weekend.*
*Alice:* *But now I'm glad that Mark is back there [At Bob and Sally's].*

Mark glanced up as Alice was speaking and it appeared to Harlene and Paul [our interpretation in viewing the video] to be pleased with Alice's comment. It is not unusual for family members to comment in session, "This is the first time I really realized how you felt" or "Now I know what you meant." Clients often tell us that they "notice" familiar things for the first time or "hear" them differently in therapy.

*Harlene.* *So you talked about the things you learned in here. You wanted to take them home with you but you would forget. What happened? Will they come back to you later?*
*Bob:* *I think that it comes back to you . . . Our normal routine at that point was total chaos. After our time visiting with Dr. Burney and at the same time us maturing a little bit—I don't know maybe just being together longer and longer and realizing that that's the way it is going to be. That's the one thing that I told him [Paul] when we first came in here. I laid this out for him. This is how to fix my family. I'm a real "let's-just-lay-it-out, let's-just-fix-it."*
*Sally:* *He tells it all.*
*Bob:* *One of the things I told him [Paul] was, because I didn't want him to be a failure, I wanted him from now on to succeed. One thing working for you [Paul] is that we truly have a belief that we will be together. It's not a this- may-or-may-not-work thing. We have faith in God that we made a commitment. Not just to ourselves but to Him. We're going to be together. Now what he [Paul] has to help us with is, are we going to be miserable together or are we going to be happy together? We want to be happy. [Everyone laughs]. He had that going for him.*
*Harlene:* *That's a very positive foundation to build on.*
*Paul:* *They were very willing in everything we talked about to making it work . . .*
*Bob:* *What was one of the first things I said to you when I met you here in this room?*
*Paul:* *I don't remember.*
*Bob:* *I said you are going to want to write a book about this family [Everyone laughs]. We know it's a challenge what we're in, it's probably not for the weak of heart. We knew that going in. We had long talks about it. Sally's brother is a pastor of a church. We had meetings with him and worked with our own pastor at the time. We knew that this was not going to be an easy road ahead of us.*
*Harlene:* *What about the kids? What kinds of thoughts are going through your minds?*
*Tom:* *I was thinking about the ropes course.*
*Harlene:* *Well, I want to hear about the ropes course.*
*Tom:* *Well, our first event was, we had to pair up. It was Mom and Bob and Alice and Megan and me and Mark. Mark and I were working real hard*

*together. We were going moving on this wire and since I'm small I could work around real easy. On the next one we had to work together as a family. We had boards and things. The long boards were the parents and The short boards were the kids. The little board was Paul.*

Megan: *The camera was on us [Smiling], so we were being nice. Then after a while it was like everyone's true feelings came out. I don't know.*

Alice: *I watched that tape not long ago.*

Sally: *Bob said, "I'm 99 percent right about that," referring to how quickly we fell into our normal ways of being with one another. We were laughing at that one. We all ganged up on Dad.*

Harlene: *How did it happen? How was it decided that you would do the ropes course?*

Paul: *Actually, I think it was when Bob and Mark were here one day. For some reason, it came up [Turning to Mark] that you had been on the ropes course before at school. [Addressing Mark] Do you remember how it came up?*

Mark: *Yes, you said something about working together as a family and I said that our school had sent some people to a thing where you learn how to work together as a team . . . I thought it was going to be fun.*

Bob: *We're very out-doorsey, anyway.*

Sally: *We do things as a family a lot.*

Mark: *I think that everyone thought we would be swinging from ropes. I think we were disappointed.*

Harlene: *Like Tarzan and Jane.*

Sally: *We talked about doing the high ropes at some point.*

Paul: *Yes.*

Mark: *And then we only got through two things.*

Harlene: *And then you watched the tape—so tell me, what kind of thoughts were you having while you were doing it and what came to mind when you watched the tape?*

Tom: *Me and Mark, mainly, and Bob was sitting there: "All right, we're going to do this, and we're going to do that" and that was when we were going across the boards and the boards couldn't hit the ground. And Bob was just mainly being the boss. And me and Mark were saying, we'll give someone else a chance. But Bob said, "No, we got to do this and follow through."*

Alice: *He was right though.*

Bob: *We got through. One thing that I remember from that day is we kept going back and forth on how some of us were competitive with each other. Dr. Burney would never tell us the rules of the game. He would say, "I want you to do this." and some of us would think, well, this team is against his team. And we were crossing on the wire and some of us would try to help each other cross and some of us would try to knock the others off. It was interesting to see all of the players played out. [Referring to their interactions and relationships in the different activities on the challenge course] Whether it is the little squares thing we did in the room or the tight rope deal.*

*Sally:* *One of the things that was interesting that day was, you know we have often talked about the boys and the fact was it seemed like Bob would side with Mark more, and I would side with Tom more. They, Mark and Tom, would pick at each other often. But when we paired up, these two paired up, you know, real quick together.*

*Bob:* *You gave us the option though.*

*Sally:* *No. No, he just said to pair up. They paired up [pointing to the girls] and they paired up [indicating the boys] and that just left us [Sally and Bob].*

One activity involved three platforms separated from one another. Working as a group, family members were asked to move from the first platform to the second and then to the third without touching the ground with either the boards or their bodies. Three boards were available as resources. They named each item using words they thought were relevant to their family roles and dynamics. They discussed how they often paired, saying the children usually paired by gender, or Sally with her children, and Bob with his son. On this occasion Sally and Bob paired since the children had already chosen their partners.

The family and Paul reflected on the platform activity. They remembered that Alice, Megan, and Mark grouped together, Tom acted alone, and Sally and Bob were together. Although they were in close proximity and helped each other to reach the third platform, Paul wondered out loud if they were three distinct teams within the family unit. Alice, Megan, and Mark offered comments or suggestions. Sally laughingly commented on their seeming to be mad at Bob during the activity because he was telling everyone what to do but was not listening to them. Tom mentioned that when he and Mark argue at home it drives Sally and Bob "up the wall." One of the children commented that they seemed "to gang up on Dad" during the activities but the children agreed that this "ganging up" was an isolated event. Megan commented in a more serious tone that Bob had been 99 percent right about ways to approach the activity.

*Bob:* *I have, and we have talked about this before, I have a belief that when we die and we all go up to to Heaven that I am the head of this household. At this stage, anyway, and I am going to be judged by how well of a head of the household I was. My job as head of the household is to get these people through life as easy as possible and safe as possible. When we were on those boards and planks, we were to get around the platforms. I don't know if you [Addressing Harlene] were aware of it, but we were to name each platform, the boards, and the ground. The platforms we named, the first one "Where We Are Now," the second platform was "The Journey," and the third one was "Happy Ending." The ground beneath the boards was, and I made the comment, it was "chaos or divorce." They [the rest of the family] did not want to use the word divorce so we used the word, "Unhappy Ending."*

*They continued, discussing how they might not still be together as a family if they had not learned new ways of communicating, being with one another, and solving their problems.*

*Bob:* *So, if you fall off into the "Unhappy Ending" it's not good. The boards were the tools to get around these platforms. I called "The Big One."*

*Tom:* *Parents, kids, and Paul.*

*Bob:* *I think it was actually, I thought it was something else. Anyway, we have to take these boards and utilize these boards to get us to these other areas. I knew in my mind, and I had no doubts, that this is the way it had to happen. Alice was the first one that actually said, "Well, I've got another idea." No, it was Mark. Mark said, "No, we need to do it this way."*

*Alice:* *I didn't have an idea. I said that the whole time, but I did want to do it Mark's way.*

*Mark:* *Just the way he introduced his idea, it was so demanding.*

*Megan:* *Just the way he introduced the idea, it was so obstructive.*

*Bob:* *Right, my idea was that this is the only way to do it, you've got to do it my way. Mark said, "No, I've got another idea. We can do this and this." It wasn't five minutes into this deal when everybody lost it.*

*Mark:* *Alice was sitting down on the ground and I was leaning up against a tree.*

*Bob:* *Alice was ready to go back now, she was done with this.*

*Mark:* *I remember Paul asked Alice what she thought of this, and she said, "It's so boring."*

*Harlene:* *How did this chaotic situation become unchaotic or did it?*

*Bob:* *Finally, I think everyone just gave in to my demanding ways. We got around the course like I said, and I got to feel like I was right once again. They all felt deflated because I was right once again.*

*Alice:* *I was very aggravated by the time we got around the course.*

*Harlene:* *It was very typical that you have the idea of how it will work and they say it is wrong? Tom: I thought it was everybody's idea of how to get around the course, everybody put a little piece in.*

*Sally:* *It did work. We did get around the course.*

*Harlene:* *Did you notice anything different about the way Bob was being head of the household?*

*Alice:* *I don't have a problem with that, I think I was aggravated at Tom that day.*

*Bob:* *That is what I visualize as our biggest problem. Where Sally and I are concerned is when it comes time to say we have two roads here and we have to choose one of them. Let's choose one—I want her to say, "OK, you're the husband, that's the road." I know that's a bad thing to say and I apologize for saying it.*

*Sally:* *No, you don't.*

*Harlene:* *You are just being honest.*

*Sally:* *He is always honest.*

*Bob:* *I apologize for saying it but that's how I feel. I will always feel that way. Because so many times I don't say that because you [Sally] want to go your way, so we go and it's the wrong way. Not that she isn't a smart person. She's a very intelligent person and knows what she's doing.*

*Tom:* *She's been on this earth longer.*

*Harlene:* *That's what we were talking about earlier while we were waiting for Alice to come. You are an assistant principle and a very take-charge person but inside the home that's different.*

*Bob:* *No, inside the home it's the same. She's a very take-charge woman. That's probably the issue. She's the one at work that everyone else wants to be the leader. When she is in a group, Sally is the captain. She has no problem in that role and does a good job. And I don't have a problem with that, that's why I married her, I didn't want a weak woman. But now I have two people. [Referring to how he sees Sally in two different ways].*

*Sally:* *So I have to be strong and I have to be submissive.*

*Harlene:* *How do you do that?*

*Sally:* *[Laughing] Not very well.*

*Alice:* *You would think that because you are so tired every day that you would just gladly say, O.K.*

*Sally:* *It would be much easier, wouldn't it?*

*Harlene:* *You both have strong personalities and jobs, careers, professions where you are very strong. You are both in charge. How do you find a balance?*

*Sally:* *We both have strong beliefs about these children.*

*Tom:* *I just follow my Mom's lead.*

*Sally:* *They are very strong-willed children.*

*Harlene:* *They come by it genetically then?*

*Bob:* *They are all leaders in their own right—Mark is a leader of a group of boys at school. Megan is on track for valedictorian, and a state track champion. Alice is studying to be a lawyer and Tom is a leader.*

*Sally:* *We are a bunch of chiefs and not enough Indians.*

*Paul:* *I think that was one of the comments they made while on the ropes course was that we are all chiefs and there aren't any Indians.*

*Harlene:* *That's interesting, Paul, because I sometimes think of a leader as a choreographer in terms of how to nurture, support, and guide—to bring out the talents of all the people you are working with, to access the talents of the artists you are working with. So I see that as a double challenge for you—how to access and nurture the leadership in your family.*

*Bob:* *If I truly felt that I was the leader in their eyes, I could see myself doing that, but that is where I fail as a leader in this situation because I still come from the old school. My interpretation of the attitudes about families in the Bible is that a man's responsibility is to run his family. I know where I am now. I am the leader. I hear myself saying things sometimes that are totally ludicrous, like when I am upset. But I believe that if I was looked upon as the leader then I would in turn say, "O.K. how do you feel we should handle this?" But Sally is always saying this should be a joint decision, we need to make it together. O.K., what do you think? Well, I think this. O.K., well, I think the opposite. How are we going to decide? Someone has to step up and make a decision. In that situation, I feel like it needs to be me.*

**Comment:** We might have been tempted to be experts and judge the family members and their values and roles, and to be lured by the seductive issues of parenting, gender, grades, and religion. We are more interested, however, in the family's expertise, and how we can facilitate members talking about what is important to them and how they want to do it rather than questioning or interpreting from our standpoint.

**SL:** *This chapter also raises a question related to the responsibility of the therapist Sometimes collaborative therapists are understood to withhold their expertise as there is often a mis-reading of Anderson and Goolishian's chapter, "The client is the expert: A not-knowing approach to therapy" (1992). Though clients are seen as the experts on their lives and the content of their struggles, therapists have expertise in many areas, as well. So, could a therapist suggest a family have a session on a challenge course, or make any other type of suggestion he or she thought would be helpful? In fact, Harlene and Harry have often said the therapist was creating new problems if he or she held back on something that might be helpful. Holding back has both ethical and practical implications. Not only might the client be disadvantaged by missing out on new and alternatives ideas and approaches, the therapist may get so absorbed with the dilemma of holding back that he or she is unable to fully attend to the client. The critical issue in making suggestions, as a collaborative therapist, is keeping them suggestions and not imperatives. Suggestions must be offered tentatively, for instance, not thought of or presented as the only next step or the imperative solution. If the therapist becomes attached to his or her idea, and the client is not interested in pursuing it, the therapist must find a way to let go and re-enter the conversation that the client prefers.*

*Harlene* *So that's what you think a leader needs to be, so you make the decision?*
*Bob* *Yes, try to. Like she said, she's not very submissive nor are they [The children]. I'll take that back. This one gives me less grief [Indicating Megan]. This one second [Alice] but the boys fight me tooth and nail.*
*Harlene* *So it is an interesting challenge the two of you are faced with.*
*Sally* *But it is wonderful.*
*Bob* *So far, so good.*
*Harlene* *So what about when you were watching yourselves? [Referring to the video tape of their session on the ropes course]*
*Megan* *It was embarrassing.*
*Bob* *We tend to watch our P's and Q's when we don't know someone real well. But it doesn't take us long to know someone well enough to let it all hang out. Megan has a new boyfriend and he is still in that P's and Q's stage, but he is probably close to hearing it all hang out and see the other side of the family.*

**SL:** *Conversations shift and turn, taking various directions and having a reflexive nature. They told of Megan's boyfriend's comments on how the family members related to one another, as he watched the family's copy of the video tape. This led Bob to talk about the ways they usually related to one another. Then they returned to the challenge course, describing how at the beginning they tried to be good mannered and proper but how quickly they slipped into their more normal ways of relating to each other as they became more involved in the activities. They said that the activities provided a focus that allowed family members to work, in their words, in an "unselfconscious manner," revealing "our natural ways of being together." In turn, the reflective aspect of the experience afforded them the opportunity to view those ways of being in their words, in a "conscious" manner and reveal "new insights" about each other and themselves.*

*Harlene:* *So, it sounds like things are really moving in a direction you want them to be moving in?*

*Bob:* *Not fast enough.*

*Harlene:* *Not fast enough, then.*

*Alice:* *I think compared to some friends, we act like we are unhappy and have terrible problems and then you wake up the next day and think we don't even have any problems or that it's not a problem. I think we are an extremely close family. Compared to people I know, we are so far ahead of it and other families.*

*Bob:* *I agree, a lot of times—when you think you are not doing too well, look at the other side and that's probably true for the most part. We get along pretty well, but have our problems.*

*Alice:* *There are problems, but—*

*Tom:* *I just wanted to say, like even though we don't visit the ropes course everyday, we are going through a ropes course everyday, I mean it is, we are going through life.*

*Paul:* *Good analogy.*

*Tom:* *We are always facing challenges like on the boards, or having to slide around each other.*

*Sally:* *But one of the things I have noticed, and I think Bob has too, is that for the longest Bob was very defensive when I reprimanded Mark or I didn't see eye to eye with him about Mark. I was the same way with Tom. For some reason I would always come to Tom's defense and he would always come to Mark's defense. I feel like we have come a long way with that, as far as being unified, decisions are made with Mark and with Tom. [turning to Bob] Don't you think we have and that it has been since Mark has come to live with us?*

*Harlene:* *Is part of it being able to talk and express yourself in a different way and to develop a way for you to be able to talk through theses things?*

*Sally:* *And I feel like, now I don't know how it is for Bob, but for me it is like Mark is ours, and he is here with us. I feel more comfortable even though he is my stepson that it is not so much like a stepchild situation anymore.*

*Bob:* *You feel that you have the right to reprimand Mark.*

The family spontaneously talked about how Sally and Bob seemed to be more supportive of one another and how Mark and Tom were more accepting of their respective step-parents. The boys no longer felt that the step-parents were "picking on them" when they were corrected. All family members believed that the children were learning to be more accepting of responsibilities and consequences in general, an issue that had been part of previous sessions' discussions.

> *Harlene:* *It sounds like all of you have a set philosophy: That it's hard work, sometimes a little more work than at other times and requires tolerance.*
> *Bob:* *Patience*
> *Harlene:* *Patience, O.K. and it sounds like each of you are confident that you are moving in the direction you want to be moving in?*

Megan, not being able to put her finger on a concrete change said, it "*feels* like something is different and Sally agreed. She further commented that there seemed to be less fighting saying, "but when we fight, its not as bad," and that her parents now stay out of the children's disagreements. The parents mentioned that the children were becoming more mature as teenagers and young adults. Tom was going through some of the things that Mark had gone through several years before. Everyone laughed as Mark said, "I look at Tom and see myself doing it!" All agreed, "We are better listeners for each other."

> **SL**: Each listener of the spoken conversation has silent thoughts about what they hear. We value bringing these silent thoughts into the room, and particularly therapists' being public about theirs. At this point Harlene turned to Paul and wondered what he had been thinking as she and the family members were talking. Paul shared that he felt that the family and he had grown together and his impressions of the current conversation. Harlene [Addressing the family] added her thoughts.

Therapy conversations like everyday conversations weave back and forth; they do not follow linear paths. Here, the conversation momentarily turned away from the family's experience on the challenge course as Bob and Sally returned to reflect on their expectations of therapy.

> **SL**: *From a theoretical perspective, we believe that there are not linear relationships between things and that meaning develops in relationship. Therefore, therapists' ideas or suggestions arise out of the relationship and the conversation—the dialogical connection and activity—and are not owned by a particular person.*

> *Bob:* *One last thing. You (a gesture to Paul) made me think of something. I remember the first four or five times—[glancing at Sally] and you probably have thought of them too—we were home after hearing and visiting with Paul. Going home and working it out, Sally and I would look at each other and say, "When is he going to give us the answer?"*
> *Sally:* *Yes! Yes! Yes!*

*Bob:* *When is he going to tell us? And we got frustrated.*
*Harlene:* *Say more about that.*
*Bob:* *Well, we came for an answer. We paid our money, and we spilled our guts.*
*Harlene:* *Well you said earlier that you came expecting him to tell you exactly what you needed to do.*
*Sally:* *In fact we each wanted him to tell us what we wanted to hear.*
*Bob:* *We wanted a prescription.*
*Sally:* *And I wanted him [Pointing to Paul] to tell me that I was right, and he [indicating Bob] wanted him to tell him that he was right.*
*Bob:* *And he did not do that. We never did open up and say, "When are you going to give us the answer?" But I think, probably after four or five times, we started hinting, "We want the answer!" And I think he handled us perfectly in allowing us to continue on because the answer was within us. He couldn't give us the answer. You know if he had given us the answer, "Bob's right, he's always right, and he is always going to be right" that wouldn't have fixed the problem!*
*Sally:* *No! We probably wouldn't have come back! [Everyone laughs]*
*Bob:* *I would have been back by myself! [Laughter]*

**SL:** People often come to therapy expectating the "experts" to tell them what to do, to have the "right" answers. Sometimes they are quite forthright in their request. Even though we think the "client is the expert," we do not ignore such requests and questions. How we learn more about and respond to their expectations, however, depends on the conversation itself. At first Sally and Bob expected Paul to give them an answer. Their expectation dissolved as they began creating their own "solutions." Currently there was no need for Paul to continue to be their conversational partner.

*Sally:* *Right. And there is no quick fix. You have to live and learn. As Bob said, everyday there are life challenges. We'll work on it and call Paul when we need to and know that he has a good listening ear.*
*Alice:* *This a good forum, all of us sitting here.*
*Bob:* *We have a movie camera and what we should do now and then is set it up and have a little family meeting and ship it off to you. [Laughter]*

**SL, Pausing Comment:** *We think of clients and therapists as conversational partners on an uncertain journey. Each may have beginning ideas about the destination and the path, but the destination and the path change along the way. We can say the same about writing and reading.*

## REFERENCES

Andersen, T. (1997). Researching client-therapist relationships: A collaborative study for informing therapy. *Journal of Systemic Therapies*, *16*(2), 125–133.

Andersen, T. (Ed.). (1991). *The reflecting team: Dialogues and dialogues about the dialogues*. New York: W.W. Norton & Co.

Andersen, T. (1987). The reflecting team: Dialogue and meta-dialogue in clinical work. *Family Process*, 26, 415–428.

Anderson, H. (1997). *Conversation, language, and possibilities: A postmodern approach to therapy.* New York: Harper Collins.

Anderson, H. (1995). Collaborative language systems: Toward a postmodern therapy. In R. Mikesell, D.D. Lusterman, & S. McDaniel (Eds.). *Integrating family therapy: family psychology and systems theory* (pp. 27–44). Washington, DC: American Psychological Association.

Anderson, H. (1992). *C* therapy and the *F* word. *American Family Therapy Association Newsletter.*, *50*: 19–22.

Anderson, H. (1986). *Therapeutic impasses: A break-down in conversation*. Adapted from paper presented at Grand Rounds, Department of Psychiatry, Massachusetts General Hospital, Boston, Massachusetts, April, 1986, and at the Society for Family Therapy Research, Boston, Massachusetts, October, 1986.

Anderson, H. & Burney, J.P. (1997, June). *Collaborative inquiry: A practical voice illustration by case study.* Published articles of the European Institute for Advanced Studies in Management and the K.U. Leuven, Department of Work and Organizational Psychology Conference: Organizing in A Multi-Voiced World: Social Construction, Innovation and Organizational Change. Leuven, Belgium.

Anderson, H. & Goolishian, H. (1992). The client is the expert: A not-knowing approach to therapy. In S. McNamee & K. J. Gergen (Eds.). *Constructing therapy: Social construction and the therapeutic process*, (pp. 25–39) London: Sages.

Anderson, H. & Goolishian, H. (1988). Human systems as linguistic systems: Evolving ideas about the implications for theory and practice. *Family Process*. *27(4)*, 371–393.

Anderson, H. & Goolishian, H. (1986). Systems consultation to agencies dealing with domestic violence. In L. Wynne, S. McDaniel, & T. Weber (Eds.). *The family therapist as systems consultant*. (pp. 284–299). New York: Guilford Press.

Boyd, G.E. (1996). *The art of agape-listening: The miracle of mutuality*. Sugarland, TX: Agape House Press.

Burney, J.P. (1998). *Challenge courses and collaboration*. Paper presented in a workshop of Texas Association for Marriage and Family Therapy 25th Annual Conference, Dallas, TX.

Holzman, L. (1999). *Performing psychology: A postmodern culture of the mind*. New York: Routledge.

Holzman, L. & Mendez, (2003). *Psychological investigations:* New York: Routledge.

Holzman, L. & Morss, J. (Eds.). (2000). *Postmodern psychologies, societal practice, and political life*. New York: Routledge.

LeFevre, D.N. (1988). New York: The Putnam Publishing Group. *New games for the whole family*. (pp. 32–33).

Schoel, J., Prouty, D., & Radcliffe, P. (1988). *Islands of healings: A guide to adventure based counseling*. Hamilton, MA: Project Adventure, Inc.

Schon, D.A. (1983). *The reflective practitioner: How professionals think in America*. New York: Basic Books.

Shotter, J. (1993). *Conversational realities: Constructing life through language*. Thousand Oaks, CA: Sage.

*Chapter 7*

# *The Client's Nonverbal Utterances, Creative Understanding & the Therapist's Inner Conversation*[1]

PETER ROBER WITH CONVERSATIONAL PARTNERS GLENN LARNER AND DAVID PARÉ

*Mother had contacted me because she was concerned about the behavioral problems of her 8-year-old daughter Elly. The family was gathered in the session: the mother, Elly and the 2 year old Art. It was the second session with this family. At a certain moment mother started talking about the possibility of having some time to talk with me individually about her painful childhood. At that moment Elly playfully gave mother an injection with a toy hypodermic needle. Mother interrupted what she was saying and we all looked at Elly.*

When this sequence happened the therapist was confronted with the question what he[2] would do next. Would he ignore Elly's action and go on listening to the story of mother? Would he ask the child what she meant? Would he ask mother what she thinks Elly meant? Would he act on some idea that popped up

[1] I want to thank Lois Shawver and everybody at the PMTH discussion list on the internet. Furthermore, I also thank Craig Smith, Tom Strong and Lynn Hoffman for their comments on this manuscript. I also want to thank my colleagues who have helped me in discussing the case: Sara Keymolen, An Nijsmans, Karin Tilmans, An Luyten, An Vanhimbeek, Mich Vanwayenbergh, Lieven Migerode.

[2] In order to avoid the discriminating use of the generic masculine, the client and the therapist are referred to with a feminine pronoun, except when there is an explicit reference to a man.

in his mind about what might be expressed by Elly's behavior? One of his ideas was that maybe the injection was a painkiller and that the girl wanted to help mother to feel less pain. This was one of those situations in family therapy practice when a therapist has to make decisions on the spot. Therapists are invariably confronted with the unforeseen, the uncontrollable and the unpredictable. Their theoretical and technical knowledge alone doesn't suffice to help them through the day. In daily practice, since there's often hardly time for reflection or deliberation, therapists have to act intuitively.

This doesn't mean that these acts of the therapist are mindless or impulsive. To the contrary, there's knowledge in our intuitive actions. Schön (1983) wrote about these intuitive actions in everyday professional life and he used the term *knowing-in-action*: "Our knowing is ordinarily tacit, implicit in our patterns of action and in our feel for the stuff with which we are dealing. It seems right to say that our knowing is *in* our action" (p. 49). But, as Schön writes, professionals don't only act on this knowledge they are not aware of, they also reflect in action. This *reflection-in-action* reveals itself in the thousands of small and ordinary questions we ask ourselves in our inner conversation during our talks with clients: "What will I say?" "What will I ask?" "To who?" "What do they expect from me?" And so on. We usually base our answers to these questions, not only on prior explicit theoretical or philosophical considerations, but also on some kind of tacit knowledge (Polanyi, 1975) and on implicit theories that inform this knowledge.

In this chapter I will reflect on ways of dealing with nonverbal utterances of clients in the family therapy session, like Elly's act of giving her mother an injection. I will propose that the therapist's reflections-in-action in her inner conversation (her thoughts, ideas, . . . ) are very useful in this context. From a postmodernist viewpoint however, there is cause for suspicion towards the thoughts and ideas in the therapist's inner conversation because of the risk of privileging the therapist's point of view. The therapist's thoughts and ideas are informed by her limited perspective; they are historically situated, and they are bound to their (conversational) context. In fact, as Bakhtin (1986) wrote, these thoughts and ideas can not even be considered as *her own* thoughts and ideas. They are constructed in the dialogue with the clients, and in the context of dialogue thoughts and ideas don't belong to one person, but to (at least) two: the speaker and the listener.

Although these postmodernist ideas reflect suspicion towards the therapist's thoughts and ideas, they could in some way also be seen as highlighting the potentialities of the therapist's inner conversation. Exactly because the therapist's thoughts and ideas are not only shaped by the therapist herself, but also by her involvement in the dialogue with the clients, they are valuable for the therapeutic conversation. The therapeutic dialogue reverberates in the therapist's inner conversation. Delicate chords are touched there and begin to resonate. These resonances can be important bridges between the sensitivity of the therapist and the vulnerability of the clients (Elkaïm, 1997), on condition that the therapist would be open, not only to so-called objective observations, but also to the personal reflections these observations evoke in her (Rober, 1999). These reflections can be theoretical speculations, philosophical contemplations, dreamlike images, curious questions (Andersen, 1995). Whatever form they take, these reflections, if taken seriously, are potentially rich resources for the therapist, since they can give access to things that haven't yet been said (Rober, 1999).

## NONVERBALS AND COLLABORATIVE THERAPISTS

In the context of discursive or collaborative therapies (Strong, 1999), it is the therapist's task to help to make space for the *not-yet-said* (Anderson & Goolishian, 1988; Anderson, 1997). The concept *not-yet-said* refers to the client's internal private thoughts and conversation (Anderson, 1997, p. 118) or, in other words, to the stories that haven't been told. The role of the therapist is described as being a *participant-facilitator* (Real, 1990; Rober, 1999). She participates in the conversation from *a not-knowing* position (Anderson & Goolishian, 1992; Anderson, 1997): "Not-knowing requires that our understandings, explanations, and interpretations in therapy not be limited by prior experiences or theoretically formed truths, and knowledge." (Anderson & Goolishian, 1992, p. 28) The traditional, structuralist expert-stance of the therapist is rejected and the client is considered the expert (Anderson & Goolishian, 1992).

When we return to the case of Elly and the injection, the question poses how a collaborative therapist would react. How can the therapist avoid an expert-stance? What would be a collaborative response of the therapist? What should she do to connect with the clients experience from *their* perspective? What would be a not-knowing stance in this particular context? What should the therapist do to be a participant-facilitator in the conversation?

At first glance, collaborative therapy literature doesn't seem to offer very much that can help the practicing family therapist to find out how to react in cases like the one of Elly and the hypodermic needle. Nonverbal behavior is hardly mentioned in the books of Michael White, Harlene Anderson, Freedman & Combs, and other important collaborative authors (Rober, 2002a). On closer inspection however, there are some interesting ideas in the collaborative therapy literature that can be used as building blocks for our attempt to generate answers to our questions. I would like to refer to Griffith & Griffith's work about mind-body problems, to Tom Andersen's ideas about signs of comfort and discomfort of clients, and also to ideas about the therapist's inner conversation.

### Mind Body Problems

Griffith & Griffith (1994) state that some things cannot be expressed in verbal language because it doesn't fit the social or cultural context. When the context is not safe, stories are not verbalized in order to protect oneself or others. These stories however are sometimes expressed in body language: "somatization is . . . a language of the body that dominates when talking is forbidden or unsafe" (Griffith & Griffith, 1995, p. 84). A somatized symptom is the public performance of an unspeakable dilemma, from which the person cannot escape, and about which there can not be conversation.

## Bodily Signs of Comfort and Discomfort

Tom Andersen (1995) states that it is best not only to discuss the things a client says, but also the way these things are said. The therapist has to watch for bodily signs of the clients that tell something about how it is for them to be in the therapeutic conversation: "There are many signs [. . . ]: talking less, looking down or away, conveying the feeling that it would be better to leave the conversation than to stay in it, and so on. We can *see* the other feeling uncomfortable" (p. 15).

Andersen (1995) gives an example of a father who sighs when he speaks about his son's sadness. This was an invitation for Andersen to start a conversation about sadness and he asked: "When your son is sad, is his sadness totally filled with sadness or are there other feelings in his sadness?" The father says "there's also anger." Andersen goes on and asks: "If your son's anger could speak, what would the words be?" and so on. With these kinds of questions Andersen is not searching for what is the real meaning behind or under the expressed. Instead, he sees nonverbal utterances as invitations for further curious and respectful questioning; the therapist uses them as points of departure for further conversation.

## The Therapist's Inner Conversation

Anderson & Goolishian (1988) stated that the therapist maintains a dialogical conversation with herself, which is the starting point of her questions. This dialogical conversation can be called the *therapist's inner conversation* (Rober, 1999; 2002b) and can be described as a polyphony of inner voices (Bakhtin, 1981, 1984; Voloshinov, 1973; Rober, 2002b). In the inner conversation there's not one voice, not one truth. To the contrary, there are many voices that can be very different, one from the other. Some voices are prominent in the forefront, others are faintly audible in the background. One voice may be speaking with confidence, another may be tearful, while yet another remains emotionally unaffected, and so on.

> *Glenn Larner: "How is the inner conversation of a play therapist or child analyst working with nonverbal communication as countertransference similar or different to what you are saying?"*
>
> *Peter Rober: Thanks for this comment, Glenn. I often work with colleagues who are child analytic therapists. I must say, although we sometimes use different words to say things, it is not so difficult to understand each other. Often when I'm stuck with a family, their ideas offer me a useful perspective that helps me to go on with my clients.*

*I'm not a child analyst myself, though. For me it is difficult to see similarities or differences between my approach and the approach of child analytic therapists. I have a hunch that the differences are not that big. Sometimes my analytic colleagues tell me that I translate analytic ideas in other words in order to make them fit a family therapeutic setting. They mention also analytic authors who have written things in line with my ideas (e.g. Thomas Ogden, Patrick Casement). I haven't read these authors though, so I don't know if it is true.*

*Sometimes I wonder that maybe we shouldn't search for the differences in the theoretical frameworks, but in the therapeutic setting. In an individual setting maybe a therapist has another position towards his/her clients, than in a family session, for instance in terms of dependency and depth of the transference relationship. I don't know.*

*Let's take an example. For instance, I teach my students to show restraint in the family session when someone starts to weep, let's say the daughter. Some students are very fast in handing this weeping daughter a Kleenex. I teach my students to wait and see how the other family members react to the weeping of the girl, and to give the family the chance to help, support, console, be annoyed or whatever... If the family therapist would rush in and take things over from the family, then this might repress the family's own resources and make the family more dependent of the professional helper.*

*I wonder: How would a play therapist react when a girl starts to cry in the session? Would the play therapist also show restraint? I guess so, but would he/she do that for the same reasons as a family therapist? Would he/she do it in the same way as a family therapist? I don't know.*

*All in all, your comment, Glenn, makes me reflect on the relationship between psychotherapeutic schools. As you write in your own chapter on Levinas, outcome research shows again and again the importance of the non-specific factors. Why then these wars between different schools about who's right or wrong? Why these theoretical discussions that seem to go nowhere useful? Why don't we all together try to understand what is necessary for a relationship between two people to be helpful?*

*GL: Let me give you a last comment about the link between inner talk in therapy and countertransference in psychoanalysis. It seems to me the child analyst and family therapist share a creative process of thinking in the presence of others that is both dialogical and relational. What the therapist or analyst thinks, comes from and is returned to the other as a sharing of meaning, a mutual exchange in constructing a common language, where as therapists our welcoming of the other or ethics comes first.*

As the therapist converses with the clients, she is simultaneously listening to her inner voices and actively preparing her responses in her inner conversation (Anderson, 1997). Rober (1999) proposed that the therapist's actions in the outer conversation would be inspired, not only by her observations, but also by the personal experiences (feelings, ideas, fantasies, memories, . . . ) these observations evoke in her inner conversation. These experiences are rich resources that can help open space for the not-yet-said in the therapeutic conversation, or give access to subjugated knowledges. Families are complex, and in order to be effective family therapists, our technical-rationality, i.e. the idea that our practice is an application of rational and scientific knowledge, has to be complimented by a more practical, intuitive knowing (Schön, 1983), or what Polanyi calls *tacit knowledge* (Polanyi, 1975). Hoffman (2001) also speaks about this kind of intuitive knowing and she stresses that it is a relational knowing or a kind of transpersonal communication, which she calls "*traveling empathy*" or "*tempathy*" for short. This kind of knowing is often reflected in the images, questions or considerations that pop up in our inner conversation while we are talking to others (Rober, 1999). If we allow ourselves to go beyond our technical-rationality, and use our relational, intuitive knowing for the benefit of our clients, we can reach a richer understanding of the stories our clients present to us.

The idea of the mind-body problems as expressions of unspoken stories, of the importance of bodily signs of comfort and discomfort, and of the importance of the therapist's inner conversation will serve as building blocks in the further discussion of a dialogical view of nonverbal utterances in family therapy practice. I will elaborate on the above-mentioned ideas and I will propose some additional ideas about ways to take nonverbal communication seriously, without falling in the trap of taking a structuralist expert-stance. Instead of making interpretations and trying to uncover the hidden meaning of nonverbal behavior, I propose that it is useful to make the nonverbal behavior a topic of conversation and to discus potential meanings of the behavior, in such a way that space is created for the not-yet-said in the conversation (Anderson & Goolishian, 1988; Anderson, 1997).

> *David Paré: Peter, you've got me thinking about the differences between the not-yet said by* you, *the not-yet-said- by* me, *and the not-yet-said by* us. *My impression is that uncovering and sharing either of the former two (client's and therapist's unspoken utterances) is a step in a process that leads to the emergence of the latter: a dialogic creation, a "never-previously-said"?*
>
> *PR: I don't know, but it seems to me that as a therapist I'm especially concerned about the not-yet-said of the clients. I'm trying to make room for the stories the family members have not told yet. Sometimes when I as a therapist say things I have not said before to the family, this makes room for what they have not said yet. So it seems to me, in a therapeutic context the not-yet-said by the therapist is secondary to the not-yet-said of the clients.*

## REFLECTIONS ABOUT POTENTIAL MEANINGS

Bakhtin (1986) maintained that any culture contains meanings that it itself does not know: "They are there, but as a potential" (Morson & Emerson, 1990, p. 55). The same holds true for families. There are a lot of unspoken, potential meanings in families that even the family members themselves have not realized yet. According to Griffith & Griffith (1994) some of these unspoken meanings may be expressed in somatic problems. Similarly, in the therapeutic conversation, they may also be expressed in nonverbal ways.

Instead of making interpretations about the so-called underlying real meaning of a nonverbal utterance, the therapist can be open to the multiplicity of voices in her inner conversation, and reflect on possible meanings of the utterance. In this way, the therapist is open to the complexity of what she observes without trying to pinpoint the simplistic *true* meaning of the nonverbal utterance. In her inner conversation, the therapist's images, thoughts and ideas may first appear as vague, chaotic constellations. Only later, and with some effort, these reflections can be articulated. Vague sensations grow into sharper images, dim ideas become accessible for conscious contemplation, and disparate elements are connected in more complex wholes that give meaning to them. In this way, the therapist's reflections structure her observations.

## OPENING DIALOGICAL SPACE FOR UNSPOKEN MEANINGS

The therapist's reflections should not necessarily be introduced in the outer conversation, but they can be, if the therapist thinks that in that way space for the not-yet-said might be opened (Rober, 1999). Introducing one of her reflections in the outer conversation, initiates a dialogue about potential meanings in which not only clients, but also the therapist, is present as a person. This means that a therapist has to do more than just listen to the client's story and try to empathically understand what it is they want to say. Empathic listening, in which the therapist tries to be open to the meanings the client tries to convey, is important in therapy, but it is not enough. As Bakhtin (1986) wrote, understanding is not a passive process in which meanings are conveyed by the client and received by the therapist. There is no duplication of the client's meanings in the therapist's mind. Rather, understanding is an active, creative process in which the meanings of the client make contact with the meanings of the therapist, in the process of which new meanings emerge that are different from the original meanings of the client. According to Bakhtin, this dialogical process of creative understanding can only take place if "the person who understands is located outside the object of his creative understanding" (Bakhtin, 1986, p. 7). This is what Bakhtin called *outsideness*.

This dialogical model of creative understanding looks very promising in the context of our theme of nonverbals and reflections about potential meanings. The therapist's inner conversation is the outsideness from which reflections about potential meanings are introduced in the therapeutic conversation. These reflections become subject of a respectful dialogue with the clients through which potential meanings may be actualized in such a way that something new emerges. The meanings the clients add to the conversation will modify as they make contact with the therapist's different meanings and with the meanings that were already there in the conversation. Paraphrasing Bakhtin (1986) we could say, both therapist and clients retain their unity, but they are mutually enriched. In that way new meanings are constructed, reflecting some of the meanings that originated from the not-yet-said of the therapist, and reflecting some of the meanings that originated from the not-yet-said of the clients (McNamee & Gergen, 1999).

The detailed discussion of the case story of Elly and the hypodermic needle will illustrate more vividly how these ideas can be put into practice.

## CASE STORY OF ELLY

*When Elly's mother started talking about the possibility of having some time to talk with me individually about her painful childhood, Elly playfully gave mother an injection with a toy hypodermic needle. Mother interrupted what she was saying and said playfully "Aw, you're hurting me!" We all looked at Elly.*

*This sequence happened in the second session of the therapy. In the first session, we had talked about all sorts of things. The children had explored the room and they had played some. Mother had told me that she worried about Elly's behavior at home. Elly was not nice, she didn't obey when her mother asked her to do things, she bullied her brother and she used profane language. Mother had also told me that she herself had been hospitalized for a depression some months ago. At the end of that first session, I had asked them to bring something to the next session that would help me to get to know them better (for more information about this task, see Rober, 1998).*

*In the next session (the second session) the children had each brought a teddy bear. Elly said that she played with her bear and that she cuddled him and that she took him with her to bed when she went to sleep. "Except when my brother can't find his teddy bear," Elly added, "Then I give him mine, and I go to sleep alone." This made me reflect in my inner conversation that this girl seemed to be very caring and helpful. I made a mental note of that. Then something strange happened. Art, who still hadn't spoken a word, took his bear and put him in an empty chair. Without speaking, we all looked at him doing that, and then we saw that he sat down in another chair, opposite of his bear. When he sat on this chair, Elly stood up from her chair and put her own bear, that was bigger than Art's, with Art's bear in the same chair. She took her bear's arm, and laid it around the shoulders of the little bear. It struck me that it looked like a very loving embrace and again I reflected how helpful and concerned Elly was. When Elly sat down in her chair again, Art stood up and went back to the chair where the bears sat. Without words, he took Elly's bear and dropped it on the floor and put his own bear in the chair again. Elly protested and yelled "Hey". She stood up and took Art's bear and dropped it on the floor and put her bear alone in the chair. At that moment mother burst in and said, "Elly, don't bully your brother."*

*All the time I had sat there observing the interactions of the children. In my inner conversation I reconstructed the scene: Elly did something warm and caring first by putting her bear comfortingly with Art's bear in the chair. She was not rewarded for it, not by her brother, nor by her mother. Then when she and her brother were playfully competing, mother gave her a reprimand. I wondered if this showed me something about this family that wasn't said yet. Maybe this scene expressed some story that lived in the family that could not be told yet. Maybe at home the same thing happened: maybe mother didn't reward Elly for the things she did for others. Maybe she only commented on the things Elly did wrong. If that was so, I thought, maybe mother in her own childhood had not been rewarded for what she had done for the family.*

*I kept these reflections to myself and I asked mother what she had brought to the session that could help me to get to know her better. She said she had brought a letter. She handed it to me and she said it was a letter she had written to her mother when she was 18 years old. At that time, her mother had been dead already for nine years. I asked her if she wanted me to read the letter. Mother said she wanted me to read the letter and she wanted to talk about it. "But not now," she added, "not with the children present."*

*I saw tears in her eyes and I remembered her telling me in the first session, without going into the details, that she had had a terrible childhood. I proposed to mother that I would keep the letter, and read it later when we had time to talk alone, without the children. Mother agreed. Then we talked some more about Elly and about her behavior that was bothering mother. I tried to get mother to talk in a more constructive way about Elly, but it was very difficult for mother to say anything positive about Elly. Then, near the end of the session, mother said that Elly was probably missing her father. Since the divorce, three years ago, she only saw him twice a year: "Maybe Elly's problems are caused by the grief she has from missing her father," mother said. Mother suggested that it might be good for Elly if she could talk alone with a therapist about her father and how she misses him. I turned to Elly and asked her what she thought about that. Elly didn't say much. But after some time she hesitatingly said that she didn't want to speak about her father because it would make her feel very sad. I said that, if she didn't want to talk about her father, I would respect that, but I added that if she would change her mind and decided she did want to talk about her father, she could. Elly nodded. Then I asked mother if she thought it was time for her to talk, without the children, about the letter to her mother she had brought to the session, and about her painful childhood. Mother said that indeed she wanted to talk about her childhood and her mother. It was then that Elly stood up and gave mother the injection with the toy hypodermic needle.*

*When Elly gave the injection to her mother, my first thought was "this is important". Although I can not say why, I felt quite confident that Elly's act was meaningful. Maybe because she initiated the act at the exact moment when mother started talking about a session alone to talk about her painful childhood. Maybe because mother interrupted her story. I don't know. But the thought "this is important" made me prolong the focus of attention of all present on this act of Elly's. In my inner conversation I tried to connect what I had just seen with some of my earlier reflections. I wondered if Elly maybe wanted to draw our attention away from the painful subject mother was talking about, to the here-and-now that was less painful. Another reflection was that maybe this might be Elly's way to symbolically help her mother feel less pain about her miserable childhood (the injection being a painkiller). Indeed, Elly had just said she didn't want to talk individually about issues that mattered to her because she would feel too sad. Maybe she thought mother would be sad too when she would talk about her childhood.*

*I asked Elly: "Do you want your mother to feel less pain?" Elly smiled and hesitated. She didn't say anything. Then I shared with her some of my reflections. I told her that she had struck me as being a very helpful person and that maybe she thought it would be painful for mother to talk alone, and maybe she wanted to give her mother a painkiller. After some hesitation, Elly answered that she didn't want her mother to talk with me alone about her painful childhood. I asked if she could help me to understand that. She remained silent. I asked, "Do you think it will be too painful for her?" She nodded yes. Mother said to Elly: "But if I would talk about it, the pain would eventually go away." Elly shook her head and said,—"If you would talk about those painful things, where would I have to stay?" At first I was confused by this remark of Elly's. Then I realized that Elly probably was referring to the three months that her mother had been hospitalized with depression. Elly had to stay in a home for that period. I asked her if she was afraid her mother might have to be hospitalized again if she would speak about her painful childhood. She nodded yes.*

*I was glad that I had shared my reflection about Elly trying to help her mother feel less pain in the outer conversation. It had helped to make space for a story that hadn't been told yet (the story about the fear of the daughter that mother might become depressed again). Of course, I still don't know, and I will never know, if Elly intended anything by giving the injection. Maybe Elly didn't mean anything by giving that injection, maybe she just wanted to play, maybe she meant something else with it... I don't know. Inspired by Ludwig Wittgenstein (1958) we could say that meanings of language relate to their consensual use in the social context. In the same way, the meaning of Elly's nonverbal utterance related, not to what Elly might have intended it to mean, but to the meaning Elly, her mother and I constructed in consensus through our dialogue.*

*The importance of this constructed meaning became evident, some weeks later, in the first individual session[3] with mother. At a certain moment I mentioned to mother that I thought her daughter was trying to be helpful to her in lots of ways. I reminded her of the injection Elly had given her, and told her that together we had interpreted it as a way of being helpful. The mother first looked at me disapprovingly and then she said that she*

[3] In the beginning of the third session Elly and mother came in and they said that Elly had agreed to talk with a therapist individually and she had also agreed that mother would talk to me individually. I asked them how they had decided that. They said they didn't know. After the previous session, they had talked some more and then Elly had agreed. I was baffled. I didn't understand where this decision came from all of a sudden, and I still don't.

*didn't agree with that interpretation anymore. She said Elly didn't help her at all. I asked her to tell me what she meant by that. She said: "Last week, for example, I was feeling very depressed again. I was lying on the couch, thinking about all the things I had missed in my childhood and I was really down. And then, instead of helping me, Elly made a lot of noise, and she started kicking her little brother. So I got really mad at her. I stood up, I yelled at her and I sent her to her bedroom."*

*My first thought was that the meaning we had constructed together was not useful anymore. It didn't fit mother's story at all. In mother's view it was clear that the girl didn't help her to cope with her depression. Then mother added: "She does that every time when I am very depressed. It's as if she deliberately wants to make me angry." This made me think about the girl's behavior in another way. I reflected in my inner conversation that this sounded as if Elly wanted to make her mother angry, as if she preferred an angry mother instead of a depressed mother. I hesitated because I sensed somehow I was moving into vulnerable territory. After some reflection, I decided to share these reflections nonetheless with mother, and I said: "Maybe Elly wanted you to be angry because she prefers an angry mother, instead of a depressed mother who is thinking of killing herself."*

*The mother was silent for a moment and then she asked me, "... as if she wants to keep me alive?" I wondered what mother meant exactly but I nodded just the same. Then, mother began to cry and after some time she said,—"I think you are right, she is trying to help me." Mother then told me that she now understood her daughter was going through the same things that she had been through as a child. As a child, she had lived alone with her mother who was often depressed and she tried to help her mother the best she could. One day, when she was nine, she came home from school and she found her mother in the bedroom. She had killed herself with a shotgun.*

*"All these months I had tried to keep my mother alive, but clearly I failed," she added. After she told me this story, mother assured me that she didn't want her daughter to have the same miserable childhood as she had had. We talked about how she could make sure her daughter would have a happy childhood.*

Elly's nonverbal behavior invited several reflections in the therapist's inner conversation. He introduced one of these reflections in the outer conversation. This is what Anderson (1997) might call *going public*. Sharing such a reflection is meant to help the therapist and the family members in their process of finding words for the not-yet-said. The reflection is offered as a theme for discussion, not as an expert explanation or as a diagnosis. That's why the therapist used questions and tentative language, and presented his reflection in an open way; doing his best not to push the client this way or another.

Another comment about the case of Elly I want to add in this chapter has to do with the verbalization of reflections from the inner conversation. Inner reflections are less fully formed than spoken comments. Spoken words have a shape that was only nascent in the internal version. But verbalization is more than finding the right sounds to express and shape inner meaning. In his book *Thought and Language*, Vygotsky (1962) wrote: "Thought is not merely expressed in words; it comes into existence through them." (p. 125). Meaning is born in its expression. For instance: sometimes when therapists want to share an inner reflection with a family and they start to talk to the family, they are surprised themselves by the words they are speaking. What they are actually saying to the family is not a mere expression of their reflections. Certain aspects of what they actually say have not been premeditated in their inner conversation. In that unpremeditated part of their message some intuitive understanding is reflected, which often proves surprisingly meaningful for families. This is illustrated in some of the case stories I published earlier (Rober, 1999), but it is also illustrated in the story of Elly. In the individual session with mother, the therapist reflected in his inner conversation that Elly maybe preferred an angry mother, instead of a depressed mother. When he introduced his reflection in the session, however, he added intuitively "... who is thinking of killing herself". This unpremeditated addition seems to have made all the difference for mother, because it connected her with her own childhood experiences that had been left unspoken until then. This is an example of those cases in which the therapist voices the tacit knowledge that Hoffman (2001) calls "*tempathy*". It's a relational, intuitive knowledge that sometimes pops up in a dialogue, but that escapes the comprehension or control of the therapist. The therapist can however welcome this relational knowledge and try to use it in the advantage of her clients. She can try to be open to this knowledge and let herself be a vehicle of it, "... [w]ith a sense of humility and astonishment ... " (Larner, 1998, p. 567).

*GL: "How is this process of inner talk that occurs in therapy different or the same to the dialogic process that occurs in any creative endeavour like novels or films?"*
*PR: My wife is an artist/painter, and I often talked with her about this fascinating question. There are of course similarities between the inner talk of a therapist and the inner talk of an artist. But there are differences too. For one thing, a therapist is always in relation to someone else. An artist is much more lonely. My wife tells me that she doesn't think about her audience when she is working. "When I'm painting, I'm alone with myself," she says, "I only start to think about my audience when I start to plan for an exhibition." That's a big difference with the way I work. During a therapeutic session, mentally I'm constantly in connection with the clients I'm working with.*

*On the other hand, there are certainly also similarities between artists and therapists. In his book Improvisational Therapy, Bradford Keeney describes therapy as a kind of improvisation, and the therapist as an artist. He writes: "Becoming an artist involves moving away from impersonating others and developing one's own style. An artist fully utilizes his or her personal resources and limitations to create a unique style that is an aesthetic portrait of self-in-context." (1991, p. 2) Described in this way, I would say that the creative process of the therapist is quite similar to the creative process of an improvisational artist like a jazz musician or a stand up comedian.*

*I strongly believe in the importance of the non-specific factors in therapy, and I see therapy as a meeting of two (or more) unique human beings, at a certain moment in time. There is no predictability, no certainty, no control over what will happen in the session. We can only do the best we can, as limited and mortal human beings, to be helpful for those coming to us in distress, doubt or pain. Although I don't have big theories or philosophies to back these ideas up, as a therapist it is something I personally feel very strongly as the ethical foundation of my work.*

*DP: Glenn, I'm wondering if you could say more about what you're thinking about the artist's dialogic process.*

*GL: On the question of how the therapist's inner talk is related to creating a novel or film, I'll go back to Kieslowski's comment that as a writer or filmmaker he directs by not knowing. In this creative not knowing process he nonetheless exercises expertise and knowing as a highly crafted scriptwriter director and likewise the curious therapist facilitates discourse as a skilled conversational expert. While there are obvious differences between the context of therapy and art, such as the intentional nature of the activity and whether others are immediately present as audience, as Peter notes (though one could argue the artist's creative voice comes from and eventually returns to a cultural context as a communal relating of ideas), this creative interplay between knowing and not knowing is what they have in common. Peter calls this 'constructive hypothesizing' and I refer to it in Levinas's terms as ethical relation, however in both therapy and art it involves a creative process of inner talk and reflection about reflection that is part of an ecstatic experience of other.*

*Thus Peter's therapy narrative about Elly reminds me of a Kieslowski film, there is an element of mystery and the unknown, a surprise about what occurs where therapists like artists are moved to think, speak and create in wonder. Peter is like a photographer taking images of the therapeutic process and freezing them in time. There is a silent beauty about Elly putting the needle into her mother and the rich meaning that unfolds as Peter begins to reflect in the presence of the family, a process that reads like a fairy tale in providing a relational key for the not-yet-said and what is unknown and surprising. The intuitively spoken words of the therapist seem to jump out of the therapy relationship as if they were in their own time and waiting to be said. This is inside outside or outer inner.*

*DP: Songwriting is the artistic craft I turn to most often for creative expression outside of my professional life. It's there that I frequently have the astonishing experience of something seemingly being "given to me", either in the form of a musical motif or a turn of phrase. This, to me, is much like the intuitive knowing of which you speak, Peter. I evaluate these gifts and sometimes utilize them, and sometimes decide they don't fit the piece I'm working on. The difference for me, though, is that my decision is mostly a personal aesthetic one—a beholden-ness to the product of my craft. Therapy is no such private affair, however. The therapist's "gift" might be the client's bane.*

*PR: Yes, David, you are right. That's a big difference. The therapeutic relationship should be an I-Thou relationship: As a therapist I have a responsibility towards thou (the client). This does not mean however that intuitive knowledge, or as Schön (1983) called it knowing-in-action, should be banned from our repertoire. Therapy is not a rational enterprise. If we like it or not some of our actions as therapists are based on tacit considerations. As Hoffman (2001) suggests, even some of our most empathic therapeutic actions are. But, as you write, there's a danger there; the danger of hurting our clients, or of not being respectful. Luckily we can also reflect in action. We can ask questions to ourselves in our inner conversation during our session with our clients, and try our best to be as responsible and respectful as we can towards them.*

## CONCLUSION

In this article nonverbal communication is considered to be an important aspect of the client's story, even though often the meaning of that part of the story may not be clear. Therapy is a complex process, in the face of which the therapist can only be very humble (Larner, 1998). As Bakhtin (1986) wrote, meanings cannot be finalized: "There are no limits to the meanings embedded in utterances." (Leiman, 1998, p. 115) The therapist will never grasp all the potential meanings of the client's nonverbal utterances. There will always be other perspectives and there will always remain things left unspoken and stories left unheard. This is something the therapist has to live with. Still, it is possible to work with nonverbals in family therapy in a way that contributes richly to the bringing forth of novel and helpful meanings. The client's nonverbal utterance is seen as an invitation for a dialogue, through which potentials can be activated in such a way that new meanings are created. In this process of creative understanding, reflection-in-action is no longer confined to the therapist's inner conversation, but, rather, becomes a joint effort of the family and the therapist in their dialogue.

## REFERENCES

Andersen, T. (1995). Reflecting processes; acts of informing and forming: You can borrow my eyes but you must not take them away from me! (pp. 11–37). In: S. Friedman, (Ed.). *The reflecting team in action: Collaborative practice in family therapy*. New York: Guilford Press.

Anderson, H. & Goolishian, H. (1988). Human systems as linguistic systems. *Family Process, 27*, 371–393.

Anderson, H. & Goolishian, H. (1992). The client is the expert: A not-knowing approach to therapy (pp. 25–39). In S. McNamee & K. J. Gergen (Eds.). *Therapy as social construction*. London: Sage.

Anderson, H. (1997). *Conversation, language and possibilities: A postmodern approach to therapy.* New York: Basic Books.

Bakhtin, M. (1981). *The dialogic imagination*. Austin (TX): University of Texas Press.

Bakhtin, M. (1984). *Problems of Dostoevsky's poetics*. Minneapolis: University of Minnesota Press.

Bakhtin, M. (1986). *Speech genres & other late essays*. Austin (TX): University of Texas Press.

Elkaïm, M. (1997). *If you love me, don't love me: Undoing reciprocal double binds and other methods of change in couple and family therapy*. Northval (N.J.): Jason Aroson.
Griffith, J.L. & Griffith, M.E. (1994). *The body speaks: Therapeutic dialogues for mind-body problems*. New York: Basic Books.
Griffith, J.L. & Griffith, M.E. (1995). When patients somatize and clinicians stigmatize: Opening dialogue between clinicians and the medically marginalized. In: S. Friedman, (Ed.). *The reflecting team in action: Collaborative practice in family therapy* (pp. 81–99). New York: Guilford Press.
Hoffman, L. (2001). *Braided voices: A legacy for family therapy*. Unpublished manuscript.
Keeney, B. (1991). *Improvisational therapy*. New York: Guilford Press.
Larner, G. (1998). Through a glass darkly: Narrative as destiny. *Theory and Psychology, 8(4)*, 549–572.
Leiman, M. (1998). Words as intersubjective mediators in psychotherapeutic discourse: The presence of hidden voices in patient utterances. In M. Lähteenmäki & H. Dufva (Eds.). *Dialogues on Bahktin: Interdisciplinary readings*. University of Jyväskylä, Centre of Applied Language Studies, Jyväskylä. 105–116.
McNamee, S. & Gergen, K. (1999). *Relational responsibility: Resources for sustainable dialogue*. London: Sage publications.
Morson, G.L. & Emerson, C. (1990). *Mikhail Bakhtin: Creation of a prosaics*. Stanfort (CA): Stanfort University Press.
Polanyi, M. (1975). Personal knowledge. In M. Polanyi & H. Prosch (Eds.). *Meaning* (pp. 22–45). Chicago: The University of Chicago Press.
Real, T. (1990). The therapeutic use of self in constructionist/systemic therapy. *Family Process, 37*, 201–213.
Rober, P. (1998). Reflections on ways to create a safe therapeutic culture for children in family therapy. *Family Process, 37*, 201–213.
Rober, P. (1999). The therapist's inner conversation: Some ideas about the self of the therapist, therapeutic impasse and the process of reflection. *Family Process, 38*, 209–228.
Rober, P. (2002a). Some hypotheses about hesitations and their non verbal expression in the family therapy session. *Journal of Family Therapy, 24*, 187–204.
Rober, P. (2002b). Constructive hypothesizing, dialogic understanding and the therapist's inner conversation: Some ideas about knowing and not-knowing in the family therapy session. *Journal of Marital and Family Therapy, 28*, 467–478.
Schön, D.A. (1983). *The reflective practitioner: How professionals think in action*. New York: Basic Books.
Strong, T. (1999). Collaborative influence. *Australian and New Zealand Journal of Family Therapy, 21*, 144–150.
Vygotsky, L.S. (1962). *Thought and language*. Cambridge (Mass.): MIT Press.
Voloshinov, V. N. (1973). *Marxism and the philosophy of language*. Cambridge (Mass.): Harvard University Press.

# Chapter 8

# Discursive Approaches to Clinical Research

JERRY GALE, JOHN LAWLESS WITH CONVERSATIONAL PARTNER KATHRYN ROULSTON

As therapists, our tools are our discursive performance. But, how do we know what our actions accomplish? When we talk about such practices as collaboration, co-construction, transparency, and gender and cultural equality, how are these constructs performed, and what consequences are achieved? While one's goal for integrity of ideology and practice may be sincere, we need to reflect upon the following question: "How does our 'talk about the talk' of therapy match our discursive performances achieved in session?" In this chapter we will present some ideas about discursive approaches to clinical research. Several analytical methods will be presented that can be used to consider how talk manages, maintains, creates, and challenges the construction of identity and social interaction, and key differences and tensions between these discursive methods will be highlighted. In particular, we note how these methodological tensions are similar to tensions between various discursive therapy approaches, and reflect epistemological choices made by researchers and practitioners. Finally, implications of discursive research for practitioners, supervisors/educators, and researchers, as well as potential concerns involved with this type of research are also provided.

## POSITIONING OUR PRESENCE

Since nothing one says or writes is neutral or comes from a non-centered position, we believe that it is important to share a little bit about ourselves—but not to make our position transparent (we do not think that is possible). We hope that it helps readers better understand our experiences, biases and preferences in choosing how we shaped this chapter, and to remind you of our presence in the text. I (JG) have been teaching in an academic setting for over 13 years. My interest in language and identity began in my childhood when I was speech impaired (Gale, 1991a), overweight, and very introverted. Born in 1953, I grew up in a middle-class environment in Detroit, the youngest of 3 children, and the only male child, in a Jewish family. Academia has exerted pressure on me to maintain a research identity and agenda, and at times this competes with my clinical persona. Also, directing an accredited Marriage and Family Therapy (MFT) program has kept me actively involved in 'American Association of Marriage' (AAMFT).

From the time I (JL) was a young child I was fascinated with how people changed their language based on the context while discussing the same issue. Growing up in a middle class white, Irish, Catholic family in Upstate New York State (Utica) with three brothers allowed me the opportunity and privilege to develop and test these conversational skills. I soon became proficient utilizing these skills but I did not question the process or context in which these skills were developed. As I began to develop a critical consciousness around sociopolitical issues and contextual variables, in my early 20s, I questioned how I utilized these skills while challenging dominant narratives about myself, how "Others" positioned me, and how I positioned "Others." These issues, skills, and challenges have remained salient in all areas of my life.

## OUR ASSUMPTIONS REGARDING RESEARCH

While many postmodern practitioners are skeptical of research claims, and distrust notions of objectivity, control, generalization, researchers' sociopolitical agendas, and grand narratives, we argue that there is a critically important place for research. While beyond the scope of this chapter to discuss in detail, our view is that research of any kind (qualitative and quantitative) can be useful, and indeed, is crucial for maintaining integrity to our practice. What is important is that there is logical consistency within the research approach between the researcher(s)' epistemology, theoretical perspective, methodology, methods, and reporting (see Crotty, 1998), and that research reporting is made user friendly for practitioners, policy makers, and other consumers. When logical consistency is maintained, the research is competently conducted, and reports are well written, research can provide important and relevant information to practitioners of all ideological persuasions.

*KR: I was initially disconcerted to have been asked to respond to this chapter, since I wondered what an "outsider" to the world of therapy talk might have to offer. However, the topic of this discussion is central to my research concerns in two ways: 1) I am a qualitative researcher grounded in the traditions of ethnomethodology (or the study of "members' methods") interested in applying conversation analytic tools to examine talk-in-interaction; 2) my teaching in higher education settings concerns the design and conduct of qualitative research studies. Many of my students—teachers, administrators and counselors—see themselves as "practitioners," rather than academics, and bring various perspectives to bear on their study of such topics as "epistemology," "theoretical perspectives," "methodology," "data analysis," and "theory." My background in elementary teaching in Australian settings provides some insight into some practitioners' initial struggle with the kinds of discursive work Jerry and John propose in this chapter: shared assumptions of conversation analysis critical discourse analysis and textual analysis.*

The discursive approaches to research that we will present include conversation analysis (CA), critical discourse analysis (CDA), and textual analysis. All of these analytic approaches share some common assumptions.[1] Identity is viewed as an active discursive accomplishment that is maintained and transformed within joint social interactions. In other words, through our social encounters, the construction of one's identified "self" is continuously being upheld, repaired, or changed.[2] From this perspective, context is not a bucket that contains our actions and identities, but rather, a performance that is accomplished through practical interpretive practices of how two (or more) people make sense of each other's communication (ethnomethodology) (Garfinkel, 1967; Heritage, 1984). These identities are organized within a social structure that is constituted within face-to-face interactions that are reflexive and refer back to the immediate and proximate context (Maynard & Clayman, 1991). From these assumptions, an analyst focuses on a micro-level view of interaction, noting such features of talk as turn taking, pauses, overlaps of turns, misspoken words, and paralinguistic features (see Table 1 for a list of transcript conventions).

*KR: What might practitioners make of the close analysis of language Jerry and John propose here? Is it useful? Why? What might practitioners learn from it? How might they enter into this type of work and engage with the "findings" of such studies?*

## Key Theoretical Distinctions for Discursive Analysts

Three salient distinctions between these analytical approaches include the issues of ontology, context, and politics. While it is beyond the scope of this chapter

[1] While there are various definitions of these three analytical approaches (see Edwards & Potter, 1992; Gee, Michaels, & O'Conner, 1992; Korobov, 2001; Potter, 1996; Potter & Wetherell, 1987; ten Have, 1999; van Dijk, 1997), and there is overlap between them, there are also important differences we wish to highlight about these three approaches.

[2] Obvert examples of this are the following statements: "no that's not what I mean," "let me explain why I said that," "I'm not sexist, but . . . .," "no, I don't think that anymore." Each of these statements work to clarify or redefine how one is perceived and understood by another. This process occurs on more subtle levels as well.

**Table 1. Transcript Notations**

| | |
|---|---|
| → | Arrows in the margin point to the lines of transcript relevant to the point being made in the text. |
| ( ) | Empty parentheses indicate talk too obscure to transcribe. Words or letters inside parentheses indicate the transcriber's best estimate of what is being said |
| hhh | The letter 'h' is used to indicate hearable aspiration, its length roughly proportional to the number of 'h"s. If preceded by a dot, the aspiration is an in-breath. |
| [ | Left side brackets indicate where overlapping talk begins. |
| ] | Right side brackets indicate where overlapping talk ends, or marks alignments within a continuing stream of overlapping talk. |
| CAPITAL | Words in capitals are uttered louder than the surrounding talk |
| ° | Talk appearing within degree signs is lower in volume relative to surrounding talk. |
| >< | Talk appearing within 'greater than' and 'less than' signs is noticeably faster than the surrounding talk. |
| ((looks)) | Word in double parentheses indicates transcriber's comments. |
| (0.8) | Numbers in parentheses indicate periods of silence, in tenths of a second. A dot inside parentheses indicates a pause that is less than 0.2 seconds. |
| ::: | Colons indicate a lengthening of the sound just preceding them, proportional to the number of colons. |
| becau- | A hyphen indicates an abrupt cut-off or self-interruption of the sound in progress indicate by the preceding letter(s) (the example here represents the word because). |
| - | Underlining indicates stress or emphasis. |
| (ˆ) | A 'hat' or circumflex accent symbol indicates a marked raised pitch. |
| = | Equal signs (ordinary at the end of one line and d the start of an ensuing one) indicate a 'latched' relationship-no silence at all between them. |

to fully explore these topics, it is important to understand how these issues shape the analytic process and direction.

Discursive research has generally focused on how semiotic processes are performed, accomplished, or organized within a context via the use of language (oral or written). The focus on language can give the impression that researchers are operating from a common epistemology (how we claim to know what we know) and ontology (what we claim to know). Harre and van Langenhove (1992), however, challenge researchers to question their ontological underpinnings. In particular, social scientists have subscribed to the ontological view that the substances (people, institutions, societies) to be examined are within a space/time grid (Harre & van Langenhove, 1992). This ontological view supports a materialistic and deterministic approach to social worlds. Harre and van Langenhove (1992) propose that another ontological view is needed for researchers exploring the social world. They suggest an ontological view that social worlds exist within a persons/conversational grid rather than a space/time grid. This new grid contains different levels of analysis but all have a unifying theme: discursive practices. This view clearly places discourse at the center of what is "reality." The focus on discursive ontology supports the growth of different epistemological stances while based within a discursive ontology. This switch has important ramifications for researchers. If researchers view "the real world" as being discursively created, then all of "reality" is a meaning making performance negotiated between people. To understand this performance, language must take center stage.

Another issue for discursive analysts is how context is conceptualized and utilized. Schegloff (1992) discusses two types of contexts, distal and proximate. Distal context refers to sociopolitical variables that can influence social interactions (e.g. skin coloration, professional status, historical events). Proximate context are those features of social interactions local to that particular social interaction, such as sequencing of talk (e.g. how what is said by one person is constrained by or indexed to what was said just prior). Some discursive researchers will focus on the distal context of social interaction while others will focus on the proximate context.

As an example of proximate and distal context, consider Exemplar A below (from Kogan & Brown, 1998, p. 500). An analysis of the proximate context might note how the therapist places Jane's controlling problem as being in the past (line 4), reflecting a big change (line 11) and indicative of changes accomplished by the wife. An analysis of distal context might consider the androcentric (male-oriented) perspective implied by how Jane uses the word "control."[3]

*Exemplar A*

| | | |
|---|---|---|
| 1 | *Jane:* | *I always was the one that was controlling I was always the one that had to* |
| 2 | | *put direction in the family um I felt that way (yeh) um and I didn't feel any* |
| 3 | | *contribution from him* |
| 4 | *Th:* | *and that's changed* |
| 5 | *Jane:* | *that's changed it's changed yeh a lot even um in the household duties (yeh)* |
| 6 | | *um he'll used to I used to say him Tom would you empty the garbage* |
| 7 | | *(yeh) and three hours later the garbage still wouldn't be empty and now I* |
| 8 | | *don't even say it say would you empty the garbage the garbage is empty* |
| 9 | *Th:* | *ahh so that's why you say as a couple you are at {a rating of} 8 {out of 10}* |
| 10 | *Jane:* | *yes* |
| 11 | *Th:* | *so that is a big change* |
| 12 | *Jane* | *yes* |
| 13 | *Th:* | *it's a big change (2.0) how did you do that? How did you make those* |
| 14 | | *changes?* |

*KR: It can be initially confronting, and perhaps even disconcerting, to see our speech*

[3]This argument is not dissimilar to Bateson's (1972) distinction between pleroma and creatura.

*transcribed with repairs, interruptions, repeated questions, pauses and clarifications. Do we talk like that? Yes, much of the time. However, close inspection of talk reveals how deftly it is composed, how finely organized it is, and how carefully we orient to what we say to one another (Sacks, 1992). But why bother investigating "micro" issues found when two or three individuals talk? What can we learn? The approaches to the investigation of therapy talk advocated by Gale and Lawless reveal how the social order is co-constructed on a turn-by-turn basis, and what meaning members make of one another's actions and utterances (Garfinkel, 1967, 2002). The primary interest in using conversation analysis (or any of the tools suggested in this chapter) as a tool to examine therapy talk then, is to investigate how a therapeutic encounter is "talked into being" and "co-constructed" by participants.*

The last issue is one of politics, which is very much tied to the previous issue of distal and proximate context. On the surface, this may seem like a simple question. Do researchers bring sociopolitical ideologies to the table while analyzing data or not? While many agree that researchers' theoretical and methodological choices reflect sociopolitical values, the question being raised here is how researchers deal with the sociopolitical constraints of the participants' talk. Should a researcher refrain from examining the data with a particular lens and let the data "do the talking" or place the data within a sociopolitical context? These questions were recently highlighted in a discussion between Emanuel Schegloff (1998a, b) and Michael Billig (1998a, b). For Schegloff (1998a) and other CA researchers, issues of power and oppression are analyzed only when the participants themselves evoke them. Billig (1998a) disagrees and argues that analysis should not wait until the participants bring these issues up before the analyst evokes them. Schegloff's (1998b) rebuff is to not let ideology come between doing good analytical work. Schegloff (1998b) states that CDA should focus more on applying these micro-analytical skills to actual discourse, rather than criticizing theory and methods. Schegloff observes that the danger for those doing CDA is that rather than doing good empirical work, critical theory becomes the work that they do. Postmodern practitioners have similarly debated the appropriateness of including macro-sociopolitical issues (e.g., race or gender) as they relate to the therapeutic context (deShazer, 1991; Goolishian, & Anderson; 1992; Hare-Mustin, 1994; White, 1997).

It is important to note that these distinctions are not hierarchically organized, but rather, demonstrate the type of questions being posed and the researcher/practitioner's epistemological choice points about what is important. A researcher's[4] choice of questions being asked and type of data to attend to presents

[4] Contrast this exemplar with exemplar B below, where a different therapist (who is a narrative therapist), with the same client, addresses this notion of control in a very different manner. In exemplar A, the therapist is a solution-focused therapist. There is a similarity between how clinicians choose to attend to proximate and distal events, as well as how researchers choose to attend to proximate or distal

what that researcher conceptually values, and reveals something about the researcher's epistemological stance. Our purpose here is to highlight distinctions in using these different discursive analytical approaches, not to advocate for one over another. We do maintain the importance of the explicit and logical consistency and integrity between one's epistemology, theory, methodology and practice (Griffith, & Griffith, 1992), and we share Schegloff's (1998b) concern not to let ideological agendas dominate our research practices. These ideological battles can lead to a dominant position that marginalizes other research, and reduces the benefits of methodological diversity. Building on these differences, we will next summarize and define CDA, textual analysis, and conversation analysis, providing exemplars to demonstrate some methodological and analytical distinctions between them.

## TEXTUAL ANALYSIS AND CDA

CDA, and to a large degree textual analysis, are action oriented research approaches that focus on social problems. CDA researchers tend to have not only the goal of scientific inquiry, but also, seek social and political change. CDA researchers view the "discourse analytical enterprise . . . as a political and moral task of responsible scholars" (van Dijk, 1997, p. 23). In comparing these two analytical approaches it is important to address the question, "What is text?" Some researchers define discourse as representative of all human behaviors that are utilized for semiosis (e.g., pictures, videos, written language, oral conversations, kinestics, etc.). Others have found utility making distinctions between these various activities, specifically between written and oral language. These researchers consider written language as an appropriate focus on research, contending that many researchers overlook the importance of written language as "stand alone" data. Examples of this type of research explore the reciprocity of how documents or records are shaped by and shape micro and macro contexts. Due to the widely varied definitions employed by researchers, we distinguish written language textual analysis and CDA based on the stated research definition of the researcher.

CDA is rooted in the arena of sociopolitical research, aiming to examine semiotic processes with an emphasis on context. While textual analysis can become a part of this, it is not necessarily focused on sociopolitical issues. Textual analysis is concerned with issues of identity, specifically: how identity is accomplished, maintained and transformed within joint social interactions. The consideration of macro sociopolitical, cultural and historical contexts borrows methodological practices from discourse analysis (Edwards & Potter, 1992; Potter, 1997; Potter & Wetherell, 1987), narrative analysis (Ewick & Silby, 1995) and textual analysis

contexts. This difference reflects what a therapist or researcher theoretically views as important for the task in hand.

(Smith, 1990; Watson, 1997). For example, Smith (1990) identifies the importance of the narrator's voice in the telling of a story as a "null point" of reference. How a narrator positions or centers herself and others has implications on both attributions and accountability of intentions and actions. Foucault (1980) also considers the centering aspect of narratives. For Foucault, the vantage point from which a story is told and the normative practices implied in the telling represent a singularity and hegemony (its "center") that leaves the margins of the story untold. From these perspectives, an analyst may consider some of the following procedures in the talk: "Whose story is being told? Are other perspectives being elided? How are characters and perspectives presented within the text, and how might that presentation lead to various constructions of meaning and interaction?" (Kogan & Gale, 1997, p. 106).

As an example of this type of analysis,[5] consider the following exemplar.

*Exemplar B*

| | | |
|---|---|---|
| 316 | *Jane:* | *And I have to say that um () that I would always I had to um be in control* |
| 317 | | *of everything () I had to be in control of (.5) of him (yeh) of our* |
| 318 | | *relationship I thought I I thought if I could keep it all under control () um* |
| 319 | | *for some reason I would be a hap happier and my contribution is to let go* |
| 320 | | *and t'own up and to take his advice.* |
| 321 | *TH:* | *(hh) When you say in control you mean like sort of take responsibility for* |
| 322 | | *(1.0) for most things o::r or feel that you are responsible for lots of things* |
| 323 | | *that what you mean by in control o::r do you mean something else?* |
| 324 | *Jane:* | *(3.0) um yeh I probably had to take responsibility () (yeh) for everything* |
| 325 | | *() (ok, yeh) mhm (yeh).* |
| .... | | |
| 330 | *Tom:* | *and I perhaps had the same problem and ykn I still do sharing the fact that* |
| 331 | | *Jane's opinion is just as valid as mine (right) and then sharing those ()* |
| 332 | | *opinions in a real meaningful way I think we we both (.5) spent a lot of time* |
| 333 | | *trying to be in control f-for different reasons (yeh) an uh now we've learned* |
| 334 | | *I think to (.5) let go a little bit* |
| 335 | | *[ ]* |

[5] While the authors of this paper defined their work as textual analysis, it could also be viewed as CDA.

| | | |
|---|---|---|
| *336* | | *[ ]* |
| *337* | *TH:* | *(inaudible) so the word the word the word is respect is that respecting each* |
| *338* | | *other's opinions and (yeh) (.) and uh (.) values and morals and so on* |
| *339* | *Jane:* | *yes* |
| *340* | *TH:* | *so respect o:r acceptance or something? I mean what's a what's a name* |
| *341* | | *for this that you say (.) would fit better with what it is like?* |

From Kogan & Gale, 1997, p. 114.

In this segment, the wife, husband and therapist are accomplishing several sociopolitical positioning and identity themes. While Kogan and Gale (1997) provide greater analytical detail of this segment (pp. 114–116), here we comment on how the concept of "control" gets negotiated. The notion of 'control' is a culturally loaded term for a female's identity in family contexts. As Bograd (1988) notes, women face the double bind of being assigned responsibility for family relationships, but yet, cannot be in the position of appearing to run things. In the segment above (lines 316–319), Jane first presents herself as 'controlling' in a way that is potentially negative, and tends to represent an androcentric (male-oriented) perspective in constructing meaning (Hartsock, 1983).[6] The therapist first works to shift the meaning of control, as used by Jane, to one of responsibility (lines 321–323). The therapist then further seeks to move out of control/lack of control relational polarity for the couple, to one of shared respect and co-privileging of perspectives by both Jane and Tom (lines 337–338, 340–341). This invites the husband and wife to both share centers of subjectivity, without having to posture for a winner or loser position.

In Exemplar B, note how the therapist's attention to Jane's use of the word "control" reflects his epistemological understanding and valuing of a socio-political issue as implied in using this word. As demonstrated in exemplar A, the therapist, when encountering Jane's use of this word, goes in a different direction. The crucial distinction here is how the word "control," is understood by each therapist. For Michael White, Jane's use of the word "control" draws upon a cultural (distal) discourse of gender politics. For the solution-focused therapist, the word "control" likely draws upon an interactional (proximate) context. This discursive analysis highlights a difference of epistemological valuing by two therapists for what each sees as important to attend to in a session.[7] It is this same epistemological choice point that is at play for CA and CDA researchers. CA Researchers tend to focus on the proximate context of the talk. This is their choice point for where "the action

[6]Consider again exemplar A, where the therapist takes for granted Jane's use of "control" and does not challenge the implication of this word usage to Jane's identity and marital relationship.

[7]This implies that there is not a fixed meaning to a word. The same word can be understood differently by different people, and used to accomplish multiple purposes.

of the talk" is located. A CDA researcher's epistemological scalpel tends to cut across the distal context and examines interpretive repertoires (Edley & Wetherell, 2001). In other words, CDA considers how words have sociopolitical meaning and as such, have different interpretations and interpersonal consequences (see Hare-Mustin, 1994 and Weingarten, 1991 for clinical examples).

> *KR: As Jerry and John show in the extract above, therapists routinely enact methods that accomplish the work of marriage and family therapy. It is these members' methods, or "ethnomethods"—ways of achieving social order or "talking the world into being"—that interest analysts. Garfinkel (2002) argues, "members of society must in fact, actually, really, have some shared methods for achieving social order that they use to mutually construct the meaningful orderliness of social situations" (p. 5). From close analysis of therapy talk practitioners can learn:*
>
> a. *how members use various conversational objects to achieve certain kinds of actions (for example, such as the mundane activities of reporting, criticizing, complaining, arguing, agreeing, praising and so forth);*
> b. *how different formulations posed by therapists generate different kinds of responses; and as Kogan and Gale have shown in the example above,*
> c. *how different epistemological assumptions may be discerned in the ways that therapists take up and work with each client's responses.*

As speakers using language to accomplish certain kinds of actions (instruction, therapy and so forth) that will hopefully yield certain kinds of responses (learning, self-reflection and change), we all have much to learn. Look again at the above transcript to further "unpack" how the talk above is co-produced by speakers. Now, let's focus on the proximate context of the talk.

| | | |
|---|---|---|
| *321* | *Th:* | *(hh) When you say in control you mean like sort of take responsibility for* |
| *322* | | *(1.0) for most things o::r or feel that you are responsible for lots of things* |
| *323* | | *that what you mean by in control o::r do you mean something else?* |
| *324* | *Jane:* | *(3.0) un yeah I probably had to take responsibility (.) (yeh) for everything (.) (ok, yeh) mhm (yeh).* |

This excerpt shows an "adjacency pair" (ten Have, 1999, pp. 14–15) in which the first pair part is a question (lines 321–323) and the second pair part is an answer. Close inspection reveals that the question actually is formulated in multiple parts, and is in fact, three questions: (1) When you say in control you feel like sort of take responsibility for (1.0) most things; (2) feel that you are responsible for lots of things?; (3) do you mean something else? The therapist has begun his response by using Jane's words seen in line 316 ("I had to be um in control of everything"). In fact the conversational object seen in lines 321–323 is also a formulation (Heritage

& Watson, 1979), in which the therapist preserves information presented by Jane, ("control"), transforms the sense of her talk by suggesting that by the use of the term "control" she could possibly mean "take responsibility," and deletes information ("I had to be in control of (.5) of him (yeh) of our relationship"). The first question posed also "downgrades" Jane's statement (which could be seen to be a criticism of Tom, since she "had" to do it) from "I had to um be in control of everything" to "take responsibility for most things". The therapist's reformulation of Jane's talk exhibits subtlety, in that, the "extreme case formulation" (Pomerantz, 1986) of "everything" has been transformed to "most things." By posing this formulation as a question, however, the therapist provides a place for Jane to disagree with the suggestions posed. Sacks, Schegloff and Jefferson's (1974) paper on turn-taking outlines how speakers adeptly allocate and take turns in multi-party talk, and locate transition relevance places (TRP) for smooth transitions to the next speaker. In response to the first question posed by the therapist, the pauses in line 322 of one second and the elongated syllable "o::r" provide points at which Jane could have taken a turn. When this is not forthcoming, the therapist offers another question ( a "downgrading" of the first question posed in addition to providing a possible response). Again, on line 323, with the elongated syllable "o::r" a possible TRP is provided for Jane. Again, she does not respond and the therapist continues with an open-ended question "do you mean something else?" It seems here that the therapist has responded to the lack of immediacy of Jane's response by reformulating the question, not once, but twice. After a pause of three seconds, Jane finally responds. In answering the question, she reclaims the sense of some of her prior utterances (which the therapist had reformulated), melding them with the formulation provided by the therapist. "I probably had to take responsibility... for everything." Here we see Jane re-asserting that she took responsibility for "everything" (line 317) rather than the therapist's "most things" (line 321). Once again, she has repeated that she "had to" do this (rather than the therapist's "feel that you are responsible"). In these short utterances, we see how participants keenly attune to one another's utterances, and how they both reformulate and take up suggestions offered by one another, yet also show resistance to one another's portrayals of their positions.

We have used this fragment of talk to show how certain conversational objects: adjacency pairs such as questions and answers and formulations are used by speakers to "do therapy". By analyzing how this gets done, practitioners can learn not only about their own work, but how clients position themselves and orient to a therapist's talk.

## CONVERSATION ANALYSIS

Conversation analysis (CA) focuses on the proximate context of naturally occurring conversations and does not bring sociopolitical frameworks to the analysis, although the results may be placed within a sociopolitical framework. CA is typically divided into two types of analysis, social institution of interaction and social institution in interaction (Heritage, 1997; Miller, 1997). Social institution of interaction is the exploration of the common thread that weaves through all social interaction. The focus is on macro language customs or "ordinary conversation" (Peräkylä, 1997). When this type of CA is utilized, context (age, sex, ethnicity of the participants) is deemed not essential for the understanding of language practices (ten Have, 1999).

Social institution in interaction is the examination of how social worlds (e.g., therapeutic interviews, judicial proceedings, medical interviews) are summoned and made into being through talk. Heritage (1984) referred to this as "talk into being." Psathas (1995) stated that social structure is traditionally thought of as having a determining affect on social interaction. Conversation analysts challenge this assumption, particularly when examining the institution in interaction. Psathas stated,

> Conversation analysis would propose to show in what ways persons orient to, take into account, and make relevant particular features of the setting; in what ways the settings' features provide enabling conditions for particular kinds of activities; in what ways the parties are engaged in what constitutes the work of the organizations and thereby are engaged in producing interaction that is context renewing and re-forming (p. 54).

In other words, how do the participants build and manage the context of the social institution in and through their talk (Heritage, 1997)? For example, for analyzing a therapeutic interview, one would wish to demonstrate the ways that the participants' (therapist and clients) talk accomplishes and creates the social institution of a clinical therapy interview. One would want to show how the speakers collaborate to create talk as therapeutic, advance it as therapeutic, and distinguish it from other therapeutic talk (e.g., talk with a friend) (Heritage, 1997).

Pomerantz and Fehr (1997, pp. 71–74) suggest five tools or questions in analyzing transcripts from a CA perspective. These include: (1) Select a sequence to analyze. (2) Characterize the actions in the sequence (what is the person trying to do in his/her turn). (3) Consider how the speaker selects what words (referencing terms) and phrasing to use as well as how s/he organizes his/her talk to provide a particular understanding to a topic. Also, consider the options the speaker has in making his/her selection. (4) Consider how the timing and turn taking provides for particular understanding of the talk and action. (5) Consider how the talk and action was accomplished and led to certain identities, roles and/or relationships for the participants. In using these tools, the CA analyst can study how social institutions are organized and constituted.

## CONTRASTING CA AND CDA

As noted earlier, one way to understand this difference is to examine how these different discursive approaches invoke contexts and assign meaning to interactions. Proponents of CA, such as Heritage (1984, 1997) and Schegloff, (1998a), argue that it is important to understand participants "in their own terms." CA focuses on how participants make sense of each other and the interaction. When considering such social categories as gender, power inequities, conflict, and oppression, the focus of CA is on the local context. Hence, CA analysts note the sequential interpretive practices and understandings that are relevant for the participants, by showing how these categories are oriented to by the participants and how they are consequential in the interaction. Utterances and the social categories they index are both context shaped and context renewing (Heritage, 1984), and treat context as the "project and product of the participants' actions" (Heritage, 1997, p. 163).

Critics of CA, however, have argued that CA is too reflexive and ignores the embedded nature of talk within a larger cultural context and conceals the contested and political nature of interactions (Pollner, 1991, Rogers, 1992). CDA, on the other hand, argues that the "context both produces and is produced by the participants actions" (Korobov, 2001, paragraph 4). The implication of this perspective as suggested by Wetherell (1998), is that the analyst needs to examine the participants' talk within a broader sociopolitical cultural context.

Applying these issues to the practice of therapy, CA tends not to include a consideration of cultural discourses that are also at play in the therapy session (Hare-Mustin, 1994; Weingarten, 1991). For example, Gale's (1991b; Gale & Newfield, 1992) CA of a therapy session examined how the participants in the session manage and make sense of the talk, and specifically focuses on how the therapist pursues a solution-focused agenda. Unlike the textual analysis of Kogan and Gale (1997) however, he does not examine how sociopolitical and gender dynamics are also impacting the couple and therapist interactions and interpretation of events. In his earlier work Gale leaves out such commentary as to how the husband's accountability for having and ending an affair is minimized in the therapist's pursuit of a solution-focused agenda.[8]

### An Exemplar of a Joint CA and CDA Analysis

The following exemplar highlights the methodological transition I (JL) have experienced within a transcript. I was interested in examining how couple and

[8] I (JG) find it interesting to talk about Gale in this way, as if I am talking about a different person. This style of writing is kept like this as it does show how written language produces descriptions of an identity. It also demonstrates how I have changed in my thinking over the years, and in a very real sense, Gale (1991) is not the same Gale as Gale (1997).

family therapy supervisors "talk" about race, ethnicity, and culture (REC) in supervision. My initial stance was not to assume that REC would be discussed. I was interested in how the participants were co-creating the talk about REC when it was overtly identified. I recruited a supervisor known in couple and family therapy (CFT) to be proactive in discussing intersections between REC and presenting problems. I analyzed eight hours of audio tapes (8 supervision sessions). Segments of supervision sessions that overtly brought forth issues of REC were initially analyzed. Take the following exemplar:

*Exemplar C*

| | | |
|---|---|---|
| 13 | T1: | *So she's a (.98) black (1.33) [woman* |
| 14 | S: | *Can we] talk about her?* |
| 15 | T1: | *Yea, A black woman [that uh* |
| 16 | S: | *I] I brought the file* |
| 17 | T1: | *44* |
| 18 | S: | *Lets see if I brought my notes with me. Wait, wait.* |
| 19 | T1: | *One of the last ones uhm She's the [she the case-* |
| 20 | S: | *oooh hold on] when did we* |
| 21 | | *speak about her?* |

From Lawless, 2001

On lines 13 and 15, the therapist brought forth the race of her client. This exemplar and others created the pool of talk to be analyzed. It is important to highlight that the analysis was focused on the proximate context with no sociopolitical ideologies being brought to the analysis.

Initially, only a few turns prior and after were utilized to create the context of the REC comment. As the analysis continued, a question regarding the genesis of the REC comment kept rising. Where is the "beginning" of REC talk? This question began an analytical movement from the overt talk of REC to the tacit talk of REC and initiated an analytic shift from a pure CA approach to a blend of CA and CDA. It was found that the conversation of REC began many turns prior to the actual utterance of REC lexicon. This finding opened up a new set of questions. How did prior conversations support the possibility for these findings? How did the contextual variables (e.g., race, ethnicity, sexual orientation) of the participants affect the supervisory conversation? Exemplar C will highlight this process. To assist in the process the reader is encouraged to first read the text starting with line 389. We will return to lines 365–388 shortly.

*Exemplar D*

| | | |
|---|---|---|
| 365 | T2: | *. . . And that's their mutual agreement that he can come and visit the* |
| 366 | | *kids at any time. And the other issue that concerned me (1.12) that* |
| 367 | | *I thought might have an impact on Jim's behavior, .hhh is that he* |
| 368 | | *was beginning to take (.68) Melissa uhm their daughter* |
| 369 | S: | *Hhm, hhm* |
| 370 | T2: | *out, he would come and pick up Melissa and take her but not Jim.* |

371 S: *Hhm, hhm*
372 *(1.14)*
373 T2: *And Sue was making a distinction between Melissa being his child*
374 *and Jim not being his child.*
375 S: *Hhm, hhm*
376 *(2.33)*
377 T2: . *hh A::nd (.91) I've heard this in a lot of other families (1.18) a real*
378 *differentiation made even if the parents are intact.*
379 S: *Hhm, hhm*
380 T2: *The father will treat the (.76) stepchild quite differently than the*
381 *biological child. .hhh uhm (.81) and (.73) s:::o I suggested to*
382 *Sue that (1.26) from Jim's perspective, he's just gotten*
383 *interested in his biological father and knows that his biological*
384 *father does not seek contact with him. And now his (1.20) his*
385 *father father, the one that he's known for the longest,*
386 S: *Hhm, hhm [rejecting him*
387 T2: *is also rejecting] him too, from his point of view.*
388 S: *Hhm, hhm*
389 T2: *Uhm In fact, I think Sue has been encouraging a differential*
390 *treatment of the two children.*
391 S: *°Oh°*
392 T2: *Uhm, that she says things, hh I have heard quite a few mothers uh*
393 *when there's a separation say this kind of thing, and > I do hear it*
394 *much more in Latino families< hh as well. > I have to let him see*
395 *so and so because after all he's her [father*
396 S: *fath-] bio-, yea=*
397 T2: *=but you*
398 *know I'm not going to let him keep seeing so and so*
From Lawless, Gale & Bacigalupe, 2001

In the beginning phases on data analysis I (JL) saw the talk of REC beginning on line 394. When I began questioning the "beginning of REC talk," the analysis began to move backward. In other words, does the talk begin earlier in the conversation? Now re-read the above section beginning with line 365. The expanded analysis revealed that the participant, T2, began to shape her talk of REC, lines 377–378, much earlier than the actual utterance on line 394. Taken together, participant T2 is beginning to delineate cross-cultural differences. T1 utilizes the generic term "families" on line 377 but becomes more specific on line 377. This process may seem overt, but in the context of a longer conversation preceding this overt gesture (approximately 20 minutes) and the talk of supervision focusing on the presenting problem, the comment "Latino families" becomes secondary. This finding sparked another question regarding the data. Are there conversations within conversations (meta-conversations) between the participants that supported this overt gesture that were not captured by the researcher? How do sociopolitical factors of the participants support or suspend the talk of REC? These questions begin to ask about the distal context of the conversation and move the researcher away from the proximate context.

## SO WHAT? IMPLICATIONS FOR PRACTITIONERS

Discursive research approaches provide a methodology to examine how our interactions relationally position one another. Shotter (1984) suggests that people's attributions and accounts of their intentions position them on moral and relational maps, which helps them assess their own and others' actions and assign social meaning. Cobb (1994) from this perspective states, "responsibility is a function of the position occupied on the moral and relational maps that emerge in conversation" (p. 178). Our communications are continuously constructing and maintaining our understanding of identity and reality. They help to define our contexts, though we agree "external reality" does constrain those conversations. We live in a world of constraints, both implicit and explicit. However, our focus is on how our interactions achieve meaning making.

Particularly, we see value of these research approaches in therapy and training. Questions such as, "How do our communications shape our experiential identity continuum?" "How do participants locate problems, attribute blame, attribute forgiveness, or exert power and privilege over another?" "How do therapists' actions facilitate (or shut down) clients' cooperation and collaboration?" "How do supervisors create contexts that encourage trainees to feel safe to express themselves, to expand their clinical boundaries?" "How do therapists value and support diversity, and not privilege particular ways of being?" "How do our actions reduce our effectiveness?" "How do we reconcile what we think, say or do with what our actions actually accomplish?"

For postmodern researchers, there are no simple answers. No methodological approach is the best one. Each method we have discussed offers different understandings and relational perspectives about therapeutic interactions. It is this very diversity of method and focus that offers clinicians reflective analytical skills regarding their practice. There is a long (and political) history of how mental health clinicians have struggled with incorporating research into their practice. This chasm between researchers and practitioners has led to separate languages, skills, and world views that at times can seem insurmountable. Discursive research may be one way to bridge this gap.

*KR: Jerry and John have outlined a number of implications for practitioners of their discursive approach to research of therapy talk. I would like to address this issue by reviewing two questions of relevance:*

*How might practitioners engage with this work? First, our ability to use language to accomplish a multitude of tasks—announce news to another on the telephone, greet our work colleagues, read a bed-time story to a child, or undertake talk in a therapy session—is a seen-but-unnoticed practice that is mostly taken for granted (Garfinkel, 1967, p. 37). Some recent research concerning how novice interviewers developed their skills (Roulston, deMarrais, Lewis, Forthcoming) indicates that knowing how to do something may not immediately translate into actual practice. As Jerry and John suggest, we also recommend close, guided analysis of interview tapes and transcripts as one of three potential ways that might be used to assist novice interviewers to reflect on talk-in-interaction in interview settings. Practitioners—both experienced and novice—will benefit from closer inspection of their own talk and the analytic procedures advocated by Jerry and John provide ways into this work. While it may be painstaking work (both in the doing of the analysis, and in learning something about one's talk), it will prove rewarding. Practitioners could benefit from this type of work in two interrelated ways, that is the training of therapists (cf. Tapsell, 2000) in addition to learning more about one's own epistemological assumptions as a therapist as they are displayed in therapy sessions. This type of work might be best thought of as a communal enterprise. That is, researchers, analysts, and therapists, might come together in group settings to share audio- and video-tapes and transcripts for repeated listening and analyses. ten Have (1999) outlines some of the key features of what are commonly known as "data sessions" and his text provides a useful text for beginners in this area.*

*Why is this work useful? Heap (1990) has specifically addressed the issue of why do this work within the "big question"—"how should I live?" Heap recommends that applied ethnomethodology utilizing conversation analytic approaches to the analysis of talk allows us to "resolve (provisionally) in some specific settings the big question of how one should live" (Heap, 1990, p. 69). In this article, Heap exemplifies this by closely analyzing transcripts of teacher repairs of students in oral reading sessions with the aim of delivering what he terms critical news ("others got it wrong as to how things are") and positive news ("X is organized this way") (pp. 42–43). Returning to therapeutic talk, close analysis of transcripts using tools derived from CA, CDA and text analysis provides a means for forwarding the multi-disciplinary effort proposed by Heap (1990, p. 69) for the purpose of examining the big question: "how should I live?"*

*In summary, I support Jerry and John's proposal that practitioners in the field of therapy utilize methods drawn from CA, CDA and text analysis to examine therapy talk. Rather than derive data, as do the majority of social science researchers, from retrospective interview and reflective accounts of "how things went," I too urge therapists to use the data of the "everyday" to make sense of the social order of therapy work, and something of "what our actions might accomplish."*

## REFERENCES

Bhaskar, R. (1978). *A realist theory of science* London: Harvester Press.

Billig, M. (1999a). Whose terms? Whose ordinariness? Rhetoric and ideology in conversation analysis. *Discourse and Society, 10*(4), 543–558.

Billig, M. (1999b). Conversation analysis and claims of naiveté. *Discourse and Society, 10*(4), 572–577.

Bograd, M. (1988). Scapegoating mothers in family therapy: Re-exploring enmeshment. In M. Mirkin (Ed.). *The social and political contexts of family therapy* (pp. 69–87). New York: Gardner Press.

Cobb, S. (1994). "Theories of responsibility." The social construction of intentions in mediation. *Discourse Processes, 18*, 165–186.

Crotty, M. (1998). *The foundations of social research*. London: Sage.

Day, J.M. & Tappan, M.B. (1996). The narrative approach to moral development: From epistemic subject to dialogical selves. *Human Development, 39*, 67–82.

deShazer, S. (1991). *Putting difference to work*. New York: W.W. Norton.

Edley, N. & Wetherell, M. (2001). Jekyll and Hyde: Men's constructions of feminism and feminists. *Feminism & Psychology, 11*, 439–457.

Edwards, D. & Potter, J. (1992). *Discursive Psychology*. London: Sage.

Ewick, P. & Silby, S.S. (1995). Subversive stories and hegemonic tales: Toward a sociology of narrative. *Law and Society, 29*, 197–226.

Foucault, M. (1980). *The history of sexuality, Vol. 1: An introduction* (R. Hurley, Trans.). New York: Vintage/Random House.

Gale, J. (1991a). The use of self in qualitative research. *Qualitative Family Research Newsletter. 5*, 1, 3–4.

Gale, J. (1991b). *Conversation analysis of therapeutic discourse: Pursuit of an agenda*. Norwood, NJ: Ablex.

Gale, J.E. (1996). Conversation analysis: Studying the construction of therapeutic realities. In D. Sprenkle and S. Moon (Eds.), *Family therapy research: A handbook of methods* (pp. 107–124). New York: Guilford.

Gale, J.E. & Newfield, N. (1992). A conversation analysis of solution-focused marital therapy session. *Journal of Marital & Family Therapy, 18*, 153–165.

Garfinkel, H. (1967). *Studies in ethnomethodology*. Englewood Cliffs, NJ: Prentice-Hall.

Garfinkel, H. (2002). *Ethnomethodology's program: Working out Durkheim's Aphorism*. Lanham: Rowman & Littlefield.

Gee, J.P., Michaels, S., & O'Connor, M.C. (1992). Discourse analysis. In M.D. LeCompte, W. L. Millroy & J. Preissle (Eds.), *The handbook of qualitative research in education* (pp. 227–292). San Diego: Academic Press, Inc.

Goolishian, H.A., & Anderson, H. (1992). Strategy and intervention versus nonintervention: A matter of theory. *Journal of Marital and Family Therapy, 18*, 5–16.

Griffith, J., & Griffith, M. (1992). Owning one's epistemological stance in therapy. *Dulwich Centre Newsletter, 1*, 5–11.

Harré, R. & van Langenhove, L. (1999). Introducing positioning theory. In R. Harré & L. van Langenhove (Eds.), *Positioning Theory* (pp.14–31). Oxford: Blackwood.

Hare-Mustin, R. T. (1994). Discourses in the mirrored room: A postmodern analysis of therapy. *Family Process, 33*, 19–35.

Hartsock, N. (1983). The feminist standpoint: Developing the ground for a specifically feminist historical materialism. In S. Harding & M. Hintikka (Eds.). *Discovering reality: Feminist perspectives on metaphysics, methodology, and philosophy of science* (pp. 283–310). Dordrecht: Reidel.

Heap, J.L. (1990). Applied ethnomethodology: Looking for the local rationality of reading activities. *Human Studies, 13*, 39–72.

Held, B.S. (1995). *Back to reality: A critique of postmodern theory in psychotherapy*. New York: W.W. Norton.

Heritage, J. (1984). *Garfinkel and ethnomethodology*. Cambridge, England: Polity.

Heritage, J., & Greatbatch D. (1991). On the institutional character of institutional talk: The case of news interviews. In D. Boden I & D.H. Zimmerman (Eds.), *Talk and social structure: Studies in ethnomethodology and conversation analysis* (pp. 93–137). Berkeley: University of California Press

Heritage, J. (1997). Conversation analysis and institutional talk: Analyzing data. In D. Silverman (Ed.). *Qualitative research: Theory, method and practice* (pp. 161–182). London: Sage Publications Ltd.

Heritage, J. & Watson, R. (1979). Formulations as conversational objects. In G. Psathas (Ed.), *Everyday Language* (pp. 123–162). New York: Irvington Press.

Kogan, S.M. & Brown, A.C. (1998). Reading against the lines: Resisting foreclosure in therapy discourse. *Family Process, 37*, 495–512.

Kogan, S.M. & Gale, J.E. (1997). Decentering therapy: Textual analysis of a narrative therapy session. *Family Process, 36*, 101–126.

Korobov, N. (2001, September). Reconciling theory with method: From conversation analysis and critical discourse analysis to positioning analysis. *Forum: Qualitative Social Research*. On line journal: 2(3). www.qualitative-research.net/fqs-eng.htm

Lawless, J. (2001). *Exploring the discourse of race, ethnicity, and culture of clinical supervision in marriage and family therapy utilizing conversation analysis* (Doctoral dissertation, University of Georgia, 2000). *Dissertation Abstracts International*, 6, 3372.

Lawless, J.J, Gale, J.E., & Bacigalupe, G. (2001). The discourse of race and culture in family therapy supervision: A conversation analysis. *Contemporary Family Therapy, 23*, 181–197.

Maynard, D.W. & Clayman, S.E. (1991). The diversity of ethnomethodology. *Annual Review of Sociology, 17*, 385–418.

Miller, G. (1997). Building bridges: The possibility of analytic dialogue between ethnography, conversation analysis and Foucault. In D. Silverman (Ed.), *Qualitative Research: Theory, Method and Practice* (pp. 24–44). Thousand Oaks, CA: Sage.

Peräkylä, A. (1997). Reliability and validity in research based on tapes and transcripts. In D. Silverman (Ed.), *Qualitative Research: Theory, Method and Practice* (pp. 201–220). Thousand Oaks, CA: Sage.

Pollner, M. (1991). Left of ethnomethodology: The rise and decline of radical reflexivity. *American Sociological Review, 56*, 370–380.

Pomerantz, A. (1986). Extreme case formulations: A way of legitimizing claims. *Human Studies, 9*, 219–229.

Pomerantz, A. & Fehr, B.J. (1997). Conversation analysis: An approach to the study of social action as sense making practices. In T. van Dijk (Ed.), *Discourse as Structure and Process: Discourse Studies: A Multidisciplinary Introduction* (pp. 64–91). London: Sage.

Potter, J. (1997). Discourse analysis as a way of analysing naturally occurring talk. In D. Silverman (Ed.). *Qualitative research: Theory, method and practice* (pp. 144–160). London: Sage.

Potter, J., & Wetherell, M. (1987). *Discourse and social psychology: Beyond attitudes and behavior*. London: Sage.

Psathas, G. (1995). *Conversation analysis: the study of talk-in -interaction*. (Vol. 35). Thousand Oaks, CA: Sage.

Rogers, M.F. (1992). They all were passing: Agnes, Garfinkel, and company. *Gender & Society, 6*, 169–191.

Roulston, K., deMarrais, K. & Lewis, J. (Under review). Learning to interview in the social sciences. *Qualitative Inquiry.*

Sacks, H. (1992). (1964–1968). *Lectures on Conversation* (Vols. 1–2), G. Jefferson (Ed.). Oxford: Blackwell.

Sacks, H., Schegloff, E.A., & Jefferson, G. (1974). A simplest systematics for the organization of turn-taking for conversation. *Language, 50*, 696–735.

Schegloff, E. (1992). In another context. In A. Duranti and C Goodwin (Eds.), *Rethinking Context* (pp. 191–228). Cambridge: Cambridge University Press.

Schegloff, E. (1999a). 'Schegloff's tests' as Billig's data': A critical reply. *Discourse and Society, 10*, 558–572.

Schegloff, E. (1999b). Naiveté versus sophistication or discipline versus self-indulgence: A rejoinder to Billig. *Discourse and Society, 10*, 577–583.

Shotter, J. (1984). *Social accountability and selfhood*. Oxford: Basil Blackwell.

Smith, D.E. (1990). *Texts, facts, and femininity: Exploring the relations of ruling*. New York: Routledge.

Tapsell, L. (2000). Using applied conversation analysis to teach novice dietitians history taking skills. *Human Studies*, 23, 281–307.
ten Have, P. (1999). *Doing Conversation Analysis: A Practical Guide*. London: Sage.
van Dijk, T.A. (1997). *Discourse as structure and process*. London: Sage.
Watson, R. (1997). Ethnomethodology and textual analysis. In D. Silverman (Ed.). *Qualitative research: Theory, method and practice* (pp. 80–98). London: Sage.
Weingarten, K. (1991). The discourses of intimacy: Adding a social constructionist and feminist view. *Family Process, 30*, 286–306.
Wetherell, M. (1998). Positioning and interpretive repertoires: Conversation analysis and post-structuralism in dialogue. *Discourse & Society*, 9, 387–412.
White, M., (1997). *Therapeutic Relationship. Narratives of Therapists' Lives*. (pp. 127–147). Adelaide, Australia: Dulwich Centre Publications.

Chapter 9

# Coming to Terms with Violence and Resistance

## From a Language of Effects to a Language of Responses

NICK TODD AND ALLAN WADE WITH CONVERSATIONAL PARTNER MARTINE RENOUX

Therapists have a direct interest in the judicious use of language and regularly grapple with the question of "which words should be fitted to which deeds" (Danet, 1980, p. 189). This question is particularly important where there is violence because both perpetrators and victims tend to misrepresent themselves (Scott, 1990). Perpetrators use language strategically in combination with physical or authority-based power to isolate and threaten the victim, manipulate public appearances, and avoid responsibility. Victims use language tactically[1] to express or conceal their resistance, evade the violence, avoid negative social judgments, and retain maximum control of their circumstances.

Misrepresentation of victims and offenders is widespread, if inadvertent, in the clinical literature as well. Although resistance to violence is ubiquitous (Burstow, 1992; Campbell, Rose, Kub, & Nedd, 1998; Epston, 1989; Goffman, 1961; Kelly, 1988; Lempert, 1996; Maisel, 1996; Wade, 1997, 2000; Zemsky, 1991), victims are typically represented as socially conditioned and passive recipients of abuse (Campbell et. al., 1998; Coates & Wade, 2002; Kelly, 1988; Ridley, 1999; Wade,

[1] Following Michel de Certeau (1984), we make a distinction between *strategies*, which involve planning and presume a base from which to operate, and *tactics*, which are improvised "on the run", so to speak, without the benefit of a secure base.

2000). And while violent behaviour is deliberate, as illustrated by perpetrators' strategic efforts to suppress victims' resistance, it is typically represented as an effect of social or psychological forces that overwhelm the perpetrator, cause him to lose control, and compel him to perform violent acts (Todd, 2000).

In this chapter we present a response-based approach to therapy with victims of violence that stems in part from a micro-analysis of the actions of victims and perpetrators of violence and a critical analysis of the connection between violence and language (Coates, Todd, & Wade; 2000; Coates & Wade, 2002). In the first part of the paper we examine four types of discursive operations that appear frequently in professional and public accounts of violence, with special attention to the distinction between the language of effects and the language of responses. We propose that the language of effects misrepresents victims' responses and conceals victims' resistance to violence. In the second part we present two case examples to illustrate key aspects of the response-based approach to therapeutic interviewing.

## FOUR DISCURSIVE OPERATIONS

In professional, academic, and public discourse language is frequently used in a manner that (a) conceals violence, (b) obscures and mitigates perpetrators' responsibility, (c) conceals victims' resistance, and (d) blames or pathologizes victims (Coates, Todd & Wade, 2000; Coates & Wade, 2002). These discursive operations are set in motion by a wide variety of linguistic devices: metaphors (e.g., cause-effect and psycho-hydraulic explanations), terms (e.g., mutualizing and eroticizing vocabulary), grammatical forms (e.g., passive and agentless constructions, nominalizations), stereotypical accounts (e.g., the passive victim, the out-of-control offender), and figures of speech (e.g., euphemisms) (Coates & Wade, 2002). In use, these operations are functionally linked: Accounts that conceal violence also mitigate the perpetrator's responsibility, conceal the victim's resistance, and blame or pathologize the victim. To illustrate how these four operations are combined in use, we examine two passages; the first by Miles Davis (Davis & Troupe, 1990), the second by Judith Herman (1997), an acknowledged expert in the treatment of trauma.

### Example 1:

In the following passage, Miles Davis describes the first of his assaults on his then wife, Frances.

> I loved Frances so much that for the first time in my life I found myself jealous. I remember I hit her once when she came home and told me some shit about Quincy Jones being handsome. Before I realized what had happened, I had knocked her down .... I told her not to ever mention Quincy Jones' name to me again, and she never did .... Every time I hit her, I felt bad because a lot

> of it really wasn't her fault but had to do with me being temperamental and jealous. I mean, I never thought I was jealous until I was with Frances. Before, I didn't care what a woman did; it didn't matter to me because I was so into my music. Now it did and it was something that was new for me, hard for me to understand. (Davis & Troupe, 1990, p. 228)

Davis uses all four discursive operations to conceal the real nature of his violent behaviour and mitigate his responsibility. He portrays his violent behaviour as an effect of overwhelming psychological forces—the jealousy that arose from his love for Frances—that caused him to lose control. In effect, Davis suggests that his violent behaviour was caused by love. In this way, Davis implies that his behaviour, no matter how destructive, was ultimately positively motivated. This portrayal also implies that his behaviour was inadvertent rather than deliberate, since people normally do not purposely hurt people they love. The claims that he "found" himself jealous, knocked her down "before [he] realized what had happened", and found his "new" feelings "hard to understand" further deny any deliberation on his part.

> *Martine Renoux: This raises the interesting and fundamental point of how we are to understand the origins or causes of violent behaviour. Often I am asked: "Why did he treat me like this?" Victims are shocked and mystified; they have no ready way of understanding the reasons for the behaviour of the perpetrators. As a psychologist it is very difficult to come up with an answer, which does not mitigate the responsibility of the perpetrators. If I say, "I understand why you are crying" I am saying that you have good reasons for crying. If I say, "I understand why you attacked her" I am saying you have good reasons for attacking her. So I cultivate a position of NOT understanding violent behaviours. After all there is no satisfactory explanation of sexualized assault, child abuse, or wife-assault. There are many possible motivating factors for attacking another person—money, power, and the desire to dominate. But to say "I do not understand violent behaviours" means "I refuse to accept that there could be any satisfactory explanation for it". This is one way in which victims and professionals refuse to accept violent behaviour.*

With the statement "[e]very time I hit her, I would feel bad", Davis acknowledges that he assaulted Frances repeatedly. As he does so, however, he mitigates his responsibility for his continued violence by simultaneously portraying himself as consistently remorseful. This enables Davis to effect a critical shift in focus from his overt behaviour, which is visible to others, to his mind, which he alone can know. Grammatically, this is accomplished by a transition from the transitive verb "hit" to the intransitive verb "feel". By dropping the object of his actions (Frances), Davis shifts attention from the harm he inflicted on Frances to how badly he feels about it all.

Davis also conceals the nature and extent of his violence against Frances. The phrase "knocked her down" does not convey the degree of force in his attack (i.e., How did he knock her down? With a gentle push or a closed fist punch?). The phrase "what had happened", an agent-less and existential construction, obscures exactly what did happen and who did what to whom. The phrase "[e]very time I hit her, I would feel bad", mentioned above, also conceals the pain he inflicted by displacing consideration of Frances' feelings. Compare Davis's construction, for example, with a phrase such as, "every time I hit her, she felt terrible pain" (Coates & Wade, 2002).

As Davis conceals the violence and mitigates his own responsibility, he subtly blames Frances. The ambiguous statement "most of it really wasn't her fault" implies that some of it was. Additionally, the word "really" qualifies the statement and suggests that the question of responsibility is more a matter of perspective, a point he might grant, than a matter of fact. The phrases "I never thought I was jealous until I was with Frances" and "[b]efore, I didn't care what a woman did" serve to both further the portrayal of a previously non-violent man caught up in an unfamiliar and overwhelming situation and to suggest that Frances was the unique element, the catalyst that incited (i.e. provoked) the powerful feelings that ultimately caused his violence (Coates & Wade, 2002).

Finally, Davis conceals Frances' resistance by simply ignoring it or describing the choices she made (e.g., not mentioning Quincy Jones' name again) in such a way that her agency is virtually invisible. The very fact that Frances remarked on Jones' handsome looks, knowing of Davis' "jealousy", might well be understood as a form of resistance. Likewise, her decision to not mention Jones' name after the beating could be understood as a further act of resistance (i.e., self-protection, denying him a pretext for abuse) rather than an act of acquiescence. As well, the fact that Davis assaulted Frances an unspecified number of times suggests that she did not willingly submit to his attempts to control her behaviour. The phrase "[e]very time I hit her, I would feel bad" not only conceals the extent of the violence (as already mentioned); it also subtly conceals Frances' resistance by omitting mention of her immediate responses. An account of how Frances felt about the violence, rather than how Davis felt about it, would further show how she refused to be contented with his mistreatment.

*MR: For clinical and ethical reasons, it is important to describe violence in clear and precise terms. In England the legal system has now formally adopted the term "grooming", presumably to describe coercion, abuse of trust, and manipulation with the intent to harm. I find it shocking that this term, which also refers to affectionate ways primates have of looking after one another and the care one takes with hygiene and appearance, is used to describe how pedophiles (another euphemism) entrap and violate children. It is such a thoughtless and regressive step. Of course, I am sometimes called pedantic for raising these kinds of issues. The attitude is: "Well, it's just short-hand and we all know what we mean by it". I find myself wondering why we would actively discourage each other from stretching towards more just and accurate ways of describing violence.*

*At first I worried that using simple and direct terms to describe violent acts and acts of resistance would be too graphic and painful for my clients. I was worried about re-traumatizing so I tried to soften the descriptions by asking questions euphemistically: "When that happened to you . . . " or "When that was going on . . . " I was surprised to find that more direct descriptions, although they can be very emotional, need not be re-traumatizing if they are asked sensitively and if greater attention is paid to the details of the victim's responses. Once the client is given the opportunity to detail their responses, it often becomes possible to talk more directly about the abuse, from the perspective of a responding agent.*

## Example 2:

The same four operations of language (concealing violence, mitigating responsibility, concealing resistance, and blaming and pathologizing victims) feature prominently in professional clinical discourse as well (Ridley, 1999). In the following passage Judith Herman attempts to explain why so many victims of child abuse are abused later in life.

> [T]he personality formed in an environment of coercive control is not well adapted to adult life. The survivor is left with fundamental problems in basic trust, autonomy, and initiative. She approaches the tasks of early childhood—establishing independence and intimacy—burdened by major impairments in self-care, in cognition and memory, in identity, and in the capacity to form stable relationships. She is still a prisoner of her childhood, attempting to create a new life, she reencounters the trauma . . . .
>
> The survivor's intimate relationships are driven by the hunger for protection and care and are haunted by the fear of abandonment or exploitation. In a quest for rescue, she may seek out powerful authority figures who seem to offer the promise of a special care taking relationship. By idealizing the person to whom she becomes attached, she attempts to keep at bay the constant fear of being either dominated or betrayed.
>
> Inevitably however, the chosen person fails to live up to her fantastic expectations. When disappointed, she may furiously denigrate the same person who she so recently adored. Ordinary interpersonal conflicts may provoke intense anxiety, depression, or rage. In the mind of the survivor, even minor slights evoke past experiences of callous neglect, and minor hurts evoke past experiences of deliberate cruelty. These distortions are not easily corrected by experience, since the survivor tends to lack the social and verbal skills for resolving conflicts. Thus the survivor develops a pattern of intense, unstable relationships, repeatedly enacting dramas of rescue, injustice and betrayal. (Herman, 1997, pp. 110–111)

Herman's account precludes the possibility of any judicious resistance by the victim, as a child or adult. Instead of describing in detail the perpetrators' abusive actions and the victims' resistance, Herman proposes that an impersonal "environment of coercive control" has "left" the survivor with a seriously impaired personality which compels her to "reencounter" (i.e., reproduce) her childhood trauma later in life. As she relegates the victim to a position of deficiency, Herman reserves for herself an objective, authoritative position of proficiency from which to judge which "conflicts" are "ordinary" and which "slights" are "minor".

Herman's highly deterministic psychodynamic view conceals violence because it proposes that the victim is not actually "dominated" or "betrayed"; she misperceives and wrongly fears she will be. Others do not act willingly as "powerful authority figures"; she transforms them into such through her distorted perceptions and dysfunctional behaviour. Nor do these "powerful authority figures" select the victim; she chooses them. Though impaired and unskilled, the victim somehow exerts enormous influence over the behaviour of well-intentioned others. She is in every respect the author of her own misfortunes. Two statements—"The survivor's relationships are driven by..." and "The survivor develops a pattern of intense, unstable relationships..."—blame the victim for the literally impossible act of single-handedly establishing interpersonal patterns that by definition require at least two participants. In this way, individuals who mistreat the victim are absolved of responsibility.

The net effect of Herman's account is to transform the victim into a perpetrator who "furiously denigrate[s]" others, over-reacts, and responds with "rage" to minor affronts. Simultaneously, she transforms "powerful authority figures" into victims who are idealized and then denigrated by a dysfunctional individual who lacks the skills for a stable relationship. Herman's image of the victim closely mirrors and directly endorses the image so often proffered by abusive husbands of the women they victimize—that of a terminally unhappy and over-reactive wife who inflicts the effects of her unresolved trauma on innocent others, most notably himself.

> *MR: How can someone intending to create a new life seek to re-encounter trauma? What an extraordinary idea! As a rule, do we not show constant urges to avoid what is painful to us? And do we not tend to seek safety? The attempt to create a new life is shown through the victim's determined protest against all forms of disrespect. It is only when we do not uncover the story of resistance that we are left with a false impression of "passivity" or "collusion" which we then seek to explain with ideas such as those advanced by Herman (and many before her). When we understand clearly the story of resistance there is no passivity to be explained. One version I have heard is that women seek out relationships with violent men in order to stop the violence and resolve their own psychological conflicts. Another version is that women compulsively provoke men to violence so that they (the women) can ultimately overcome it. Either way, women are to blame. If we want to think in terms of drives and unconscious*

*mechanisms, I want to propose that resistance to violence and oppression is integral to our psychological makeup: When violated, we act compulsively to preserve our basic human dignity. And I believe there is ample evidence for this view.*

## THE LANGUAGE OF EFFECTS AND THE LANGUAGE OF RESPONSES

In the clinical and research literature concerned with interpersonal violence, victims are represented almost exclusively in a language of effects (Burstow, 1990; Kelly, 1988; Ridley, 1999; Wade, 2000). There is good reason for this emphasis on effects. In the late 1970's, when feminist and other justice-oriented activists publicized the high rates of violence against women and children, manifestations of the harm caused by sexualized assault and wife-assault were widely misinterpreted as symptoms of mental illness (Bograd, 1988; Burstow, 1992; Caplan, 1995; Herman, 1997; Kamsler, 1990; Kelly, 1988; Walker, 1979, 1984). In addition, social myths and conventional treatment models tended to blame victims and mitigate the responsibility of offenders (Bernardez, 1991; Bograd, 1988; Burstow, 1992; Herman, 1997; Kamsler, 1990; Kelly, 1988; Wade, 2000). The focus in research and clinical work on the short and long term effects of the different forms of violence was in part a counter-measure inspired by the desire to prevent victim blaming, elucidate the full extent of the harm suffered by victims, and demonstrate the need for specialized treatment methods and resources. It was assumed that the treatment of victims of violence would center on the treatment of its effects.

But the language of effects encodes a number of interpretive biases that warrant careful examination. We propose that it misrepresents victims' responses to violence, conceals victims' resistance, and portrays victims as passive recipients of abuse. Resistance is a response to violence and cannot be encoded in a language of effects. The interpretive biases encoded in the language of effects become apparent when contrasted with an alternative, the language of responses. A response is a volitional act that demonstrates judgment, imagination, and will; an effect is the strictly determined outcome of a previous event/cause. A response is a social, communicative act that plays a part in on-going social interaction; an effect is an end-state, the last link in a causal chain. Resistance to violence is positive or constructive in that it signals the individual's desire to escape the violence and improve their circumstances; logically, a negative cause such as violence can produce only negative effects.

From this perspective we can see that the problem with the language of effects is not only that effects are conceptualized in an overly negative manner, as enduring psychological variables: It is that the effects of violence cannot be conceptualized in any other way. Questions about the effects of violence ask respondents to represent their behavioural and mental responses as non-volitional, asocial, and inherently negative end-states. What transforms victims' resistance and other responses into problems, and problems into symptoms, is precisely their representation as effects. The language of effects constructs the victim as a passive site of damage.

*MR: Some consequences of physical trauma, such as broken bones can be described as effects. However, even here, the accompanying pain, swelling and bruising can be more aptly described as responses. When it comes to mental or emotional events, it is even more important to consider seriously how the victims' actions and subjective experiences can be understood as responses to rather than effects of abuse. Yet I know that many of my colleagues would worry that shifting to a focus on responses would mean ignoring the harm caused by violence. But does it make sense to say that some effects of sexual assault are that many victims become depressed, dissociate, or lose their self-confidence? Or is this kind of analogy faulty because a person cannot be reduced to a physical object? Individuals produce a multitude of creative mental and behavioural responses to attacks, unlike bones that just splinter or break. My own experience is that viewing emotional pain as a response to abuse leads to a more subtle and contextual understanding of the victim's circumstances and choices. I believe emotional pain and humiliation are responses that arise from and signify the victims' immediate comprehension of the meaning and implications of the perpetrators' actions. Emotional pain in response to violence signifies and registers a protest in that it shows that the victim is refusing to be contented, relaxed, and comfortable with abuse. When I am safe, I respond by relaxing. When I am threatened, I respond with fear, hurt and bewilderment. In this way we can acknowledge the diverse forms of distress victims suffer as responses, many of which are intelligible as forms of resistance.*

## A RESPONSE-BASED APPROACH TO THERAPEUTIC INTERVIEWING

From a response-based perspective, therapy consists in part of practices that reverse the four operations of language to (a) expose violence, (b) clarify perpetrators' responsibility, (c) elucidate and honour victims' resistance, and (d) contest the blaming and pathologizing of victims. This is achieved in part by focussing on the details of victims' responses to particular incidents and circumstances. Through a focus on responses, many actions and subjective experiences that were previously ignored or constructed as effects of violence are accorded new significance as responses and forms of resistance. The following case study of a woman we shall call "Yvonne" illustrates this process.

*Yvonne sought therapy for feelings of depression following the breakup of her marriage. She was having difficulty sleeping, concentrating, and remembering. She had gained weight and was inactive by her usual standards. Her friends and family were very worried. And although her husband of 25 years was abusive, she missed him and grieved the end of the relationship.*

*Yvonne was quite concerned about the fact that she would cry whenever family members pressured her to leave or remain in the marriage. Even close friends seemed to believe it was their duty to provide Yvonne with advice about how best to live her life. Yvonne wanted to stop this interference, to confront friends and family in a firm but respectful way. However, each time she tried, she wound up crying and feeling "pitiful". Her crying seemed to prove that she needed help.*

*Yvonne initially described herself and her difficulties almost exclusively in a language of effects. She suspected that her unwanted crying and inability to stand up for herself were the effects of mistreatment she had endured in her family when she was young. She wondered if she was depressed because she had failed to "deal with" the "baggage" carried over from her childhood.*

*Yvonne was the youngest of seven children. As a child, she was criticized and called names by her siblings on virtually a daily basis. No matter what she tried, she seemed powerless to make them stop. If she got mad, they laughed; if she fought back physically, they beat her. However, when she cried they would usually just leave her alone. For some reason, Yvonne's crying made it very difficult for people to continue their abuse.*

*I (AW) noted that Yvonne had resisted the abuse in several ways; for example, by getting angry, fighting back physically, and crying. With some further questions about Yvonne's responses to specific incidents of bullying, I learned that Yvonne had also tried avoiding her siblings, calling them names, and telling her parents. Although these forms of resistance did not stop the abuse (with the exception of crying), Yvonne was pleasantly surprised to realize that she had in fact been standing up for herself all along, even as a youngster, when she had felt so vulnerable and afraid.*

*I then asked Yvonne how she had responded to her husband's abusive behaviour. Yvonne described how she had asked him to stop, pleaded with him to get help, refused to drink with him, told her friends, avoided him, withdrew her affection, protected the children, secretly saved money, cried, defended herself physically, and separated herself emotionally long before it was safe to do so physically.*

*Yvonne remembered that she sometimes cried at the least provocation from her husband, so quickly in fact that he sometimes left her completely alone. Playfully, with an expression of mock embarrassment, Yvonne admitted that she used the same tactic with family members before they had a chance to get started in their criticism. Yvonne agreed, however, that crying was much more than a tactic. For her, it was a way of expressing her feelings and refusing to be silenced. Yvonne said that she had not seen crying in this way before. Instead, she had seen it as a sign of weakness.*

*Three weeks later, Yvonne reported that she had had several successful confrontations with family members without crying. She was surprised at how calm and resolute she felt. She had cried on one occasion unrelated to confrontation, and had felt that this was the type of crying that she wanted to be able to continue in her life. Yvonne said that these successful confrontations, combined with her gaining more effective control of her own crying, were evidence that she was "a lot stronger" than she had realized. She was walking, sleeping better, eating healthier foods, and finding much more comfort in the company of her family and friends.*

Yvonne initially used a number of negative abstractions (e.g., depression, inability to stand up for herself, baggage) to describe herself and the problems she faced. She presented these problems as the effects of previous abuse and herself as a passive recipient of that abuse. The therapist responded to this account with simple questions about recent events, Yvonne's important relationships, and the details of the problems that occasioned therapy. The purpose of these questions was to contextualize the negative abstractions by eliciting accounts of interactions in particular situations.

When Yvonne suggested that her problems might stem from abuse, the therapist asked some quite general questions, such as "Can you say a bit more about what you mean by abuse?" When Yvonne mentioned specific forms or incidents of abuse, the therapist asked questions about how she had responded: For example, "When your brothers and sisters started tormenting you, how did you respond? You know, what did you do?" These questions shifted the focus from a language of effects, in which Yvonne was represented as a passive and socially conditioned recipient of abuse, to a language of responses, in which Yvonne was represented as a perceptive individual who actively opposed mistreatment.

As Yvonne's responses were examined in relation to her siblings' abusive behaviour, many of them became intelligible as forms of resistance. In Yvonne's case, the therapist introduced the vocabulary of judicious resistance casually, in a tone of piqued curiosity, as though this new perspective was obvious but still very interesting. After listing some of Yvonne's responses verbatim, the therapist commented: "So, you did all kinds of things to resist this abuse, even though you were little". This acknowledgment of Yvonne's childhood resistance provided a basis for examining her responses and resistance to the abuse by her husband.

> *MR: As you describe it, in coming to terms with violence, victims may have little choice but to draw upon terms and metaphors that conceal their resistance and portray them as passive, dysfunctional, and ultimately as partly responsible for the violence. But is there a risk of imposing a new and equally rigid interpretation that does not do justice to the complexity of events and the victim's experience.*
>
> *I (MR) remember one client who told me that every night in the privacy of her room she silently recited all the wrongs her parents did to her during the day. How are we to understand such an act? Why should we understand it as an act of resistance? Could we not understand it equally well as an act of poetic creativity, for example?*

The issue of not imposing particular interpretations of events is always important, but especially so with people who have been subjected to violence or other forms of abuse. In order to appreciate how particular mental or behavioural acts might represent forms of resistance it is necessary to take into account the precise nature of the perpetrator's actions, at minimum, and often the larger social and political context in which those actions occur. For example, if the perpetrator attempts to isolate the victim, any means by which the victim refuses to be isolated and retains a connection to others can be understood as a form of resistance. Officials in the church and state run "residential schools" tried to separate aboriginal children from their families, communities, and cultural practices. Children retained their connections by secretly speaking their own languages, playing traditional games, making silent prayers, and gathering around new arrivals to smell the smoke on their clothes, to name but a few examples. These acts can all be understood as forms of resistance.

Similarly, if it was the case that the parents of Martine's client denied their verbal and physical cruelty, or defined it as "discipline", the act of privately reciting her parents' wrongs each night, perhaps as a way of expressing and preserving her own truth, can certainly be understood as an act of resistance. It might also be understood as an act of poetic creativity: After all, poetry is a time-honoured medium of dissent. The attention we pay to the details and "situational logic" of each individual's complex responses takes us away from imposing interpretations, which often stem for theories about the mind of the victim or the offender, and into a process of building accounts of responses that are always situated and unique. We introduce the vocabulary of judicious resistance in a tentative manner and ask clients to evaluate the accuracy and usefulness of that interpretation.

Moreover, we do not view this process as a type of reframing. Rather, resistance is just as real as violence. Questions about victims' responses to particular acts of violence tend to elicit more complete and accurate accounts in which certain responses become intelligible as forms of resistance. Additionally, acts of resistance should not be confused with survival, coping, or resilience. While these terms acknowledge the resourcefulness and determination of victims, and make sense of certain behaviours that might otherwise be interpreted as symptoms of pathology, they do not explicitly acknowledge, and in some cases actually conceal, victims' spontaneous resistance.

The account of Yvonne's responses and resistance to abuse by her siblings and husband provided a factual basis for contesting each of the negative attributions (i.e., depression, passivity, crying as a deficit, inability to stand up for herself) that occasioned therapy. While Yvonne initially stated that she could not stand up for herself, the accounts of her resistance showed that she had been standing up for herself all along. Although Yvonne could not stop or escape the abuse, the accounts of her resistance showed that she did not "let it happen". It became clear that crying was not an unwanted effect, signifying damage and deficiency, but rather an inherently healthy response and form of resistance signifying chronic mental wellness. Similarly, depression was not a psychological disorder caused by violence but a form of protest signaling Yvonne's steadfast refusal to be contented with abuse and unwanted interference.

*MR: The pathologizing of victims with the language of effects can be quite subtle. A clinical psychologist recently told me that she had noticed a pattern in the behaviour of victims of abuse. She said, "Whenever I do a relaxation activity with victims of abuse, they can't find a safe place". She saw this as an inability on the part of victims, and as a long-term effect of the abuse. This view fits neatly with the commonly expressed view that victims are overly anxious, hyper-vigilant, and unable to trust others. But it seemed to me that the psychologist was pathologizing the victims she was treating by assuming that their persistent concern with safety was not appropriate in the exercise she had constructed. I replied, "Is it that they can't find a safe place or that they are naturally concerned with safety? When you guide a relaxation and ask victims to think about a safe place, it is to be expected that they will respond by remaining alert to possible intrusions". Of much more interest therapeutically is the question of how victims manage to retain just the right level of awareness and vigilance even when an expert suggests that they relax.*

The second example is an interview transcript reconstructed from sessional notes to illustrate a response-based approach to several concerns frequently presented by women who have been subjected to abuse by their male partners. "Jill" attended therapy after she called the police to report that her husband "Bob" had assaulted her. Bob was arrested, charged, and released with an undertaking to avoid contact with Jill. Several weeks later, Bob returned home. Shortly after, Jill met alone with the therapist. The transcript is broken into three segments, interspersed with commentary.

## Segment 1:

| | |
|---|---|
| *C (client):* | *I've been pretty depressed lately.* |
| *T (therapist):* | *Okay. Well . . . what do you mean by depressed?* |
| | *[asks the client to provide more detail about specific behaviours]* |
| *C:* | *Just kind of mopey, not doing very much.* |
| *T:* | *When did you start doing less?* |
| | *[emphasizes volition of the client]* |
| *C:* | *Well, it's been worse the past few days.* |
| *T:* | *Really? What's been happening lately?* |
| | *[focuses on context]* |
| *C:* | *Well, it's been pretty bad at home, with Bob, lots of fighting.* |
| *T:* | *What kind of fighting?* |
| | *[begins to contextualize the abstraction 'fighting', a mutualizing term that is often used to conceal the unilateral nature of abuse]* |
| *C:* | *Arguments about drinking, housework, that kind of thing.* |
| *T:* | *What's your side of the argument and what's his?* |
| | *[breaks down the mutualizing term 'argument']* |

C: *Well... I feel he drinks too much and doesn't help out enough. He tells me to quit nagging, then maybe he wouldn't drink so much.*

T: *So he kinds of blames you for his drinking. [identifies blaming as a strategy for avoiding responsibility]*

C: *Yeah, he does that a lot.*

T: *Does what a lot?*

C: *Blames me. It seems he always has an excuse for everything. I'm always to blame for how unhappy he is.*

T: *So, you ask him to be accountable and he makes excuses. Am I getting that right? [redefines 'argument' in terms of her taking a stand on equal sharing of relationship responsibilities; asks the client to evaluate the reformulation]*

In segment 1, Jill encodes her concerns in a language of effects, as negative abstractions (e.g., depression, mopeyness). It becomes apparent that these concerns are related to difficulties with her partner, Bob. However, Jill describes these difficulties in mutualizing terms (e.g., fighting, arguments) which imply that she is partly responsible. The therapist contextualizes these abstractions and contests the mutualizing terms by eliciting an account of actual behaviour in specific interactions. On the basis of Jill's account of these interactional details, the therapist exposes the strategies Bob uses to avoid responsibility, and elucidates some of Jill's responses (which are later identified as acts of resistance). The therapist uses active grammatical constructions (e.g., "So he kind of blames you...") that convey who did what to whom and, in so doing, clarify responsibility. The question "When did you start doing less?" suggests that doing less is an active response to circumstances, not a form of inactivity (which is often seen as a symptom of depression). The phrase "... you ask him to be accountable..." suggests that she was, in a responsible manner, refusing to accept his irresponsible behaviour

## Segment 2:

C: *Yeah, but it doesn't do any good.*

T: *What do you mean?*

C: *He just ignores me and does exactly what he wants.*

T: *Well, yelling at you to shut you up isn't exactly ignoring you. So, how do you respond to that, when he tries to ignore you and does what he wants anyway? [acknowledges that Jill's response represents a significant challenge to Bob's irresponsible behaviour; defines yelling as a method of suppressing resistance; clarifies responsibility for perpetuation of the problem]*

C: *It makes me mad, but I don't say anything because he'll get angry.*

T: *Okay, so you keep quiet sometimes when its too dangerous not to. But, what do you mean by angry? What does he do when you try to say something about him not taking you seriously?*

*[defines Jill's quietness as a prudent form of resistance; contextualizes the abstraction "angry"; defines Bob's actions as efforts to suppress her resistance]*

C: *He gets really loud and shouts in my face that I don't care about him, that I never stop bitching.*

T: *Oh. So, he tries to bully you into shutting up.*
*[defines shouting and intimidation as abuse; further highlights Bob's attempts to suppress Jill's resistance]*

C: *Yeah, he does that a lot.*

The therapist continues to focus on interaction. It becomes apparent that, far from ignoring Jill, Bob tries to shut her up by becoming increasingly aggressive. Jill refuses to shut up and presses forward with her concerns in a respectful manner until Bob threatens to escalate his aggression. She then chooses to be quiet, for her own safety. The therapist reformulates the phrase "I don't say anything", which suggests inaction and might be misinterpreted as submission, as "you keep quiet sometimes", which suggests action and highlights Jill's volition and tactical awareness.

T: *Why do you think he uses aggression to try and keep you from speaking your mind?*
*[indirectly acknowledges that she presents a significant challenge to his efforts at control, exposes the abuse by defining aggression (i.e., "anger") as a tool he uses deliberately for a purpose]*

C: *Well, I never thought of it like that. I thought he just had a bad temper.*

T: *Is that a fair description of what's been going on? I mean, his using aggression deliberately to shut you up?*
*[asks her to evaluate the accuracy of this re-description; acknowledges the importance of being fair to her partner]*

C: *Yeah, I think it is.*

T: *Okay. Well, what's it like to think of what he does in that way?*

C: *It makes me mad! I really don't like bullies. If that's what he's doing... I don't know.*

T: *Well, if that's really what's going on, then its no wonder you've been refusing to be happy or do things for him.*

C: *Yeah, I guess so.*

T: *Would you expect any person to be happy and feel good about doing things when this kind of thing is going on?*

C: *Well, no. I guess not.*

T: *You know, it sounds to me like you've got some really good reasons to be sad and mopey. But I don't see how this means you're depressed. You've certainly refused to be happy. And you've refused to shut up because these are legitimate and important concerns you have. So... I don't quite understand why this would be called depression. You know, it seems that the problem is not in your mind, it's in how you're being treated. Does that fit?*

The therapist draws attention to both the deliberate nature of Bob's aggressive behaviour and the determination evident in Jill's resistance. On close examination, it becomes apparent that "arguments" and "fighting" are in fact mutualizing terms that conceal a pattern of aggressive behaviour by one party and judicious resistance by another. Jill recognizes the significance of clarifying Bob's responsibility ("I thought he just had a temper problem") and re-considers her own responses. The problems "depression", "mopeyness", and "not doing very much", which were initially presented as effects of "arguing" and "fighting", are recast as responses and forms of resistance. Based on a more complete and accurate account of the circumstances and the conduct of both parties, the very problems that occasioned therapy are intelligible as expressions of mental wellness.

> *MR: When I first started using this approach I found that I lacked the vocabulary to acknowledge resistance. I remember writing a lexicon to help me formulate a language of responses. It's quite stunning to see how quickly significant changes can occur with this approach to interviewing. I have heard comments like "I knew I was not weak" and "I feel more capable now to deal with what is thrown at me". I wonder why it makes so much difference to acknowledge the individual's responses and resistance to the violence. It is as though there is something restorative in the process. It removes blame because the account of the individual's resistance shows that she or he did not "put up with it" or "let it happen". It acknowledges their countless efforts to maintain their dignity.*

## CONCLUSION

Misrepresentation[2] is integral to crimes of violence. For therapists, the question of how the actions and subjective experiences of perpetrators and victims of violence are constructed in discourse is always at issue. In professional and public discourse, language is often used in a manner that conceals violence, mitigates perpetrators' responsibility, conceals victims' resistance, and blames or pathologizes victims. The language of effects is a particularly powerful discursive machinery that misrepresents victims' responses and, more specifically, conceals victims' spontaneous resistance to violence. In this chapter we briefly outlined an alternative, response-based approach to therapy with victims of violence that is based in part on a close analysis of interaction between victims and perpetrators in particular instances. From a response-based perspective, therapy consists in part of discursive

[2] In 2001, the newly elected government of British Columbia held a referendum ostensibly so that the people of the province could express their opinions on several questions concerning the government's negotiations with First Nations regarding so-called land claims and self-governance. The government deliberately ignored the fact that several of the questions on the referendum concerning aboriginal rights and government fiduciary responsibility were already answered by the Supreme Court of Canada. In effect, the people of the province were asked to propose guidelines for the land claims and self-governance negotiations that would, if enacted, be in violation of Aboriginal rights under Canadian law.

practices that expose violence, clarify perpetrators' responsibility, elucidate and honour victims' responses and resistance, and contest the blaming and pathologizing of victims. In the process, therapy with victims of violence shifts from a focus on treating effects to a focus on elucidating and honouring responses.

## ACKNOWLEDGMENTS

We are grateful to Dr. Linda Coates, whose ideas permeate this paper, and to Martine Renoux, psychotherapist, for many helpful suggestions and questions, and for contributing as our conversational partner.

## REFERENCES

Bernardez, T. (1991). Adolescent resistance and the maladies of women: Notes from the underground. In C. Gilligan, A.G. Rogers, & D.L. Tolman (Eds.). *Reframing resistance: Women, girls, and psychotherapy* (pp. 213–22). New York: The Haworth Press, Inc.

Bograd, M. (1988). Feminist perspectives on wife abuse: An introduction. In K. Yllo & M. Bograd (Eds.), *Feminist perspectives on wife abuse* (pp. 11–26). Newbury park, CA: Sage.

Burstow, B. (1992). *Radical feminist therapy*. Newbury Park: Sage.

Campbell, J., Rose, L., Kub, J. & Nedd, D. (1998). Voices of strength and resistance: A contextual and longitudinal analysis of women's responses to battering. *Journal of Interpersonal Violence, Vol. 13(6)*, 743–762.

Caplan, P. (1995). *They say you're crazy.* New York: Addison-Wesley Publishing Company.

Coates, L., Todd, N. & Wade, A. (2000). Four operations of language. Workshop overhead. *Bridging the Gap Conference.* Victoria, BC.

Coates, L. & Wade, A. (2002). *Telling it like it isn't: How psychological constructs obscure responsibility for violent acts.* Manuscript under review.

Danet, B. (1980). Baby or fetus?: Language and the construction of reality in a manslaughter trial. *Semiotica, 32,* 187–219.

Davis, M. & Troupe, Q. (1990). *Miles: The Autobiography.* New York: Simon and Schuster.

Epston, D. (1989). *Collected papers.* Adelaide: Dulwich Centre.

Goffman, I. (1961). *Asylums.* New York: Doubleday.

Herman, J. (1997). *Trauma and recovery.* New York: Basic Books.

Kamsler, A. (1990). Her-story in the making: Therapy with women who were sexually assaulted in childhood. In M. Durrant & C. White (Eds.), *Ideas for theapy with sexual abuse* (pp. 9–36). Dulwich: Dulwich Centre Publications.

Kelly, L. (1988). *Surviving sexual violence.* Minneapolis: University of Minnesota Press.

Lempert, B. (1996). Women's strategies for survival: Developing agency in abusive relationships. *Journal of Family Violence, 11,* 269–290.

Maisel, R. (1996). *You've really got a hold of me: Deconstructing and re-viewing past experiences with survivors of persistent and severe childhood mistreatment.* Paper presented at the Narrative Means & Therapeutic Practice Conference, Vancouver, February 24, 1996.

Ridley, P. (1999). *The language used to describe victims of sexualized violence in therapy.* Unpublished manuscript, University of Victoria.

Scott, J. (1990). *Domination and the arts of resistance.* New Haven: Yale University Press.

Todd, N. (2000). *An eye for an I: Response-based work with perpetrators of abuse.* Unpublished paper: Men's Crisis Service, Calgary, Alberta.
Wade, A. (1997). Small acts of living: Everyday resistance to violence and other forms of oppression. *Journal of Contemporary Family Therapy, 19*, 23–40.
Wade, A. (2000). *Resistance to interpersonal violence: Implications for the practice of therapy.* Unpublished doctoral dissertation, University of Victoria, Victoria, BC.
Walker, L. (1979). *The battered woman.* New York: Van Nostrand Reinhold.
Walker, L. (1984). *The battered woman syndrome.* New York: Springer.
Zemsky, B. (1991). Coming out against all odds: Resistance in the life of a young lesbian. In C. Gilligan, Rogers, A.G., & Tolman, D.L. (Eds.). *Reframing resistance: Women, girls, & psychotherapy* (pp. 185–200). New York: The Haworth Press, Inc.

# *Chapter* 10

# *What's Love Got to Do With It?*

## Managing Discursive Positions and Mediating Conflict within a Heterosexual Love Relationship

GERALD MONK AND STACEY L. SINCLAIR WITH CONVERSATIONAL PARTNER CRAIG SMITH

### INTRODUCTION

Standing at the altar, two persons united in love prepare to begin their new life together as a married couple. The groom wears a black tuxedo with a white vest and white tie, while the bride wears a white silk satin strapless gown. Both bride and groom are flanked by their respective bridesmaids and groomsmen. As the string quartet plays "Here Comes the Bride", the father escorts his daughter down the aisle while the groom waits expectantly. The pastor guides the bride and groom through the ceremony, inviting them to proclaim a set of vows, "The Book of Common Prayer," to one another:

> I, *(name)* take thee, *(name)* to be my wedded *(husband/wife)*,
> to have and to hold from this day forward,
> for better, for worse, for richer, for poorer,
> in sickness and in health, to love and to cherish and to obey,'
> 'til death do us part,
> according to God's holy ordinance;
> and thereto I give thee my troth.

This couple has just participated in a ritual that is enacted on thousands of occasions everyday in the Western world. Despite the taken-for-granted nature of this routine Christian ceremony, there are several discursive features worth pointing out. For example, several discourses are privileged within the above interaction, including the discourses that "a man and woman who are in love should marry," "a proper bride wears white," "a father should present his daughter, the bride, to her new husband," "a couple who are in love make a commitment to be together for their whole lives," and "the community witnesses and sanctions the union of two people within a wedding ceremony". These discourses reflect what is often considered "common sense" about how couples in love should proceed, and in particular, about how husband and wives should behave. Moreover, these discourses exert a powerful influence in the day-to-day interactions of husbands and wives specifically, and of men and women in intimate relationships generally.

The Christian wedding ceremony we have described brings together powerful discursive features, which on the one hand provide a promise of stability, certainty, and nurturance, and on the other hand, create the potential for misunderstanding, contradiction, and conflict. Let us explain. The commitment of the couple to be together in good times and in bad for the rest of their lives is a widely held cultural idea in marriage. In fact, the Western marriage ceremony is intimately tied to the discourses of romantic love that dominate the courtship, decision to marry and the period of time that is often termed infatuation. Discourses of romantic love often include the following notions: "My partner is a wonderful human being", "I don't want to change my partner in any way", "I expect my partner to take care of me forever", "My partner is my true soul mate", "My partner understands my dreams, thoughts, wishes, hopes and desires, even when not spoken", and "My partner provides all that I will need in life".

While these traditional ideas promise a lifetime of companionship and support, there are emerging cultural assumptions that are in contradiction to these outcomes that create the potential for prolonged and destabilizing conflict. To be more exact, in the Western world, the notion that marriage and long-term heterosexual relationships should be based upon the equality of rights and responsibilities for the parties committing to live together is becoming increasingly prevalent. This view of equity suggests that men and women should be equally responsible for the major duties and responsibilities in making a long-term relationship work. The viewpoint gathers momentum as the number of women in the paid workforce continues to increase. As women increasingly play a significant part in contributing to the financial viability of the couples or family's future, so the expectations grow in relation to men participating more fully in the domestic tasks in the home, the shared socio-emotional care of the partner and the parenting responsibilities for those couples with children.

The traditional and still widely popular wedding vows, however, embody cultural practices that, to some extent, do not fit with equitable social positions and responsibilities. For example, the act of the father of the bride "giving her away" to the groom, the statement that the couple will "obey" one another (which, at an earlier time was expressed by the bride and not the groom), and the symbol of vulnerability and purity, conveyed by the white satin gown, support the patriarchal arrangements that have so powerfully shaped heterosexual relationships over many centuries. These vestiges of patriarchy in the Christian ceremony reinforce discourses that are in stark contrast to emerging discourses of equality of rights and responsibilities in a couple relationship. In these ways, we can see the potential for conflict to emerge.

In this chapter, we explore the idea that the concept of discourse can be used to facilitate conversations and relationships within mediation. In particular, this chapter offers a useful framework for negotiating conflict in a heterosexual love relationship by highlighting the manner in which individual's expectations are mutually emergent from particular discursive spaces. We outline specific discursive practices and approaches for mediators that make more visible the cultural production of conflicts; thus providing more freedom to couples in heterosexual relationships to explore conflicts with less totalizing descriptions of the other as blameworthy. We set the scene by briefly outlining the experiences of a couple in the midst of a serious conflict, who, a few years earlier, were enamored with one another. The following account represents a composite of our professional experiences working with couples in mediation.

## DEAN AND ANDREA

Dean (33) and Andrea (29), an Anglo-American middle-class couple sought help from a family mediator after talking about separating after a four-year marriage. Over the last three years, both have experienced prolonged painful conflicts about parental and partnership duties in the home. Both are in a state of shock and fatigue. It didn't seem very long ago that they were madly in love and filled with excitement about their impending wedding. They were fully immersed in the state of romantic love or we would say mesmerized by the discourses of romantic love.

For Andrea, Dean was a fulfillment of her childhood and adolescent dreams. He was a sensitive, responsible, hard working and intelligent man. During their courtship, Andrea found Dean to be a charming, thoughtful, kind and generous person. Dean found Andrea to be nurturing, generous, spontaneous and tender. As a recent graduate in mechanical engineering, Andrea's fiancée was offered a generous salary with significant benefits in a position in a large company three hours flying time from where they were living. Andrea had graduated from a program in applied physics. She had completed a highly successful thesis on the application of laser technology in navigation and was offered a position in a high-powered research lab funded by a U.S. military contract in the city where they courted. During this whirl-wind courtship of six months, Andrea made the decision with some reticence that she would be prepared to support Dean's career moves and sacrifice her own. There were no facilities to support her work in the city they moved to. Dean was immensely grateful for Andrea's willingness to put aside her own career prospects for his.

It was a difficult adjustment for Andrea in their move to their new home. While Dean was loving his job and especially enjoying the male friendships he was making in his new company, Andrea felt very socially isolated and professionally dissatisfied. Her part-time job as a lab-technician was unrewarding and boring. At the end of their first year of marriage, Andrea and Dean decided that they would like a child. Two and a half years later, with now two young children to care for, Andrea is depressed, resentful, and feels overwhelmed by the parenting tasks and burdened by what she feels are her partnership duties. Dean is feeling angry towards Andrea and blamed by her constant negative responses about being alone at home with the children for long periods of time and being responsible for all the household duties. On Dean's current salary, they cannot afford extensive child-care or maid-services.

Early in the first interview, Andrea describes a lack of support from Dean and states he should be taking an equitable share in the parenting of the two children and participating more fully in the domestic tasks in the home. The mediator asks Andrea to address Dean.

> Andrea: *Dean you seem to be totally oblivious to what I am going through. I feel totally unsupported by you. I moved to Delaware for your career, and set my own career aside. I'm at home most of the day with the kids on my own and when you come home you hardly provide any help with the kids and barely lift a finger to help with dinner preparation. You've never so much as picked up a vacuum cleaner...*
>
> Dean: *I can't believe you're so angry and resentful all the time. You were the one that encouraged me to move here. You wanted kids right now and you're blaming me for you deciding to put your career on hold. You expect me to work all day, do yard work on the weekends and be at your beck and call when I get home. I am sick of you being depressed and expecting me to do it all.*
>
> Andrea: *Dean, you've become so mean and selfish. We agreed you'd help out at home. On the few occasions you do, you do it with a scowl on your face. Can't you see I have enough to do and that it's too much to do on my own I'm just sick of all of this.*
>
> Dean: *I'm sick of you being so damned ungrateful for how hard I work and how I contribute to this family.*

From any perspective, this couple is in trouble. Listening to this dialogue, it might even be too late for this couple to survive this level of despair and stay together. However, the mediator has to do something. What does he or she do? There are a multiple set of possibilities about how the mediator can proceed and many theories about conflict that guide what needs to be done in order to assist this couple.

## THEIR CONFLICT

Conflict can be considered from a multitude of perspectives. Given liberal-humanism's dominance in mainstream counseling, psychology, and psychotherapy over the last three decades, it is not surprising that conflict has traditionally been viewed from this framework. That is, with its celebration of individualism, liberal-humanism has tended to locate conflict between individuals as distinct and separate from the social, cultural and political contexts in which they live (Neimeyer, 1998; Winslade, Monk, & Drewery, 1997). This dislocation of individuals and their conflicts from the larger cultural context reflects the humanistic focus on intrapsychic processes occurring *within* people. From this liberal-humanist perspective, conflict in intimate relationships is most often conceptualized in essentialist terms, as arising from discrepancies in partner's biological needs or underlying interests (Winslade & Monk, 2000; Winslade, Monk, & Cotter, 1998). The term essentialism is embedded within liberal-humanist traditions that depict things as having essential natures and promote a quest of fundamental truths. In much of the psychological literature, there is the tendency to discuss conflict in essentialist terms. This leads to viewing parties in mediation as having problems that need to be fixed: They have communication difficulties. They don't know how to empathize. They need to own their feelings, take responsibility, and quit blaming. With a more balanced view, their behavior will improve. They need training in paraphrasing and "I" statements. Another mediator influenced by the essentialist notions accompanying many scientist-practitioner approaches may suggest that this couple need to learn some problem-solving skills. They need to be proactive. They need to agree upon specific problem definitions. They need to identify some specific goals, to brainstorm possible solutions.

Other mediators might make efforts to identify mutual needs and interests the couple shares. Both Dean and Andrea want support, acknowledgement, validation, and appreciation. They could work out a plan on how to do that and practice with the mediator.

The one characteristic that all the above approaches share is the location of the problem as residing *within* the couple or *in* the relationship. Increasingly, liberal-humanism is being critiqued and challenged for its naïve and uncritical privileging of the individual and his or her inner process as distinct from the socio-cultural context (Jenkins, 2001; Parker, 1998; Sampson, 1988). When conflict is conceived as arising from *within* individual or couple deficits, it tends to invite a universal, totalizing, essentialist description of the problem(s). What follows is often a blaming interaction whereby partners are pitted against one another's "truth- based" assumptions about desirable human behavior. In Dean and Andrea's conflict, each partner is accusing the other of not living up to their expectations about parental and household responsibilities and these "failures" are situated as intrapsychic limitations, (i.e., "[you] are so mean and selfish").

To address these concerns, it has been suggested that conflict be re-conceived from a discursive perspective whereby partners' expectations are viewed as thoroughly dependent upon and impacted by the socially constructed world (Winslade & Monk, 2000). A discursive view of conflict is strongly influenced by the philosophical positions associated with postmodernism and poststructuralism which emphasize the enormous variation in how people live their lives due to the quite different discursive contexts that surround them. Given the great diversity in the way we make meaning in our lives, it follows that differences will result and conflict will arise from time to time within or between people.

In paying special attention to the multiplicity, contextuality, and active construction of meaning, a discursive approach offers itself as a useful framework for understanding the cultural location of conflict within heterosexual love relationships. Specifically, this approach recognizes that, in fact, conflict is socially constructed and positioned within particular social and historical cultural settings, or discourses. In this way, mediators locate the conflict not as a result of a personal deficit in the other, but as a result of cultural viewpoints that we are required to negotiate and manage.

When we think about Andrea and Dean's conflict in cultural terms, we notice a clash of discourses emerging on the one hand from the cultural assumptions of romantic love and on the other hand from the assumptions of equality and equity in interpersonal relationships. In our mediation work, we emphasize the discursive backdrop to the conflict and how this positions Dean and Andrea in an inevitable clash of viewpoints, experiences, feelings and behaviors.

*Craig Smith: Do you think that we're mostly living out discourses in a non-intentional manner? Is therapy/mediation about promoting more reflexivity and intentionality?*
*Gerald Monk and Stacey Sinclair: We think that most of the time most people are living their lives within the maze of cultural prescriptions that are unique to the cultural contexts in which they inhabit. Often, it is in times of crisis, deeply troubling moments or during prolonged periods of despair that we begin to examine why we are doing what we are doing. Even then there is the likelihood that we will locate the origin of our despair in the hands of our perpetrator, the evil one, the other person who is intent upon harming us. Seldom do we stand back from the discursive sea that constantly flows over us. We think mediation and therapy are about creating a context where we can examine, sometimes for the first time, how we are encapsulated by the cultural prescriptions that are present in our communities. The practice of deconstruction is a useful tool to help us examine the discursive positionings shaping our way of being in the world. When we examine why we are doing what we are doing, we are in a better position to engage more intentionally with the possibilities that are presented within our cultural worlds.*

## DISCOURSE AND POSITIONING

Discourse is both the process of talk and interaction between people, and the products of that interaction. Intimate relationships are of course embedded with discourses. In this chapter, there are elaborate descriptions about how discursive contexts not only shape intimate human interaction, but also are inscribed in thought, behavior and affective responses. In fact, we opened the chapter with a description of the multiple discourses that are privileged within a popular set of marriage vows. Indeed, to know anything is to know in terms of discourse (Davies & Harré, 1990). That is, we speak from discourse, feel from discourse, and behave from discourse. In addition, there are multiple discourses circulating at any one time and discourses can compete with one another.

It is important to note that people are capable of exercising choice in relation to discourses. In other words, individuals are not rendered passive by discourses. A useful metaphor used to describe the fluid and dynamic relationship between people and discourse is positioning (Davies & Harré, 1990). Positioning is a spatial metaphor that emphasizes the relationship between words and the forms of life that they physically point to and propel us into (Winslade, 2003). The metaphor highlights the manner in which individuals are located in conversations as active participants in producing varied realities. That is, individuals always speak and act from "some place, some time, some social context" and in response to other conversational moves that have gone before (Winslade, 2003). Therefore, discourses are manifest in how we go forward in our conversational moves. There is a dynamic back and forth quality about how we are positioned in discourse and these discursive moves influence the changing assumptions and expectations we have about one another and ourselves.

In emphasizing the subjectivity that is produced through the discourses we take up (or are located in by others), the concept of positioning helps focus attention on the dynamic aspects of interactions (Davies & Harré, 1990; Drewery, 2002; Winslade, 2003). Our view is that the discursive fields within which people live inevitably provide some degree of subjectivity and thus an agentic position (Monk, 1998). In other words, as Winslade (2003) has pointed out, "as we move from conversation to conversation, we are offered a 'panorama' (Davies and Harré, 1990, p. 47) of different positions that in effect create multiple subjective experiences from which we can draw in understanding our potential choices in life" (p. 42). Thus, to the extent that there are always multiple discourses at work in our positioning, people have choices in the discourses they decide to take up or refuse (Davies & Harré, 1990; Winslade, 2003).

In the complex field of gender relations, we can see how positioning is a useful tool to describe how discourses are acted out in a heterosexual relationship and the intricacies involved in mediating conflict within this relationship. We use the following interaction between Andrea and Dean to illustrate this point.

*Andrea:* *Dean, you seem so unaware of what it takes to take care of the kids. You are so focused upon work and oblivious to what this family really needs.*

*Dean:* *This is what's driving me crazy. You really don't get it. I am working 70 hours a week right now and have been earning decent money for the family and you say I don't know what the family needs.*

In this moment, Dean is expecting Andrea to continue to respond in the way she did early in the courtship and expects her to recognize his contribution to the well-being of Andrea and now to the children through the income he is generating. In this interaction, Dean's response is illustrative of the discourse of man as primary income earner and woman as responsible for most domestic tasks and socio-emotional caregiver. He is challenging the notion of what Andrea means "to take care of the kids" and thus rejects this position invited by Andrea's demand for more equity in the socio-emotional care of the children and her desire for him to assist with domestic duties. Dean's discursive positioning in this moment leads him to assume that Andrea should perform nearly all the domestic duties in the household and be grateful for his contribution. This assumption or expectation produced within this position leads Dean to feel betrayed and underappreciated by Andrea's request for more help.

In this conflictual interaction, Andrea is no longer beholden to the cultural mandates of romantic love. Rather, Andrea's response reflects the discursive position of equity that each partner share the socio-emotional care of family members and share household responsibilities. These competing discursive positions within this interaction have significant influence in determining how Dean and Andrea respond to one another and how they interact with the mediator in the next part of the mediation. However, the presence of these discourses and the positions that are produced for Dean and Andrea within this conflict are not as static and unyielding as they seem. Even in this conflict where Andrea and Dean appear to be constrained by very rigid and seemingly inflexible positions, there are, in fact, multiple discursive positions that can be expressed within these interactions.

For instance, while Dean appears to be taking up strongly the position of a traditional discourse whereby women are primarily responsible for children's care-giving, at the same time he may also be positioned by numerous other discursive influences. For example, Dean prides himself on his ability to share the financial management and decision-making of the couple's domestic income and expenditures. For Dean, to share financial decision-making with his wife is a very different arrangement than the one his parents and many other families modeled for him in his parent's generation. Dean's father, like many men in the 1950s and 1960s, took full responsibility for all financial decision-making so that his mother had no access or interest in information about domestic financial matters. In this regard, Dean is positioned within an equity discourse about financial matters in his relationship with Andrea.

The salience of Dean's "preferred" traditional positioning reflects the notion that some discourses become foregrounded in interactions. Along these lines, Winslade (2003) refers to particular orders of discourse (Fairclough, 1992; Foucault, 1972) that have a profound bearing on social interaction. He describes a class of discourses that have endured across the centuries (within a particular civilization) and are so persuasive and in a community that they are completely taken-for-granted about how life should be lived. These dominating discourses shape every aspect of human functioning embracing thought, behavior and affective responses. Dean's engagement with Andrea is reflective of such a dominating discourse regarding gendered responsibilities.

On the other hand, there are discourses that do not typically bear such a great influence in people's interactions. These alternate discourses challenge the more dominant discourses and are often representative of marginalized cultural ideas circulating within a context or community. For instance, the sharing of financial management and decision making within the home is indicative of the presence of an equity discourse in a relationship. So, while Dean continues to be seduced by the traditional gendered discourses about family duties and responsibilities, he at the same time, is positioned by discursive influences that are in stark contradiction to patriarchal patterns of relating. His sharing of financial decisions is one such alternate discourse that is in juxtaposition to the positioning of men as primary income earners or men as heads of households.

## TEMPORARY ESSENTIALISM

A mediator using a constructionist understanding of conflict embraces ambiguity and indeterminacy in an escalating conflict, and nurtures a spirit of informed curiosity about what is unfolding. From this perspective, there are no universal truth-based approaches to rely on in guiding the mediator's actions. That is, the mediator is not relying on liberal humanist philosophy that suggests that one can know the truth about the human experience. This ambiguity poses an ethical crisis for the mediator. The mediator, like the parties, cannot avoid not being positioned discursively in the conflict they are mediating. The question is from which discursive position will the mediator work?

For example, will the mediator take up a position in a patriarchal discourse or an equity discourse? There is wide consensus that dominant gender discourses have tended to privilege the interests of many men over the interests of many women. Will the mediator understand and know how to respond to the effects of cultural imperatives that leave many women exhausted by the duties they feel in taking responsibility for the socio-emotional and domestic care of the families? Will they be curious about why many women, even today, sacrifice career opportunities in favor of supporting their husbands? Will the mediator be sensitive to and understanding of the cultural prescriptions on men that they should be primarily responsible for the family income to fulfill their role as a 'good provider.' To find a way forward with these difficult ethical challenges is to position oneself as a mediator from a declared ethical stance.

The practice of remaining curious and open-minded, yet choosing to take an overt ethical stance has been referred to as temporarily essentialism (Spivak, 1990). It provides a basis to act from an ethical position or moral standpoint without falling into the abyss of anarchy or naked relativism. From a position of informed curiosity, mediators consistently review their identifiable position that shapes how they practice, and modify their theory and practice in the light of new experiences and challenges. This act is similar to Paré's (in press, 2003) notion of discursive wisdom which suggests that practitioners act upon their knowingness, while at the same time acknowledging the limits of their knowing and, if necessary suspending this knowing in the face of other voices.

Within this framework of temporary essentialism, the mediator is invited to view professional knowledge as provisional, temporary, limited, and tentative. This stance allows practitioners to hold their professional knowledge lightly and through the encounters with their clients, be prepared to revise their therapeutic efforts, and perhaps in some instances, examine and then change previously held assumptions about some aspect of their clients' viewpoint. The mediator from this standpoint is fully prepared to acknowledge that her or his ethical and professional stance will shape and influence the direction of how the conflict will be addressed. The mediator is mindful that each move they make in the mediation emerges from a discursive position that will influence the questions that Dean and Andrea will be asked and how responses from Dean and Andrea will be acknowledged.

For example, the mediator has to ask him or herself, "How can I do better in both taking an overtly moral position and at the same time being curious and respectful about Dean and Andrea's experience and the meanings they associate with this experience"? Reviewing the discursive positioning of the mediator can be achieved by considering the questions the mediator asks Dean and Andrea. For example, take the question, "Dean, what do you think is going on in our community where many women want their husbands to be more involved in the social and emotional care of the children than they currently are?" Choosing Dean to answer the question, embedding the statement "what . . . is going on . . . where many women want their husbands to be more involved in the . . . care of the children" in the question, and asking Dean "what do you think?" in front of Andrea is an example of the mediator being positioned by the discursive shift that propels men to demonstrate more equity in childcare.

In this conversational move, the mediator is not merely asking a random question, but rather is making a choice and taking a moral position regarding equity in relationships. Our view is that it is legitimate to privilege an equity discourse over and above a patriarchal discourse insofar as the mediator is taking a position that is in alignment with an emerging collective and normative ethical stance regarding equity. As Larner (1999) points out, "to not take a position is itself an act of violence, implicitly condoning the injustices suffered by the client (p. 48). Moreover, this privileging of equity is further justified in that the mediator is open to modifying his or her position if this position is not working for the couple. The challenge for the mediator is to take an ethical position in the face of potentially socially unjust or socially destructive interactions exhibited by clients while at the same time remaining open minded. Taking an ethical stance and being curious are not mutually exclusive.

## DISCURSIVE EMPATHY

Liberal-humanism invites mediators to believe that empathy and understanding is present if he or she is able to connect with his or her own humanity. Since the reference point for empathy is the universal human condition, mediators utilizing a humanist approach are likely to believe that everyone has the capacity to "walk in another's shoes". One of the important factors in the mediation process is the ability of the mediator to monitor the extent to which he or she can engage in an empathetic understanding of the couple in conflict. However, from a social constructionist perspective, there are domains of human experience that may not be understood or translated between mediator and his or her clients. That is, contrary to liberal-humanism's claims of universality, there are discourses that position the clients that cannot be known, shared, or understood by one or the other partner in the conflicted couple. For instance, many people on the planet do not participate in dominant Western cultural practices but rather participate in cultural practices lived in uniquely diverse contexts from the ones that are portrayed in the mainstream media. Thus, it is problematic to assume that mediators who have not shared the profoundly different life events experienced by their clients can inherently know the problems their clients struggle with or understand the lives their clients have lived.

This approach invites mediators to develop what we call discursive empathy: an orientation to practice that involves a constant review of the discourses influencing their relationships with clients, and clients' relationships with each other. In this way, mediators do not presume to understand their clients' experiences; rather, they spend time "unpacking" the cultural knapsack that each partner carries. So, while humanist empathy is captured in the question, "How would you [Dean] feel if you were staying at home with the kids all day?" discursive empathy is captured in the questions, "What ideas were influential in you having two children at this point in your marriage?" and "How were you thinking about who would care for them and what that would look like?" This attempt at discursive empathy may assist mediators to avoid inappropriate cultural impositions on their clients. This is easy to say and hard to do. Mediators who have spent much of their lives positioned in discourses that are predominantly racist, classist, or sexist, for instance may experience a difficult challenge being empathetic with clients who have been targeted by those very discourses.

In fact, one of the difficulties of mediation is that by oneself, it is difficult to identify discourses if one is coming from a completely unconsidered and unexamined framework. Building upon the concept of temporary essentialism, the practice of discursive empathy enables the mediator to be much more open to the cultural assumptions that parties hold that are initially difficult to grasp. In other words, discursive empathy points to developing an awareness of the discourses and positioning of ourselves and of our clients. And in the process of developing this discursive awareness, the temporary essentialist practices of remaining curious and open minded are helpful in negotiating conflict.

Overall, the questions that the mediator should pursue are the ones that relate to identifying the parties' assumptions that guide their behavior. The mediator also has the task of helping the couple identify the expertise that this couple has that can be drawn out and used to assist them with their difficulties as well as identify the local knowledges that might be relevant to their needs in this context at this time. Discursive empathy calls on the mediator to demonstrate a willingness and openness to locate the conflict not as a naturally occurring, independent object, devoid of cultural significance, but rather as an outcome of various positions taken up amongst a sea of discourses.

## DECONSTRUCTION

Deconstruction refers to the practice of exploring the taken-for-granted assumptions and influential discourses underpinning our conversation, behavior and emotional expression (Derrida, 1978; White, 1992). Deconstruction builds upon the framework of temporary essentialism and discursive empathy. Where temporary essentialism suggests taking a moral (discursive) stand with curiosity, and discursive empathy suggests identification and review of particular discourses, deconstruction begins to provide us with a specific therapeutic act, intervention, or method for responding to the impact and influence of these discourses and discursive backdrops (Paré, in press, 2003). In this regard, deconstruction is conceived as a *tool* of temporary essentialism and discursive empathy. The mediator utilizing a deconstructive approach to conflict is interested and curious about how his or her work is influenced by the possible prejudices, dogmatism, biases, and therapeutic certainty which shuts down avenues of exploration and inquiry with clients. When using deconstructive approaches in conflict resolution processes, mediators ask themselves "What interactions am I having with the people I am working with that demonstrate I am jumping to conclusions and too easily accepting prior assumptions about the nature of the problem?" and "What limitations are produced by the positioning of my own cultural frameworks and how is this influencing my understanding of the cultural contexts impacting upon the parties and their difficulties?"

Deconstruction invites a tentative, curious, deliberately naïve posture. For example, it asks of any therapeutic engagement, "What was left out? What was covered over? What was paid attention to and what was not?" (Monk, Winslade, Crocket, & Epston, 1997). Discursive mediation focuses on the contextual staging of problems to assist professionals in keeping things moving and becoming less preoccupied with seeking definitive and objective answers that fail to consider the larger background of their lives as well as the lives of their clients. During mediation, practitioners are invited to engage in the deconstruction process that challenges the ways in which cultural systems maintain the status quo. When deconstruction is applied successfully, the mediator questions his or her own preoccupations and preferred points of reference, familiar habits, social practices, beliefs, and judgments which are often regarded as common sense.

The social constructionist practice of deconstruction is differentiated from other forms of mediation, including what can be considered "good practice sense", in that it appreciates fully the extent to which people are seduced by culture and its imperatives to behave in certain ways. Deconstruction practices are especially helpful to address some of the more subtle effects of dominant discourse on the mediator, "because dominant discourses are so familiar, they are taken for granted and even recede from view" (Hare-Mustin, 1994, p. 20).

After deconstructing their own discursive positioning, mediators must then begin to deconstruct the discourses that position their clients. For instance, below the mediator begins to deconstruct the cultural imperatives that may be shaping of the conflict that Andrea and Dean experience, asking "Andrea, where did you get the idea from that it was a good idea to sacrifice your career prospects and move to Delaware to support Dean's career?" This question seeks to expose the romantic love discourses that led to Andrea putting aside her own professional aspirations. The naming of the discourses of romantic love expose Andrea and Dean to the cultural notions that were present in their courtship but are no longer applicable in their present state of relationship. Through this deconstructive question, Andrea is confronted with the extent to which she was positioned by the cultural ideas that Dean would provide for all of her needs, understand deeply her dreams, hopes, and desires, and take care of her forever.

Similarly, Dean is exposed to the cultural assumptions accompanying notions of romantic love that Andrea would take care of him, provide for all of his needs, and deeply understand him. Andrea and Dean can be invited to reflect upon the value of these cultural ideas of relationship and how this has impacted upon their relationship. They can also be asked about the extent to which these cultural ideas have assisted them in their relationship. Further questions deconstruct the potency of romantic love discourses. For example, "Andrea, how did you expect that Dean would show his gratitude to you after you had sacrificed your career prospects?" Assisting the couple to evaluate the impact of dominant discourses that position them in their relationship may help them move away from the intensity of the blame that each has for the other and instead bring to the foreground the cultural assumptions that underpin their current despair. For example, this question may assist them in this process. "Dean, what did you think the costs were on Andrea when she decided to sacrifice her career and move to Delaware to support yours?" This question invites Dean to contemplate the repercussions of the cultural assumptions of romantic love that positioned Andrea and Dean's decision to move to Delaware.

While there are a number of discourses that are operating in Dean and Andrea's conflict which are open for deconstruction, one of particular salience is the discourse that "Women are meant to be the homemakers and caregivers of the children". This discourse is one of interest insofar as it positions both Andrea and Dean in a mutually blaming stance. Dean blames Andrea for not happily fulfilling this dominant cultural idea of how a mother should be. Andrea internalizes the blame, is depressed, and experiences shame that she is not able to successfully fulfill this cultural imperative. The following question attempts to deconstruct this discourse: "Andrea, what does it mean for a woman in this society to realize that being primarily responsible for taking care of the children and the domestic duties in the house is stressful, depressing, and unfulfilling?" The mediator in this question is inviting Andrea to consider the impact of the nurturing mother discourse on her well-being. Inviting Andrea to identify with the potency of the discourse rather than blaming herself or Dean for making her feel so depressed and angry provides an inroad into defusing the intensity of the blame within this couple conflict.

The mediator gets at some of the other discursive influences that position Dean and Andrea by asking the following deconstructive questions: "What is going on in many relationships today where many men are confused with the request by many women to get more involved with domestic help and social and emotional care of the children when they are putting in long hours in their paid work to earn money for the family?" and "What are the consequences on couples of women wanting more contributions from their husbands to take a more active role in the domestic help in the house and to provide more attention to the children?" These deconstructing questions are further examples of the methods employed by a mediator to open spaces for the couple to interact with less blame and judgment as they begin to identify the discursive positions that shape their wishes and hopes of how they would like things to be.

*CS: Do you think we generally select from existing discourses in mediation or therapy, or is there room for creating new and original ones that stand outside dominant ones?*

*GM and SS: We think that when temporary essentialism, discursive empathy, and deconstruction are utilized, then people are not completely and utterly dominated by existing discourses. That is, these practices, which are embedded with abundant and genuine curiosity, invite clients to consider other discourses that stand outside dominant ones. In fact, because existing discourses are so dominant, appearing "natural" and taken-for-granted, much of the work in mediation and therapy is centered on challenging these discourses and creating opportunities for new discourses to emerge. These new alternate discourses challenge more dominant discourses and often become representative of marginalized cultural ideas circulating within a context or community. To help new and original discourses emerge, practitioners must be resourceful and persistent in their genuine curiosity about cultural ideas and lived experiences with which their clients are only slightly acquainted.*

*CS: While reading your chapter, I've been thinking about the fact that you two recently got married. In your title, you borrow a phrase from Tina Turner's song, "What's love got to do with it?" So, I'd like to play with combining these two events and ask, "what role might 'love' play here?" Karl Tomm talks about "therapeutic loving". He uses Humberto Maturana's definition of love as "opening space for the existence of the other." I'd enjoy hearing whether you think this sort of "love" or compassion might have a sustaining role in helping couples endure all the rocky roads traditional gendered discourses can include. Is this sort of "love" different than "romantic love" and closer to the "spirit of informed curiosity" you talk about? Might this connect up with an "equity discourse"?*

*GM and SS: Both our early lived experiences of romantic love have so much to do with closing space down. This love is preoccupied with possessing and being possessed. It is about finding some kind of psychological completion in the other which is most clearly illustrated by the phrase "my other half." This love is pregnant with expectation about how one's partner should perform. When expectation fails to be fulfilled, blame and criticism are often evoked. Romantic love is often experienced as the real truth about how things are and should be. There is a quality to this that is all consuming as it invokes powerful cultural myths about what it means to "be in love", "find one's soul mate" "live happily ever-after." Despite the fact that we are aware that these discourses continue to make their presence felt, we still have to work at not being captured by what they promise. The cultural idea that my wife or husband will keep me safe from physical and psychological dangers continues to be a seductive culturally promoted idea about love. These discourses always want to sneak into the relationship and hang about, ready to be activated by anyone of a thousand stimuli. Discourses of romantic love are promoted in most movies, the television shows shown on most channels, and in the magazines and books that are available. Romantic love discourses hang about like a skunk's smell. We work at catching them when we begin acting from them in ways that present obstacles in our relationship. Our challenge is to be curious about how they manifest themselves. What doesn't help is to blame one another when they appear in our way of relating. We seek to bring forth the kind of love you describe. Opening space for the existence of the other embodies an open and curious posture. This kind of love is characterized by respect, the willingness to take risks, trust, honesty, genuineness, compassion and understanding, and understanding that so many aspects of our way of being are culturally induced. The challenge is to not take things personally as what comes from us does not come from us alone. Even more importantly, we work at not making assumptions of the other. This is where the spirit of curiosity and openness is essential to keeping our relationship enlivened.*

## SUMMARY

Our aim in this chapter was to introduce conflict as a discursively produced phenomenon. We presented a conflict within a heterosexual relationship to explore the workings of discursive positions in the production of conflict. In our personal and professional lives, we have found that using a discursive analysis of conflict has provided us with resources to avoid or minimize the tendency to produce totalizing descriptions of the other. To be more precise, a discursive approach with a focus on positions affords opportunities to engage with a high degree of reflexivity about one's conflict. It invites couples and mediators to be more intentional and socially responsible in negotiating conflict and encourages these parties to examine and renegotiate various cultural assumptions and meanings. When the mediator is working from within a discursive framework, he or she is invited to be openly tentative and respectfully curious. This fosters an ongoing exploratory posture rather than seeking definitive conclusions about a clients' experience.

We have argued that the practices of temporary essentialism, discursive empathy, and deconstruction have provided us with tools for "furthering talk" in ways that are more open and honest, and less dominated by blame and judgment. While we have targeted heterosexual couples and families, we feel the ideas presented in the chapter have relevance in all forms of human conversation and interaction. We look forward to developing and adopting further strategies for managing discursive positions and mediating conflict.

## REFERENCES

Davies, B. & Harré, R. (1990). Positioning: The discursive production of selves. *Journal for the Theory of Social Behaviour, 20(1)*, 43–63.

Derrida, J. (1978). *Writing and difference*. Chicago: University Press.

Drewery, W. (2002). Everyday speech and the production of selves. Unpublished manuscript.

Hare-Mustin, R.T. (1994). Discourses in the mirrored room: A postmodern analysis of therapy. *Family Process, (33)*, 19–34.

Fairclough, N. (1992). *Discourse and social change*. Cambridge, England: Polity Press.

Foucault, M. (1972). *The archaeology of knowledge* (A. Sheridan-Smith, Trans.). New York: Pantheon Books.

Jenkins, A.H. (2001). Humanistic psychology and multiculturalism: A review and reflection. In K.J. Schneider, J.F.T. Bugental, & J.F. Pierson (Eds.). *The handbook of humanistic psychology: Leading edges in theory, research, and practice* (pp. 37–45). Thousand Oaks, CA: Sage Publications, Inc.

Larner, G. (1999). Derrida and the deconstruction of power as context and topic in therapy. In I. Parker (Ed.). *Deconstructing Psychotherapy* (pp. 39–53). London: Sage.

Monk, G. (1998). *Developing a social justice agenda for counsellor education in New Zealand: A social constructionist perspective.* Unpublished doctoral dissertation, University of Waikato, Hamilton, New Zealand.

Monk, G., Winslade, J., Crocket, K., & Epston, D. (Eds.) (1997). *Narrative therapy in practice: The archaeology of hope.* San Francisco: Jossey-Bass.

Neimeyer, R.A. (1998). Social constructionism in the counseling context. *Counselling Psychology Quarterly, 11*(2), 135–149.

Paré, D.A. (in press, 2003). Discursive wisdom: Reflections on ethics and therapeutic knowledge. *International Journal of Critical Psychology.*

Parker, I. (1998). *Social constructionism: Discourse and realism.* Thousand Oaks, CA: Sage Publications, Inc.

Sampson, E.E. (1988). The debate on individualism: Indigenous psychologies of the individual and their role in personal and social functioning. *American Psychologist, 43*, 15–22.

Spivak, G.C. (1990). *The post-colonial critic: Interviews, strategies, dialogues.* New York: Routledge, Chapman & Hall.

White, M. (1992). Deconstruction and therapy. In D. Epston & M. White (Eds.). *Experience, contradiction, narrative, and imagination* (pp. 109–152). Adelaide, Australia: Dulwich Centre Publications.

Winslade, J. (2003). *Discursive positioning in theory and practice: A case for narrative mediation.* Unpublished doctoral dissertation, University of Waikato, Hamilton, New Zealand.

Winslade, J., Monk, G., & Drewery, W. (1997). Sharpening the critical edge: A social constructionist approach in counselor education. In T.L. Sexton & B.L. Griffin (Eds.). *Constructivist thinking in counseling practice, research, and training* (pp. 228–248). New York: Teachers College Press.

Winslade, J. & Monk, G. (2000). *Narrative mediation.* San Francisco: Jossey-Bass.

Winslade, J. Monk, G., & Cotter, A. (1998). A narrative approach to the practice of mediation. *Negotiation Journal, 14*(1), 21–42.

## Chapter 11

# Certainties v. Epiphanies

## Forensic Therapies and Adversarial Assessments

THOMAS CONRAN[1] WITH CONVERSATIONAL PARTNERS
TOMS STRONG AND BRADFORD KEENEY

> "Ambiguity is the warp of life, not something to be eliminated. Learning to savor the vertigo of doing without answers and making do with fragmentary ones opens up the pleasures of recognizing and playing with pattern, finding coherence within complexity, sharing within multiplicity. Improvisation and new learning are not private processes; they are shared with others. The multiple layers of attention involved cannot . . . be brushed aside or subordinated to the completion of tasks. We are called to join in a dance whose steps must be learned along the way, so it is important to attend and respond. Even in uncertainty, we are responsible for our steps." (Mary Catherine Bateson (1994, p. 9).)

> "A leader is best when barely known to exist.
> Not so good when praised or acclaimed.
> Worse when feared and disdained.
> The leader's purpose is fulfilled when the people say,
> 'We did it ourselves.'" (Lao-tse, Tao te Ching, Chapter 17, 6th century BCE.)

[1]Thomas Conran, PhD, Epiphany Partners, 533D Colebrook Drive, Saint Louis, MO 63119. 314.607.8401 Voice 314.962.07342 Fax *TJC@Earthlink.net*. Appreciation to Sue Ashwell, LCSW, Sharon Bonner, LCSW, Ellen Cowell, MA, Judith Chavers, LCSW, Andrea Clark, LCSW, Mario Dollschnieder, PhD, Barbara Kelly-O'Neil, LCSW, Tracy Kern, LCSW, Cynthia Kluzak, LCSW, Barbara Flory, LCSW, Jonna Mason, LCSW, Tom Lovinguth, PhD, Tom Weber, LCSW, Elizabeth Wilson, MA, and Andrew Zemcuznikov, MA all current or past leaders and workers with Saint Louis County Family Court's services to families, and especially to Joe Pfeffer, PhD, former court psychologist and patriot of the postmodern.

## INTRODUCTION

In a rural county, I once assessed a woman who murdered her husband. He kept a rifle next to his bed, the same rifle he used to brutalize her, the same rifle used to shoot up her mother's home, and the same rifle he showed the sheriff's deputy as he and the deputy drank beer after she had made a domestic abuse call in the early 1970s, her last call to the authorities. He had ruptured her colon with a kick, had tattooed his name near her genitalia, and had threatened her mother with rape if she tried to help.

She shot him because she knew she would never get another chance. He had her serve him dinner in bed while he watched TV. He would whistle down the hall for her to bring his food, whistle when to change the channel, and whistle when he wanted his tray taken away. This night, when he was done, he uncharacteristically turned away and fell asleep. She noticed the rifle, leveled it, and shot him in the head.

As she narrated her tragedy, I attempted empathy. I said, "It was so terrible the way he treated you. He treated you like you were his remote control for the TV . . . " She interrupted, saying, "Oh no, you're wrong, he whistled at me like a dog!"

At trial, her defense counsel had her plead guilty to the crime. I offered my analysis of how she felt that her only chance to break out of the concentration camp was to kill the commandant in his sleep. The prosecutor was not impressed. Why then could not we declare open season for wifely vigilantes? Were there not other ways she could have sought for help? It is the 1980s, not the 1880s, are there not women shelters everywhere and every other Sunday night movie and talk show about how women leave abusive relationships? She had me look at the pictures of the gruesome corpse. She said that ten bullets had done the damage. How could I testify with any professional integrity that this was anything other than cold-blooded murder?

I said that the many shots revealed years of rage. It was both defense and vengeance. However, in terms of risk, she had no other priors than two DWIs five and two years before. I said that alcohol is used by many battered women to dull their pain and escape their torment. I recommended probation, to include both regular counseling and attendance at a women's group for substance abuse.

The prosecutor snorted, "I don't know how you can say that. This woman has killed a man. How can you sit there and say that she is not a danger?" The prosecutor's face flushed a crimson flame.

I responded, feeling my own emotions rise, "I believe that she is no danger, except maybe to another man who might hurt her. Actually, to me she is depressed and is more at risk for hurting herself or developing a more serious drinking problem. I believe we owe it to her to help her heal from all she's been through. I think this will benefit not only her but all of us."

Now, the judge chimed in, "So, you're saying that you believe she is a reasonable risk for probation?" Judges rarely speak from the bench in this way.

I fumbled, "Yes, your honor. I think if she has a reasonable treatment program, she will do okay." The attorneys said there were no more questions. I left the courtroom crucible, glancing at the lady. We smiled at each other, and I drove home. Later, I heard that she was granted probation.

## FORENSIC PSYCHOLOGY AND FAMILY THERAPY, DECONSTRUCTED

The above vignette illustrates how therapists have become the "new informants" (Bollas & Sundelson, 1996) of our culture. We are asked to assist in the determination of guilt, punishment, employment, security clearance, child custody, termination of parental rights, and foster placement. Some therapists, especially collaborative, client-oriented clinicians, find this alliance all too painful and problematic. We are overwhelmed by heated adversarial disputes managed by grim specialists in rhetorical competition. We are frustrated with how our findings are twisted, and disgusted at miscarriages of justice. How can we claim to be collaborative when the very role given us is that of "expert witness?"

However, we deconstruct the adversarial nature of forensic work when we understand legal systems as languages (Goolishian and Anderson, 1987). Legal systems grow around a complaint, and imbricate complaint into investigation into allegation into mediation into litigation into judicial determination into the implementation of court orders. Power flows through persuasive narrations and, upon convincing guardians, judges, and juries, artificially constructs life altering realities such as child custody awards or prison time. Lyotard (1979), in a depiction of modern language systems, well describes a legal language system,

> It excludes in principle adherence to a metaphysical discourse; it requires the renunciation of fables; it demands clear minds and cold wills . . . it makes the "players" assume responsibility not only for the statements they propose, but also for the rules to which they submit those statements in order to render them acceptable. It brings the pragmatic functions of knowledge clearly to light . . . the pragmatics of argumentation, of the production of proof, of the transmission of learning, and of the apprenticeship of the imagination. (p. 62)

Lyotard's last phrase, "apprenticeship of the imagination" applies to therapists immersed in forensic work. When we imagine ourselves through the lens of the rhetorical moves of lawyers, we can and will be saturated with competitions over certainties. Every rhetorical move has illocutionary possibility. For example, a primary distinction is made in legal systems between narrative and evidence. All involved forcefully state their narratives and judges must rule on what narratives constitute evidence. Attorneys spend many hours comparing statements for consistencies, additions, or omissions, and they scour to find supporting documentation or multiple attestation from other witnesses for their preferred narratives. The presentation of evidence occurs in a theater styled ritual known as a hearing, where the judge hears the narratives and determines what actually constitutes "evidence." Each side presents their preferred narrative and to deconstruct their opponent's narrative. The ritual of transformation from narrative to evidence is the accomplishment of forensic power. Whomever the judge or jury believes gains not only the victory of a positive judgment but is also often able to write the details of the final judgment.

If we see courts as a kind of theater, we can perhaps work with more confidence. We can participate in the illocutionary process by accepting and respecting it, but not becoming too much of a co-competitor for truth and power. For example, I noticed how the prosecutor in the above story was becoming upset and emotional in her interview of me. I thought of her more as a sister of the deceased. This allowed me to speak with her about her concerns, the safety of the community. Weaving her concerns into my own narrative, I attempted to bridge the divide separating her from the accused woman. For a clear example of such cooperation, see Johnston and Roseby, (1997).

Such experiences have allowed me to see legal journeys as another kind of therapy. Judges become authority figures, lawyers become strong advocates, reports become therapeutic letters, and everyone is seen as trying to do their best with what they believe they know. Shamanic cultures have integrated both community building and personal healing into therapeutic rituals for many years (Keeney, 1994; Krippner, 2002). As Jerome Frank noted in his comparisons of psychotherapy, any context can be healing in which the interactors conspire together to persuade each other to accomplish personal insight, change, and social benefit (Frank & Frank, 1991).

## ACCOMPLISHING COLLABORATION IN MILIEUS OF ESCALATION

Harry Goolishian taught for many years the value of questions. He had an ability to adopt an intersubjective, "we both have valuable points of view," stance in therapy (Anderson, 1997; Goolishian & Anderson, 1987). Lawyers, judges, social workers and especially family members can welcome appreciative inquiry that respects each person and offers space for each view. As noted by McNamee and Gergen (1999) postmodern conversation can open up fresh possibilities,

> As relational inquiry takes place and each of the interlocutors takes on different voices and entertains alternative intelligibilities, so is their relationship

> subtly transformed . . . For example, to move from the position of authority to questioner, from the assured to the ambivalent, or from the angry to the sympathetic invites an alternate identity from the other. To become the questioner invites the other's authority; to be ambivalent opens the way for the other's ambivalence, and to replace anger with sympathy enables defensiveness to be replaced by goodwill. If effectively pursued, relationally responsible inquiry has transformative potential for the participants. (p. 27)

Furthering this kind of dialogue in incendiary assemblies demands firm commitments to collaborative principles. Most of these have been well and thoroughly articulated elsewhere (Friedman, 1995; Hubble, Duncan & Miller, 1999). From these traditions, I have articulated four specific intentionalities that inform my work with arduous disputes: transparency, multiplicity, commensality, and epiphany.

## TRANSPARENCY

First, when we embrace client views and understandings, even if those views are dangerous or distasteful, we encourage maximum transparency and mutual cooperation. Yet, the more we know of someone's tragic or possibly despicable actions, we may recoil in fear[2] and disgust. If we view everyone involved as a "heroic client" (Duncan & Miller, 2000), we may be able to sustain sincere and appreciative inquiry. It is important to not become alarmed, certain, or confused. Patient, steady, and slow inquiry should continue until clients, lawyers, and colleagues can be understood from their own perspectives. A Buddhist parable (Kornfield, 1993) may offer guidance:

> Develop a state of mind like the earth . . . For on the earth people throw clean and unclean things, dung and urine, spittle, pus, and blood, and the earth is not troubled or repelled or disgusted. And, as you grow like the earth no contacts with pleasant or unpleasant will lay hold of your mind and stick to it. (p. 26)

For example, when a psychiatric nurse was referred for sexually assaulting and mutilating three women, we spent four sessions studying a six inch case file. We read together every police report, every psychological examination, and I inquired in detail what he knew and thought about each item and how he understood his own situation. He explained how his mother had been a prostitute when he was a boy and how her patrons would, in his words, "Do her and then do me." The narrative was horrific, in the detail he could tell of his childhood, how it interested

[2] For example, in my work with families in custody disputes, $25,000 (US) to $50,000 in legal fees are common, and some families I have served have each spent more than $500,000 in legal fees over years of hearings and allegations.

him in psychiatric work, and how the feelings turned monstrous when he thought that wives or girlfriends had betrayed him. Over time, he began to soften and wonder if he had not become that which he hated. The benefit of such inquiry showed later when he called the police upon himself when tempted to be violent again with a new girlfriend.

Also, in legal systems, clients often need and demand to know in detail the therapist's own understandings and beliefs about the situation. Few therapists are prepared for such detailed requests for their own thoughts. For example, in a child custody[3] evaluation, I was collecting detailed information from a mother about her beliefs that her soon to be ex-husband was trying to take her children from her. She had been reported as overly volatile with the children, especially showering them with negative affect and ideas about Father. I said something like, "I understand this is hell on earth for you. But, it may be you have bonds with the children. What are you doing to keep good relations with the children despite whatever your husband is doing?"

She sat up calmly, and said, "You've been asking me all these questions, I think you must have some ideas. I'd really like to know what you think I can do. I think I'm fine and have been doing everything well. It's my husband that's the problem. Do you think I have a problem?"

We debated around a little bit, and then I put my clipboard on my desk and put my pen down. I said, "Well, what I really think is that you are very intelligent and that you love your children immensely. I hear them say they are disappointed in you because you express so freely so much anger at their father, but I think they still have the strongest of feelings for you. They wouldn't be so angry with you if they didn't care. I think you have a lot of potential, no matter what your husband does. I worry that you are so traumatized by what he's doing that it's like you're hypnotized into believing you have no power here when in reality you have a lot of options."

Theoretically, this is Gergen's (1994) concept of supplementation in social construction. The communal construction of meaning occurs as,

> Lone utterances begin to acquire meaning when an other or others coordinate themselves to the utterance, that is, when they add some form of supplementary action . . . The supplement may be as simple as an affirmation ("yes," "right) . . . Or it may extend the utterance in some way . . . We thus find that an individual can never "mean"; an other is required to supplement the action and give it function within the relationship. (p. 264–265)

We should be free to have these more natural, less pathologizing conversations with family members, attorneys, and court social workers (Kovarsky, Duchan & Maxwell, 1999). Some guidelines:

[3]Judith Chavers, Barbara Flory, Jonna Mason, Joe Pfeffer, and I formed the usual core of this team.

- When asked for diagnoses, all responses should be technically accurate within current DSM systems, and all pathologizing should be balanced with contextualization of the apparent "disorder" and be further balanced by as detailed a description of competencies as of weaknesses or problems.
- When beginning a consultation, let everyone know that you will have a goal of "no surprises." You will keep everyone informed of important information. If you have a strong concern about someone, they will hear about it from you.
- Care should be taken to avoid using or encouraging negating terms like "denial," "personality disorder," or "addict." Offer language such as paralleling the above, "private personal reality," "stuck pattern or bad habit," and "struggling with addiction," which acknowledges a problem without predicting or totalizing a finality that precludes possibility of change (Anderson, 1997).
- Caution should be taken to avoid a perception of strong advocacy for a particular person or "side" in a dispute. However, advocacy of general principles of safety and respect are needed. This distinction may be subtle, but it is important, such as saying, "I'm sensing that both parents agree that the violent stepfather needs to leave Mother's home for the time being. However, Mother seems to find it difficult to agree to this openly. Maybe we can help her by making it a court order so that she can inform him that it was not her decision alone, nor was it her ex-husband's alone." This should not be strategic or paradoxical. When we really believe that someone's best interests can be served by relieving them of responsibilities they can not, without undue shame, lay down themselves, our imagination of their reduced-stress future can be appreciated and implemented.
- The ethical responsibility of the above point must be emphasized. I am not saying that we "help" clients with "diminished capacity." I am suggesting that we offer the option of a face saving exit from a previously strongly held position. For example, once I suggested an alternate religious perspective to a father whose "Christianity" to his son included both loving hugs and shoves into walls, both homework help and retrieval from the trash of a half eaten banana, then shoved into his son's mouth. I suggested he consider himself a missionary to his son and offer standard compassionate evangelizing practices such as comforting, nurturing, and encouragement. I said clearly that I would recommend to the court that he only use positive and warm religious methods of communication with his son. He left, sadly, the consulting room with scathing words and voluntarily dropped his custody suit. He said, "I have never, ever been so insulted in my entire life. I will do with my son what I will. He may never return to me, but I will stay the same." In fact, he continued to see his son at family gatherings. The son came in later and spoke proudly how he liked seeing his dad now and would debate him about religion over fried chicken.

- Clarity in findings and recommendations is needed. Most assessments have 98% of their material on problem description, and a few general sentences of recommendations. I am finding that if I work to be clear on my recommendations, that then my reports are about 50% discussions of fresh ideas, possible plans, and helpful suggestions, often suggested by clients themselves. And, I leave room for further questions and invite reflections and modifications. I frequently say, "These are my best thoughts for now. We'll probably both want to change them later when we know more."

## MULTIPLICITY

In legal systems, the accomplishment of transparency leads quickly to the storms of multiplicity. The reality marketplace of legal systems calls forth an escalating differentiation of memories, observations, and preferences. Clients attempt to persuade their attorneys of the accuracy of their claims, lawyers advocate for their understandings of client wishes, extended family members and friends all offer variations, professional helpers such as physicians, ministers, and counselors weigh in, court appointed expert witnesses offer supposedly objective contributions, and judges have the privilege of agreeing with whomever they find persuasive or inserting their own interpretations.

And, most participants find that they change their truths quickly as opponents develop creative responses to any assertion. The goal is to maintain ascendancy of persuasion, and narrations are modified or cast aside as needed in the quest. The high cost of legal controversies is often due to the need for ongoing expertise in this reality management. As one veteran observer said, "Anyone who likes the law or sausages should never watch either one being made." In his analysis of modern efforts at "finding the truth," Bauman (1993), states,

> It was a characteristic, a defining feature of modernity that the aporia [a contradiction that can not be overcome] was played down as a conflict not-yet-resolved-but-in-principle-resolvable; as a temporary nuisance, a residual imperfection on the road to perfection, a relic of unreason soon to be rectified, a sign of not-yet-fully-overcome ignorance of the "best fit" between individual and common interests. One more effort, one more feat of reason, and the harmony would be reached—never to be lost again. (p. 8)

Most attorneys and legal professionals would recoil at being characterized in such cynical terms. Most in my experience understand that there is no actual truth, no absolute best to achieve. But, most have fairly "thick skins" for the process of multiple reality competition. Most clients find the process excruciating, and even the best therapists can be overwhelmed with faced with two, or as many as five or six, hotly contested variations of absolute certainty. The forensic search for an end to multiplicity can be shattering. For example, a six year old child having been medically examined to end debate over whether she had been sexually abused said, "I hated the talkative chair, they strapped me down and spread my legs apart. It hurt. I screamed for mommy, but they wouldn't let her come."

And so, most participants in the controversy appreciate the presence of a caring, listening resource, assisting each party to receive some benefit from the encounter (Cobb, 1993). Parents are so used to being interrupted and interrogated that their relief is palpable. Lawyers warm to the chance to talk with someone who is interested in hearing their thoughts. Social workers value the opportunity to be taken seriously. Judges especially welcome those who cast their voice as broadly informed by all competitors. One boy, who had endured multiple hospitalizations and was taking five separate medications, said in a family interview with his divorcing parents, "Shake hands." They did, and he flushed red, shivered, relaxed, and smiled. Respectful multiplicity in action can lead to profound moments of peacefulness amid the storm.

However, when we offer empathy and understanding to each person to whom we meet in the process, they can, understandably, come to believe that we are "on their side" in their dispute. I have often been challenged, "I can't trust you. My lawyer said that you sounded sympathetic to the other side." After I have checked out if there is some specific concern, I try to say, "It's my job to listen to everyone. If I have a serious concern about you, I will let you know. If and when I need to make a strong opinion or recommendation, I will tell you personally. I promised no surprises. I have to try to work with everybody."

And then there is the challenge of conjoint interviewing and courtroom testimony. The shift of the position of the therapist in the legal system from therapist as asker of questions to provider of answers is mirrored by shift in conversational format from personal, individual interviews and phone calls to more conjoint and public encounters of therapist and system participants. Initial interviews and family meetings often expand into consults with attorneys, schools, and physicians. And, extensive networking grows into report writing, depositions, courtroom testimony, and at times, further individual and conjoint family therapies after legal proceedings.

And, there are numerous safety and comfort issues involved. For example, battered women should not be placed in compromising situations where they are expected to join in a conversation with an abuser who can intimidate by sheer personal presence. Divorcing spouses can rarely have productive conversations with both in the same room at the same time. Siblings may be in custody in different placements. Many parents are allowed visits with children only with a supervisor, and a court appointed social worker or relative may have to be included in interviews. Some family members may be in hospitals recovering from wounds and others may be incarcerated. Certain cases demand that clients do not talk with each other so as not to "taint" testimony.

I have found it helpful to build toward more conjoint and public interactions with legal systems through a step-by-step process where therapy and assessment format matches the level of conversational comfort and desire:

- Initial interviews are often best accomplished individually. Each person then has a free opportunity to express themselves without fear and without intimidating others. During these meetings, plans can be made for beginning to connect each person's story. We have used letters, videos, and speakerphones to help slow the interaction process enough to avoid emotional escalations and quick judgments about another's views. For me the goal is to assist each person in, slowly and carefully, answering the questions and needs of other family members and legal professionals. The cross-connecting builds slowly, with frequent checks and invitations for reflection.
- A critical step in the process occurs when the therapist is asked by some participants about the other participants. For example, I often talk with the attorney guardian of a child after conversation with the child and each parent. I try to inform, delicately and cautiously, the guardian of the views of each person. I usually offer general comments on broadly therapeutic themes. I am reluctant to provide exact details. Each parent is very curious what the other says and everyone wants to know what children have to say. They often say, "I can't have anyone find out what I really think!" The best paradigm is to offer reassurance when possible and clear information on differences when necessary. I try to say, "I am working with the other party to help them answer you. What would you like them to reflect upon?"
- And, I have shared notes, children's drawings, video or audio recordings, charts, custody calendars, etc. produced in individual sessions with other participants in other sessions. For example, asking a father what he thinks of a picture drawn of him by a child in another session can help build cross-understandings. I have made digital pictures of people and events in sessions to share with others that have been helpful, e.g. children's drawings on a marker board. And, having families draw their own custody calendars has often been useful.
- None of my tapings are ever available for court subpoena as all are erased or can be erased upon any hint of interest by an attorney. And, my case notes are written very generally so that little if any information is available in a raw form for attorney inspection. When asked to make statements in conjoint settings, I need the freedom to improvise what needs to be said at that time, and base my perceptions and opinions on the sum total of my interactions with all participants. Many attorneys dispute this stance, since they are trained to undermine any legal participants' position by finding counter examples to current statements in past events and statements. I

respect attorneys' tasks in this area, but I compensate them for a lack of raw data with in-depth reports and depositions and testimony as needed.
- I often encourage use of email (letting clients know that this is or will be a public document). Clients in serious disputes often can use the more plain text communication of email to provide each other with information and options. We sometimes will email directly from sessions.
- And, I sometimes will have some members of a family have an appointment then depart for part of a day to have some interaction with each other and then have some or all the family or service providers convene again later to discuss the events and hopefully progress of the day.
- In written reports I make a point to discuss each family members' own views of themselves and to chart how their all too sincere perspectives lead to conflict. Every family member also has notes on strengths and areas for further development. I also note any degree of convergence, any unity, and suggest that there may be building blocks of solutions and conversations for the future.

The above formatting alternatives are helpful, but sometimes not sufficient to address forceful multiplicities. I have found reflecting team (Friedman, 1995) formats most useful in addressing potentially damaging, unsafe, and volatile legal and client systems. Reflecting teams are the best response to multiplicity dilemmas because team members can illustrate subtly how difference can be non-threatening, and even occasionally helpful.

For example, several family therapists and psychologists formed a team at the Saint Louis County Family Court in the mid-1990's. We assisted each other, offering reflecting teamwork with families who were in serious distress. We saw twenty six families, some for more than one reflecting session, and about seventy percent of the people reported that the addition of reflection to their ordinary therapy was helpful. As Joe Pfeffer, a court psychologist and team member said, "A good reflecting team session is worth about four or five individual sessions." What we learned from our successes, and even more from our failures, is distilled below:

- It is essential to craft an invitation to team reflection that distinguishes the process from usual and typical group staff meetings, mediations, hearings, and investigation. Reflection is an opportunity for understanding, not planning, deciding, or judging.
- And, it is important for legal systems to understand that reflectors, therapists brought in for one or two sessions, are not to be subpoenaed or forced to make statements in writing. Only the primary therapist should have those responsibilities. Also, attorneys should be informed that tapes will not be available for subpoena. We made it clear we erased or would erase all tapes.
- Reflection can include many members of legal systems: attorneys, social

workers, extended kin, and extended family members. We are careful about safety and respect in all invitations. Our largest crew was 18 and smallest was two. More time needs to be allotted for larger groups.

- Reflections most often were staged as "living room conversations" where all therapists and clients were all together in the same room at the same time. And, while it is helpful for reflectors to most often talk with each other and the primary therapist, the openness of the conversation allows any clients to talk with any therapist. As long as the therapists avoid becoming entangled into an "interview" or what we called a private debate with one client, the whole room conversation usually moves smoothly.
- Behind the mirror efforts can best be used for safety and respect concerns. Clients who have been violent can sit behind the mirror with a therapist and absorb the talk of the person they hurt. Also, behind the mirror organization is useful for children to observe parents attempting to listen to each other's ideas about parenting, for step-parents to observe their spouses trying to hold a civil conversation, and for social workers to observe efforts at mutual understanding.
- All formats noted above, speaker phone, tapes, notes, letters, etc. can be folded into reflections. Families can watch or make tapes. Emails can be co-authored.
- And, reflection offers opportunities to have "breakout" sessions with one or more family members. Sometimes, a family member can be overwhelmed and will leave the room. Having a therapist to talk with briefly can help the person re-engage or be more prepared for their own personal consultations later.
- As a team, it is important to review tapes of your work and to find ways to make each other a little uncomfortable. This may sound counter-intuitive, but the ability to share difficult, emotionally laden experiences and ideas with each other is a hallmark of the work. We also often ask families what they think, and children are frequently invited to grade us. One child said of me, "Tom only gets a C-because he keeps twisting my words." The team had a field day with that.

## COMMENSALITY

The immersion into multiplicity becomes the ethical foundation, the information saturation necessary to the task of commensality, the collection of mutual actions taken by all parties for, hopefully, the benefit of all. Commensality derives from ecological studies, economics, and the anthropology of human communal eating (Hirschman, 1998). It denotes the state of relations when all somehow benefit from the interactions of all parties to the relations. Therapists encourage commensality though actions which simultaneously benefit clients, agents of authority, and themselves. By refusing to think of ways to benefit one client over another, to prefer one social authority over another, or to elevate our welfare over another, we place ethical boundaries on ourselves which encourage the kinds of actions which result in practical safety, motivate client self-interest in change, and dissolve negative interactional escalations.

A menagerie of disparate examples may illuminate commensality:

- [Initial interview with a man who seriously threatened his wife.]
"I understand how angry you can be thinking she is having an affair. I know the last counselor said he didn't care if she fucked the whole football team. I just know that there's got to be a better way to deal with this than killing her. What can you do other than murdering the mother of your children?" [He eventually voluntarily signed away his rights to see his children saying he just could not take the stress of seeing her in the future.]
- [After an hour initial interview with a couple where the abusive husband explained how he thought it was okay to use drugs and see other women.] Anne said, "I thought these were his problems. All this time I've been trying to help him." I said, "He isn't talking about problems. He's describing his lifestyle. It sounds like the way he really wants to live." John said, "Right." [Later, Anne stopped him in the parking lot and said, "Did you really mean all the crap you said?" He said yes. They divorced without further violence.]
- [In a custody hearing where each attorney showed me an email.]
Yes, sir. I see both emails from father. One is threatening, and the other is an effort at collaboration. I believe that they represent sides or temptations of father's thought. He is both angry beyond all measure and hopeful that he and Ellen can work together for their son. No, this is not inconsistent. Most of us have countervailing impulses. Yes, the emails from Ellen indicate that she has conflicting inclinations as well. The time has come for collaboration based upon their more positive hopeful confidences.
[Both accepted the judge's ruling and have continued therapy.]
- [In a hallway outside a courtroom, a lawyer threatened to report me for malpractice if I testified in a case. He said mediators could not testify. He showed me a letter I had written and he had highlighted the phrase, "I attempted to help mediate a dispute . . . "]

  "I know you are trying to help your client. I have some good things to say about both him and his ex-wife. I also have some firm suggestions. If you are going to use a technicality to keep me off the stand because I used the word "mediate" in a letter about my help to them, that is wrong. I am going in there to testify. My brother is an attorney and you can call him."

  [I was scared, but determined. The judge was impressed with my "no nonsense" testimony and assigned me to work with the family for a longer period. I went to the lawyer who accosted me, and shook his hand, promising to work with him in the future. He smiled back.]

In addition to "happy endings," what I have found especially interesting in this work is that many relationships, both family and therapeutic, have ended, often not a happy goal for a family therapist. But, safety has been the highest value, and if a client's epiphany is to separate permanently from a context of their own unhappiness, then the greater good has been served. With enough pre-conversations, with the slow accumulation of informing points of view, with carefully nurtured affirmations of all, and with an apparent devotion to the common good, sometimes commensality is not sneered away, but grasped in a dance of the future, even if the dance is sad and slow.

## EPIPHANY

With the achievement of transparency, the management of multiplicity, and the establishment of commensality, the ground is prepared for the kinds of therapeutic epiphanies that we love to celebrate. Epiphanies are perhaps most clearly seen in the ecstatic rituals of shamanic practices around the world (Frank & Frank, 1991; Keeney, 1994). In highly charged legal systems, freedom from the terror of adversarial competition is as exhilarating as an all night healing dance.

For example, after a long court testimony over child custody, a father came to me and said, "That was like a half-day therapy session. I never really realized why you did what you did. My lawyer said you just did things your own way and to give you time. I now appreciate why you took so long to do certain things, why you wanted us to talk with each other only after we emailed. I think I can do this now. I've never felt like this, I actually think we can do this. I appreciated the compliment, even more the epiphany of the client. And decisions to end relationships also are epiphanies, even if they are tragically sad. Several clients who decided to leave spouses, children, careers, and lives have said, "This was completely crap. You all are idiots. I'm going to get on with my life and quit wasting my time. The slow process allowed a tragic, but fairly final exit for them.

As e. e. cummings wrote, "Always the more beautiful answer that asks the next difficult question." Legal work poses questions with few answers. As one young lady, fifteen years old, who had suffered brutal sexual assault at the hands of a step-father who also brutalized her mother and dealt internationally in cocaine, said at the end of our consultations, "What happened to me was horrible and I'll never forget it, but now its only like one percent of my whole life."

*Tom Strong: Tom, what I most like about your work is its inclusive and integrative features, in a relational ecology that engages all who seem relevant to each other in terms of problems and solutions. It dovetails some of the work I've seen in bringing postmodern ideas to such areas as restorative justice and 'program evaluation'. That said, there is a huge public sentiment that sees these issues, especially criminal ones, as unresolvable and that the answers should be punishment or worse. What do you say to those who have experienced grievous harm or loss about the kinds of processes you might ask them to join?*

*Tom Conran: I hope that my work serves the community by helping dangerous individuals become less of a threat. Most criminal offenders are released from prison more socialized into violent thought and relations. Most mothers who have their children taken away become pregnant again. Formerly battered women largely re-marry. Many who receive adverse findings in divorce cases re-file new motions within a year or two. Harsh attitudes and punishment only serve to reinforce an epistemology of "dominate where you can and submit when you must." The crime and punishment system is all too tautological. Family therapists learned long ago that the "revolving door" of mental hospitals needed to be unhinged, perhaps we can learn to do the same with legal systems. Invitations to self-protection and collaboration may often go unheeded, and many individuals must be imprisoned or sanctioned. Yet, for those who are willing to hear and respond, shall we not provide a path toward safety where they make the safety of others their own wish and concern? For example, the Coordinated Community Response system for domestic violence intervention in Duluth, Minn, incorporates legal, medical, social work, and therapeutic interventions into a collaborative effort, with much less recidivism.*

*TS: Tom, some might see what you're describing as uneconomic, and inexpedient. In other words, a tough sell, if practitioners here wanted to emulate your work. What can you say to those who might feel inspired by these ideas, and want to develop such processes in the contexts of their work?*

*TC: The economics are indeed difficult. For divorce and defense services, clients often spend large sums on legal fees, and counseling or assessment fees are a small part of their overall expense. Other kinds of services often receive grants and community funding, such as child abuse interventions funded by state authorities. The key is training and trust. Obtaining extensive experience and slowly building relations with attorneys allows the freedom to charge reasonable fees. Apprenticeship is probably the best method of entry, or involvement in an existing grant program.*

*TS: I am curious about the implications of your work for professional codes of practice for psychologists, psychiatrists, psychiatric nurses, social workers, and family therapists? It seems your work brings us to a new ethical frontier when it comes to collegial practice.*

*TC: The possible good to be achieved is significant enough to encourage us to achieve truly professional collaboration. I believe that transparency is best evoked with full informed consent. Once all involved know that all involved will be sharing information that potentially could be shared with others, a chain of decision making about how to respectfully achieve openness unfolds which challenges the secrecy, triangles, and gossiping which is pandemic and deadly in these systems. Traditional confidentiality has often been used in forensic systems to protect the interests of individual professionals rather than to advance the good of the client system. The key is a careful, slow, deliberate fashioning of ethical consent. The hunt for "evidence" often skews and distorts clinical information and clients can be offered the opportunity to break free of the excruciating process by becoming part of a mutual exploration of each other's views and beliefs. Openness does not have to focus on embarrassing details and dirty secrets. It can, if we wish, focus on visions of the future and beliefs about solutions and possibilities. Because people in legal systems are so focused on preventing access to potentially damaging information, they often lose any chance to learn potentially helpful information. If an ethical stance is taken that client welfare can be best promoted by cautious transparency, especially in regard to belief systems and future goals, then the murky waters of ethical dilemmas can be avoided.*

*Bradford Keeney: I applaud Tom Conran's noble quest to ambiguate the social construction of so-called "evidence" in the heated disputes of courtroom drama. Implicitly and wisely respecting the constitution of narrative as loosely knit fragments of communication that may shift with each telling, Conran avoids the lazy moral dualism (and low ethical ground) that demands a false choice between therapist and legal respondent. He knows he's in the territory of the shaman: an undercover coyote trickster dancing with the somewhat arbitrarily drawn, fear-ridden and anger-laden dualities of victim-perpetrator, right-wrong, justice-injustice, that are too mindlessly cast by the self-righteous (and profit-making) industry of litigation.*

*To enter into this arena of complexity, suffering, and madness with the intent of breaking forth any kind of liberating moment that releases the bondage of adversarial competition is, in my opinion, a spiritual calling. The way Conran practices forensic therapy gives us new reason for hope.*

*Whirling inside the winds of ambiguity, he shows us how to evoke transparency, multiplicity, and commensality. When the rhetorical storm clouds are calmed, epiphanies and grace are born out of authentic suffering, giving light to all involved. I am moved by Conran's dedication to reminding us that the oldest lessons of reconciliation and healing can be re-learned in the midst of our contemporary muddles of courtroom intimidation and terror.*

## REFERENCES

Anderson, H. (1997). *Conversation, language, and possibilities: A postmodern approach to therapy*. New York: BasicBooks.

Bateson, M.C. (1994). *Peripheral visions*. New York: Perennial.

Bauman, Z. (1993). *Postmodern ethics*. Oxford, UK: Blackwell Publishers.

Bollas, C. & Sundelson, D. (1996). *The new informants: The betrayal of confidentiality in psychoanalysis and psychotherapy*. New York: Jason Aronson.

Cobb, S. (1993). Empowerment and mediation: A narrative perspective. *Negotiation Journal*, *9*(3) 245–255.

Duncan, B.L. & Miller, S.D. (2000). *The heroic client: Doing client-directed, outcome-informed therapy*. San Francisco CA: Jossey-Bass.

Frank, J.D. & Frank, J.B. (1991). *Persuasion and healing: A comparative study of psychotherapy* (3rd Ed.). Baltimore MD: Johns Hopkins University Press.

Friedman, S. (Ed.), *The reflecting team in action: Collaborative practice in family therapy*. New York: Guilford Press.

Gergen, K. (1994). *Realities and relationships: Soundings in social constructionism*. Cambridge, MA: Harvard University Press.

Goolishian, H. & Anderson, H. (1987). Language systems and therapy: An evolving idea. *Psychotherapy 24(3S)*, 529–538.

Hirschman, A.O. (1998). *Crossing Boundaries*. New York: Zone Books.

Hubble, M.A., Duncan, B.L., & Miller, S.D. (1999). *The heart and soul of change: What works in therapy*. Washington: American Psychological Association.

Johnston, J.R. & Roseby, V. (1997). *In the name of the child: A developmental approach to understanding and helping children of conflicted and violent divorce*. New York: Free Press.

Keeney, B. (1994). *Shaking out the spirits: A psychotherapist's entry into the healing mysteries of global shamanism*. Barrytown, NY: Station Hill Press.

Kornfield, J. (1993). *Teachings of the Buddha*. Boston, MA: Shambhala.

Kovarsky, D., Duchan, J. & Maxwell, M. (1999). *Constructing (in)competence: Disabling evaluations in clinical and social interaction*. Mahwah, NJ: Lawrence Erlbaum Associates.

Krippner, S. (2002). Conflicting perspectives on shamans and shamanism: Points and counterpoints. *American Psychologist 57(11)*, 962–977.

Lyotard, J. (1984). *The postmodern condition: A report on knowledge*. Minneapolis, MN: University of Minnesota.

McNamee, S. & Gergen, K. (1999). *Relational responsibility: Resources for sustainable dialogue*. Thousand Oaks, CA: Sage Publications.

*Chapter* **12**

# *Mesmerizing Violent Offenders with a Slice of Life*

## Drama and Reflexivity in the Treatment of Men who Abuse their Spouses

BILL HANEC WITH CONVERSATIONAL PARTNER DON BAKER

Many men who are referred to treatment programs because of their abusive behaviour towards marital partners are resistant to this therapeutic experience as a result of authoritarian attempts to get them to explore their problems. When it comes to family violence, it could be argued the community is the client, and public awareness campaigns have made violence against women and children a taboo. Unfortunately, regardless of how well the community has attempted to raise public consciousness with respect to violence, men usually enter treatment fearful, which creates fear and promotes an escape from responsibility. When these men are mandated to seek counselling through the courts or given an ultimatum by their partners, they experience a wide range of emotions, including shame and blame. In this context, the use of face-saving explanations of behavior is a typical response.

Within the therapeutic forum, therapists brace themselves for frustration and it is all too easy to condemn the men speaking defensively as "unworkable". This chapter was written to describe one approach to engage men who are who are confused over the consequences of their abusive behaviour. The work described here is founded on a collaborative working relationship between clients and therapists. It involves the use of drama therapy techniques to generate and examine a "slice of life", and to invite clients to examine their choices for action based on the dilemmas role-played before their eyes.

There are many dedicated clinicians working to resolve the serious problem of spouse abuse. Their creativity has led to different and varied tactics to influence clients. Models of group intervention target specific participants, with varying degrees of stringency, based upon the content of the model and the perceived capacity of potential participants to fit the model's criteria. A question frequently asked is "Is there a good fit between client and program?" The answer frequently involves an assessment of clients' cognitive or emotional capacities as they relate to structured tasks built into the program curriculum. I have named this an "attitude of exclusivity" because it excludes many potential participants based on a perceived mismatch with the program. In our work, we[1] have opted for an "attitude of inclusivity", on the premise that we as clinicians are not "expert" enough to know which men would benefit from participation in our program to stop violent behavior.

The stance we deliberately choose is one of humility and respect. We find that group members know more about their circumstances than we do, and that they have the ability to be strikingly inventive in devising strategies to combat violence. We listen and incorporate their ideas about non-violence and use these to co-construct interventions with the men which will bring about better consequences in their relationships through the practice of respectful behaviors. This gives the men a sense of ownership of the therapeutic process. It also creates a discursive context that helps to foreground or construct non-violent identities, and to promote respect over the use of force. We've discovered that many men develop an interest in the program curriculum as they became engaged in a collaborative relationship with the clinicians running the group. Many men who are initially resistive eventually want to be included in group participation because they can see certain benefits for themselves and their families in the non-violent behaviours and values which emerge by the group. For us, an inclusive stance is more than a means of accommodating large numbers of participants; it's an attitude that helps us embrace men who are initially disinterested and hostile towards receiving any form of help.

## THE DISCURSIVE CONTEXT OF VIOLENCE

The men who come into treatment have typically been indoctrinated with ideas about the use of force in the resolution of differences. This is the discursive context they are most familiar with and it guides their decisions around conflict. In many of their families of origin, alcohol abuse and violence were common. Many of the men I have worked with saw their fathers dislocate from their partners in times of conflict. If there was an argument, the exercise was to eradicate the threat by winning the debate or overpowering the opponent. As a result of this

[1] Throughout this chapter, the pronoun "we" refers to our male/female therapy team which facilitates our groups. The makeup of these teams varies from group to group.

behaviour, many of the men walking through our doors have a great deal of difficulty with empathy and often tell stories of victimization with respect to their partners' behaviour. Their accounts of their lives and their actions are lacking a sense of personal agency which might portray them as dealing with conflict in a deliberately respectful manner. The discourses that dominate tend to focus on retribution and punishment, rather than justice and reconciliation. Empathy is hard to identify in these stories: understanding seems to be a one-way street, with the perpetrator needing assurance and the victim being pressured to provide understanding and compliance, albeit with covert resentment and fear which can rebound into hostility. There's a sense of loneliness with many of the men; their difficulties accepting responsibility for their actions isolate them from those around them. As a clinical team, our task is to support these men in a healing relationship without colluding with their discussions of retaliation. In this respect, we seek to invite them into a new kind of conversation, to perform new discourses associated with respect and compassion.

## Drama Therapy, Narrative, and Collaboration

The performance of discourse is something we most often do unthinkingly. For the men in our groups, most of their abusive or violent actions are not meditated upon—they are experienced as expressions of the usual practice of daily life. I believe the value of drama therapy in a group setting lies in helping to dislodge participants from these automatic views and the behaviours associated with them, to adopt a reflexive position and to look back on past actions from a detached perspective. Our therapy team's task is to bring key scenes of conflict into the room, and to create the opportunity for the men to think and act differently in response to them. This change in thinking and acting is more than a momentary behaviour shift; we view it as the beginning of the construction of new identities associated with fairness in relationships.

Our part in that construction process is to highlight the men's competence in relation to issues of power, control and violence. This is a co-authorship process (White, 1989) in which we contribute our views, as evidenced by my use of the word "competence". I do not believe a therapist can escape bias no matter how much we may talk about neutrality. Nevertheless, this process is not directive. Despite our preference for certain strategies of dealing with conflict, we recognize that the ultimate choice about how to act rests with the men themselves. It is our hope that we can support them in developing ways of dealing more effectively with conflict, and thus avoid the possibility of re-arrest and more criminal convictions.

Our intention in re-creating dramatic scenarios within the room is to move beyond mere discussion of issues to the actual performance of alternative responses to conflict situations. The drama provides an opportunity to explore through the use of imagination, and to try out alternate ways of interacting which may bring about consequences that these men would prefer in their lives. The men we work with act out their ideas of hetero-social relationships not only in their interactions with their partners, but with the female co-therapist in our group. It is not uncommon for group participants to indicate that my "abuse" of the female co-therapist/actor is justified; they engage in a great deal of blaming the victim. At first, this was a shock to the therapy team as we were surprised that the men could not see how my behaviour towards my "partner" was abusive and violent. We have come to realize that for the men, their response to these actions of verbal or physical abuse fits with both the meanings they attribute to these scenes in life and to the feelings attached to those meanings. In other words, actions which the therapy team identifies as inappropriate or incompetent, coming from a discourse of mutuality and respect in relationships, may make complete sense when nested in contrasting discourses.

Group participants use words to describe embodied, feeling states that fit with their perceptions of situations. A partner "attacks them", they get "ballistic", they "give it back". The choices for action the men make in response to their feelings are coherent within their discursive framing of events, but have consequences that are not in line with the men's stated preferences. By highlighting the negative consequences in a non-judgemental way, we create an opening for exploring the beliefs which promote those consequences, many of which have been handed down, so to speak, from their families of origin.

Moving beyond drama therapy, psychodrama, socio-drama and theatrical improvisation, it is my opinion that narrative and social constructionist therapies contribute a critique of expert knowledge and an emphasis on collaboration which open up promising new possibilities for change with clients not initially motivated for therapeutic engagement. Perhaps the idea of drawing in "expertise" to "treat" a client makes sense when the client is actively seeking input. However, perpetrators of abuse are not initially in the role of a consumer when they come into our clinic. They are not seeking help for their relationships, nor is it apparent to them that their choices in dealing with conflict may not be conducive to their relationship goals. We draw on narrative ideas (White and Epston, 1990) to adopt a collaborative stance, using Socratic questions to help clients explore their meaning-making around violence and conflict. A large part of this exploration occurs as therapists and participants comment on the dramatic scene played out between the therapist-actors. Clients hear about the beliefs of the characters involved in the scene, and view various versions of conflict escalation and resolution. Assumptions are queried as the process is deconstructed (White, 1991), inviting the participants into new ways of performing relationship in conflictual situations.

*Don Baker: I really like the dynamic quality of what you're doing Bill. I'm wondering if you see this approach as mainly action or behavior oriented? In addition to focusing on what the men do, I find it important to join with them in examining where their beliefs come from—to look at how their various contexts (cultural, socioeconomic, gender etc.) have impacted on their experience of power and their use of power. This gives me a chance to validate their views but also to question them.*

*Bill Hanec: In this approach "action" is given the task of stimulating discussion. It isn't the case where action serves the exclusive purpose of role modeling. Action's sole aim is to capture the attention of the group participants. Action gives texture to the dialogue of ideas around abuse and how to perform respective behavior. It is our position that the action which someone performs springs from affect which is grounded in belief. Throughout the acted scenes there are numerous pauses which occur as the therapy team recedes into their seats to carry on a discussion with participants on their beliefs with respect to specific practices of relating in human relationships. Some of these practices reflect what we describe as respectful interacting and other practices reflect what the community sees as violence. Our discussions do take the form of historical assessments as the participants explore the evolution of sex roles as they were taught by men in their lives as well as the community at large. One handout from Kivel's book, Men's Work (1991), we have used in the past is called The Man Box (p. 25). It is a diagram where participants can put all their ideas of what it means to be a man. This also a metaphor useful to exploring ideas as to what it means to be a woman. Structured exercises such as this allows participants to explore how their ideas lead to feelings and how this combination of belief and affect has resulted in action which has led to different consequences. One of the linguistic tools we have employed is the phrase, "psyching yourself up" for violence as opposed to "calming yourself down" in terms of dissipating anger arousal. These terms seem to describe a chain of ideas about belief, affect and choice concerning action which is designed to affect one's relationship with others. In this way we use language tools to form cues for behavior only after we have explored the cognitive processes associated with that specific behavioral practice.*

## IN THE DIRECTOR'S CHAIR: THE IMMEDIACY OF IMPROVISED SCENARIOS

The men who come to our group are weighed down by their own ideas about their situations, and indeed their lives. Many have been directed to our program through probation officers who are enforcing a court order which mandates counselling. It is not uncommon to have 15 to 20 men there on opening night feeling once again that they will be told how to run their lives. Unfortunately, this defensive posture restrains the men in accepting new ideas. It's a challenge to promote trust and stimulate engagement in this climate of fear. The improvisatory nature of our enacted scenarios helps us in this respect: it prompts the men to sit up and pay attention, to become curious about what's going on in the room. "What's happening here? Here is our therapist handcuffing himself while his co-therapist—or is it his "wife"—yells at him that he will never see the kids again?".

Daniel Wiener (1994) believes that theatrical improvisation has the ability to free clients from the constraints of social reality and allows them to explore alternative realities. It is a way of using play to discover something new. Weiner suggests this form of engagement bypasses our habitual tendency to avoid danger and censor anxiety-provoking situations. The drama unfolds without introduction, and without formal invitation to watch. It happens in a non-linear fashion; a postmodern pastiche of imagination which juxtaposes itself against the lives of group members. The therapy team constructs a composite based on the men's accounts of their own acts of violence. It is as if their own memories are movie projectors and those enacting the scenarios are film actors portraying their lives.

These improvised scenarios last only as long as needed. When the men become engaged in discussions about their restraining ideas and possibilities of new ideas/practices around the practice of non-violence, the therapy team sits. Once the co-construction of new realities is underway, the characters fade away in mid-scene to their chairs and contribute to the conversation. Men in the group may stimulate a new scene by wondering what a specific course of action would look like in the flesh and blood. Below is an example of a typical sequence, represented in script format.

Therapist in Role of Abuser
(voice rising with anger)
*So I've been working all f—day and I come home and there she is on the couch, watching TV, while the house is a complete mess.*

Therapist out of Role talking to Group
*What should I do now?*

Therapist in Role of Abuser
*So I say to the bitch, "you never should have taken that job at the lawyer's office! Your place is here to look after me and the kids!"*

Therapist out of Role Talking to Group
*Is this the right approach? Do you think I'll have a warm response? How do you think she's feeling?*

Therapist in Role of Abuser
*I'm the one who earns the salary and pays the bills; you're the one who agreed to stay home. Going to work just proves you aren't responsible and besides, before you know it you'll be sleeping with one of those lawyers.*

Therapist out of Role Talking to Group
*Do you think she'll do what I want? Will she be content in the role I've given her; the jobs she has to do?*

Female Therapist in Role of Wife
(hurt and upset voice)
*I can't stay in this house all the time. I need a life too! How come you never let me go out and you stay home with the kids?*

Therapist in Role of Abuser
*You just want to go out to find another guy. You always want everything . I married a spoiled bitch.*

Therapist out of Role talking to Group
*Do you guys have any ideas about how I could act differently? There she is crying and I'm feeling like crap.*

Various Spontaneous Responses from the Men
*"You have no right to tell her what to do." "You're a jerk, you don't care about her feelings." "She'll probably leave you for a lawyer then he'll help her take you for everything you've got."*

Typically, vignettes like this elicit a range of suggestions, some earnest, and some facetious. While some are unconstructive, they contribute to an imaginative and playful atmosphere that is itself helpful. The men respond from their chairs: "Tell her you were earning grocery money while she watched soap operas", or "Tell her to go shopping" or "Ask her how she's feeling now". The therapist-actors may pick up any of these suggestions and play them out to another choice point where the men are again asked for input. The scenarios are short embodied illustrations of the men's experience which they can manipulate like videotape. The group can fast forward, stop action, reverse to replay. It is as if the group is in one giant sandbox with a few toys and their imaginations to design how life has looked, could or should look.

## THE UNFOLDING PROCESS OF ENGAGEMENT

In this section I will outline the process of engagement which commences with the initial meeting of participants and the clinical team in session one and proceeds through the conclusion of our 12-session course. It is best to view this with a both/and perspective: many of what we refer to as "stages" are intertwined and may run simultaneously. Nevertheless, the notion of stages helps in breaking down various aspects of the work.

### Stage One—Establishing a Base of Non-violence

Now it's time for you the reader to use your imagination. My female co-therapist and I are starting the group; going over some guidelines for how the group should proceed. Many of the men are anxious; more likely resentful they've been forced to come by the criminal courts or as a last chance to save their relationships. I take out my handcuffs and to the surprise of those in attendance, place one of the "silver bracelets" on my wrist. "Ouch, it hurts!" I exclaim. I ask if the police will take them off or at least loosen their clasp. I ask the men if they would rather be in control of their lives or have their lives controlled by the police, a judge or a probation officer? We enter into a dialogue about how we can commit ourselves to specific courses of action.

We begin to consider the consequences of physical, mental and sexual abuse. Irresistible invitations (Jenkins, 1990) begin to get the group participants motivated about consequences which might come from respectful actions which they hope will bring them the loving relationships they desire in life. Do you want a relationship in which your partner respects you out of care, or acts compliant but only out of fear? What would the consequences be if your partner just reacted out of fear? How would you feel? Is this a preferred feeling?

## Stage Two—Initiating the Trance of Drama

Using the Irish concept of the Fifth Province (McCarthy & Byrne, 1988), the clinical team establishes a linguistic process which promotes an ambivalent disposition. According to Irish mythology, the Fifth Province refers to an imaginary meeting place where ordinary things could be seen in an unusual light. It essentially involves establishing some type of mutual ground where things can be seen from a detached perspective apart from partisan perceptions.

Drawing on a sketch we have planned previously, I begin to spontaneously act as an abusive man to my female co-therapist. Roles are blurred; the men are mesmerized by the confusion of identities. Within confusion there is the quest for understanding which can only come about through focused attention. The group puts forth their views of what's happening. I am confronted with my abuse as I, in the role of one of their peers, request their help in asking about my own violent behavior. I ask about my partner. What is she experiencing and how does she feel in relation to my abuse? Within the Fifth Province there is no defensiveness, no judgement, only inquiry to understand what is unfolding before us.

## Stage Three—Breaking Down the Fourth Wall

Although the clinical team may be quite directive during the preliminary stage of a new group, being "one-down" by primarily asking questions flattens the hierarchy within the group and does not place the clinicians in an expert stance. The theatrical concept of breaking down the fourth wall encourages engagement; the actor carries a scene forward and simultaneously requests guidance, or makes comments to the audience. The interactive aspect of these sketches promotes agency on the part of the men because it invites them to act as directors in addition to being audience members.

This approach has been influenced by Tom Andersen's work with the process of creating a different stance in viewing experience through the use of "reflecting" (Andersen, 1991). The men comment on my actions, questioning me and also providing me with different scenarios. Hit her; yell at her; leave her alone; listen to her. I try all four. The scene is rewound and replayed. It is within the dialogue of this curiosity that the group sees and feels the different textures of decision making within a situation of conflict.

## Stage Four—Reflexivity Amid Dilemmas

Reflexivity is the process whereby the therapist as actor is continually moving to a meta-level and looking back on his actions, motivation and feelings in an effort to understand them. Within the violent scene I'm acting out I continuously stop and ask, "What next? Act or react? Make a violent or a non-violent move? Discuss my feelings?".

> *DB: Speaking of feelings, I wonder about your views on focusing on these as a way of understanding how abuse gains entry into the men's lives. I often find in my work with men dominated by abuse that anger becomes the catch-all emotion for all feelings, and that it's important to get at more vulnerable feelings and other beliefs that go along with the anger.*

> *BH: We usually discuss anger as a "secondary feeling". That is, there a variety of ways men can describe how they've been affected by the environment. In our culture, women are better practised in using a larger variety of feeling words in their dialogue with others. Men on the other hand seem to focus on ideas of arousal with respect to its application of power. We support them in increasing the breadth of their vocabularies for describing what some have labelled as "primary feelings", so that they be more mindful of their arousal levels without getting caught up in them. These might include descriptions such as "I am sad, fearful and lonely". Within the roles we play in the dramatic scenarios, men can explore how their language influences their ability to communicate effectively. The greater the flexibility in terms of vocabulary, the more accurately one can talk about how things are perceived. This can also create the opportunity to describe a variety of feelings related to the beliefs one holds about different aspects of a relationship. Unfortunately, many men select an audience which reinforces talk of "power over others" rather than the exploration of feeling words to convey how they're responding to the world around them. However, it has been our experience that men welcome these other types of discussions, because discussions of non-violence eases the pain caused by not being able to engage their loved ones intimately.*

As the scenario continues, I throw out other options for responding: "Insult her mother? Help me guys: what should I do?". This process whereby the therapist questions his behaviour and asks questions of other group participants allows the men to teach me to pause and reflect. In dialoguing with me, they encourage me to have these same dialogues in my mind. I thank them for assisting in my evolution as a problem solver. And perhaps they too begin to develop a reflexive detachment, with our talks becoming their own inner voices. Courtney (1990) discusses this in more detail in his book, *Drama and Intelligence*, where he explores the cognitive theory behind the value of drama in allowing us to learn new ideas.

## Stage Five—Developing an Appetite for New Knowledge

We talk and become a unit in deconstructing conflict. The group's curiosity is piqued at this point. I tell the men I have some ideas other men have used to help them deal with anger arousal. "What do you think? How can we use it? Direct me as a conflicted man and I'll try putting the ideas to work". At this stage I tell the men I have handouts containing ideas from published authors as well as notes from other group participants who have shared their views. They are free to take. Handouts are not automatically given nor are men forced to take them. Our team does not dictate knowledge in a hierarchical fashion. The handouts themselves are co-created with the men: I ask their permission to include their ideas for sharing with other group participants in the future. The documents live on as a testimony to the work they have accomplished.

## Stage Six—Co-authoring Progress by Highlighting Unique Outcomes

As the group evolves and becomes more cohesive in their quest to learn non-violent behaviour, the therapy team is in a position to notice what Michael White (1989) describes as "unique outcomes". White uses the idea of a unique outcome—a positive development in a client's struggles with a particular issue or problem—to highlight those areas of competence which clients have performed but may not be able to distinguish.

Drawing on the work of White and Epston (1990) we have found it useful to use letter writing as a way to reinforce positive developments and engage men in considering their progress. My co-therapist and I fuss over the gains we hear but that the men have yet to distinguish. One man says he discussed a time-out with his partner. Another was able to articulate feelings of remorse or grief. We enter into dialogues about the identities we see reflecting a commitment to non-violence. We talk to the group about their ideas for letters we can both construct on progress for their probation officers. "What ideas do you have about this group? What can we say about you and what do you want to say about your participation in this group?" The men's progress is highlighted in the accounts of their emerging non-violent identities.

> *DB: Do you worry that there's a risk of colluding with these men, that in your effort to validate them you might "get them off the hook" so to speak? I'm thinking about the issue of accountability to the victims of their abusive behaviour.*
>
> *BH: The treatment team does not endorse the use of violence. We do try to listen to the men in our group with the hope that we can role model acknowledgement, even though we have our own beliefs about respectful human relationships. Listening to participants has a mirroring effect in modelling how they can listen in return. When men discuss tactics of violence we extend their chain of action steps towards natural and logical consequences. So what happened next? How did she feel? Who called the*

*police? What happened to you? How did you feel? Within this respectful discussion where all points of view are favoured the participants come to see on their own that certain steps lead to consequences they themselves do not want in their lives. This includes the effect of violence on their partners and children. The aftermath of violent behavior usually contradicts what the men hope for in their relationship goals. Many men have an adverse reaction when asked how they would feel if their wife left them for good or if their son were arrested later in life for actions he role modelled from his father. This is one way to have men begin to develop accountability to their families for violent actions. We do not stop with self-centred concern but strive to achieve explorations in empathy. When the men develop a language for speaking about feelings, they are more able to appreciate that others with whom they relate also have feelings which are influenced by the men's actions.*

### Stage Seven—Soliciting an Audience

Towards the latter half of the course as group members begin to talk more openly about their successes and dilemmas, we find it helpful to ask if their partners or other interested parties have noticed their movement towards a lifestyle of non-violence. White (1989) and Epston (1989) stress the importance of an audience to notice behaviours typically not acknowledged or distinguished by a client. I will ask the men if I can negotiate bragging rights for their stories of success. "Can I borrow your story to help another man who is struggling?" Without breaching confidentiality, stories are traded which tell of problem solving strategies and choices based on respect.

## VOCABULARY OF CHANGE

As a practicing clinician much of what we do comes from a place of tacit knowledge. Just as it can be awkward converting new ideas into practice, so can it be difficult putting our practice into words. Acknowledging these challenges, I have attempted to formulate a working vocabulary for our group therapy model. The following are some of the key elements in our current practice of therapeutic drama in working with men.

### Plasticity

This approach is both supple and spontaneous. The drama moves forward and moulds itself around specific needs of group participants, rather than a preordained agenda. Men are not typically asked directly to supply information as they find this process threatening; however, the men do volunteer their experiences or argue points, and these provide personal examples we can dramatize. Spontaneity is vital for this creative process. It frees the imagination and allow ideas to flow without censorship. While we provide a scaffold for the process, the men act as both "script writers" and "directors".

## Reflexivity

The clinical team communicates not only directly but through the therapist as actor who questions his own behaviour and invites comments from other group participants. This enables the actor to demonstrate the art of self-reflection, giving group members the chance to simultaneously reflect on their own behaviour. A reflexive stance encourages the consideration of alternate forms of action and allows for a multi-levelled form of communication and examination to occur in the group.

## Biphasic Direction

The group is initially directed by the clinical team to a point in time where the participants have established a rudimentary commitment to non-violence and there is a cohesion in the group around this goal. At this juncture, a second phase evolves where the therapy team recedes into the background or is no longer in role as group participants direct the process of dialogue as they question each other and offer suggestions on how to resolve the dilemmas participants describe. Our team contributes to this forward momentum and keeps the group from deviating or regressing by continually focusing on the purpose of our enterprise. In a sense, we are both directive and non-directive. We are directive in keeping the group focused on the quest for non-violent ways of relating, and we are also non-directive in making space for the men to explore the consequences of their own choices.

## The Reflecting Team

Following Anderson (1991) we have found it useful to discuss the progress and dilemmas of group participants with other members of the therapy team as well as other group participants in front of the party we are speaking of without immediately inviting him into the conversation. Anderson suggests this is less threatening than speaking directly to a person, and allows him to be in the "listening position" instead of having to answer questions or account for his actions. This reflecting process does not point to deficiencies, label or pathologize participants. Instead, we highlight areas in which the men are succeeding, and speculate about possibilities for potential growth.

## Collaboration

Following from much of the work done in narrative and social constructionist therapy, we have found it useful to establish a context of cooperation rather than coercion. Although the men have been mandated to attend, we do not force individuals to participate while in session. We feel that by inviting group participants to speak we diffuse reactivity in the room, building respect by not establishing a hierarchy. Collaboration is more evident as the group matures and the clinical team becomes involved in co-authoring progress notes and letters to probation officers. Instead of evaluating or diagnosing members, we invite them into a dialogue, noting competencies and expressing concerns, primarily through the use of questions. We differentiate ourselves from the court system and position ourselves as allies to the men in their struggles with outside influences.

## Humour

The use of humour is valuable to decrease tension in the group as well as deliver curriculum topics. It also serves to bond group members with each other and with the clinical team. Although the topic we deal with is a serious one, humour has a way of establishing a less threatening context which reduces defensiveness. Among other approaches, we use irony, sarcasm, practical jokes, and the exaggerated portrayal of certain behaviours.

## The Fifth Province

As mentioned earlier, we deliberately engage in dialogic processes that help to detach participants from partisan and prejudiced views. McCarthy & Byrne (1988) refer to the Fifth Province as "an archetypal, imaginary meeting place" (p. 189). In other words, it is a mutual ground whereby individuals can reflect on things without focusing on vested interest or defending one's actions. Our dramatic scenarios blur the lines between what is real and unreal, unbalancing the audience and creating an opening for new meanings and actions.

*DB: You mention meaning here, but my impression is your approach is more skills oriented. Do you think there's a risk that the men could develop new skills but not shift their meanings of beliefs—that they could learn new ways to avoid going to jail but continue to abuse?*

*BH: The use of drama, although physical in presentation, is just one aspect of learning which occurs in the group. There are many discussions which occur around the acting and these are more prevalent during the second half of the group where the men take ownership of their own relationship dramas, and seem less concerned about the different scenarios acted out by the treatment team. Although men do discuss ideas of how they could act differently in their current relationships, within these discussions are conversations about feelings. Feelings and beliefs form the bedrock off which the participants plan future actions. As the men participate in discussions, they come to value other practices such as "problem solving" and "compromise" strategies to deal with conflict over practices of using power over another person. They experience different consequences when they can give and receive feedback, and in many cases this style of interaction is more in line with their goals for family relationships. As the men perform new behaviors which are respectful, they receive feedback from their partners and others which influence their beliefs on how to act in relationships. Instead of reliance on formulas of abuse, they discover a variety of options for relating to others. The men begin to choose those practices which promote the goals they'd hoped for and which do not bring about consequences such as police involvement, which has caused them a great deal of pain.*

## Choice and Consequence

We communicate the notion that liberation comes at the cost of responsibility, that freedom equals choice and consequence. The purpose of this is to reinforce personal responsibility. The dramatic scenes continually portray decisions and their repercussions. This linkage is key to building a foundation for non-violence: it means making choices that are not abusive and will not infringe on the rights of others. Most of the men are aware of the legal consequences of their previous actions—they appreciate that, regardless of how justified they think they were, they nonetheless broke the law and were held accountable by the judicial system. By playing out actions to their natural conclusions, we borrow from White's (1991) idea of "collapsing time". The natural progression of the action serves to preview the outcome of a particular course of behaviour.

## Deep Play

David Epston (1989) advocates for the use of play as a way of freeing the imagination and allowing the creative endeavour to move forward. The idea of playfulness as leading towards new ways of behaving has been explored by Blatner and Blatner (1988) and Landy (1993), who view drama as a process for exploring alternative ways of being and increasing one's repertoire of social behaviors. Many times therapists are constrained by the theoretical model they work under and when they get stuck with a case, blame the victim instead of expanding their repertoire of behaviours beyond the limitations of the model they are using.

*DB: This statement rings very true for me regarding traditional approaches for dealing with men and abuse issues. How do you avoid slipping into that blame?*

*BH: We usually discuss the beliefs men have around blame. Many participants have felt they were victims of other people's actions. This stance leads them to believe they have had little influence in affecting others. Men come to see that blame is actually the practice of disempowerment. When I blame I give all power to you because only when you change can it have a positive influence on me. Instead, we endorse ideas about personal responsibility, respectful relating, and problem solving. These latter ideas usually have a more positive impact because men experience confidence in guiding a constructive talk rather than waiting in a vulnerable state in the hope that someone else will change their behavior.*

A disposition of "deep play" helps our team convey the idea that problem resolution can unfold in many different forms. It might be simpler to say that playfulness equals inventiveness, and that playful curiousity makes room for invention.

## Role Modelling

Whenever the male and female therapists interact, they provide an example of male/female interaction which group members can copy. The men have an opportunity to see both adversarial communication and cooperative communication between a man and a woman. Often times we will use the dramatic scene to illustrate how a man can discuss a new behaviour or anger control technique with his partner who is not available to be a group participant. The use of a hetero-social team helps to embody male/female cooperation. The presence of a male therapist is also important in his role as a "mirror". It is through his actions that many group participants are able to identify their feelings associated with violent behaviour. The male therapist illustrates how to describe feelings and to use techniques such as a time-out when negotiating a compromise. These demonstrations within the room surpass a cognitive understanding that might be obtained by reading workbooks or handouts.

## Detachment

As groups develop, participants are more able to stand back and think about consequences before acting. We call this "detachment"—the discipline to focus on the big picture rather than one's immediate feelings in a situation. Many of the men we work with have developed the habit of responding by reflex in moments of strong emotion. Their reactivity often causes further problems: it upsets the other party involved, which leads to an adversarial escalation of their interaction. Detachment does not deny feelings, but makes room for an intermediate step which involves a focus on choice before responding.

## Orientation to Competence

Our focus is on what the men are doing right, rather than on naming deficiencies or excavating for causes (typically pathological) for actions. This is not to say we don't believe one can make mistakes or act inappropriately. We simply find it more helpful to highlight and dialogue about progress towards non-violence rather than adopting a moralizing stance and coercing confessions of guilt. We find that when the men are not in a position of saving face or protecting their esteem, it is easier for them to own their own limitations. Men will often spontaneously describe their own poor choices in managing certain conflict situations. We also find a competency-based approach flattens the hierarchy and makes room for solutions to evolve.

## Focus on the Receptive

In order to reduce tension in the group and to avoid confronting members who are feeling defensive and threatened, the therapy team focuses on those more receptive to engaging in constructive interaction. This sensitivity is particularly crucial during the beginning phase of the group. At that time, there is little cohesion among members, and anxiety may lead to collusion among group participants focusing on rationalizing or what we call "glorifying violence". By focusing on more receptive group members, we avoid adversarial encounters with men preoccupied with face-saving arguments. We also like to acknowledge the "silent participation" of members who are watching the group proceedings but are perhaps too shy to say anything. We acknowledge their more passive engagement while respecting their right to remain silent. Our intention is to establish a context of respect which we hope men will match in their own intimate relationships.

## Reframing

Reframing could be simply described as the process of context alteration. It involves the linguistic manipulation of a comment to alter its meaning and thereby open a new way of considering things for an individual. It is the goal of the therapy team to establish a context of acceptance and respect. This is not to say that we condone violent behaviour. What it does mean is that we accept someone's comments as an offer to consider and then discuss choice and consequence. Reframing occurs when we re-interpret a comment by a participant to connote a healthier, more respectful disposition. In effect, we attend to the men's expressions of non-violent intentions and we decline invitations (Jenkins, (1990) to be audience to arguments in favour of violent confrontations and abuses of power. The reframing makes space for collaboration: rather than engaging in debate and trying to counteract expressions of violence, we can team up with the men in exploring the possibilities of non-violent interactions. For example, if we reframe blame into concern it allows us to consider various ways an individual can show his concern in a non-violent or non-adversarial manner. A context of blame may only fuel an individual's rationale for becoming adversarial and possibly violent.

## CONCLUSION

The practices described in these pages reflect a work in constant progress. No sooner did I dictate an earlier draft of this chapter that I wished I had included ideas from a couple of books I have recently read. We continually modify our approach in response to client feedback and our own observations of the process. The specific and detailed input of the men is a benefit of our collaborative relationship and is vital to our creative process: it helps us to abandon ideas that seem exciting on the page, or over coffee with colleagues, but simply don't perform well in practice. Sometimes we wish we could hold tightly to one unvarying model, but these are changeful times and it seems best to reflect that impermanence in our practice. Flexibility and responsiveness are what we promote in the groups we facilitate, and are qualities we also strive to embody in our work with men.

## REFERENCES

Andersen, T. (1991). *The reflecting team*. New York: W.W. Norton & Company.

Blatner, A. & Blatner, A. (1988). *Foundations of psychodrama; History, theory and practice*. New York: Springer Publishing Company.

Courtney, R. (1990). *Drama and intelligence; A cognitive theory*. Montreal: McGill-Queen's University Press.

Epston D. (1989). *Collected papers*. Adelaide, South Australia: Dulwich Centre Publications.

Jenkins, A. (1990). *Invitations to responsibility*. Adelaide, South Australia: Dulwich Centre Publications.

Kivel, P. (1992). *Men's work* New York: Ballantine Books.

Landy, R.J. (1993). *Persona and performance*. New York: The Guilford Press.

McCarthy, I.C. & Byrne, N.O. (1988). Mis-taken love: Conversations on the problem of incest in an Irish context. *Family Process, Vol. 27*, June, 181–199.

White, M. (1989). *Selected papers*. Adelaide, South Australia: Dulwich Centre Publications.

White, M. & Epston, D. (1990). *Narrative means to therapeutic ends*. New York: W.W. Norton & Company.

White, M. (1991). *Deconstruction and therapy*. Dulwich Centre Newsletter, 3, 1–21.

Weiner, D.J. (1994). *Rehearsals for growth*. New York: W.W. Norton and Company.

# *Chapter* 13

# *Radical Youthwork*

## Creating and Becoming Everyone

HANS SKOTT-MYHRE WITH CONVERSATIONAL PARTNERS
JESSICA SKOTT-MYHRE, KATHY SKOTT-MYHRE
AND REGGIE HARRIS

### INTRODUCTION

This chapter is the result of a project that failed. In the spring of 1994, the Bridge for Runaway Youth began an experiment. It was an attempt to engage postmodern service work and accountability within the confines of a multi-program youth service agency serving runaway and homeless youth. The parameters of the project, based on postcolonial perspective, which we will expand upon later, included a definition of the work to be engaged as: based in language, deconstructionist, expert free, reality relative, interested in exploring constraints on narrative, inclusive of non-dominant narratives and an expanding field of voice. We wanted to "promote an open dialogue between all members of our agency community. We wanted to diminish any notions of clinical ownership of other human beings" (Reed, Skott-Myhre, & Wade 1996 p. 41).

It was a powerful vision and one we were committed to both personally and as members of an agency community. However, by 1999, the agency was in turmoil. Many of the staff who had originally created the vision had left and those who remained were badly damaged both professionally and personally. In short, it was a revolution that failed.

So what does this have to do with a book on recent innovations in dialogic therapy? From our perspective, dialogic therapy, as an outgrowth or manifestation of postmodern or post-structuralist therapy, is also a revolution betrayed. It is our contention that many of the same forces and problematics of power, privilege, race gender, sexuality and class that eroded the revolutionary potential at the Bridge have also eroded the collaborative potentials of dialogic or postmodern therapy. Further, our attempts to rethink youth-adult relations at the Bridge, despite failing as a project, have potential for rethinking the interactions of the therapist within an office or clinic. We believe that dialogue, as avenue to liberation, holds tremendous force. However, it is our contention that such conversations need to be thought through carefully and contextually within the domains of postmodern regimes of power outlined above.

This chapter is an attempt to think within these domains about this work. It has an unusual structure as a result of our effort to have the structure of our writing match our style of work. In that regard, a note about who we are and how we work together might be useful. The four of us are representative of a group of people who have worked and lived together on and off for a number of years in St. Paul and Minneapolis, Minnesota. Currently our community is centered in an old big Victorian in St Paul where Hans and Kathy live full time while Jessica and Reggie live there on and off. The house is a sort of transit point for people and ideas and is often full of assorted youth subcultures, left wing adults, musicians, poets and family members. Gatherings on the porch or in the kitchen are opportunities for rich conversation and dialogue about the kinds of topics engaged in this chapter. In this regard, what goes on in this chapter is an attempt to capture some of the conversations and dialogues that we have been struggling with for the past few years. One could say that this chapter is a form of dialogical therapy in and of itself and in many sense mirrors the kind of work we do as activists, youth workers and teachers.

Here we present a conversation about how we do our work. The conversation begins with writing from Hans on youth and youth work and served as a stimulus for Jessica, Reggie and Kathy to think out loud about their work with young people. Together we have created a collage or pastiche of conversations that weaves in and out of the original writing in a way that we hope will be both informative about our work and evocative to the reader in terms of his/her own work.

For us, ours is a work of family, culture, liberation and community. We have intentionally written this together as a family, because we hold that therapy cannot be accomplished outside of family and community, however those connections are constructed. In that sense, we four are a constructed family consisting of different biological connections, racial identities, gender constructions, cultural and geographic backgrounds, alternate life practices and ages. For our family, it is in the richness of such collisions that the potential for actual liberatory connection and dialogue[1] can occur.

Finally, we offer a prefatory note about the theoretical orientation we will undertake in these pages. Our way of thinking and writing about therapy/youthwork is rooted in a neo-Marxist framework. We subscribe, each in a different way, to the

[1]A full description of the project can be found in Reed, Skott-Myhre and Wade (1996).

understanding that capitalism is not the final or best socio-economic formation. For us, capitalism, in its current 'post-colonial' or 'post-modern' form, contains and deploys sophisticated and dangerous regimes of control and discipline. However, in deploying its disciplinary means, it inadvertently produces and revitalizes new forms and political formations holding tremendous potential for human liberation. Our therapy/youthwork aims to overtly and intentionally subvert these disciplinary regimes of capital, and to amplify and accelerate efforts to overcome them.

The style of the language some of us use, in this writing, is philosophical and as such is involved in the creation of concepts and exploring how they might be used in constructing youthwork and youth-adult relations. It can be a complicated and difficult language seemingly essentially foreign, and we have tried to make it accessible through explanation and example. This format we hope will allow the chapter to be read poetically and evocatively.

## *HANS*

It could be said that working with people is best done in the space between things. This space comprises a zone of indeterminacy that is pure potential. This location is home to a moment in which that which has happened is over, and that, which is to come, is not yet. In such an opening, between the solid edifices of history and knowledge, lies a highly mobile encampment of nomads, gypsies and refugees from all that is known to be the truth. Somewhere in this shifting terrain of hazy vision and uncertain movement, lie incomplete and unfinished revolutions of the past. Deep within this libratory potential (or space) resides the un-recuperated alternatives to all that comprises the empire of now. Or, put differently, in the present moment one finds both the narratives of the current regime of power and those of the failed struggles and revolts that have ever been launched within and against it. These failed revolts and revolutions—because they never reached their full potential or realization—contain infinite possibility for new and alternative social forms and[2] structures.

These alternatives can only be developed in spaces outside of dominant forms of knowledge and discipline—by those who inhabit these spaces. Any space produced within the boundaries of the dominant culture is filled with those social forms and structures that have succeeded at the expense of these alternatives. Any and all actual alternative possibilities are to be found in the cracks and margins in the social fabric. This is the power of the minority; those created as "other", and who live between the lines that order and structure the dominant culture.

[2]By the time of this publication, Hans and Kathy will have moved to Brock University in Ontario. However, the house is now occupied by Reggie and a new collaboration of poets, writers, activists etc.

Youth are created as part of this "otherness", and as such (along with other minorities) hold, in tension, the un-recuperated and abandoned alternatives left behind by the victors of cultural, economic, and political struggle. This residue of past struggles for equity, dignity, and liberation are encoded within the performances of youth-identity.

These performances of youth, however, are immediately appropriated, interpreted and over-coded, by the dominant culture. Such encoding is based on the cultural positioning of both the speaker and the message, without their local meanings being fully investigated. Messages, from the edge, whether from prophets, visionaries, madmen or youth, are often ignored, interpreted or appropriated. "Helping" professionals are often trained and expected to encode these performances (through diagnosis, developmental models, models of social disease such as gangs etc.) as forms of deviance needing restoration back to the dominant culture's norms. Those who work with youth live between the potential for liberation implicit in youth performance and the dominant society's mandate to capture and[3] control it.

Antonio Negri, discussing the advances of capitalism, states that "Every innovation [of Capital] is a revolution which failed-but also one which was attempted" (1996 p.158). This applies to the regimes of youthwork as well. Most innovations in youthwork can be seen as failed revolutions, attempts to 'assist' young people, by appropriating (i.e., not honoring or joining) their revolutionary struggles. Youth work would not exist without the struggles of youth; the entire field is premised on the continual production of youth in struggle with the dominant culture. Each new innovation of the field is built out of an attempt by youth to subvert the constraints of adult society. The more effectively and powerfully youth escape the confines of cultural discipline, the more the field of youthwork expands to enclose them. This is the same dynamic that Antonio Negri describes in his work on the relation between capitalism and labor. "The more radical the innovation is, the more profound and powerful were the antagonistic proletarian forces which determined it and therefore the more extreme was the force which capital had to put in motion to dominate them" (Negri, 1996 p. 158)

In *A Thousand Plateaus*, Deleuze and Guattari (1987), outline the difference between a limit and a threshold. They describe a limit as a condition in which a project reaches a crisis, but one that can be attempted again in a different way or in a new form. A threshold requires an inevitable and radical change in the project (p. 438). I would argue that the "helping professions" generally attempt to extend their own limits without crossing the threshold that would change them—and their power relations to those served—radically and irrevocably. In this way the helping professions remain instruments of a dominant culture, subordinating the innovative efforts of those they purport to serve. The appropriation of the

[3]See Negri, & Guattari, (1990), Negri (1984), Makdisi, Casarino & Karl (1996), Virno & Hardt (1996).

revolutionary impetus of youth by the knowledge regimes of the "helping professions" has traditionally functioned along this axis. The question is can youthwork become something else?

Tensions between those believing that youthwork should socialize youth into the dominant norms of adult society and those who believe it should address youth as an oppressed and marginalized class constitutes an ongoing struggle in any institution, organization or practice involved with youth-adult relations. These radically differing views have a direct bearing on the lived experience of youthworkers and their subsequent co-constructions of youth. They impact youthworkers' conceptions of themselves and the work they do. These "knowings" shape the youth worker's world and lived experience. Perhaps even more importantly, they furnish the lens through which they view youth, and how to make sense of what "youth" means.

*Interlude with Jessica:*

*We started going to see therapists because we had a problem and the therapist would help us work through the problem. However, what started to happen in therapy, and in youthwork, is that the individual is turned into the problem and the therapist is turned into the solution. What we do outside of those places is concentrate on being there for each other and giving each other what we need, what we need to feel empowered and positive and especially that we don't define each other, that we define ourselves and accept that.*

*If it was different, in that way, inside the therapy office, you would allow the person to say who they were and what they were working on, asking questions about what's important for them to change. You would work with them on that and explore ways that they could do that work without being seen as the problem. Instead of the therapist being seen as the solution, you could sit down and decide what you have in common and what can be done from there.*

*I think a lot of the reason social work and therapy don't work is because kids, in particular, don't see themselves the same as adults. Or, the kids think that therapists don't see them as people and that's a problem. So even outside of therapy, say social work, the kid comes in and if they don't have a home, it's a problem. The kid is the problem and they have to find a solution to that problem—nobody wants to be treated that way. Especially if you are desperate you need support and you need somebody to say, " I understand the way you are feeling, this is how I have felt that way or just that people feel that way. How can I help you, what do you need", instead of "here's what you need to do and I'm going to facilitate that". I think that's not happening right now. Most therapists doubt youth definitions of their own situations and often see youth problems as rebellion or the youth as being difficult; or just being a teenager.*

*What needs to happen is for therapists to ask young people seriously about who they are and to let them identify what is making them uncomfortable. Ask them about their parents and how their parents identify and how their parents are involved. Then you can begin to see and help the youth to unpack the situation, instead of wondering why the youth are rebelling, the whole situation needs to be taken into account. In working with people, issues of cultural, racial and sexual orientation,*

*gender lines factor into our conflicts more than we like to see because we don't like to see our lives as political. In any case, asking the person you are working with who they are is just a huge question because that's really what people want to talk about. That's what opens people up. They want to talk about who they are, they want to explain—to share with you. You can't really connect with anyone until you make an effort to figure out who they are. I think people are scared that they are going to cross a line, but I think it can be done. The best way to connect with people who are feeling isolated (which youth always feel and especially youth who are dealing with other identity crisis) is by making sure they know they are not alone and that they are ok and that what they are feeling is alright and then you can work from there.*

## HANS

The divergent views of youth work between the impetus toward liberation or the impetus to discipline stem out of what Michel Foucault (1972) has called a "fellowship of discourse". This kind of discourse is involved in the production of "truths" that yield certain kinds of power (p. 227). The identity of the youth worker is comprised of these intersecting discourses that affect their descriptions of themselves, their roles and how they come to understand their relationship to the youth they serve. Many focus on the marginalization, categorization, normalizing, pathologizing and de-politicizing of youth while others construct "truth regimes" and "disciplines" found in discourses about professionalization, maturation, progress, rationality, science, medicine, expertise and social control. This induction into certain kinds of knowing about youth, constructs youth work within the frameworks of European modernity, the colonial/imperialist project and Euro-American capitalism. This maps youth and youthwork as a process of accommodation, exploitation or resistance, as part of 'normal' processes of development and acculturation commonly portrayed in modern psychology and sociology textbooks. Such ways of knowing make youth observable and modifiable objects, harnessing their resistance or assimilation to dominant structures of modernist knowledge or capital development. In this sense, youthwork is developed and sustained within a system designed to penetrate the private lived experience of youth and colonize it to its own ends. Choosing to join this modern approach to youth work—of helping youth fit into the dominant culture or considering them deviants for resisting the impetus to belong to dominant society—is a false choice threshold we feel youth work must push beyond.

*Interlude with Reggie:*

*The entire youthwork field that I am aware of and come in contact with, is interested in assimilation and bringing youth into the dominant structure—that is not what I am interested in. I am interested in suggesting that there is an alternative. Even though this system and the way things are now, seems to be working for us as youthworkers, case managers and directors (or seems to be working for us) it can't work for everybody. If we can step away from rationalizing this system, then we could go into how could it work for this person, what would make it work better? Then we can support them in doing that. By support I mean by really being selfless in our work with the youth. In other words, you might not agree with what youth are trying to do and you may not agree with the future that they are envisioning, but be selfless in the fact that maybe this will work for them and encourage that.*

## HANS

The theoretical foundations of dominant modern views of youth and youthwork, are being radically altered, as we move from the Colonial and Modern, to the Postcolonial and Postmodern. In this sense, "Post, in fact, marks an end, and the beginning, of a new field of inquiry which unsettles and undermines previous theoretical discourses and forms of inquiry, while drastically providing an open-ended field of possibilities" (de Toro & de Toro, 1995, p. i).

This shift into "post-ality" enables a reconceptualization of youth and youthwork within an entirely different framework; one where youthwork is no longer focused on regimes of truth through which youth can be known in some essential or singular way that can be discovered. Instead, we can bypass authoritarian systems of control based on solid definitions of identity and social position, for indeterminate possibilities created and explored by youth and adults together. There are two implications of this shift that I would like to outline briefly.

First, as deToro points out (1995, pp.17–18), the relations of power between the center of dominant culture and the periphery shift. This shift in relations recodifies and re-centers history by including multiple, mixed and heterogeneous versions (or stories) of the past and present—a world where places and identities are no longer defined necessarily or solely by geography, race, gender, sexuality, age, and so on. Instead identity reflects an intersection of possibility produced by such influences, or ways of being 'located'. These locations constantly change as people increasingly move around the globe, and as their self-definitions become more mutable and less stable through cultural collisions and the destabilizing forces of post-modernity. For example, Western society often unconsciously thinks of the center of normality as located geographically in Europe or the United States. All other forms of identity are considered as "other" or "alternative". This difference is embedded in how we speak, act and view ourselves, occluding and obfuscating other localities and identities (Said, 1979). Exploring these occluded/obfuscated alternative localities and identities requires a profoundly different approach.

*Interlude with Reggie:*

*There's essentially two ways to do youthwork, either I am trying to bring them into a system that already isn't working for them—that is actually oppressing them socially and economically—or I'm trying to work with them to recreate and imagine something different. That doesn't mean that today I do that work and tomorrow all the oppression is gone.*

*What it means is that both you and the youth expand. In other words you become more than individuals. You become each other and that makes it easier to do things with the "other" because you are always really working for yourself. If you are constantly expanding, then you are not static in your ideas of who you are. You can become the person in the next city, the person in the next country, youth, adult etc. Then you can avoid the neo-colonial problematic of regressive and rigid definitions of race, gender etc. which reify colonial identities within the revolutionary movements of the previously oppressed.*

*Because, even though people may think that the system is working for them, it's not really working for anyone. Some people are getting more gasps of air than the others, but everyone is drowning. So if everyone is drowning, then working with that youth becomes about us and how we save all of us together. All of a sudden this space between is collapsed, there is no such thing as a bridge, all of a sudden we are all going down together. So now, how do we get out of this?*

*When I am talking to youth, I am always paranoid that the staff will discover that I am someone who should be receiving, not giving services. I am afraid that I will be seen; that I will be visible. My fear is that slowly because the dreams are being manufactured now, at an early age our revolutionary potential is being snuffed out and that at an earlier age we are making a decision to want to be part of this system that oppresses and exploits others. We become convinced that there are no alternatives because there are no examples being given of how else it could be. We don't see any pictures of it, no movies about it, no songs about it. The only thing we hear and see on a daily basis is the reality that is working for some and not for most.*

## HANS

The second relevant postcolonial feature relates to how traditional youth work in residential programs, schools, family studies, and education tends to focus on how to discipline youth effectively. This disciplinary focus reflects the fact that such youthwork operates within the frameworks of colonial modernism. The practices and social machinery of youthwork as a discipline are an integral part and not an exception to the reproduction of capitalist democracy.

The French philosopher, Gilles Deleuze (1990, pgs 178–180), however, argues that we are moving beyond a disciplinary society, to a "society of control". This society of control has several parameters: it "no longer operates by confining people but through continuous control and instant communication" (p. 174), it works through "open sites" and "continuous training" (p. 175). Its people are constantly monitored and speech and communication are "corrupted" or captured by capital (p. 175). Identity is achieved through consumption and debt—tied to our credit rating and accessible wherever we are 24 hours a day.

Within such a society, the concern with resistance and discipline outlined in contemporary youthwork is no longer relevant. The modes of analysis utilized by most youthwork practice orientations do not account for the rapid mutations inherent in any new regimes of control. By the time resistance or challenge can be mobilized, all the definitions have shifted to accommodate, enclose and incorporate the new knowledges made available from youth or youthwork. We need to break past the insularity and circularity of this threshold.

*Interlude with Kathy:*

*A lot of the ways in which the youth I have worked with are resisting—like those used by punks, gangs etc.—are appropriated by capital. However, by the time their resistance is appropriated they are already in a different place and what was appropriated is no longer relevant to me as a youthworker, because they continue to keep moving. It's lines of flight like this that I am interested in pursuing with young people, not appropriation.*

*I don't think I ever joined in resistance with the young people I work with. I think instead, I have had conversations that were more creative than that. I would listen for things that ordinarily would slip through the cracks. For example, I am thinking about a young woman who I worked with in a drop in center for homeless, exploited and at risk youth. This young woman came from a family full of chemical dependency, physical and emotional abuse, yet she didn't fall into the same trap her family was in. She didn't use chemicals and she just said this in passing as she was listing off the traditions of her family. And that really struck me and so I asked her, "How was it that you managed to break the tradition of chemical use in your family?" She thought about that for second and replied that she had never thought of it in that way. That allowed her a whole new perspective on her role in her family and in her own life that she hadn't considered before. I could have framed this as resistance "so how are you resisting. . . ?", "how are we going to keep you drug free, chemical free?" Instead of, "How is it that you have managed to escape from or take a different route than the rest of your family?" I wasn't interested so much in her maintaining her sobriety as much as I was interested in the road she was on and how she managed to take that road. I didn't see it nor did she see it as "resisting" chemical dependency. She saw it as a way out of what her family had been in for generations.*

## HANS

Deleuze proposes that "the first given of a society is that everything takes flight" (1997, p. 189) and that lines of flight are "objective lines that cut across a society" (p. 189). "Lines of flight" suggest infinite possibilities of escape from ever-changing dimensions of cultural control. In fact flight itself might be defined as the idea that " . . . effective escape is nothing less than the perception of one's vitality, one's sense of aliveness or changeability (often signified as freedom)"(Massumi, 1996 p. 229 The definition of flight as the expression of life itself allows for a flexibility, energy, and stamina that are most probably required to engage in flight from an ever shifting landscape of control.

*Interlude with Jessica:*

*If you have people that don't fit into what capital is marketing to, then the marketplace is not working exactly the way capital might hope. If you have this trans- boy listening to this popular music, what he is getting out of it is not what capital is putting out. It's a totally different community and perception that isn't being marketed to, so even if that person is looking towards popular music or popular clothing how it is used can be outside the way its being marketed.*

*Just being outside of "being marketed to" is a step back from the control of the "dividual" talked about by Deleuze, (1990) Communities are being created with a different way of living that is perhaps a more loving lifestyle that caters to politics much more than an individual lifestyle does. What happens when you have these communities of people that are different and need that community is that they become inherently political. Even if they begin by only caring about one issue they may become involved in other related issues. There is a much greater tendency to work on political issues and to work on accepting people for who they are and who they say they are inherently and that is political. Just that different way of living is political.*

## HANS

In the society of control, people become "dividuals", rather than individuals. The individual has an identity made up of the actions and relationships of lived experience. The "dividual"'s identity is strictly that of a marketing niche. Such a niche is constantly under revision as capital redefines identity according to its value as a commodity for sale. In this sense, capital captures identity and uses it to its own ends. However, this flexibility of identity can be used to other purposes. For example, a youth-work of flight can use this mutable identity toward liberation from market place efforts to further control youth. In other words, the infinite mutability of youth identity can develop lines of flight outside of those proscribed by capital. Through this alternative mutability, youthwork can provide youth and adult collaborations the ability to cultivate a multiplicity of identity possibilities; to circumvent marketplace controls.

Such lines of flight cannot be found in the existing metaphors of capital, or the confines of disciplinarity (family, work, school etc.), but in creative conversations that explore infinite and preferred possibilities for shifting identity. These lines of flight can offer multiple exits in the face of a society of control attempting to appropriate and assimilate any new identity. A youthwork of flight could creatively engage youth in collaborating with adults in developing fluid identities that can flee any particular static identity benefiting a society of control.

*Interlude with Reggie:*

*Being multiple selves takes a lot of courage. There is no safety in multiplicity; it's where our 'contradictions' lie. Multiplicity of self is when the youthworker can acknowledge if they have enough courage to admit that sometimes: I "do drugs", I practice unsafe sex, I can't manage my bills. Things I am supposed to be helping you do or showing you how to do, I need help doing. Having a conversation like that would be significant, in fact revolutionary, but we generally don't have those conversations. Instead we stay in our positions of illusory safety as "case managers" or "youthworkers". We don't agitate, we just conform and just smooth everything over and try to get the youth to come in and do the same thing with us.*

*But, I am more interested in what Hans talks about as the undreamt dreams and we have to dig for that. And because our dreams are being produced and manufactured by conglomerates a part of us is dying every day. The work then, is to join with youth in imagining something different than what we have known. For the youth I work with, every day there is a gun; every day there is a death; every day there is a new chalk line on the ground where someone got killed. It's imagining something different than that. For me, that's where I'm at. That's why the work needs to be done together. That's why there's no difference between us. Then, once we can imagine something, trying to believe in that. What kind of meaningful youthwork can be done if people can't get truly vulnerable with each other? If they cannot say you know what, your life is fucked, my life is fucked. You're having issues with that, I am too. Maybe you know something about the issues I got and I know something about the issues you got. Maybe together we can do something a little different.*

## *HANS*

In *Control and Becoming*, Deleuze wrote, "We've got to hijack speech. Creating has always been something different from communication" (1990, p. 175). Youthwork must move beyond "informative communication", to creative or poetic conversations that inspire and differently mobilize youth/adult relations. Our conversations could break apart and explore the myriad possibilities inherent in each word, finding or creating lines of escape in each turn of phrase. Deleuze said that, "The key thing may be to create vacuoles of non communication, circuit breakers so we can elude control" (Deleuze 1990 p. 175). In other words we have to go beyond making sense in order to escape. We must not stop at the point at which something seems to be known or makes sense and instead continue to create new meanings that cannot make sense yet. We must bust up the world of the known and sensible and collaborate with youth to become incomprehensible. Conversations and frameworks for youthwork should not merely make sense (in the conventional modern sense), but *break sense* from the language of the marketplace. Its definitions must be mobile and transitory, evocative not definitive.

*Interlude with Reggie:*

*I really love the phrase hijacking speech. It puzzled me for a while, but I really like it. Hijacking speech is, for me, is what the really creative circles of the GLBT community are doing with queer theory. People are taking words and forcing them to go other places. That to me is the epitome of hijacking speech. This word or that word has traditionally meant or symbolized something particular to people—all of sudden you take and redirect it into an area it isn't supposed to be in and it's a struggle because its going unwillingly, not like the word wants to be in this new space, wants to represent something different. Words, like most people, want to stay where they are at and symbolize what they have always symbolized. When you hijack speech, you take a language- you take a word against its will—and make it say something different. In this respect, they are slipping the "Borg", they are evading capture/appropriation/marketing by doing this chameleon type thing where they keep shedding and going to something different.*

## *HANS*

Finally, new codes or passwords are required in our conversations with youth, to generate lines of flight counter to marketplace efforts to close off such lines of flight. Evidence of these new codes and passwords may be found in how youth subcultures perform their many ways of resisting being captured by capital or other means of societal control. We can join in their efforts to flee such control.

*Interlude with Jessica*

*I want to talk about how definitions should be transitory, evocative not definitive. New codes and passwords must be constantly generated within the idiosyncratic life world. We use that a lot in the work that I do, especially with gender, because right now, gender is a new thing being worked on and it's a really small community of people that are working on it. So, we are constantly coming up with new terms to redefine ourselves through what we are doing. If you have someone who is trying to come out as "trans" but they don't want to get stuck in being either male or female, then you have different words that go into that. We have created different pronouns like ze or hym or hir that talk about these people. They are constantly changing and evolving as we decide that they don't fit people and we are not satisfied with them. So it's like we are constantly rebelling against the terms that we create for ourselves just moving along. As we do that, as long as we can be unified in finding those terms in looking for those terms we're continuing to mutate in a way that can't be followed completely by the lines of capitalism. If you can't anticipate something being, you can't market to it. So if we have people waking up every day and they create different forms of identity, capital is not quick enough to keep up with that.*

*If you have people everyday coming to the realization, I'm not a woman, I am a man, then all of sudden you have this trans community. However, before capital can catch up with the trans community, you have people who realize and say I'm not really a man or woman, I'm in between or you have people who have transitioned and want to go back to their original gender, or you have people like a really masculine woman who transitions to become a man but when they become a man they realize that they are a feminine man and there is nothing in capital that can market to that. Capital cannot come close to marketing to these kinds of gender transitions.*

*In the general culture we are still trying to work out the genders of man and woman. It is really important for us to keep doing radical transition because capital cannot follow those transitions. Because there's no market it forces people outside of its usual dichotomies to look to alternative communities and to look within themselves. And they communicate with each other to continue doing that so they have a way of belonging because they look to alternative ways of communicating with each other to stay positive. They find their own ways of role modeling and reaching out to youth and stay a little bit outside.*

## *HANS*

In *Control and becoming*, Deleuze (1990) states that we have lost the world and our sense as a people. Radical youthwork would concern itself with the recovery of both a people and a world. Its creative conversations would explore the struggles and evocative histories that might be pastiched together to develop agile cultures and people resourcefully capable of finding and creating their necessary lines of flight. This would be an artistic project that has to do "with a particular way of occupying, taking up, space time, or inventing new "space times": revolutionary movements" (Deleuze, 1990 p. 172). Such an approach to youthwork favors conversations where collaboratively constructing culture as an art form would be a focus.

*Interlude with Kathy:*

*Recently, I worked with a group of young women on a Christian campus. I began to hear stories from the young women I was seeing, about a certain identity for Christian women, that was defining who they felt they were supposed to be on that campus. The Christian woman image, as related to me, was being a very godly woman who was really there to earn a degree but not to any particular purpose. The real reason that she was in college was to become educated enough to be a good wife. There was also a physical image that they were supposed to be striving for and that was to be thin tall and beautiful if possible. It was this image of perfection that was driving a lot of these women to struggle with eating disorders and anxiety and depression. It was a very covert message that the campus and other women were giving to them but it was pretty clearly articulated by a lot of the young women who came to see me.*

*At one point during the year, I was on a board of women who were trying to decide what we were going to do for women's history month and we started having a conversation about this image and we called it "The Bethel Barbie" image. We were interested in debunking that image which these young women were striving for. We had a public conversation called "Deconstructing the Bethel Barbie", which ended up being probably one of the most well attended events on campus in a long time. There were a lot of women concerned about what it meant to be in the process of becoming a woman. And so we spent a considerable amount of time talking about just what that word woman meant to them. It wasn't that we came to any conclusions in those conversations but it got something started on campus. Conversations started about why we are trying to live up to this particular image and this image is really damaging to a lot of the young women who are on the campus. For example, in order to be thin enough and beautiful enough a lot of women quit eating or they were throwing up after eating or they were over exercising, studying all hours and being a member of every committee to look like they had the cheerleader image. They felt like they were putting on this mask and no one really knew who they really were. The conversation really got people on campus talking in the cafeteria, in the dormitories, in the lounges and that's what we had hoped. Young women really began to take a different look at who they wanted to be.*

*I hate the term working with people because it is really more creating a space for them to explore the potential that they have as a group and as individuals through the group. We have become a very individualized society and started just counting on ourselves. But I think we have to start recognizing how powerful it is to be exploring and creating within a group of people who have similar parameters, a group of young women, a group of Christian young women, black young women, a group of punks, a group of skinheads—they all have their own expertise which I don't think is voiced otherwise. I mean it can be done within the walls of a little therapy room but I think voicing that among a larger group is a much more powerful experience. In a way, I wasn't even a therapist in that situation. I mean I wasn't running a group. I was simply facilitating a conversation. I was only there to make sure that as many voices as possible would be heard and just to keep the ball rolling. I wasn't there to give answers or conclusions or resolve dilemmas or anything else. I was just there to keep the space open for alternative ways of being or alternative ways of thinking. However, I was definitely a participant as well, in that I could see this conversation I was having with these women who were 17, 18, 19, 20 years old having a huge impact on me in how I understood being a woman, and my practices of becoming a woman. Sharing the impact of the conversation on me with them was an important part of the conversation in that it showed that I wasn't necessarily the expert—that I was moved just as much by the conversation as they were. That I was also in the process of becoming a woman in a different and in the same way they were. It was a transformative process is all I can say.*

*Traditional therapy is all about resolving problems, finding solutions and as a result there is always a termination point—you have done the work they came in to do. In creative conversation, on the other hand it's a very different way of working with people in that it opens up all kinds of alternatives. You are not just focusing on one or two solutions; you are creating what you might call lines of flight, if you will. You are opening infinite possibilities instead of narrowing to a few. Traditional therapy often times closes down certain possibilities. Creative conversation focuses on a number of different ways of becoming or of being.*

*Interlude with Jessica:*

*In terms of the therapist's position, where I have seen that work (especially in feminist communities) is when there may be older persons or some influential people in the community who really reaches out and encourages young people in their activism, in feeling the way that they are feeling. They give them information if they need it, give them emotional support if they need it, help them become involved in their community, help them access resources such as money or time; in essence just really be there. I have seen that make a difference for a huge number of people, with one person really doing that in the community, and so I think that's what therapists need to be looking at.*

*I also think that these therapists can be up in a room somewhere in the middle of the city and they are not talking to the community people. So, you have a bunch of kids who are coming in from the ghetto and dealing with all these racial issues but these therapists and social workers are not in contact with the community –or the people who run programs; they are not in contact with people who work in the community. If you take someone totally outside their community, tell them to get a job, then give them one somewhere (without putting them back into their community)—what happens when they go back to their community: of course its going to break apart. Therapist and social workers need to have links to the community.*

*In terms of lines of flight, one of the really important things we're doing is going outside of all of that and just saying, I care about everyone no matter what. I care if you are hurting; I care if you don't understand who you are; I care if you have this horrible pain in your life. To just take that and just put that forth and to fight to understand all the suffering that is going on that you can comprehend is a big thing. As part of caring I am suggesting that people in the helping professions willingly accept pain into their lives. Much pain you can see and feel and still help and move through with the people you are serving, so that when your time with them is over you've moved farther as well as they've moved farther. You feel progress in them and yourself and the community and what's going on. So that you are grounded in the fact that you are helping even though you are joining with this pain you are also alleviating it.*

## HANS

Youthwork is, in the end, an encounter between youths and adults. What kind of an encounter is engaged here? Perhaps we could say an encounter of potential, that is to say a tentative, provisional encounter. It might be characterized as an exchange between guerrillas whispering in the dark, a subversive encounter that points the ways out, reveals nothing and in fleeing closes the entrances off behind itself. The dialogues of such an encounter hold tremendous potential to re-write our future and our present world. In a moment in which the forces of control and exploitation seem to be all pervasive and indomitable, it is important to stay cognizant of the fact that their power derives from the multitude. It is only through the capture and exploitation of the life force of the peoples of the world that capital can prevail. But capture and exploitation are never final outcomes. They are a transitional moment in which life hesitates before fleeing; before taking flight into the infinite creativity that is our birthright as a global multitude. Such flight can be discovered in the encounter between those in the world of dominant adults who yearn for freedom and those in the minoritarian world of youth who constantly flee. Of course there is no safety in such an encounter. It is unstable and decentered.

Such a dangerous encounter is the one comprising the world of youth work. In this age of post-ality and encroaching regimes of global control, there are many arenas of possibility for building the force of global alternatives; politically, culturally, spiritually and creatively. To do this, however we must leave our old colonial selves behind. We must create ourselves differently. In a sense we must abandon the self that we know until finally there is no one; no single person there. In flight we can escape the bondage of the individual body of industrial labor and the theft of creative identity in post-modern capital. Through flight we can join in the force of fully collaborative creation. In such acts of creativity, finally we all become everyone.

## REFERENCES

Deleuze, G. (1997). Desire and Pleasure (D.W. Smith, Trans.). In A.I. Davidson (Ed.), *Foucault and his interlocutors*. Chicago IL: The University of Chicago Press.

Deleuze, G. (1990). *Negotiations*. New York. Columbia University Press.

Deleuze, G. & Guattari, F. (1987). *A thousand plateaus: Capitalism and schizophrenia*. Minneapolis, MN: University of Minnesota Press.

de Toro, F. & de Toro, A. (1995). *Borders and margins: Postcolonialism and postmodernism*. Madrid: Iberoamericana.

Foucault, M. (1972). *The archeology of knowledge & the discourse on language* (Trans. A.M. Sheridan Smith). New York: Pantheon.

Makdisi, S., Casarino, C., & Karl, R.E. (Eds.) (1996). *Marxism beyond Marxism*. New York: Routledge

Massumi, B. (1996). The autonomy of affect. *Deleuze: A critical reader*. Cambridge, MA: In P. Patton (Ed.). Blackwell Publishers.

Negri, A. (1984). *Marx beyond Marx: Lessons on the Grundrisse*. Massachusetts: Bergin and Gravey.

Negri, A. (1996). Twenty theses on Marx: Interpretation of the class situation today. In S. Makdisi, C. Casarino & R.E. Karl (Eds.), *Marxism beyond Marxism*. New York: Routledge.

Negri, A. & Guattari, G. (1990). *Communists like us: New spaces of liberty, new lines of alliance*. New York: Semiotext(e).

Reed, Skott-Myhre and Wade (1996). *We mean to do this: An experiment in post modern social service work and accountability* in *New designs for youth development*.

Said, E.W. (1979). *Orientalism*. New York: Vintage.

Virno, P. & Hardt. M. (Eds.). (1996). *Radical Thought in Italy*. Minneapolis, MN: University of Minnesota Press.

*Chapter* **14**

# *Response-able Practice*

## A Language of Gifts in the Institutions of Health Care

CHRISTOPHER J. KINMAN AND PETER FINCK WITH CONVERSATIONAL PARTNER LYNN HOFFMAN

Understanding human and natural worlds to be filled with gifts, calling us and others to respond in turn with endless movements in every place, exposing us everywhere to others. Ross (1996). P. 1

*Did we initiate this change, or did the other?*
*Perhaps we could even argue*
*This change was initiated by a distant ancestor*
*Either mine, or hers*
*Or both, or all*

*Perhaps all outcomes*
*Positive/negative*
*Both or other*
*Are results of complicated*
*And indecipherable*
*Knots or histories, legacies*
*Intentions and interactions...*
*Gifts are given*
*Gifts are received*
*In never-ending*
*Ever-bending circles*

At the beginning, some questions. Where are we going? What are our intentions?

We call for a response-able practice. We invite a re-languaging[1] of human services practices, with a specific emphasis upon the practices of health care. We depict these practices as occurring amidst processes of gift-exchange, and propose that this re-languaging enables the practitioner to collaborate in communal and responsive acts and move away from practices that are closed and institutional in flavor. The work is not limited to practice with clients and families, but is also a rewarding way to work with institutions and communities, as we have discovered through our own involvement with the public health nurses and their leadership.

## THE PUBLIC HEALTH NURSE STORY

This story is told with a specific emphasis on the experiences of a group of public health nurses[2] in the Fraser Valley of British Columbia, Canada. In their work and their lives they developed a relationship to something we call a language of gifts. We (Christopher Kinman & Peter Finck) were contracted to work with the public health nurses of the Fraser Health Authority, through the organization Rock the Boat.[3] Our task was to assist the nurses and their management in a quest to incorporate a language of gifts into their organizational culture, practices and documentation. Here, in the public health nurses' own words, we present their journeys with a language of gifts.

## WHAT IS A "LANGUAGE OF GIFTS"?

What do we mean by a language of gifts? Particularly in the context of human service and health care practices, we are suggesting that helping professionals enter each situation with an attitude or a spirit that receives the person or group being served as an entity bearing gifts. Even when the discourse surrounding the person or group is permeated with deficit and problems, the practitioner sees her work as one of distinguishing abundance and receiving the fruit of that abundance as gifs

[1] "Languaging" is a word used by Maturana and Varela (1987). The term invites an imagining of language as an active, constantly transforming process enabling a building and rebuilding of human connections within shifting

[2] Public Health Nurses in Canada provide in-community nursing care that includes community vaccinations, in-home support for new babies and their moms, among numerous other community health tasks.

[3] Rock the Boat is an organization dedicated to the honoring of the gift-exchange in people's lives, communities and workplaces. For more information see www.rocktheboat.ca.

offering enrichment and healing. The practitioner believes that if anything good will come for the people s/he works with, it will not come, from their deficiencies and problems, but from the very abundance that surrounds them. The practitioner's own skills, techniques and knowledge become tools that enable community recognition (of the gifts distinguished) and response (to the gifts distinguished). These are gifts from the practitioner's own abundance, thereby enabling a continuation of the exchange. Any form of "human service" entails collaboration between community and practitioners, and involves the circulation of a series of gift exchanges. Problems are not ignored within a language of gifts, but they are illuminated in a different light in that a problem is only a problem when it restrains significant gifts from circulation in community life.

This circulation of gifts, with its overtly social orientation, encourages an assortment of collaborative actions, and an honoring and re-generating of community. Kiernan O'Rourke-Phipps (2002) recently attended a conference in Surrey, British Columbia (called Honoring Community) where the work of the public health nurses was highlighted. Through her own experience of listening to the stories of the nurses, she is able to clearly articulate the effect on a particular community of a language of gifts.

> *I saw community change being created through person-to-person interactions, rippling outward in rhizome connections as tough and resilient as crabgrass... That is, when two people interact in language in a way that is mutually beneficial, open, and transparent, they are exchanging gifts. By consistently and overtly referring to their behavior toward each other as a "gift exchange," rather than referring to it as solving a "problem," two people can begin to transform the language used by their community. Soon more members of the community start to use this language to describe their own activities. As the language is transformed, community members start to see themselves differently. In other words, as the members of the community focus on using the language of gifts, the community will be transformed through language.*
>
> Karen Bath, Public Health Nurse, Langley, B.C.: *What I like about this, when we are thinking in terms of gifts, is that there is this exchange. So, it really isn't about the family, and it isn't really about me. It's about an interaction that's happening between humans. You know what I mean? And it really does change things. It certainly changes the way we work.*
>
> *I had gone to see a mom. All her children, up to that point, had been in the care of the government. But she had just brought her new baby home and she was really proud that she had the baby. That was almost a year ago, and now I was reconnected because she has just moved back to this area. However, when I went to see her, while I was in the car, I found myself in deficit thinking. As I got to her house I realized—no, I needed to just go in there looking to get to know her and hear what her story has been for the last year. After all, I hadn't known her for these last months. So, instead, I went in just wanting to know her, and then I discovered that she had so many wonderful things to say.*

*When I went to the home, I met this nine-month old who's walking all over the apartment, who was into absolutely everything. So I pointed out some of the things I noticed—his curiosity, how stable he was on his feet, and how interested he was in the world. She said, "Oh yeah, well he's really interested in the world because I never put him in a play pen. I knew that he needed to know his world. I just sensed that". Here's this mom who for drug-use reasons had lost all her other children, but now she's sensing with this baby that he needs to know his world. I mean—that's beautiful. So then I said, "Oh, that's a wonderful thing you've identified and now look he's nine months old and he's already walking"... Then she turned to me said—"I did that!" Isn't that beautiful? She said, "I did that". I responded, "You did that!" You know, that's what its about. "You are so right—you did that". And this was the child's first week, since he was born, of not being under supervisory order with the Ministry. The mom said, "I did that".*

*You need to make the basic assumption that there are all kinds of gifts. It's a basic assumption. If you don't make that assumption you won't find the gifts. I know that if I had come in that front door in the same deficit thinking that I had in the car we would never have got there. I would never have heard things like "I did that" and "he had to discover his world". I wouldn't have heard all that. I came away most energized. (Karen Bath, Public Health Nurse, Langley, B.C.)*

Before further exposing the richness of a language of gifts as it informs the work of health care, we should also discuss the institutional economies that influence the worlds of human services, and how these have given form and direction to practice. Three particular facets of these restricted economies[4] are discussed—bifurcation, accountability and legislation.

## THE POLITICS OF BIFURCATION

It appears to us that institutional languaging on practice has been subject to extensive processes of bifurcation. Bifurcation is a term used to describe a splitting that occurs in time-bound lines such as rivers, trees, roads, etc. It entails splitting into two new directions. Particularly with institution discourse, this process splits organizations, communities, human actions and people themselves into repeated hierarchies of two, much like the branches of a tree.

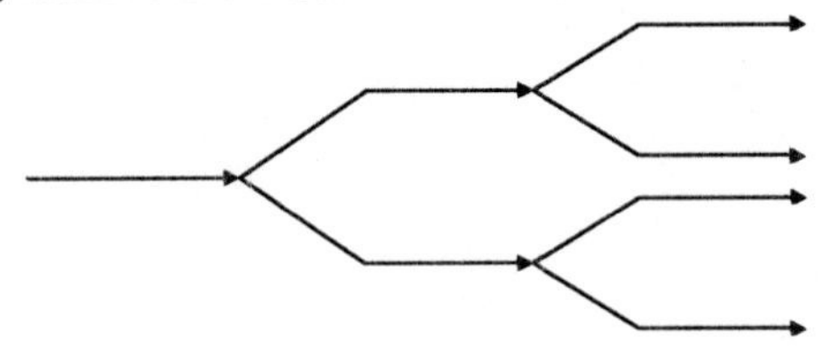

[4] Restricted Economy is a term used by Ross (1996, 1998) to refer to economic systems that assign value to those things embedded in scarcity and restriction. Institutional economies—whether built on a left-wing or right-wing foundations, whether the institutions are public or private, profit or non-profit—all come from this restricted economy background.

There are several bifurcations that emerge in the languaging of practice. One could say that these bifurcations are structurally formative, in that they organize the arrangements necessary for the assembly of human services institutions. Most contemporary, Western human-service activities, including health care and therapeutic practices, are embedded within the structures created by these processes. Several of these bifurcations are described below.

- Professional/Client—Practice, in human services, is that which is performed by professionals upon human bodies. This language entails a distinction between professionals and lay-people/patients/clients and engenders a world where some are entitled to take action while others are supposed to be more or less passive recipients of the action.
- Professional/Paraprofessional—The processes of bifurcation also produce a distinction between professionals and non-professionals, paraprofessionals, or other lower-ranked helpers. The work of these individuals is not given the same weight as the work of the professionals. Generally the roles of paraprofessionals and non-professionals are to be supportive to the professional. These hierarchical distinctions also form between professional groups, as in the bifurcations that emerge between doctors and nurses.

  Within these bifurcation processes institutional hierarchies and their accompanying politics certainly surface. It must also be noted that once the politics of bifurcation appear in institutional settings, bifurcation processes become entrenched and repetitive.
- Management/Front Line—The institutional hierarchy is further split by a line between front-line work and management. We use the term management loosely to include executives, bureaucracy, middle management, those who train the workers, and anyone considered in leadership. Management is supposed to be able to see the "big picture" and give direction to the organization as a whole. Included in this role is the task of giving direction to the practices of front-line workers.
- Thinking/Doing—The language of practice leads us to another bifurcation. Practice is conceived as something that people do, as opposed to something people may think or talk about. If the institution were a body, professional practice would be the "hands" of the institution. Ideas, critical thinking, reflective thought and theory are what management is supposed to engage in. Management is therefore perceived as the "head" of the organization.

As the following quote illustrates, the public health nurses in our project were committed to undoing these bifurcation processes, particularly the thinking/doing bifurcation. They undertook the work of "thinking through" their practices as a vital professional and personal task, and they pursued this task against challenging odds. One of the first practices they challenged was the Problem-Oriented Record, which they were required to use as an intake tool.

*Marjorie Warkentin, Public Health Nurse, Langley, B.C.: We were uncomfortable with going into a family and having our practice shaped by the documentation that focused on problems. And so we started questioning that whole documentation process. We decided we were going to change. We were going to do something different with our documentation. So we did research. We started collecting articles, and had a variety of people come and talk to us. We realized that there really wasn't anything that we could use. We started looking at our own model. We began looking at how we could document things for ourselves, not necessarily being bound by what other people were doing. Rebecca and Amrit started looking at the documentation. They worked with charts. They looked at "Goal Oriented Record" rather than "Problem". And they looked at strengths and client capabilities, resiliencies, all these different words that we were using and playing with. We actually had a chart that we were going to start using. But by this time about two and a half years had past, three years, and we got discouraged. We felt all of us were doing this, as nurses say, "on the side of their desk". We didn't get extra hours for this. We were feeling like there was a lot of interest but we weren't really getting the time we needed, and we didn't have the financial support. I mean if you're going to start doing this you need to have some research, you need to have the time and the money to really know that this is valid. And so we, a couple of us, were actually ready to quit.*

*Joyce Walters, Public Health Nurse, White Rock, B.C.: Our office met with a group of social workers with the Ministry of Children and Families group. Each person introduced herself, talked about caseloads and what special interest each one had. It was my turn. So I started to tell the story, how we were at this point where we really needed help to implement this change we needed for our practice that better reflected what we did in our work. So I was describing this and someone got very enthusiastic across the table and said, "I know exactly whom you need to talk to. You need to talk to Chris Kinman and Peter Finck from Rock the Boat". And she scurried out of the room and returned in a few minutes with a document called a Collaborative Action Plan. It was very exciting because it started with gifts, went to potentials. It also talked about problems, but in a way of using roadblocks. This seemed like a real opportunity and a real fit to me so I took it back. I guess it was to Jean, who was also on the committee. Jean said, "Well, call Chris". So Chris and Peter came out to White Rock to meet with us. And that's how our relationship with Rock the Boat began.*

## A CULTURE OF ACCOUNTABILITY

There is one word we hear much of, a word that circulates extensively within human service settings, and certainly within worlds of health care—that word is accountability. This word does much to unpack the institutional settings for most human service practice. Accountability, accountable, countable, accountant, counting . . .

The word drives us into a world of numbers, a reduced world, a digital location. It takes us to places like Enron and Exxon, places where individuals, families, ocean eco-systems, and numerous other entities become, if anything, numbers for accountants, lawyers, auditors, judges and other counting professionals to play with. And the playing can be deadly, for while life seems starkly absent, death, as well as death's colleagues like violence and depression are close at hand. Whether it is seabirds in Prince William Sound, children in Iraq, First Nations men in prison, patients in a hospital, or families on a caseload, all are repetitively reduced to numbers in the name of accountability.

> *Loa Vanderburg—Public Health Nurse, Langley, B.C.: I think of the number of times we have worked with families who were overwhelmed with difficulties. It was so hard for us as nurses to go back to the office and write down all the problems, which is what we were supposed to do. It tended to burn us out. What do you think it was doing to the families? What we needed was to take the families away from those problems and focus on what could help them change that negative focus they had to live with all their lives. Well, the language of gifts gives us just that. It gives us a language. And it gives us permission to give them hope. Hope is a wondrous thing. Without it life is bleak and discouraging.*
>
> *The business of contemporary health care is imbued with the language of accountability. Any person who has experienced first-hand the administration of health care upon one's own body or the body of a loved one is more than likely familiar with the de-humanizing sensation that comes with being reduced to numbers and equations. While it may be argued that the purpose of accountability is to ensure that work done is the highest quality possible, we are not at all convinced that the language of accountability is able to lead to this state of excellence. We argue that accountability, while often framed with noble intention, can have paradoxical and devastating effects upon the health and healing of human bodies and souls.*
>
> *A Public Health Nurse, Mission, B.C.: I remember a mom who came in; she was the kind of person who would tell you everything. She told the story of living in Vancouver on the streets. It was a rough life. I asked her what helped her come to the place that she was able to look so glowing. She told me it was some worker who came across her in an alley. This person gave her a coat and told her where to get a meal. This was enough for her. This just changed things for her . . . When we get wrapped up in being "accountable", these little snap-shots are difficult to assign a value too.*

## LEGISLATION AS INSTITUTIONAL LIFESTYLE

Accountability takes another direction, different, but all too related. Or you might say that accountability has a Siamese twin, tied at the hip. That twin is legislation. Legislation is a task that all modern institutions are required to engage in. It matters not whether these institutions are government or corporate, profit or non-profit. Legislation is a main task of the modern institution! And, the effects of modern legislative processes are so pervasive on the human experience that they become engulfing.

> Unlike other civilizations, modernity legislated itself into legislation—legislation as a vocation and duty and as a matter of survival. (Bauman, 1995, p. 34)

Where does the gift exchange fit into this legislative fixation? Legislation insists that all remnants of the gift be forgotten, legislated away, or, at least, trivialized. A cold, calculated, restricted[5] economy emerges, a far cry from an exchange of gifts. Also, rather than searching for those gifts and goods currently in circulation, legislation is preoccupied with problems and deficits, those things that irritate, annoy, leave us indebted and overwhelmed. But here we discover a serious dilemma, for the problems that legislation tends to focus upon are repetitively those that cling like lint on black velvet—they are all-too visible and they refuse to disappear.

> *Rebecca Straforelli, Public Health Nurse, Surrey, B.C.: We didn't see families as a list of problems and it was really hard to fight because we had to come back and write it down as a list of problems. So it's that whole idea of fighting the power of written text. It's the idea that when you write something down it becomes powerful and it has the power to be truth because it's written down. And, we knew, instinctively inside, that families aren't a list of problems. They are so much more. And the way the "Problem Oriented Record" was set up and designed was that problems superseded and cancelled out the gifts and the good that families had.*

> *Rebecca Straforelli: We are conditioned to believe that we are the professionals and therefore we must know best. I have heard many nurses say "I like this (problem-based) framework because it gives clear guidelines for what I'm supposed to do. The score tells me whether or not I should follow the family." Other comments have been "I liked it as a new nurse because I didn't have experience to fall back on and by following the guidelines I felt I was doing the right thing." "We need clear instructions for new nurses to know who to follow and how many visits we should do." I can't help but feel this is a false sense of security. It takes away the responsibility of the person to listen, to hear, to experience the relationship, to be moved and touched by the humanity of the people's lives we are inspecting.*

[5]Steven David Ross (1996) compares the economies of the gift to what he refers to as restricted economies. I use the term restricted to specifically refer to those economies that function by increasing value through restriction. The less there is of specific item, and the less access people and institutions have to this item, the more value it develops. Value becomes quickly associated with scarcity. Gift economies, in comparison, tend to increase the worth of an item, not with restriction, but to the contrary, in accordance with the items relation to abundance. The most treasured or valued (if I may use an accountability term to discuss the gift economy) items are those that are found in abundance (see also Hyde, 1979).

## THE ETERNAL RETURN OF PROBLEM/LEGISLATION

An eternal return[6] surfaces. This eternal return is compellingly reminiscent of the sin/law dynamics discussed by Paul in the New Testament. The contemporary eternal-return hides its tiresome repetition by somehow inspiring expectation, by encouraging the belief that the problem/legislation process, if only done right, would truly lead to a secularized salvation. Yet over and over again problem/legislation creates more of the same, hence an eternal return.

The failure of problem/legislation is typically defined as a failure to get the right formula of problem/legislation. This leads to the conclusion that more, not less of this problem/legislation process is needed. Contemporary political movements and upheavals are based on this process. Organizational restructuring is argued on this basis. C.E.O.s are repetitively recycled because of this eternal return and its failed hope. Over and over the task of this eternal return seems simple—develop awareness that the other person, party or position is in deficit and sinking with problems; persuade those with institutional influence that what is needed is a newer, better code, brought about by newer, better leadership that could lead people to some sort of legislative promised land. In the end, what does one usually get, not a promised land, but more of the same. And, that "more of the same" just leads to even more of "more of the same".

This problem/legislation interaction also mimics the very therapeutic processes that many of us are professionally involved in. Is this really what we do when we do good work? Do we identify a problem or deficit, attempt to understand the depths of the problem then put a plan or an intervention in place to fix it? Or, when we do good work, are we doing something else?

Much of human service practice is already embedded in layers of code, policy and procedure. While this may often be necessary, it should also be a cause of worry. Meaningful human service work occurs in response to human beings and human faces. Layers of legislation can never replace respectful practitioners responding to people and community.

## INTERRUPTED BY THE GIFT

If leadership, bureaucrats and executives were to do less restructuring, and instead focus their attentions on showing an honest recognition of the gifts of their workers, as well as providing ways and means that would enable the workers to continue responding to individuals and communities, they would discover a

[6]Eternal return is a term used extensively by Nietzsche (1967). We use it to describe any process that repetitively repeats itself, that causes itself to return again and again. These processes are not necessarily undesirable, but can be meaningfully productive, devastating, or somewhere in between.

realistic vision of effective human services work. This vision would not be waiting to transpire, but would happen before their eyes.

To our delight this is exactly what we saw in the Fraser Health Authority, with management leadership shown by individuals such Catherine Kidd and Margaret Gander. We saw leadership that eschewed the typical institutional bifurcations, honestly admired the work of the public health nurses, and worked hard to enable them to continue their productive practices.

In the New Testament this eternal return of sin/law is to be interrupted by charis, grace, or gift, so in the problem/legislation world the gift interrupts.[7]

## RESPONSE-ABLE PRACTICES

Jacques Derrida (1995) introduces another word that takes us in very different directions to bifurcation, accountability and legislation. He opens us to responsibility. While reminding us of the work of the Czech writer, Patocka, Derrida states that responsibility, in Czech, is tied to the word "response". Certainly this tie is evident in English, too. Derrida draws much from this connection, claiming that responsibility is too often tied to truth claims, to dogma, to knowledge, whether religious, political, scientific or other. He utilizes Patocka's phrase to suggest that the "discounting of responsibility" is to "subordinate responsibility to the objectivity of knowledge" (p. 24). Instead of submitting to the long-standing Christian and secular traditions that connect responsibility to the objectivity of knowledge and dogma, Derrida invites us to enter a world where human action is a *movement of response*. He suggests that responsibility demands response, and, more precisely, response to an other. Responsibility awakens us to a person, to a face. Responsibility inherently ties us into relationship. Relationship and response demand the other; always lead us to the other. Derrida quotes Patocka.

> In the final analysis the soul ... is not a relation to an *object*, however elevated ... but to a person who fixes it in his gaze while at the same time remaining beyond the reach of the gaze of that soul (as cited in Derrida, p. 25).

> <u>Marjorie Warkentin, Public Health Nurse, Langley, B.C.:</u> *I like the word "responding". When I go into a clinic I know I have tasks to do. But our work is really about responding. When I go into a home it is about responding—I am therefore much more relaxed.*

[7] In the New Testament grace and gift represent the language of a new world outside of that world created by the language of sin and law, so in contemporary times the gift and the gift exchange become language that enables the creation of more engaging and liberating worlds that extend outside of the institutional language of legislation and accountability.

## AWAKENING TO THE FACE

Bauman (1995) is also committed to this emphasis on response to the other. He reiterates that legislation and relation/response are two very separate experiences. He escapes the objectification of relationship by writing extensively about an "awakening to the face" (p. 60). And, it is about how we respond together, in the context of that face.

Following up on Derrida and Bauman, responsibility becomes something that is not about following rules; it is not about giving obedience to some predefined order, it isn't even about gaining knowledge and acting on that knowledge. Responsibility is about how we act in a rhizome[8] world. It is about decisions that are made in connection with others, in conversation, in relationship. Responsibility is a constantly shifting quest about how we respond to those people around us, or more precisely, that person facing us. It is about face. It is about how we look someone in the face. It is about whether we look someone in the face. And, it is about how do we respond, together, in the context of that looking.

Irresponsibility, on the other hand, is about refusing to look someone in the face. Let us never forget the discipline of the soldier; how s/he is trained to not see the face of his enemy, to be more productive in his/her killing. An example of the "irresponsible", at the time of this writing: America and its allies insist on maintaining sanctions on Iraq, and in preparing for war, a military type discipline is needed to ensure the irresponsibility not to see the faces of perhaps one million Iraqi children who lost their lives as a result of the sanctions. Not just their faces, what about the faces of their moms and dads, grandparents, brothers and sisters? Of course, the regime in Iraq also survives through irresponsibility, through erasing faces. It is infamous in its erasure. But, erasure, in various forms and intensities, seems almost a default task of institutions. Irresponsibility erases all these faces, and in this erasure it eventually erases our own faces, and even the faces of our own children. It erects bureaucracies and institutions, policies, procedures, problems and deficits, and legislation upon legislation. But, most tragically, it erases faces.

> Rebecca Straforelli, Public Health Nurse, Surrey, B.C.: *I could never feel completely comfortable telling the family that I had decided that they had a high score (which means they are plagued with problems) and therefore I felt they needed me to come into their home and continue to assess them. How must that feel?*

[8]Rhizome is a botanical term used extensively by Deleuze and Guattari (1983b) to describe a non-institutional network of lines and nodes that connect the lines. We define this rhizome place as community, not an institutional community, but a rhizome community, that place of multiple and shifting relations where the meaningful elements of life emerge (Kinman, 2000).

## PRACTICING THE GIFT

Is health care about faces? Is it about responsible practice? Is it about the gift? It was for these public health nurses. They could paint in rich language the contours and lines on the lives and faces of the people they worked with. Tied to these faces were stories, tied to the stories came understanding, and with all of this came a sense of gift.[9] An important point—the gift exchange for these public health nurses was not focused on their giving, but rather, through the faces of the people these nurses worked with came a gift for the nurses. And, in response, in the nurses' ability to respond (response-ability) to these gifts, a transaction occurred. The faces these nurses worked for also saw faces. They saw and experienced the faces of the nurses. A face-to-face interaction, the gift exchange circulating—this is what responsibility is.

We propose that anything good that occurs in health-care comes in the form of gift exchange, and it comes with a face. Ask anybody about good experiences receiving services from health professionals (and most people have some of these stories to tell); the face and the gift are always present. Once more, this is what responsible practice is.

> Nurse quoted in Local Wisdom: *Looking back, I realize that my client was a gift to me—a gift that I didn't recognize at first. Sometimes she comes back and almost haunts me—in a good way. I feel that I have evolved in a way.*
>
> Maryanne I, Public Health Nurse, Surrey, B.C.: *The mother is a single mom with two kids and she is just having a really hard time. She has no family or anyone here so I've been going in probably about once a month and just visiting her. She's very negative about herself and her family and the way her life is going. I see so much potential in her and I saw a lot of gifts. I wanted her to be more aware of them and focus more on them rather than the negative. So, slowly every visit I would write down a couple of gifts that I'd noticed during those visits. About a month ago I went to her place and we went over them all together. I had a full page. I probably had fourteen or fifteen gifts that I could share with her. And it was a real good experience, seeing her expression and hearing her, "Wow, thanks!" I typed these gifts out on the computer. She put them up on her fridge so she can go over them. I think it gave her more a sense of a self, more a sense of family and a feeling that she is doing something right for her family.*
>
> *I don't think anybody had ever sat her down and told her anything good about her—because she had been into drugs and prostitution. To have somebody sit down and tell her good things about her was really amazing. It's wonderful now. When I go see her it's like I'm part of the family. It's just a really nice experience. Even the kids love having me there. I really, really enjoy it.*

[9] For more reading on the gift exchange see the following: Fox (1994); Godbout & Caille (1998); Hyde (1979); McKnight (1995); and Ross (1996, 1998).

## THE GIFT OF DEATH

Derrida (1995) associates the gift and responsibility with death. Death, according to Derrida, reminds us of the irreplaceable, of uniqueness, of absolute singularity. Death has an effect on us only because it takes away something irreplaceable. If it were not irreplaceable, it would not seem like death to us. When the replaceable disappears, it is simply replaced. When the irreplaceable disappears, we experience death.

> The gift of infinite love comes from someone and is addressed to someone; responsibility demands irreplaceable singularity. Yet only death or rather the apprehension of death can give this irreplaceability, and it is only on the basis of it that one can speak of a responsible subject (Derrida, p. 51).

Look at faces around you- is there not an absolute singularity about these faces? Can these faces be replaced? If your child, or your mother, or your lover's face were erased would this not be an experience of death? The irreplaceable gift is only such in the context of death.

In a similar manner, Derrida connects the acts of love to the finite and to the ruin. Ruin is not a negative thing... What else is there to love anyway? One cannot love a monument, a work of architecture, an institution as such except in an experience itself precarious in its fragility: it has not always been there, it will not always be there, it is finite. And for this reason one loves it as mortal, through its birth and its death, through one's own birth and death... through the ghost or silhouette of its ruin, one's own ruin... How can one love otherwise than in this finitude? Derrida (2000, p. 278).

Where does the gift not more belong than in the realm of health care? Death and ruin, in health care, maintain a steady presence. The irreplaceable face is most treasured at those times when death presses upon a human community the very irreplaceability of that face. Nurses repeatedly find themselves in the presence of the gift of an irreplaceable human life in the very face of death and ruin. Are they able within the face of death to engage in a response-able practice? Story after story confirmed, for the nurses, the answer: an unambiguous "yes"!

> <u>Nurse quoted in Local Wisdom:</u> *I remember a family who had a baby born with Down's syndrome along with a serious heart condition. The baby couldn't come home right away. When the baby was able to return home I met with them. Unfortunately the baby died at 4 months... I wrote the gifts down and sent them in a card. It was a very positive experience. I met her in the mall at a later time. She told me that she appreciated it so much that she called all her friends to read it to them.*

> <u>Nurse quoted in Local Wisdom:</u> *This phone call I just got, it was to do with a teenage boy addicted to crystal-meth. He just called to say that he turned down some speed. You could look at this boy and see how miserable he had made his world and those*

*around him, or you could choose to see some good in him. I chose the later. And, it just paid off.*

*Often when we talk of a language of gifts, people respond as if the gift should only be spoken of in places that are cheerful and positive, in places where death is far away. But why? Is this not a gross trivialization of the gift?*

*A friend recently asked me how the gift fit into a specific, real situation where children who were being abused were not removed from the home to a safer setting. Her question implied a sort of inappropriate placement, where the gift seemed out of context in light of such injustice. Derrida, however, places the gift right on the doorstep of such places. Pain, suffering, frustration, and even death—these are the places where the gift becomes most evident. These are the places that expose the gift. If we stop to face these experiences with people, to listen, we discover that the pain exists only because much more precious things are very real to them. For example, troubled parents are typically only troubled because they have a relationship with an irreplaceable human being, their own child. Without this relationship, they could not be troubled or parents. Death of a relationship only hurts because the relationship is valued and loved—it is a gift. If we connect with a person, or a family in the time of pain, will not the gifts emerge in light of the pain they are experiencing? Is not our job, as human service professionals, one of connecting people to the very gifts that give significance to the pain itself? Will these gifts not carry people through?*

## HEALTH CARE PRACTICE AND A LANGUAGE OF GIFTS

The languaging of gift exchange in health care, just like other communal tasks, is not something that is passed down in a hierarchical manner. It cannot be taught, legislated, controlled or insisted upon. But, it can be awoken. It can be touched. It can be shared across a table. It can be invited. It spirals and escalates, transforming and re-transforming actions and practices. The languaging of gifts exposes rich and productive ways of interacting with clients, with colleagues, with management, with our own families and communities.

In the heart of health care—whether it is the weighing of a baby, the cut of the surgeon's knife, cleaning a wound, vaccinating a child, listening at a bedside—all involves hands, all demands a face to face. Health care, if it is truly about health and care, can be nothing else but a gift exchange. Health, as well as safety, community, justice, and so many other goods come to life within that social exchange—the languaging of the gift.

### The Watcher on the Hill

### *Reflection by Lynn Hoffman*

*I have this image of sitting on a hill on one side of the continent while Chris Kinman has been sitting on a hill on the other side. We kept exchanging smoke signals, and on a few occasions I flew across the country at his expense. This connection kept surprising me as it germinated, grew, then burst into bloom. Let me tell the story of my connection with the unusual partnership called "Rock the Boat," directed by Chris Kinman, family and community therapist and former minister, and criminologist Peter Finck.*

*Back in 1994, Chris phoned me and asked me to come out to do a workshop in British Columbia. When I came, we had a small workshop (not more than 25–30 people attended). I was quite disappointed. However, Chris brought me into contact with the powerful traditions of First Nations culture, and particularly the art of the Haida from the Charlotte Islands. Chris was working with First Nations youth and families, and had been greatly influenced by the ritual of the potlatch, where the idea is to give rather than to acquire. During a break in this workshop, which was being held near the university in Vancouver, I went into a hall and noticed a room full of green light. There, in the midst of ficus trees and bamboo, was an astonishing object. It was a greenish bronze canoe, half the size of the room, and in it a variety of totemic animals were struggling and biting each other, the raven with the bear, the wolf with the eagle, while half-human creatures like the Dogfish Woman, or the Bear Mother, paddled, watched over by the Village Chief with his temple-shaped hat. I learned that this was the achievement of a sculptor called Bill Reid, who was himself descended from the Haida. In this work, titled The Spirit of the Haida Gwai, Reid represented himself as the Ancient Conscript, paddling along with the rest.*

*Chris also took me to the university bookstore, a favorite haunt, and introduced me to a number of philosophical writers like Gaston Bachelard (1994), who came up with the concept of "reverberation" as an alternative to "causation". Another two French writers, Deleuze and Guattari (1983a, 1983b), had used the image of the "rhizome" to counteract the tree-like hierarchies that permeate Western professions, and which Chris was seeking to dismiss. At this time, he told me that one of his interests was the literature on "the gift". He said he wanted to work from the idea of abundance rather than the idea of lacks and disabilities.*

*Chris showed me some of the journals he had put together that he called Local Wisdom. Some of the titles were Local Wisdom of the Mothers, or Local Wisdom of Some Parents, or Local Wisdom of the Kids. He would transcribe what people said to him and put it into a journal that would represent in writing what was spoken. Sometimes he would intersperse their comments with passsages he wrote, or quotes from writers he admired. I felt it gave the people he worked with a special dignity to be set down in print like that. These documents then informed the future, in what I was beginning to call a "Rolling Conversation."*

*Another innovation Chris showed me was what he called a Collaborative Action Plan. This document was an alternative to the usual problem oriented record, widely used by services in that area. What was special was that it was organized around a "language of gifts." The first page asked, What are the gifts this person and the community around them are giving. The second asked, What are the potentials this person and community can offer. The third page read, What are the roadblocks to these gifts and potentials. This was the gist of it, although it varied over time. Chris told me that just using this document drastically altered his relationships with the people he worked with for the better.*

*In his wish to acquaint me with his environment, Chris took me to an old time resort hotel in the Canadian Rockies, showing me as we drove all kinds of wild life. It was only one night, but it must have cost a pretty penny—well worth it, if the idea was to impress me. I asked about the work he was doing with First Nations young people and their families, and he told me touching stories about his efforts to see the world as they did. One memorable thing he told me was about a teen-age girl who said to him, "Therapists try to get into your head; counsellors help you bear your burdens." Or, as he put it, "What the mountain cannot bear, the river takes away." I liked the idea that therapy might be like the river. We closed our time together with a trip to the Anthropological Museum, the repository of so much First Nations culture and its splendor. I bought a book on the work of Bill Reid, and said goodbye.*

*A year went by, and Chris asked me out again. He had organized a meeting that represented the "systems" he was working with: some parents of kids he was seeing; a group of his trainees; and a few of his colleagues. At the time I was much influenced by Tom Andersen's ideas about reflecting process, and thought we could use such a format for our meeting. What I did was to ask Chris to sit and listen while I interviewed each "pod" in the circle about their experience with Chris very different way of working. The parents said that Chris was not like the usual social service worker because he made them feel like helpers and partners. The students were pleased, because the tools he gave them made connecting with clients so easy. His colleagues had similar things to say. During all this, Chris fidgeted horribly, but every time he tried to break in, I stopped him. When all had their say, I turned to him and asked about the impact on him of what he had heard. He was obviously full of emotion by this time, and turned to the notes he had taken, offering each persons' idea as if it were a line in an extended poem. I talked about our relationship, and how close I felt to him at that moment, and he responded similarly. Then we thanked the company and broke to have refreshments and further discussion.*

*A couple of years later, Chris asked me to come back again to preside over a meeting that was called Honoring Community. This time the gathering was more formal, and Chris introduced me to his new partner, Peter Finck. Present were representatives of various health services: some foster parents, two members of a biker gang (they actually rode bikes and had tattoos) who directed homes for troubled boys; a probation officer (the only one there who had a degree); some social work trainees; and a group of adults brought over from Vancouver Island by psychiatrist Robin Routledge that was called The Mood Clinic. Chris gave an orienting talk, and introduced me, and I then sat with each subgroup and asked about their work. I was very touched by the different experiences that were presented, and the ideas offered, and because most of the people present would not have otherwise known about the worlds of the others, it became a fascinating conversation, both for those talking and those listening.*

*The day before, I had sat in on a weekly conference attended by the men directing the youth homes. They all had vivid tattoos on their forearms and looked menacing, but their talk was not. Nobody had introduced me, so I felt like a foreign object, but I sat and listened with interest. A large dog under the circular table kept going from one set of feet to another, finally settling on mine. At this point, the leader of the group asked me for my opinions. I said that what had most impressed me was their tenderness. Then I ventured to say something outrageous: I said "To me, you are just a bunch of fairy Godfathers." A moment of appalled silence, and then the whole group burst into a huge roar, looking especially at the leader, who was clearly the chief honcho of them all. Luckily he was laughing too. This leader and a colleague came to the conference, and commented powerfully on their personal experience of social class prejudice within the service professions. But what most caught my eye was a small tag pasted on the shirt of the leader, saying "Fairy Godfather."*

*The conference finished with all of us listening to the people from the Mood Clinic who had made the long trip by ferry, getting up at an ungodly hour to do so. This was an informal club organized with the help of Robin, which played an advocacy role between patients and medical doctors on issues to do with medication and treatment. Their stories enlisted both our sympathies and a feeling of hopefulness. The event as a whole had given me a depth knowlege of the helpers and workers who toiled, you might say, in the shadows of desperately troubled clients, and who kept their optimism intact. Again, this was an example of a rolling conversation.*

*But that in no way prepared me for the next time I was asked to the Vancouver area. I had kept in touch with Peter and Chris, and every once in a while Chris would email off to me another one of his journals. Once he used up a whole roll of my fax paper—yards of fax came pouring out of the machine, like an endless Chinese scroll. But now there was a new wrinkle. This was a new Local Wisdom called The Wisdom of the Public Health Nurses. Speaking by phone, Chris had told me that some nurses from the Fraser Valley Health Area had come to Rock the Boat for advice because they had become disenchanted with the problem-oriented record that they used for their assessments. They had heard that he and Peter Finck had been experimenting with a "gift oriented" alternative. Apparently, the Collaborative Action Plan fit the bill. Chris told me how these women had taken this format and were fitting it to their own practice. Then it seemed that their supervisors and the bureacracy were supporting them, that the teaching program in public health nursing at the University of Victoria was also changing.*

*Sitting on my hill a continent away, I noticed a lot of smoke signals, but I still had no idea of the profound implications of the shift that they attested to. Without much warning, Chris and Peter asked me out one more time. It seemed that they were going to have another Honoring Community built around the achievement of the public health nurses. So I flew across one more time, and what I found really staggered my mind.*

*As soon as I got there, I began talking to the nurses who were the frontline workers, and meeting with the program managers who had supported them. They told me about their plan for the meeting the next day. First Chris Kinman would give a slide show with the nurses' own commentary (he stayed up all that next night to finish it). Then I would get to speak to a group of the nurses and hear their story. Then came a group from the bureaucracy, including their chief sponsor, Catherine Kid. Next came a group that represented the teaching program at the University, which included field advisors as well as professors. And finally, I sat with one of the nurses who helped spearhead the change, Marjorie Warkentin, and a young mother who was recovering from a postpartum depression and had agreed to add her voice.*

*What all this represented to me was the first time in my 40 years in the field that I had been present at a change that effected each level of a complex health system, from front line workers to managers to teachers to clients. That last was a particular group usually excluded from such conferences, except as exhibit A in a Grand Rounds. I thought about all the families that had been interviewed by experts in demonstrations of family therapy to huge audiences since my field began. But this young mother, Rose, was not there as evidence of some clinician's ability, but as another voice in behalf of change. She and Marjorie spoke movingly as they described their experience with this "gift-oriented" approach to human difficulty.*

*The conference itself was a rolling conversation, but like all such events, transitory in time. The changes that it attested to were real—for the moment. When I got back to New England, Chris told me that Catherine Kid had been moved to another health area, and that a new bureaucrat had replaced her. I have not learned whether this system-wide change has persisted, or if not, what else has happened. But I am here to bear witness to the newness that shone forth so brightly in the Fraser Valley Health Authority on this one occasion at least. This kind of change will happen again, despite the reductive mantle of managed care, and continue to inspire hope in those of us who believe that the language we use makes all the difference. And there are many of us who continue to be watchers from that hill!*

## REFERENCES

Bachelard, G. (1994). *The poetics of space*. (M. Jolas, Trans.) Boston, MA: Beacon Press.

Bauman, Z. (1995). *Life in fragments: Essays in postmodern morality*. Oxford: Blackwell.

Deleuze, G. & Guattari, F. (1983a). *Anti-Oedipus: Capitalism and schizophrenia*. Minneapolis, MN: University of Minnesota.

Deleuze, G. & Guattari, F. (1983b). *On the line*. New York: Semiotext(e).

Derrida, J. (2002). *Acts of religion*. London: Routledge.

Derrida, J. (1995). *The gift of death*. Chicago, IL: University of Chicago.

Fox, N. (1994). *Postmodernism, sociology and health*. Toronto, ON: University of Toronto.

Giving Voice to the Work of Public Health Nurses. *Local Wisdom* (Online Journal) (2002) www.rocktheboat.ca/lw_0204_nurses.html

Goudbout, J. & Caille, A. (1998). *The world of the gift*. Montreal, QC: McGill-Queens University.

Hyde, L. (1979). *The gift: Imagination and the erotic life of property*. New York: Random House.

Kinman, C. (2000). *A language of gifts*. Vancouver, BC: Rock the Boat.

Maturana, H. & Varela, F. (1987). *The tree of knowledge*. Boston, MA: Shambhala.

McKnight, J. (1995). *The careless society*: Community and its counterfeits. New York: Basic.

Nietzsche, F. (1967). *On the genealogy of morals*. New York: Vintage.
O'Rourke-Phipps, K. (2002). *The gift exchange: Lynn Hoffman and the Public Health Nurses in British Columbia. A Guest Editorial*. http://www.rocktheboat.ca/sf_rhizome_0209.html
Ross, S. D. (1996). *The gift of beauty: The good as art*. New York: State University of New York.
Ross, S.D. (1998). *The gift of touch: Embodying the good*. New York: State University of New York.

## Chapter 15

# Therapy As Social Construction

## Back to Basics and Forward toward Challenging Issues

SHEILA MCNAMEE WITH CONVERSATIONAL PARTNER LOIS SHAWVER

Perhaps the most useful way to enter into the conversation about discursive therapies is to address what I see as a central issue that we must confront as spokespersons of therapy as social construction: What does it mean to approach therapeutic practice from a constructionist stance? What do we do, as therapists, once we propose that meaning emerges in the on-going flow of persons in situated activity? This concern gives rise to a related issue which I will touch upon as an exciting and vitally important direction in which we must now move: how do we assess or evaluate our therapeutic practice if meaning is understood as a local achievement? This question emerges as we confront both the continuing conversation around therapeutic practice and its relation to a constructionist orientation[1] (e.g., this volume stands as one illustration). Our discussions *might be* well focused on appreciating conversations that challenge us to articulate what we mean when we talk of therapeutic practice as social construction.

[1] In this chapter, I am focused on therapy as social construction. I will use the term social construction or constructionism to refer to theory and practice that others in this volume call postmodern or discursive.

## THERAPY AS SOCIAL CONSTRUCTION: RELATIONALLY ENGAGED PRACTICE

First it is necessary to note that while there are many available models of therapy that draw on, or are conversant within, a constructionist philosophy, my own consideration is focused more broadly than any specific model. Solution focused therapy (de Shazer, 1985; Berg, 1994; O'Hanlon & Weiner-Davis, 1989) and narrative approaches to therapy (White & Epston, 1990), to name two, are discussed as constructionist therapies. I do not talk explicitly about either these nor other specific approaches to therapy. I certainly accept them as *elaborations* of therapy as social construction, and others in this volume directly address how this is the case. My own concerns are broader in that I want to explore the question of what we mean when we talk about *therapy as social construction*. What are the implications of this way of talking for practice, for training, for assessment? And, more to the point, what does it *mean* to talk about therapy as social construction?

For now, let me briefly state that therapy as social construction centers attention not on any particular form of practice, nor on any specific activity a therapist might bring into the therapeutic context. Instead, therapy as social construction centers on *how* a therapist might bring particular forms of practice or conceptual bases into the conversation. In short, it is an issue of *how* not (necessarily) *what*. Does the therapist *impose* his or her way of working with clients or does the therapist approach the conversation with clients as a moment of invitation and construction—a moment when all members of the conversation draw upon their histories, their relations, their familiar ways of acting and *gently* introduce them into the therapeutic dialogue. As I will argue here, allegiance to any particular model or technique risks throwing any *gentle* participation in the therapeutic conversation out the window and imposing a domineering or colonizing form of instruction.

If therapy from a constructionist stance lacks specification of a particular therapeutic technique, what is it, precisely, that constructionism has to offer in the therapeutic context? Related is the question of what we teach if there are no set methods or techniques emanating from a constructionist orientation. Perhaps the most useful way to talk about the relationship between constructionism and therapy is to recognize that there are no constructionist therapies *per se*. Rather, constructionism, as a philosophical stance, positions us to view therapeutic process as a *conversation* or *dialogue*.[2] This marks the central distinction between what we

[2] The title of my 1992 volume, co-edited with Kenneth Gergen, speaks directly to this important issue. We titled that volume, *Therapy as Social Construction* rather than *Social Constructionist Therapy* to indicate our focus on a stance or orientation with which we approach therapeutic process as opposed to a focus on any specific type of therapy (e.g., a model). As constructionists, we are interested in

have come to call constructionist (or discursive) therapies and others. However, this point has not been well articulated to date in the constructionist literature.

For the constructionist, language is the focus of our concern. It is in language that we create the worlds in which we live. Thus, it should come as no surprise that in therapy, we are focused on the discourse of participants and how particular discursive moves constrain or potentiate different forms of action and, consequently, different realities. This is a liberating stance because when we become curious, as opposed to judgmental, about *how* people engage with each other, we open ourselves to the consideration of alternatives. This particular feature is often associated with the postmodern/constructionist focus on uncertainty. Attention to language (which, to the constructionist includes all embodied activities) positions us in a reflexive relationship to our own actions as well as to the actions of others. We are poised and prepared to ask, "What other ways might I invite this client into creating a story of transformation?" "How is she inviting me into legitimating/transforming/challenging (etc.) her story?" "What other voices might I use now? Would the voice of a behavioral therapist be useful at this point? Of a friend? Of a parent?" "What other voices might he use? Perhaps I could ask him to answer me as if he were his wife responding, as if he were his fear speaking, or as if he were speaking as the person he wants to imagine himself to be when he doesn't have this problem any more."

## HOW DO WE UNDERSTAND LANGUAGE?

What is the place of language and its relation to the meaning making process? Language and meaning are, after all, central to psychotherapy. As long as there remains confusion about language and meaning making, therapy as social construction will be misconstrued as a particular school or model of therapy rather than a way of positioning oneself towards social life in general, and toward therapeutic process more specifically.

One of the byproducts of conceptualizing language as a system we use to represent or picture the world is that it reduces our activities with each other to a technique. Specifically, if language is a system of symbols we use to represent the world, then in any conversation we are generally entering into a debate about my representation of things versus yours. The byproduct of this is that we attempt to claim the truth by using language accurately (according to us and the standards of our significant communities—which very likely differ). This form of persuasive discourse, which we try to justify by an appeal to a reality that already exists,

exploring therapy (and any other context or phenomena) first and foremost as a conversation wherein realities are crafted.

permeates our institutions (education, government, health, etc.) as well as our intimate relationships. The difficulty is that this view raises the question of what reality is that is "out there" and independent of our ways of talking and acting. Here opinions differ. While most would agree that accurate or truthful representations must be rationally or logically formulated, the question is *which* or *whose* logic or rationality is appropriated. This question is pertinent because it calls to the fore the difficulty of *actively responding*[3] to any discourse (particularly those that are incommensurate with our own) in a way that is consistent with a constructionist sensibility. Can our responses, our justifications to those who question us serve as invitations to ***future*** coordinations rather than as claims to the truth?

One arena in which constructionism is consistently questioned, for example, is the arena of evaluation and assessment. Here, critics want to know whether therapy, when situated as a process of social construction, has standards by which we can evaluate the success of both the therapy, itself, and the professional competency of the therapist. If we can engage with our critics on this topic in a manner that invites further coordinations and conversations, we engage an aesthetic consistency between our theory and our practice. The aesthetic consistency is engendered when we, as constructionists, attempt to coordinate our activities with our critics rather than debate them. It is this unity or consistency of theory and practice that gives way to the identification of constructionism as a practical theory and thus affords an aesthetic quality to our work. In simplest form, it is to practice what we preach. And, in this practice there is an aesthetic harmony due to our resisting opportunities to tell others how it is or should be and rather, to engage others in attempts to coordinate our multiple views.

To be able to have such conversations with our critics is an achievement that varies dramatically from the modernist goal of winning the skeptic "over to the other side." In fact, this issue opens the door to the very purpose of a constructionist discourse. That is, it centers on how we might *bridge incommensurate discourses* in such a manner that we can create meaningful and ***useful*** ways of going on together. Isn't this, after all, what therapy is all about? This purpose is dramatically different from the tradition of debate where the goal of conversation (argument) is to decide which expert has the facts straight. But, again, straight by whose standards? It also underscores the central distinction that approaching therapy as social construction offers: our emphasis is on *coordination* and not on *shared meaning*. This bridging or coordinating of incommensurate discourses is the process of co-construction. It does not yield my truth over yours but ours.

Let me address this point in more detail. Because we are interested in the construction of meaning, many believe that it is a particular meaning, a shared meaning, or a form of *commensurate* meaning that therapy as social construction

[3]Later in this chapter I will discuss the centrality of active responsivity—what I call relational engagement—in constructionist practice.

strives to achieve. In fact, adopting a non-representational view of language, we must pause to ask, *"What does **going on together** mean if not agreement on meaning?"* Is it possible to go on together without shared meaning or a common discourse? These questions are most often left unanswered in the constructionist literature and consequently many make the erroneous assumption that bridging incommensurate discourses means not only sharing the *same* discourse, but the same meanings as well. It is here that the distinction between coordinated activities and unity of action and meaning becomes central. People can perform well coordinated scenarios with little or no shared meaning. I can disagree strongly with all that you hold dear while still engaging you in dialogue full of potential. I think here of the dialogues orchestrated by The Public Conversations Project (Chasin, et al., 1996; Chasin & Herzig, 1994) where the aim is to bring people with diametrically opposing beliefs and values together not for purposes of debating contentious issues but to engage in well coordinated conversation (i.e., dialogue). What emerges in these dialogues is not common understanding but *coordinated respect* for differences. I call this form of respect coordinated because participants are *responsively with* each other in the moment. They are not focused on coming to some unified position but hope, instead, to grant each other the *right* to be coherent.

Like the Public Conversations Project, a constructionist emphasis is on ***bridging*** incommensurate discourses, *not* on ***making incommensurate discourses commensurate***. Unfortunately, many read the constructionist literature as implying an emphasis on making differences commensurate. It is not difficult to see that when language is viewed as a representation of how things really are in the world, the penchant to make differences unified is tempting because, by definition, there can only be one reality. Yet, the constructionist emphasis on the ***activity*** (bridging) and not the ***entity*** (reality or one, unified discourse) is, as Bateson (1972) says, *the difference that makes a difference*! Here we find the distinction between debate and dialogue akin to the distinction between determining what the entity is, what the reality is (which requires debate) and constructing connections, bridges among previously incompatible ways of being (which requires dialogue). Let's examine very briefly the dialogue/debate distinction.

## THE DIFFERENCE OF DIALOGUE

An impetus for my work as a constructionist is to try to find ways of talking and writing that alert people to the possibility of the unknown, the surprises, the newness that might emerge in conversation. Certainly, therapy is a context which shares these emphases. To talk of any kind of conversation (not just therapeutic) in terms of openness, uncertainty, surprise, newness reminds me of the pioneering work of the Mental Research Institute (e.g., Watzlawick, Weakland, & Fisch, 1974) who talked about first and second order change. Any comment or action in a given conversation can be an opening to something entirely different. Unfortunately, we most often treat another's comments and actions (as well as our own) as part of anticipated rituals. Thus, an action that could invite an entirely different way of relating and creating meaning together could be interpreted as a variation on the on-going theme, the same old thing. The constructionist view is that second order change (i.e., change of entire patterns) is always potentially possible. Yet, our tendency to act into relational rituals actually constructs sedimentation of our realities or first order change (simply substituting one action for another similar action thereby maintaining the overall pattern or meaning). An important step that dialogue offers is the opening of possibilities for people to pause and consider various alternatives—or, second order change.

I find that Wittgenstein's (1953) focus on how we go on together shifts our focus from debate to dialogue. Human engagement requires attention to how we craft liveable futures together. In the simplest terms, the focus on how we go on together suggests the need to create the conversational space where *different* kinds of conversations can transpire. This implies that the preparation for generative dialogue should be central. How can we invite participants to engage in dialogue from a stance of coordination and not co-optation and therefore, with *different* voices. Often in conversations, we find ourselves speaking from abstract positions. This frequently takes the form of statements like, "This is what I believe," "This is true," "This is right," "This is wrong." These abstractions serve as invitations to debate. Yet, inviting others to speak from a personal or significant story tends to invite dialogue, newness, and surprise. While I may disagree with your position on something, I can't tell you that your story is wrong.

*Lois Shawver: At this point, your words evoke in me a story about my recently feeling trapped in a conversation in which I was tempted to debate, and even continuously struggling with the temptation. Since your words evoked this story in me, would you say that you successfully invited me to want to initiate dialogue with a story? And does my saying I have such a story in any way invite you to tell one, thus creating a dialogue? I am not asking you to tell me your story, necessarily, but wondering if this relates to what you mean by "inviting dialogue" rather than dispute.*

*Sheila McNamee: As I was writing the above passage, I was thinking about how often we tend to make broad, sweeping statements and make them with a air of certitude. I challenge myself by continually pausing to notice the ways in which my own knee-jerk tendencies to speak "as if I* ***really*** *know" (after all, I am an academic!) actually close down dialogue. I want to be aware of how those sorts of actions invite a classical form of argument. I do not mean to say that classical argument is bad or wrong. I simply want to open up some space for engaging differently together. I find that I do this most by telling stories or anecdotes about my own life, my family, my insecurities... not in a mode of self deprecation but rather in the spirit of inviting those with whom I am speaking to fully engage* ***with*** *me. So, yes. I suppose a story does beget a story!*

This opens a possibility for us to be in a different kind of conversation than one in which we would otherwise find ourselves. Often, people are responsive to what they imagine the other person will say based on the relationship's history. But, that is not what *has* to happen and that is where conversations go awry quite often. If I'm truly being attentive to the process of relating—that is, being relationally responsible (McNamee & Gergen, 1999)—no matter how many times you and I may have had into an argument about something, when I'm talking with you now I will not necessarily listen to what you are saying *in that frame*. Rather, I might be attentive to what we are doing *right now*. The history of that becomes a part of it, but does not dominate it. Again, this leaves space for the creativity.

The question is how can we build in Bateson's (1972) notion of the difference that makes a difference? How can we position ourselves in relationships such that we are either waiting to understand another's "same old" comments or activities in slightly different ways *or* willing to do things ourselves in slightly different ways? It has always been interesting to me to notice how we talk about dialogue as a natural activity. We engage in dialogue every day. And in contrast, we think of debate as something in which we must be trained. In debate, we have rules and procedures. There is an order to debate. Ironically, in order to make a difference (to invite dialogue not debate), in order for the newness to emerge, we must make the ordinary unusual, make the familiar, unfamiliar. We can do so formally as illustrated by public dialogue models such as the Public Conversations Project, and we can do so in a more intimate relationship. It is not so difficult to say, "Let's make a rule before we have a conversation that we won't talk in this way or we won't be too quick to judge each other." Personally and intellectually I find that those operations remind us that dialogue is full of potential. But we need to be reminded by making it into something that is foreign. I will return to the importance of making the familiar unfamiliar later.

A poignant illustration is repeated each year in my courses. Students engage frequently in simulations of families, colleagues, couples, and so forth. The first thing that happens in these simulations is that students look for the "script" and their "part." I inform them that there is no script, there are no parts. They simply need to begin, for example, being a family. They start by drawing on extremely stereotypical images. Yet, slowly they create an identity that is beyond any one of them—a beautiful illustration of the performative notion of developing into who you will become. They engage in precisely the sort of creative, unusual, and spontaneous reality that marks the distinction between dialogue and debate. They create identities, relationships, and even *histories* that are part of all of them but not identifiable with any single one of them. They engage in a conversation and questions are asked and accusations made and things happen. And then, if those of us observing ask them questions, we find that our questions can change or arrest the direction or nature of what is being created and so forth. This all becomes so powerful that, in every single instance, there has been at least one person in the simulation who has felt it necessary to declare openly to the class, when all is said and done, "I am not like that! That is not who I am. I don't act that way. I don't believe in those things."

This activity is an opportunity for all of us to see the power of dialogue. It also provides us with the opportunity to reflect on how infrequently we question *how* we accomplish the creation of beliefs, values, and identities in this ordinary practice called dialogue. Participants in simulations might believe that it is ordinary to be a mother this way or be a father that way, but very quickly it becomes unusual, not ordinary. It becomes an incredibly unique and unpredictably dynamic. The interactive moment[4] constructs the identity of the family, of each individual and so forth. To me, this is an illustration of the tension in dialogue to recognize our routines and our assumptions while also recognizing the open potential for transformation, for something beyond the usual.

## THERAPY AS SOCIAL CONSTRUCTION

As therapists, we are not interested in persuading clients to see their difficulties as we do from our "expert, professional position." Therapy as social construction is not concerned with debating what is healthy or unhealthy in dialogue with clients. Nor is it concerned with debating what counts as constructionist technique and what does not at the level of professional, academic and clinical dialogue. Therapy as social construction concerns itself with an ethical obligation to coordinate disparate logics or discourses. The simplest way to articulate this constructionist ethic is to say (again) that reality, truth, and values are neither mine nor yours but they are ours. Yet *ours* to the constructionist does not imply a common discourse nor shared meaning. *Ours* refers to the relational construction of a joint space where participants can *coordinate* their activities together. It is the creation of a conversational domain where respect for divergent rationalities is coordinated—the *coordinated respect* of which I spoke earlier. This ethic helps constructionists articulate theory and practice in a manner that is closer to an invitation to practical dialogues aimed at creating new futures together, rather than a closed pronouncement of how things already or *really* are. This ethic assures the *aesthetic consistency* of constructionism—not a reliance on convincing (debating) others how things are or should be but a way of *engaging* in relational coordination with others that does not separate theory from practice.

[4]The interactive moment refers to the moment by moment engagement of persons in their situated activities. This focus on what people are doing *together in the moment* is not, however, devoid of the historical and cultural resources available to them. In other words, social construction, with its focus on the interactive moment, does not move all social interchange to either a level of abstraction such that there is little left to inform participants how to go on nor does it move to such a singular level of activity that any interchange is capable of being viewed as a-historical and/or a-cultural.

To maintain a focus on *therapy as conversation* (another way to say "therapy as social construction"), I find it useful to be attentive to how we might focus on our activity with others. We should be able to offer our critics the sort of responsiveness and engagement in the relational process of constructing realities together that we offer our clients in therapy. Furthermore, we should be able to do so without waving the banner of "better." Discursive therapies are not better. They are not techniques. They are orientations to therapeutic process that privilege what is happening in the conversation. The focus is on dialogue, not on individuals, psyches, situations, problems, or relationships divorced from the conversations that construct them. This is a significant difference because it positions the discursive therapist in an open manner to *any* method of therapy.

Specifically, approaches to therapy, as well as theoretical models, are most typically taken as incommensurate or in competition by most practitioners. Working from one model usually implies allegiance to that model and not to others. Such an attitude ensures that the virtues and values of one over another will be continually debated. The constructionist focus on *how we engage with others* in crafting possible futures, pasts and presents, allows us to attempt *coordinated respect* for all models. The constructionist focus on dialogue facilitates bridging (i.e., coordinating) different discourses at the expense of arriving at one answer (i.e., adopting one truth/model over all others or *making the incommensurate, commensurate*). Behavioral, cognitive, psychoanalytic, narrative, solution focused, and all other models become ***potentially*** viable and generative ways of becoming relationally engaged with clients. For example, one client might find a psychoanalytic understanding of his problem as useful in "going on" while another might find the same form of understanding exceedingly pathologizing, only making the situation worse than it was before therapy. The point is that a therapist can not know ahead of time how to engage with clients. We can not know what will resonate for any particular person. At the same time, as therapists, we can not enter into a therapeutic conversation without our own historical traditions, relations, and forms of discourse. To hold on to the idea that any discourse (any that could be potentially offered by the therapist as well as any that could be offered by the client) *could be* generative underscores the way in which any model, theory, or technique can be potentially viable and transformative.

Social construction serves as a philosophical stance one adopts in relation to meaning construction. As noted, emphasis is on language in use. My attempts to talk about social construction *in action* have led me to the term, *relational engagement*. While this term, itself, may appear unspecified or vague, it *must* remain so if it is to be first and foremost situationally sensitive. At the same time that constructionists find unilateral and scripted use of a given technique antithetical to constructionist work, we also find reliance on abstract concepts and categories equally unresponsive to the interactive moment. Thus, one way of describing relationally engaged activity (i.e., relational practice), is to characterize any theory or technique as an option for action rather than as an essential truth or means toward truth. The challenge is then one of coordinating creative possibilities among various options.

## Theories and Techniques as Discursive Options

Any particular discourse (or in this case, any particular theory or model) becomes a potential resource for transformation rather than a tool that will *bring about* (read: cause) transformation. Social construction, as a therapeutic stance, tunes us into the interactive moment where therapeutic change might be possible. The challenge, of course, is that there are no specific techniques, nor are there any desires, to determine which ways of talking are therapeutic and which are not. The question of what is therapeutic remains open and indeterminant, just like conversation. When therapy is understood as a *conversational process*, we can never be certain where it will go. I can never fully predict another's next move and consequently, the potential for moving in new directions, generating new conclusions and possibilities (and constraints) is ever present. What we can do, however, is remain open and attentive to what conversational resources we select and which ones might serve as useful alternatives. It is important at this point to emphasize that (1) we make no attempt in constructionist practice to act in a particular manner beyond adopting the stance of responsivity and relational engagement. One can not know ahead of time what *should* be done. Like improvisation, however, the professional who embraces therapy as a process of social construction will "prepare to improvise" by remaining respectfully curious about differences, (2) we become relationally engaged by focusing attention on the conversational processes of those involved (rather than on individuals, objects, problems, or specific strategies), and (3) we can not "know" what forms of relational engagement (what specific actions) will contribute to therapeutic change ahead of time. Relational engagement can only take place in the situated moment; not in the abstractions of universal or disembodied techniques.

> *LS: I am recalling that earlier you spoke of "relational rituals" constructing "sedimentation of our realities" and to such a sedimentation you are contrasting, it seems, improvisation, or performance that is tailored to the moment. But can't improvisation be improved by training or practice? Are we ever acting totally in the moment? For example, I have heard people improvise on a musical instrument. I believe my ability to improvise this way is greatly limited by the fact that I do not play such an instrument. And, surely, learning a language helps me to improvise in that language just because I better understand what is being said. Do you think there are things that therapists can do to improve their abilities to improvise in the situated moment?*

> *SM: Absolutely. This is precisely what I am trying to say (but I think it is difficult to convey the both/and quality I am trying to get at here). Instead of studying a technique, for example, so we can* **use it properly**, *we need to study a technique*

> *so we can* **integrate it into the dance we are doing with our clients**. *Musicians who improvise, as you say, need to first be exceedingly familiar and accomplished performers of a piece of music. One can only improvise* **from** *a stance of familiarity. So, our challenge when we are consulting, doing therapy, teaching, and training is to give the message, "take this and make it your own again and again and again (because it will never be consistently the same over time, across relationships)" rather than "take this and use it correctly."*

Focus on situated activity rather than disembodied techniques can be very unsettling for many of us (and our clients as well as for review boards). But remember, therapy is conversation. We can never anticipate precisely the outcome. Is this a problem? I don't think so. If we remain attentive to the process of relating, itself, we will be attentive simultaneously to the additional voices we all carry (friends, colleagues, family, culture, and so forth). In so doing, we are more likely, I believe, to engage in inquiry that encourages multiple stories, multiple possibilities, and thus, the potential for therapeutic transformation.

In the context of training, we can explore with students the multiple options for action in any given moment. Yet, we do so *not* for purposes of categorizing good and bad actions (of course, this would be impossible). Rather, we do so for purposes of illustrating (1) that in any given moment, there are multiple resources for action and (2) each of these resources has the potential to generate wholly different realities, possibilities, and constraints. Learning to move in and out of these possibilities develops the constructionist stance that marks discursive therapies from other models.

Selecting a theory, technique, or conversational theme as a practical option for action enhances our ability to be relationally engaged with clients. We become sensitive to their stories and our own in ways that allow us to be responsive and relationally responsible (McNamee & Gergen, 1999). There are many ways in which we might pragmatically achieve such a responsivity. In the remainder of this chapter, I would like to identify three conversational themes that could usefully focus our attention on relational engagement rather than on proper methods. Surely, many more themes can be added to the list. These three simply serve as useful in achieving relationally engaged therapeutic practice: (1) moving familiar conversational resources into unfamiliar settings, (2) focus on the future, and (3) languaging[5] the ideal.

In identifying these themes, my hope is to find that space between prescriptive techniques and abstract concepts. My suggestion that a therapist and client might engage in a conversation about the future, for example, is not meant to dictate how or when such a focus might be invited. It is also not to suggest that it *must*

[5] I use the term languaging here to emphasize the *activity* of relational engagement and to distinguish this constructionist notion of language from the traditional view that language is an object of sorts (a system of symbols) that is used to represent the world

*be* an element of all therapeutic conversations. The same stance is adopted for the remaining resources offered here. Let's take a brief look at these themes and consider how each might be useful in approaching *therapeutic process as a conversational activity*. In doing so, we must explore the ways in which each theme assists us in coordinating or bridging incommensurate discourses.

## Using Familiar Resources in Unfamiliar Places

Tom Andersen (1991) talks about introducing not too much change and not too little change but just enough change. He echoes Bateson's well-known phrase, "the difference that makes a difference" (1972, p. 272). Here, I am suggesting a variation on this common theme. We all carry with us many voices, many differing opinions, views and attitudes—even on the same subject. These voices represent the accumulation of our relationships (actual, imagined, and virtual). In effect, we carry the residues of many others with us; we contain multitudes (McNamee & Gergen, 1999). Yet, most of our actions, along with the positions we adopt in conversations, are one dimensional. They represent only a small segment of all that we might do and say. The challenge is to draw on these other voices, these conversational resources that are familiar in one set of relationships and situations but not in another. In so doing, we achieve *just enough difference* as Tom Andersen proposes.

Using familiar resources in contexts where we do not generally use them invites us into new forms of relational engagement with others. If we think of all our activities as invitations into different relational constructions, then we can focus on how utilizing particular resources invites certain responses/constructions in specific relationships and how it invites different responses and different constructions in others. All represent various attempts to achieve coordinated respect for the specificity of a given relationship and situation. Let me elaborate by focusing attention, for the moment, on the issue of professional identity.

We inherit from modernist discourse the expectation (assumption) that there is a proper way to be a professional therapist. We often see this in trainees when they begin seeing clients. They are more likely to talk as they believe a therapist *should* talk thereby ignoring those conversational resources that are familiar and unique to each of them (i.e., the way they might talk with a friend, a family member, or a co-worker about a difficulty for example). Trainees' ideas about how a therapist *should* talk will vary, of course, by tradition. It might be paraphrasing (What I hear you saying is . . . ), it might be empathizing (Oh, that must be quite difficult . . . ), it might be interpreting (What that really means is . . . ). Trainees are actually in the process of *adding* these "professional" conversational moves to their already developed repertoire. This is not necessarily a problem except to the extent that, in so doing, they silence the very ways of relating that are most comfortable, familiar, and thus natural for them. The familiar becomes alienated and what has previously been alien (e.g., being a "therapist") is miraculously supposed to be instantly familiar!

This reminds me of my own clinical training. As a researcher of therapeutic process, I spent years interviewing families, couples, and individuals about their therapy. After many years as a researcher, I decided to boldly plunge into my own training. The initial stages of this training were difficult and frustrating. I found myself frequently speechless with clients. Not only did I have a hard time thinking of questions to ask (regardless of how much pre-session time had been spent generating hypotheses and questions), but I was constantly monitoring myself for *how* I asked questions. I wondered endlessly about whether or not everything I did or said was "right," given my new identity as therapist. My difficulties were not at all unlike those of my students engaged in a simulation with no "script" or specified "role."

One day, while sitting with a client, my supervisors called me out of the room. They asked one very simple question: Are you comfortable and confident when you interview people for your research? My response was affirmative. They said, "Then go back in there and act like a researcher." This directive was so liberating for me that I forgot my fear of *acting like a therapist* and simply engaged in conversation with the client. What I realized in this moment was how our attempts to be good professionals actually can prohibit our ability to be relationally responsive (as professionals) in our conversations with clients. I also realized the benefit of using a familiar repertoire in a context where I would not expect it to serve as an appropriate resource. If we can encourage ourselves (and others) to draw broadly on the conversational resources that are already familiar, perhaps we can act in ways that are *just different enough* to invite others into something beyond the same old unwanted pattern. To the extent that we can invite the use of the familiar in unfamiliar contexts, we are coordinating disparate discourses. What we are avoiding is co-opting one discourse as right and another as wrong. The novelty of enacting the old in a new context becomes, I believe, fertile soil within which to craft generative transformation.

## Focus on the Future

If you examine the field of psychotherapy, you will note that a good deal of therapy talk hovers on the past. Therapists and clients alike explore the history and evolution of the problems that clients bring to therapy. When did the problem begin? How long has it been a difficulty? How have you come to understand (make sense of) the problem? What do you think causes the problem? What do others say about it (and you)? What have you done to try to solve this problem? The questions that therapists ask direct the therapeutic conversation to the past, as do the expectation that many clients bring to therapy. Most cultural presentations of therapy (consider any Woody Allen film) portray client and therapist locked in a conversation about the past (childhood, adolescence, etc.).

With such an emphasis on these past-oriented questions, there is little room for imagining the future. The potential to sediment the past, to reify the story, and thereby make it static and immutable is tremendous. Probably more important, is the logic inherent in the therapeutic focus on the past. By focusing on what has already transpired, we unwittingly give credibility to causal models that are the hallmark of modernist science. We privilege the logic that claims that what went before causes what follows.

Constructionists do not necessarily want to argue for a disconnection between past, present and future. We simply want to raise the issue of narration. The past is always a story. And we all know that there are many ways to tell a story. Not only do we harbor many voices, each with a different set of possible narrations, but others involved in the same "history" will very likely narrate it differently. Thus, the causality of past to present (and implied future) will take different turns, highlight different features, and pathologize or celebrate varied aspects depending on which story is privileged.

One reason that future-oriented discourse can enhance relational engagement is because we all understand that we do not yet *know* the future. We have not embodied it yet. And thus, to the extent that we engage *with others* (our clients in this situation) in conversation about the future, we underscore the relational construction of our worlds. We fabricate together what we might live into.

This is not to suggest that talk of the past is wrong or emblematic of non-constructionist therapy. Instead of privileging a particular way to talk and/or particular themes or topics for therapy, constructionist therapy emphasizes the collaborative, situated creation of possibilities and *one way* to achieve this is with future-oriented discourse. In our talk of imagined futures, we invite coordination of many convergent and divergent understandings of the past and the present. Again, this form of relational engagement moves toward coordinated respect for multiplicity and difference.

## Languaging the Ideal

Perhaps more than an additional theme, the notion of embodied languaging simply puts another description to our attempts to be relationally engaged. In addition to being responsive in the interactive moment, entertaining ideal scenarios offers us a way to engage in dialogue with clients. Often we associate ideal talk with talk of the future. It is, after all, fantasy-like in that it is usually unknown—like the future. However, we can invite our clients to talk about how things would be for them in the present if the past had been ideal. Ideal talk can enhance relational engagement by honoring a painful or sedimented client story. Asking how things ideally would have been, should be, or might be does not disregard how they are presently narrated by a client and thus do not further pathologize the client. I am thinking here of Carla Guanaes's (2003) research on group psychotherapy. She describes a client who offers a very well articulated story about how her problem was rooted in the past. In an attempt to help the client change her story and begin to see that she could actively participate in her own transformation, the therapist and other group members persistently offered many different interpretations about this client's past (e.g., maybe you were just lazy?). The client could not accept these interpretations. She was convinced that her story of her problem was precisely how things really were. The more she referred to this horrible past that had made her mentally ill, the more the therapist and group members attempted to persuade her to give up her interpretation and look at the many other ways she could make sense of her situation. It could be the case that if the therapist and group had engaged this client in inquiry that was focused on how the story of her past would ***ideally*** be told, the client would have felt less pathologized. Perhaps to this client, the past *is* what it is. But asked how it *could have ideally been* is a very different sort of question. Had the group been sensitive to the significance of this story for the client, they might not have attempted to (essentially) tell her she was wrong. This attentiveness to the story of the client fosters a relational sensitivity. Here, however, I am not discussing relational sensitivity as a strategic stance of the therapist but rather as an embodiment of the constructionist focus on language and conversational process. The suggestion here is simply that the language of the ideal can serve as a bridge between stories of despair and stories of hope.

## THE PROVOCATIVE ISSUE ON THE TABLE FOR DISCURSIVE THERAPIES

Thus far I have tried to articulate that constructionist therapies are not free-floating, whimsical opportunities for therapists and clients to create meaning *as they choose*. All strands of discursive therapies hinge on the very important notion of ***relational engagement***. We are all accountable not only to those with whom we engage in the therapeutic context, but we are also ***relationally responsible*** to a myriad of others within our professional, personal, cultural, and global communities.[6] Yet, talking about therapy as conversation raises an interesting question

[6] Of course, this raises a significant issue which deserves much more discussion. How can any person or set of relationships be simultaneously responsible (as in relationally responsible) to competing and divergent communities? If a therapist is relationally responsible to his or her client, does this mean he or she is also relationally responsible to a professional review board? What happens when such relational responsibilities are incommensurate? In the age of managed care, this issue is clearly negotiated on the side of the insurance companies often at the expense (psychological, physical, relational, and financial) of the client.

about evaluation that requires serious discussion. I believe such discussion will be exciting and re-invigorating for our work.

## Assessment

As with the topic of education and training, the topic of assessment is enormous. Let me use the remaining space here to simply suggest the important and exciting re-construction that is needed on this topic.

Some critics fear that the constructionist appreciation for multiplicity denies the very idea (and possibility) of evaluation standards. If standards and values emerge within situated communities, then the standards can well be expected to vary. If these standards vary, by what criteria do we recommend, promote, and help advance professionals? Equally important is discussion of the standards used to claim positive outcome in therapy. Aren't there some common standards to which we should hold all psychotherapists, regardless of philosophical or theoretical orientation?

These are important questions. They are questions that are asked professionally, but personally as well. Am I really performing as a competent therapist? Did I have the client's best interest in mind when I shared a particular story or suggestion? These sorts of questions can plague both therapist and educator alike. If we are supposed to *know*, but knowing is a relational achievement, then professionalism must also be accomplished relationally. I can not be a "good therapist," nor can I *know* that I am a "good therapist," in the abstract. I can only *know* in the very local, therapeutic relationship. A good therapist, a good trainer and educator, is one who remains open and *responsive* to the interactive moment—one who is ***relationally engaged***. There are several implications of this focus on relational engagement for both personal and professional assessment. The future of discursive therapies demands attention to this issue.

The implications are not minor. They lurk in the background (foreground for some ardent critics) of all that we do and say. Currently, it seems that we use modernist criteria to assess our professional competency, our teaching, and the outcomes of our therapy. How can we reconcile this with our dialogical work with our clients (and trainees)?

There is a fear that postmodernism at large, and constructionism specifically, can not and will not provide any standards by which we can make meaningful decisions about who is or is not a good therapist, what is or is not a successful therapy outcome, and what practices are or are not useful in promoting therapeutic change. Postmodernist practitioners can not provide such standards, critics believe, because they eschew the very notion of foundational reality. What this critique misses is that constructionist practice, by emphasizing the relational creation of meaning, *continually* and *rigorously* committed to issues of accountability and therefore to issues of ethical concern. To the constructionist, an outsider can not possibly know when a therapist is being relationally responsive. Relational engagement requires participation in the situated moment. If this is the case, then does this mean that there can never be an outside evaluation of therapeutic competence or success?

These issues must be addressed if discursive therapies are to remain viable options within the profession. They must be addressed in the spirit of relational engagement. This does not mean elaborating a constructionist evaluation. Specifying a uniform method for constructionist evaluation would only invite divisiveness (e.g., constructionist vs. modernist evaluation methods). The challenge we now confront is how we might *generatively* work together within the psychotherapy profession to collaboratively construct multiple forms of *relationally engaged evaluation*. Just as discursive therapies focus on conversation, so should evaluation. Can we create evaluative processes that are sensitive to the variation in what counts as success and what counts as useful? Can we draw on various theories and techniques as practical options in crafting situated evaluations? Can we envision a relationally engaged evaluation process by integrating the three themes proposed here: (1) moving familiar conversational resources into unfamiliar settings, (2) focusing on the future, and (3) languaging the ideal? A challenge indeed!

*LS: Your concern with the challenge of meeting not only the requirements of a postmodern conscience but also bridging with the more modernist review boards concerns me, too. Review boards could assess postmodern therapists' abilities to re-story pathologizing self-stories that clients present in less pathologizing ways. At first glance this seems to me like a hybrid practice which reifies the ability of the therapist to avoid reification. Is that good enough for a social constructionist like yourself? Or do you think that a postmodern sensibility requires us to stay closer to the ideal of tailoring even assessment to the situation with improvisation and relational responsibility?*

*SM: I'm not sure I would describe your suggestion as a reification of the ability of therapists to avoid reification. I see it more as a move toward both/and rather than either/or and, to that end, it serves as a potential bridge between incommensurate discourses. It is an attempt to say, "OK, we recognize that there can be utility in assessment of therapeutic practice but we also recognize that therapeutic practice and ways of thinking about psychotherapy in general vary dramatically from person to person. Can we generate some assessment tools that are coherent with our view of co-creating more generative meanings with clients?" Of course, that sort of activity also, to me, achieves what you raise at the end of your question—namely, being relationally responsible in any form of assessment by remaining sensitive to the situated aspects of meaning making.*

## REFERENCES

Andersen, T. (1991). *The reflecting team.* New York: W.W. Norton and Company.
Bateson, G. (1972). *Steps to an ecology of mind.* New York: Bantam.
Berg, I.K. (1994). *Family-based services: A solution-focused approach.* New York: W.W. Norton.

Chasin, R., Herzig, M., Roth, S., Chasin, L., Becker, C. & Stains, R. (1996). From diatribe to dialogue on divisive public issues: Approaches drawn from family therapy. *Mediation Quarterly*, *13*, 323–344.

Chasin, R. & Herzig, M. (1994). Creating systemic interventions for the socio-political arena. In B. Berger-Could & D.H. DeMuth, (Eds.). *The global family therapist: Integrating the personal, professional and political*. Needham, Massachusetts: Allyn and Bacon.

de Shazer, S. (1985). *Keys to solution in brief therapy*. New York: W.W. Norton.

Guanaes, C. (2003). Unpublished manuscript.

Lewin, K. (1951). *Field theory in social science*. New York: Harper.

McNamee, S. & Gergen, K.J. (Eds.) (1992). *Therapy as social construction*. London: Sage.

McNamee, S. & Gergen, K.J. (1999). *Relational responsibility: Resources for sustainable dialogue*. Thousand Oaks, California: Sage Publications.

O'Hanlon, W. & Weiner-Davis, M. (1989). *In search of solutions*. New York: W.W. Norton.

White, M. & Epston, D. (1990). *Narrative means to therapeutic ends*. New York: W.W. Norton and Company.

Wittgenstein, L. (1953). *Philosophical investigations*. New York: Macmillan.

# Author Index

# Subject Index